Praise for *Ever*

MW00774019

"*Everyday Wisdom* is a unique and creative scholarly addition introducing the recent academic field of interreligious studies in a careful balance with civic interfaith engagement. As a seasoned researcher-practitioner, Hans Gustafson demonstrates a mature understanding of how these two overlapping fields can best reinforce each other 'to advance peaceful relations across diverse religious identities and societies.' Based primarily on a lived-religion experience in the USA, this book is certainly useful for all pluralistic societies worldwide. Diverse audiences of scholars and students in the humanities and social sciences will greatly benefit from its everyday wisdom, whatever their institutional context—secular or religious, private or public. *Everyday Wisdom* is extremely useful to anyone teaching any kind of courses related to contemporary religions, whether rooted in theology or the critical study of religion. The book also provides practical knowledge for the leadership of religiously diverse professional and civic spaces."

—Patrice Brodeur, PhD, professor of religious studies,

Université de Montréal

"In the growing and complex field of interreligious studies, *Everyday Wisdom* offers a much-needed clarification of terms and orientations. But beyond that, the book also provides a set of principles or virtues for a holistic engagement with religious diversity. *Everyday Wisdom* is a great guide for anyone entering the field."

—Catherine Cornille, professor of comparative theology,

Boston College

"Synthesizing a field of expanding scholarship, packed with data on religious diversity, and charting strategies for engagement, Hans Gustafson's book provides a detailed road map for navigating interreligious studies. An excellent text to sharpen the scholar's understanding, shape the instructor's teaching, and introduce students to the multifarious reality of religious identities, belonging, and encounter. If there's one text you read for orientation to the field and its future, it should be *Everyday Wisdom*."

—Jeannine Hill Fletcher, author of *The Sin of White Supremacy: Christianity, Racism, and Religious Diversity in America*

"Timely, smart, and expertly researched and written, *Everyday Wisdom* is the book for anyone (whether scholar, teacher, practitioner, or the generally curious) looking for a comprehensive analysis of the interreligious studies and interfaith engagement fields. But this work does not stop there. Culminating in Hans Gustafson's four dimensions of 'Interreligious Phronesis' (practical wisdom), it also shows a way forward."

—Barbara A. McGraw, JD, PhD, author of *Rediscovering America's Sacred Ground: Public Religion and Pursuit of the Good in a Pluralistic America*; founding director of the Center for Engaged Religious Pluralism and professor of social ethics, law, and public life at Saint Mary's College of California

"Religion is so messy! Hans Gustafson's book expertly guides the reader through the complexities of religious/interreligious studies and encounter to discover practical wisdom for our collective journey on the earth."

—Rachel S. Mikva, author of *Interreligious Studies: An Introduction* and *Dangerous Religious Ideas: The Deep Roots of Self-Critical Faith in Judaism, Christianity, and Islam*

"Scholars and students in the field of religion will find this a particularly helpful book as they navigate the complex field of interreligious relations. Hans Gustafson does an excellent job in mapping the different scholarly debates and introducing a wide variety of topics related to religion, religious identity, and interfaith dynamics. His lived-religion approach is unique and succeeds in avoiding the problems of essentialization and reification of religious differences. Readers will also appreciate the way he complements the scholarly reflections in part 1 with an introduction to interfaith engagement in part 2. Like no other, Gustafson weaves theory and practice together and thus exemplifies what this book seeks to argue for: a wise and practically informed approach to the study of religion and interfaith relations. Speaking as an interreligious scholar and educator, I cannot wait to use this book in my classroom."

—Marianne Moyaert, professor of comparative theology and interreligious dialogue, Faculty of Theology and Religious Studies, KU Leuven

"*Everyday Wisdom* is an excellent introductory text to the nexus between religious studies and interfaith engagement, a volume that takes on some of the more challenging intellectual problems in these fields, and a book that introduces compelling new concepts. People at all levels—from students to faculty, new practitioners to seasoned professionals—will find this a fruitful read."

—Eboo Patel, founder and president of Interfaith America,
and author of *We Need to Build: Field Notes*
for Diverse Democracy

"*Everyday Wisdom* represents an important leap forward for the fledgling field of interreligious studies. With great clarity and balance, Hans Gustafson explains and addresses the central defining issues the field faces. Gustafson's proposals for how interreligious studies can inform and engage a world of diverse groups with competing commitments reflect the very wisdom the title promises."

—Brian K. Pennington, director of the Elon Center for
the Study of Religion, Culture, and Society

EVERYDAY WISDOM

EVERYDAY WISDOM

Interreligious
Studies
in a
Pluralistic
World

Hans Gustafson

FORTRESS PRESS
MINNEAPOLIS

EVERYDAY WISDOM
Interreligious Studies in a Pluralistic World

Library of Congress Control Number: 2023008312 (print)

Cover design: Joe Reinke
Cover image: Skyline city view with reflections on water. Original oil painting on
canvas - stock photo ©Elen11 | Getty Images

Print ISBN: 978-1-5064-8694-9
eBook ISBN: 978-1-5064-8695-6

Contents

Introduction   1

Part I: Interreligious Studies (IRS)

1. "Religion" and Interreligious Studies   9
2. Global Religious Identities   39
3. Messy Religion   63
4. Multiple Religious Orientations   79
5. Lived Religion   95
6. Lived Interreligious Encounter   119
7. (Inter)Religious Literacy   139

Intermezzo: IRS & IFE

8. Spider Silk, the Rock Climber, and Rocky Balboa's
   Broken Nose   165

Part II: Interfaith Engagement (IFE)

9. The "Interfaith" Lexicon   197
10. Encountering Religious Diversity   213
11. Pluralism(s) and Secularism(s)   235
12. Theological Encounters   255

13. Friendship across Difference   273

14. Practical Interfaith Wisdom   287

15. Everyday Leadership   311

   Acknowledgments   337

   Bibliography   339

   Index of Names   369

   Index of Subjects   381

Introduction

Neither avoid nor seek encounters, but be open and when an encounter arises, respond to it while it is still manageable. There is no virtue in delaying until heroic action is needed to set things right. In this way, potentially difficult situations become simple.[1]

—The Tao of Leadership

This book introduces interreligious studies (IRS) and interfaith engagement (IFE)—and the relationship between them—for instructors, students, and scholars seeking not only to understand foundational contours, concepts, trends, and approaches, but also with an eye to teaching courses, building foundational knowledge, producing scholarship, and navigating religiously diverse societies with practical everyday wisdom. This book is not about "the religions," nor is it about how to study the religions. Rather, through a framework of practical wisdom (*phronesis*) for everyday encounter, this book examines the contemporary study of the relations that take place between, among, and within the various religious, nonreligious, and spiritual traditions, ways of life, and worldviews from micro levels (e.g., person-to-person) to macro levels (e.g., community-to-community).

David Roozen, director of the Hartford Institute for Religion Research, observes that "the dominant American attitude toward other faith traditions is indifference."[2] Among the several recent definitions of IRS[3] popular in

---

1 John Haider, *The Tao of Leadership* (Palm Beach, FL: Green Dragon Books, 2015), 125.

2 Michelle Boorstein, "Interfaith Movement Struggles to Adapt to Changing Religious Landscape," *Washington Post*, August 16, 2013.

3 Paul Hedges defines interreligious studies at the basic level as "studies involving two or more religious traditions or groups." "Interreligious Studies," in *Encyclopedia of Sciences and Religion*, ed. Anne Runehov and Lluis Oviedo (New York: Springer, 2012), 1077. Oddbjørn Leirvik suggests it "is something essentially relational in that it focuses on what takes place between religious traditions and their living representatives, on a scale from

the pedagogy and scholarship of the contemporary field, the civic-oriented and practitioner approach of Eboo Patel, Kate McCarthy, and others has gained significant traction, especially at the bachelor's and master's level in the United States. For Patel and Interfaith America (formerly Interfaith Youth Core), interfaith studies[4] (and IRS) is an "an interdisciplinary field that examines the multiple dimensions of how people who orient around religion differently interact with one another, and the implications of these interactions for communities, civil society, and global politics."[5] Furthermore, for Patel, the "research agenda for a civic approach to interfaith studies focuses on how interactions among diverse orientations around religion—both in the lives of individuals and in the practices of institutions—impact civic space."[6] In complementary fashion, McCarthy argues that IRS "serves the public good by bringing its analysis to bear on practical approaches to issues in religiously diverse societies"[7] and "must frame its values and goals in terms appropriate to the secular academy, aimed at the cultivation of civic rather than religious dispositions."[8] Marianne Moyaert recognizes that these approaches to interreligious learning in academia are not unique

---

acute conflict to trustful dialogue." "Interreligious Studies: A New Academic Discipline?" in *Contested Spaces, Common Ground*, ed. Ulrich Winkler, Lidia Rodriguez, and Oddbjørn Leirvik (Leiden: Brill Rodopi, 2016), 37. Hans Gustafson defines interreligious studies as "an academic field of inquiry [that] examines, by one or several disciplinary methods, encounters that take place and relations that exist or exists, in the contemporary world or historically, between, within, and among groups with significant difference in worldview or lifeway, including religious, nonreligious, and secular traditions." "Introduction," in *Interreligious Studies*, ed. Hans Gustafson (Waco: Baylor University Press, 2020), 4. See also Hans Gustafson, "Defining the Academic Field of Interreligious Studies," *Interreligious Studies and Intercultural Theology* 4, no. 2 (2020): 131–54.

   4 Not all scholars have the same definitions in mind for both or either "interreligious studies" and "interfaith studies." Some use them interchangeably, others exclusively use one over the other, and still others use them both to distinguish between distinct fields. The American Academy of Religion group combines them ("Interreligious and Interfaith Studies") and the North American academic society AIIS front-slashes them ("Association for Interreligious/Interfaith Studies"). For more, see chapter 1 and Gustafson, "Introduction," 1–14.

   5 Eboo Patel, "Toward a Field of Interfaith Studies," *Liberal Education* 99, no. 4 (Winter 2014): 38–43.

   6 Eboo Patel, "A Civic Approach to Interfaith Studies," in *Interreligious Studies*, ed. Gustafson, 30.

   7 Kate McCarthy, "(Inter)Religious Studies," in *Interreligious/Interfaith Studies*, ed. Eboo Patel, Jennifer Howe Peace, and Noah Silverman (Boston: Beacon Press, 2018), 12.

   8 Kate McCarthy, "Secular Imperatives," in *Interreligious Studies*, ed. Gustafson, 172.

to the United States but also shape current trends in Europe: "Universities increasingly agree that for students to become successful, responsible citizens of pluralized societies they need to acquire interfaith skills, to sensitively and effectively relate to people who believe and practice differently."[9] If these two premises hold true—that is, the dominant American attitude toward religion is indifference and that needs to change, and IRS at the undergraduate level is primarily about knowledge acquisition, skill building, and practice for civil society—then a primary aim for students, scholars, and instructors of IRS should be to develop practical knowledge in preparation for potentially difficult situations in everyday life, especially for the "weighty matters" of resolving disputes with neighbors, partners, coworkers, and clients.[10] These capacities are described and labeled in a variety of ways, including leadership, skill, competency, wherewithal, literacy, craft, and so on. Jenn Lindsay contends that knowledge acquisition remains a "front-line task"—even prior to the basic building blocks of developing attitude and skills—for this capacity-building project.[11]

This book assumes a particular orientation concerning the role of academicians as arbiters and generators of knowledge. Hence, it approaches knowledge production by IRS in the spirit of how Daniel Cabrera perceives his relationship to knowledge production in his role as scholar-practitioner at the renowned Mayo Clinic in Minnesota:

The moral and societal duty of an academic healthcare provider is to advance science, improve the care of his/her patients and share knowledge. A very important part of this role requires physicians to participate in public debate, responsibly influence opinion and help our patients

---

9 Marianne Moyaert, "Interfaith Learning in Academic Spaces," in *Pluralisation of Theologies at European Universities*, ed. Wolframm Weisse, Julia Ipgrave, Oddbjørn Leirvik, and Muna Tatari (Münster: Waxman, 2020), 35.

10 Robert J. Sternberg, "Where Have All the Flowers of Wisdom Gone?" in *Applying Wisdom to Contemporary World Problems*, ed. Robert J. Sternberg, Howard C. Nusbaum, and Judith Glück (Cham, Switzerland: Palgrave MacMillan, 2019), 17.

11 Jenn Lindsay, "Growing Interreligious and Intercultural Competence in the Classroom," *Teaching Theology and Religion* 23 (2020): 17–33. Lindsay argues, "Rather than emphasizing a change in *attitude* first, we argue a different strategy for improving intercultural and interreligious competence: *knowledge* of other cultures must come prior to the development of skills to interact with them, thereby paving the way, finally, for the area of competence most deep-seated in cognition and the most resistant to change: the attitude" (22, italics original).

navigate the complexities of healthcare. As Clinician Educators our job is not to create knowledge obscura, trapped in ivory towers and only accessible to the enlightened; the knowledge we create and manage needs to impact our communities.[12]

This book affirms the frontline task of knowledge acquisition in a practical manner for everyday encounter. It proposes *interreligious phronesis* (IP), which is the confluence of *know what, know who, know how,* and *know why.* IP draws on lived experience, basic religious literacy (*know what*), and awareness of self and of others to efficiently assess (inter)religiously complex situations, empathetically account for the various and often competing needs of the stakeholders involved (*know who*), and proficiently discern and act with skill, craft, art, and technique (*know how*) in the moment toward the right outcomes for the right reasons (*know why*) for the common goods of all parties involved. Developing IP is not a quest best kept outside the ivory tower of academia and solely reserved for the ambitious self-improvement-obsessed citizen. Rather, it remains a first-order task for students and scholars seeking to be scholar-practitioner leaders. Nicholas Maxwell advocates, "the key thing we need to do to save humanity from disaster is bring about a revolution in academia so that the basic aim becomes wisdom, and not just knowledge."[13] In the multidisciplinary field of the study of religion and IRS, Maxwell's challenge may be taken up to develop IP in service of common public and personal goods.

Leadership plays an important role in this book. In 1965, John W. Gardner, secretary of health, education, and welfare under United States president Lyndon Johnson, declared, "there are serious issues of leadership facing this society, and we had better understand them."[14] Over fifty years later, the global view of leadership exemplars does not offer much more hope, if any. Gardner recognizes that we need leaders to "conceive and articulate goals that lift people out of their petty preoccupations, carry them above the conflicts

---

12 Daniel Cabrera, "Mayo Clinic Includes Social Media Scholarship Activities in Academic Advancement," *Mayo Clinic Social Media Network*, May 25, 2016; cited in Andrew J. Hoffman, *The Engaged Scholar* (Stanford, CA: Stanford University Press, 2021), 132.

13 Nicholas Maxwell, "How Wisdom Can Help Solve Global Problems," in *Applying Wisdom to Contemporary World Problems*, ed. Sternberg et al., 337.

14 John W. Gardner, "The Antileadership Vaccine," in *Contemporary Issues in Leadership*, 2nd ed., ed. William E. Rosenbach, Robert L. Taylor, and Mark A. Youndt (London: Taylor & Francis, 2014), 287.

that tear society apart."[15] Utilizing IRS for practical everyday wisdom in the contemporary world is ultimately an invitation to students, scholars, practitioners, and citizens to discern their specific roles as leaders and stakeholders in the increasingly religiously diverse global society.

This book is for students and scholars seeking a scholarly introduction to the contemporary study of interreligious relations and to the recent scholarship that continues to shape the field. For students new to the study of religion, this book serves as a complement to the growing list of textbooks that introduce the study of religion and the religious traditions of the world, and to books with theological approaches to encountering religious diversity. Offering a "lay of the land" upon which to build, critique, and grow the field, chapters serve as reference points for scholars and students to commence their literature review for research as well as for developing their own scholarship.

This book is for instructors considering teaching a course in the broad multidisciplinary field of interreligious and interfaith studies, regardless of whether their academic home discipline is in religious studies, theological studies, sociology, or elsewhere. To be clear, this is not a theology book or a book on theology; however, it is not dismissive of doing theology or the academic discipline of theological studies. Chapters 1 and 12 address the function of theological approaches vis-à-vis IRS. Hence, to some degree, the book will be of use for scholars of religion (or scholars in religious studies) seeking an introduction to critical academic theological approaches relevant to IRS. This book also strives to complement the interests of scholars, students, and syllabi grounded in theological studies by providing chapters on contemporary trends and critiques in the general critical study of religion relevant to IRS.

Chapters may serve as reference sources for developing curricular modules, planning lectures and discussions, increasing familiarity with the influential literature that shapes the field and contemporary pedagogy, and assigning directly to students' reading schedules to "fill in the gaps" of knowledge or to foreground class discussions. The book is suitable for various institutional contexts, ranging from public secular universities to small private liberal arts or religiously affiliated colleges to graduate programs. It is suitable for courses that focus on the general critical study of religion, courses with constructive

---

15 Gardner, "The Antileadership Vaccine," 295.

theological emphases, courses that address encountering religious diversity, and courses that address leadership in religiously diverse professional and civic spaces.

The book is structured in two parts with a transitional intermezzo chapter. Part I introduces interreligious studies (IRS) within the broad scope of the academic study of religion. Part II introduces essential topics and trends in interfaith engagement (IFE), which refers broadly to the more normative and civic project to advance peaceful relations across diverse religious identities and societies. The reader will discover the boundary between IRS and IFE to be porous and blurry at best. The transitional chapter 8 sketches this mutually interdependent relationship between IRS and IFE, including its tensions and alliances.

Part I addresses the category of religion and approaches to the study of religion and defines common family resemblances to scholarly approaches to IRS (chapter 1); offers a quantitative overview of the global religious landscape, especially in North America and Western Europe, and dissects the category of religious identity (chapter 2); discusses the complicated nature of religious traditions and identities as fundamentally dynamic, blended, and syncretic (chapters 3 and 4); introduces the Lived Religion (LR) approach to the study of religion (chapter 5) and its indispensable utility for scholars of IRS (chapter 6); and investigates the promise and limits of the religious literacy movement (RLM) for civic education and social cohesion (chapter 7).

Part II addresses the language of IFE (chapter 9); maps the various micro and macro responses to diversity in the context of religious difference and encounter (chapter 10); covers the enduring influence of pluralist and secular movements (secularity, secularization, secularism) for engaging religious diversity (chapter 11); introduces the dominant and relevant theological approaches to religious diversity and interreligious encounter (chapter 12); investigates the vital human element of relationships and friendships in the context of interreligious encounter and data on their promise for sustainable bridging across difference and for inter- and intrapersonal changemaking (chapter 13); and proposes a model of interfaith wisdom as Interreligious Phronesis (IP) in service of common goods (chapter 14), and for personal and professional leadership in everyday contexts (chapter 15).

Part I

Interreligious Studies (IRS)

1

"Religion" and Interreligious Studies

Chapter Outline

I. Approaches to "Religion"
    a. *Essentialist*
    b. *Functionalist*
    c. *Family Resemblance*
    d. *Critiques and Conclusions*
II. Interreligious Studies
    a. *Descriptive*
    b. *Normative and Prescriptive*
    c. *Self-Implicating*
    d. *Multi-, Inter-, and Transdisciplinary*

Utilizing interreligious studies for everyday wisdom in religiously diverse societies begins with the basic question of "What is 'religion'?" Similarly, before asking about *inter*religious studies, first inquire about *religious* studies, or the general academic study of religion. The first part of this chapter presents the major approaches to defining religion before concluding with common critiques about the process of defining religion. The second part introduces the academic field of interreligious studies by identifying common characteristics that distinguish it from other fields of study. By providing a sense of the myriad ways "religion" is used and interreligious relations are investigated, one can better navigate and lead in religiously diverse contexts.

APPROACHES TO "RELIGION"

While the guiding aim of this book is to introduce the academic field of interreligious studies for the purpose of navigating and leading in the contemporary religiously diverse world, the journey begins with an examination of the category of religion: where it came from, how it is defined and used, and how it is studied. Reflecting on the category of religion is common soon after encountering religious traditions and identities other than one's own, with questions such as: What is religion? What counts as a religion? Who gets to decide? What stakes are involved?

Scholars trace the roots of the contemporary English word "religion" to the Latin *religio*, which has two major verb uses: the older *relegere* and the more common *religare*. The former refers to the repetition and careful consideration of performing and continuing the rituals and duties passed down from one's familial and community ancestors in a particular context (place and time). The latter usage refers to the binding or yoking of an individual or community to the divine. While the latter usage was eventually more influential for the contemporary English word "religion," in the fourth century Christians were familiar with both. Hence, *religio* referred to the duties and rituals people carried out in order to yoke themselves to God. These duties and rituals, far from being considered irrational magical duties performed by outsider fringe groups, were socially accepted duties within the mainstream (e.g., offerings and official sacrifices at a public temple[1]). Scholars point to the influence of Christians and theologians over the centuries that have contributed to the more current usage of religion. For instance, fourth-century Christians argued that *religio* referred to interior thoughts, and Augustine argued for the importance of *religio* to be aimed at the correct object (i.e., aimed at the proper God and not at false idols).[2] The word "religion," as it is understood today, changed from the original usage, which was tolerant, pluralistic, and human-directed, and became more intolerant, exclusive, faith-centric, and divine-directed.[3] Needless to say, the category of religion, definitionally and

---

1 Andrew M. Henry, "What Is Religion?" Religion for Breakfast (YouTube channel), January 12, 2016 (video), 01:15–01:18.

2 David McConeghy, "Where Does the Word Religion Come From?" in *Religion in 5 Minutes*, ed. Aaron W. Hughes and Russel T. McCutcheon (Sheffield, UK, and Bristol, CT: Equinox, 2017), 8.

3 Paul Hedges, *Understanding Religion* (Oakland: University of California Press, 2021), 21.

functionally, remains a heavily debated and an "essentially contested concept" because there is no universally agreed-upon meaning.[4] The ongoing task to adequately define religion continues to keep scholars busy, especially in the past century. In almost every major contemporary textbook on the religions, the opening pages discuss the problem of defining religion. It is not unusual on the first day of a course on the study of religion or the so-called world religions[5] for the instructor to present a dozen or so definitions of religion from well-known (often Western) thinkers from the past one hundred years. The definitions are all very different, and perhaps such an exercise can leave a student in despair with seemingly no adequate definition of religion in sight. Definitions range from the very broad, such as Paul Tillich's proposal that religion is the "state of being grasped by an ultimate concern,"[6] to Leonard Swidler's suggestion that religions, or better yet "worldviews,"[7] "ways," or "life-ways" are explanations "of the meaning of life and how to live accordingly."[8] These broad definitions can include ideologies such as Marxism, political movements, social causes, support groups like Alcoholics Anonymous,[9] or

---

4 Walter B. Gallie, "Essentially Contested Concepts," *Proceedings of the Aristotelian Society* S6, no. 1 (1956): 167–98; also cited in Hedges, *Understanding Religion*, 29.

5 Suzanne Owen argues that the "World Religions paradigm" should be done away with because it "conceptualizes religious ideas and practice as being configured by a series of major religious systems that can be clearly identified as having discrete characteristics." Instead, it should be replaced with a more critical approach to the study of religion to better reflect the constructed nature of the category of religion and to mitigate the assumptions and importation of liberal Western Christian values into non-Christian traditions. Suzanne Owen, "The World Religions Paradigm," *Arts & Humanities in Higher Education* 10, no. 3 (2011): 253–68; citing Jacqueline Suthren Hirst and John Zavos, "Riding a Tiger?" *Contemporary South Asia* 14, no. 1 (2005): 5. See also Hedges, *Understanding Religion*, 46.

6 Paul Tillich, *The Future of Religions* (New York: Harper & Row, 1966), 3.

7 Ann Taves argues that "conceptualizing religions as worldviews and ways of life offers a framework for rethinking various problems in the study of religion, including the religious/secular binary in relation to the growing interest in secular and 'non-religious' studies; the relationship between indigenous traditions and so-called 'world religions' in situations of contact, conquest, and/or global communication; and the challenges inherent in relating biological, cognitive, and cultural processes." Ann Taves, "Studying Religions as Worldviews and Ways of Life" (Gunning Lectures, University of Edinburgh, Scotland, March 19, 2018), abstract.

8 Leonard Swidler, *The Age of Global Dialogue* (Eugene, OR: Wipf & Stock, 2016), 6.

9 Ann Taves observes, "Alcoholics Anonymous is happy to call itself spiritual . . . as embodying a spiritual path, or a spiritual way of life. They actually use the way of life kind of language, or call themselves a fellowship." Ann Taves, "Worldviews and Ways of Life," interview by David G. Robertson, *The Religious Studies Project*, May 21, 2018, podcast transcript by Helen Bradstock, version 1.1, May 16, 2018.

anything of "ultimate concern." Other definitions are more narrow, such as Edward Burnett Tylor's view that religion is "belief in Spiritual Beings"[10] or Rudolf Otto's idea that religion grows out of and gives expression to the experience of "the holy," which Otto famously termed *mysterium tremendum*,[11] an awesome fascination of mystery. These definitions can limit what qualifies as a religion. For Tylor, belief is the major criterion, and, what is more, it is the particular belief in "Spiritual Beings!" Many Buddhists, then, who may not ultimately believe in Spiritual Beings, would be excluded from this definition. Nor is there any mention of practices, behavior, or belonging to a community. Otto reduces religion to a feeling, and a particular feeling at that. Scholars approach the study of religion in several ways. Three well-worn approaches emerge: *essentialist, functionalist,* and *family resemblance*.

Essentialist

Approaches of scholars such as Tylor and Otto are termed "essentialist" because they articulate a common essence of religion (e.g., belief in spiritual beings or the feeling *mysterium tremendum*). Also referred to as the "substantivist" approach because it focuses on the principle internal substance or the core meaning religion has for people who identify with and practice it, this approach boils religion down to a particular aspect without which it would not be properly deemed a religion.

The problems with this approach are well documented, such as that it can easily exclude traditions that do not have the particular predefined essence. For instance, if the essence of religion is deemed belief in God or the Gods, then many (perhaps most) forms of Buddhism cannot be properly understood as religions since there is no God (or Gods) to believe in. The category of God either simply does not exist for many Buddhists, or it is not a useful question for the pursuit of enlightenment. A consequence of the essentialist approach—and, in particular, of the insistence on the necessity of a divine God or Gods for a tradition to be a religion—is the tired refrain of deeming Buddhism a philosophy, not a religion. However,

---

10 Edward Burnett Tylor, *Primitive Culture*, vol. 1 (New York: G. P. Putnam's Sons, 1920), 424.

11 Rudolf Otto, *The Idea of the Holy*, trans. John W. Harvey (New York: Oxford University Press, 1958).

just about every textbook on religions includes Buddhism among the major global religious traditions.

The question then becomes who gets to decide the essence of religion. Scholar of religion Russell T. McCutcheon argues that the quest for an accurate essence of religion is bound to fail since "there may be as many essences as there are essentialists."[12] Even essentialists do not agree on the essence of religion. Essentialism is not only a problem for defining the category of religion, but it also raises challenges for defining individual religions themselves. In the attempt to define the essence of a particular religious tradition, essentialism will likely exclude many who identify with that tradition when they do not look like or live up to the predetermined essence of that tradition. For instance, if it is determined essential for a Christian to believe in the Trinity, then those Christians who reject the doctrine of the Trinity are placed outside of what it means to be a Christian. This is no trivial matter, for it can lead those with certain degrees of power to erect guidelines for what it means to be a "real" Christian or a "real" Muslim, and so on. Likewise, in many nation-states religious communities benefit from tax exemption or even government subsidies, and religious individuals enjoy a spectrum of religious freedoms. Therefore, if a governmental body determines that a particular community or tradition is not "religious," then there are real-world implications of finances and freedom. Furthermore, especially for constructive interreligious relations, essentialism can foster genuine misunderstanding by those outside particular traditions and lead to unfair and inaccurate oversimplification and stereotyping of religious traditions and individuals.

Functionalist

Functionalist approaches to the definition of religion inquire not about what religion is (essence), but about what religion does (function). Well-known functionalists include political economist Karl Marx, psychologist Sigmund Freud, sociologist Emil Durkheim, and anthropologist Clifford Geertz.

The function of religion for Marx is to respond to suffering, but it ends up responding to the wrong source of suffering. Rather, Marx contends, religion pacifies society by distracting the majority of people from the roots

---

12 Russell T. McCutcheon, *Studying Religion* (New York: Routledge, 2014), 29.

of suffering and conflict. For Marx, "Religion is the sign of the oppressed creature, the heart of a heartless world and the soul of soulless conditions. It is the opium of the people. The abolition of religion as the illusory happiness of the people is a demand for their true happiness."[13] The function of religion is that of a drug, an opiate: to soothe, calm, placate, and distract from the realities of the world.

For Freud, "religion is comparable to childhood neurosis";[14] that is, it functions as a mild form of mental illness. Religion "is an attempt to master the sensory world,"[15] but ultimately it "is an illusion and it derives its strength from its readiness to fit in with our instinctual wishful impulses."[16] Religion functions to serve psychological human needs by convincing us that supernatural objects exist, which in reality are only natural objects. In short, religion is an invention of the human psyche, which, similar to dreams, assists individuals with expressing their repressed desires through the performance of symbolic rituals in social groups.

Durkheim argued that religion functions to bring societies together by shaping communal and moral life. A religion is a "unified system of beliefs and practices relative to sacred things, that is to say, things set apart and surrounded by prohibitions—beliefs and practices that unite its adherents in a single moral community called a church."[17] Durkheim provides here a functionalist social theory that explains how religion operates in society. As a modern sociologist of religion, he held that scholars make sense of society by understanding its parts and functions, and religion is one of those major

---

13 Karl Marx, *Critique of Hegel's* Philosophy of Right, trans. Annette Jolin and Joseph O'Malley (Cambridge: Cambridge University Press, 1970), 131. Marx's famous assessment of religion as "the opium of the people" is possibly influenced by Hegel's depiction of Hinduism. In *Philosophy of History*, Hegel describes the "whole life and ideas of" the Hindus as "one unbroken superstition" akin to someone who finds their "existence altogether stupid and intolerable, and is driven to the creation of a dream-world and a delirious bliss in Opium." G. W. F. Hegel, *Philosophy of History*, trans. J. Sibree (Mineola, NY: Dover Publications, 1956), 167.

14 Sigmund Freud, *The Future of an Illusion*, trans. Gregory C. Richter (Peterborough, ON: Broadview Press, 2012), 188.

15 Sigmund Freud, "Lecture 35: The Question of a *Weltanschauung*," in *New Introductory Lectures on Psycho-Analysis*, trans. James Strachey (New York: W. W. Norton, 1965), 207.

16 Freud, "Lecture 35," 216.

17 Emil Durkheim, *The Elementary Forms of Religious Life*, trans. Carol Cosman (Oxford: Oxford University Press, 2001), 46.

parts, especially in how it reflects the values of the society. In short, everything considered religious (stories, practices, institutions, rituals, beliefs, etc.) functions to construct and maintain group identity and cohesion in a fragile world that constantly threatens to shatter the group.[18]

Geertz's definition of religion is perhaps one of the most popular in the history of the Western study of religion. He famously wrote that religion is "a system of symbols which acts to establish powerful, pervasive and long-lasting moods and motivations in men by formulating conceptions of a general order of existence and clothing these conceptions with such an aura of factuality that the moods and motivations seem uniquely realistic."[19] Common criticisms of Geertz's definition include its assumptions that: (1) "religious beliefs are false,"[20] (2) "belief is a basic grounding factor for religion,"[21] and (3) religion is "a fairly static idea."[22] These assumptions are problematic because (1) it is difficult to determine the truth value of a religious belief, (2) some (or many) religions do not privilege belief as a central tenet, and (3) religious traditions are dynamic and fluid, changing over time with the cultures, languages, and symbols within which they are embedded.

In the social sciences, functionalist approaches to understanding religion are popular because they avoid articulating an inner essence or religion, thereby allowing scholars to focus more on religious behaviors and expressions of individuals and groups. However, functionalist approaches have drawbacks. Scholars do not agree on which functions of religion are the most basic (most *essential*?). Functionalists (and essentialists) are routinely accused of reductionism; that is, they reduce religion (or try to "explain it away") by relegating it to deeper, more genuine, nonreligious impulses, causes, needs, and beliefs. In the way essentialism assumes "that there is an essence behind the religion, its 'real' form," functionalism similarly reduces religions "to something outside the religious system, that is, to society or the mind."[23] In this manner, both essentialist and functionalist approaches can be reductionary. For example, a reductionist might argue that if a prison grants special privileges to inmates who participate regularly in religious services, then the

---

18 McCutcheon, *Studying Religion*, 35.
19 Clifford Geertz, "Religion as a Cultural System," in *The Interpretation of Cultures: Selected Essays* (London: Fontana Press, 1993), 90.
20 King and Hedges, "What Is Religion?" 14.
21 King and Hedges, 15.
22 King and Hedges, 15.
23 King and Hedges, 3.

inmates' religious expressions can be interpreted, in the least, as simply a way to garner privileges or, at most, a coping mechanism in the rough-and-tumble life of prison. Such accounts, antireductionists might argue, ignore the possibility that some inmates may participate in religious services out of their deep religious beliefs regardless of any special privileges received.[24]

Family Resemblance

Ludwig Wittgenstein famously wrote about "family resemblances," which refers to the phenomenon of when an individual initially perceives a common essential feature to things, but when analyzed properly they do

> not see something common to all, but similarities, relationships, and a whole series of them at that. . . . the result of this examination is: we see a complicated network of similarities overlapping and criss-crossing: sometimes overall similarities, sometimes similarities in detail. I can think of no better expression to characterize these similarities than "family resemblances"; for the various resemblances between members of a family: build, features, color of eyes, gait, temperament, etc. etc. overlap and criss-cross in the same way.[25]

Just as members of the same family often share similar traits and characteristics (e.g., facial features, speech intonation and accent, personality) but not always, family resemblance approaches to religion, as the name suggests, attempt to identify various traits that most if not all religions have, but not always or to differing degrees. The approach assumes that while no single trait may be uniquely present in all religions (there is no universal essence), there are identifiably common features that run across the traditions. In university-level courses on the introduction to religion, Ninian Smart's dimensions of religion are among the most popular. Smart proposes six (later nine or ten[26])

---

24 Andrew Johnson, *If I Give My Soul* (New York: Oxford University Press, 2017), 5.
25 Ludwig Wittgenstein, *Philosophical Investigations*, trans. G. E. M. Anscombe (Oxford: Blackwell, 1958), §66–67.
26 To the six mentioned in this sentence, and depending on how one counts, Smart, in later writings, adds (1) material, (2) political, and (3) economic. See King and Hedges, "What Is Religion?" 15, 28n35.

dimensions of religion: (1) doctrinal (philosophical), (2) narrative (mythic), (3) ethical (legal), (4) ritual (practical), (5) experiential (emotional), and (6) social (organizational). Typical of a family resemblance approach, Smart admits that although these aspects generally apply to all religions in some manner, they do not exhaustively capture religion. The aspects cover "facets" of most traditions. Furthermore, he maintains, aspects do not carry equal weight in various traditions nor in various historical periods of the same tradition.[27]

Smart's "dimensions" are but one example among several attempts to define religion by listing family resemblance characteristics.[28] The spirit of this approach affirms the intuition that the definition of religion cannot be pinned down to one single trait or characteristic. Rather, it argues that the best hope is to identify several traits, for this allows for more latitude and generosity with identifying worldviews as religions.

Family resemblance approaches, though perhaps steering a middle course between essentialist and functionalist approaches, are not immune to criticism. McCutcheon draws attention to their basic difficulties: (1) they often fail to define religion due to their use of ill-defined terms in their list of characteristics (e.g., sacred, profane, holy, supernatural, religious feelings), and (2) they are often based on and therefore privilege a particular tradition. For instance, the characteristic "belief in god or gods" obviously privileges traditions with central and robust concepts of god or gods and thus leaves one to question, for example, the many Buddhists who do not have a concept nor belief in a god or gods. McCutcheon articulates this common critique to the family resemblance approach in his summary of Alston's definition, which suggests that because Christianity is considered a religion and it has these various components, then all religions will have some or all of these components as well. This claim assumes Christianity is a religion to begin with and reinforces it every time it applies these components to other potential candidates for religion. However, as McCutcheon rightly observes, "Why it gets to count as a religion—rather than, say, a mass socio-political movement—is never explored."[29]

This concern is echoed in Ann Taves's critique of Ninian Smart's approach. With great appreciation for Smart's influence on the move from the study of religions to the broader study of worldviews, Taves unveils the limitation of Smart's

27 Ninian Smart, *Worldviews*, 3rd ed. (Upper Saddle River, NJ: Prentice Hall, 2000), 8.
28 Other well-known lists include Bruce Lincoln's "four domains" and William Alston's "characteristics." McCutcheon, *Studying Religion*, 62.
29 McCutcheon, *Studying Religion*, 64.

approach, which "is that he never defined what he meant by worldview. . . . what he did was simply import his six—or later, seven—dimensions of religion from the study of religion to the study of worldviews."[30]

The family resemblance approach is popular among common university textbooks that introduce the world religions. For example, after introducing several famous definitions of religion, the popular textbook *Invitation to World Religions* proposes to the reader: "Let us agree, then, on a working definition for purposes of our study: religion is a cultural system integrating teachings, practices, modes of experience, institutions, and artistic expressions that relates people to what they perceive to be transcendent."[31] This definition embeds religion in culture and recognizes several dimensions of religion. Similarly, Michael Molloy's *Experiencing the World's Religions* teaches, "We may accept as a religion whatever manifests a reasonable number of these characteristic [sic]. Scholars do note, however, that what we ordinarily call religions manifest to some degree the following eight elements":[32] Belief system, Community, Central myths, Ritual, Ethics, Characteristic emotional experiences, Material expression, Sacredness.[33] Stephen Prothero, in his bestselling *God Is Not One*, tests the following common definition to determine whether atheism may be considered a religion: "According to one common formula, members of the family of religions typically exhibit Four Cs: creed, cultus, code, community. In other words, they have statements of beliefs and values (creeds); ritual activities (cultus); standards for ethical conduct (codes); and institutions (communities)."[34] One might sift through textbook after textbook, and scholar after scholar, to curate an extensive list of proposed definitions of the term "religion." The point of such an exercise would not necessarily be to prove the impossibility of defining the word "religion," but simply rather to show that religion can be, and has been, defined in countless ways by various individuals and communities over time. Likewise, the student of religion need not necessarily despair and conclude that the term is useless. People can still talk about religion in meaningful ways.

---

30 Taves, "Worldviews and Ways of Life."
31 Jeffrey Brodd, Layne Little, Bradley Nystrom, Robert Platzner, Richard Shek, and Erin Stiles, eds., *Invitation to World Religions* (Oxford: Oxford University Press, 2012), 9.
32 Michael Molloy, *Experiencing the World's Religion*, 4th ed. (New York: McGraw Hill, 2008), 3–4.
33 Molloy, *Experiencing the World's Religions*, 4–5.
34 Stephen Prothero, *God Is Not One* (New York: HarperOne, 2011), 324.

Critiques and Conclusions

The fact that there is an endless list of definitions of religion shows just that: (1) religion can be defined in many different, sometimes very different, ways, and (2) the definitions of religion, and approaches to the study of religion, can change over time. McCutcheon suggests that the usefulness of the category of religion can be likened to that of a tool designed for specific tasks. Religion, like all tools, "must continually be re-tooled."[35] It is designed and used to understand and make sense of the world. However, new tools may come along that are more efficient or more appropriate for particular tasks. Despite the shortcomings of the various approaches and definitions of religion above, one need not conclude that all definitions are worthless, but rather that religion as a category is like a tool designed to accomplish various tasks in various contexts.

Jonathan Z. Smith is one of the most well-known twentieth-century American scholars of religion. He famously suggested that "Religion is solely the creation of the scholar's study. It is created for the scholar's analytic purposes by his imaginative acts of comparison and generalization. Religion has no existence apart from the academy."[36] For Smith, the category of "religion" is a convenient category created for the feeble attempt to describe what is going on. This is not to say that people did not practice rituals, articulate mythological narratives about the cosmos, or hold worldviews that included belief in the transcendent, God, or the Gods. Rather, Smith's argument is that religion, as a category, did not exist until it was created by scholars (i.e., the academy) and foisted upon people's beliefs and behaviors.

Some scholars push back against Smith's thesis by pointing to evidence of analogous terms to religion used by non-Christian and non-Western peoples and nonscholars prior to colonial contact.[37] These scholars contest the idea that religion is a category that only belongs to modern Western scholarship, reject the argument that the word should be discarded just because there are problems with it, and argue that long before Western scholarship encountered religions outside their own, non-Western and non-Christian traditions were

---

35 McCutcheon, *Studying Religion*, 65.

36 Jonathan Z. Smith, *Imagining Religion* (Chicago: University of Chicago Press, 1982), xi.

37 See Will Sweetman, "Against Invention,'" interview with Thomas White, *The Religious Studies Project* (podcast audio), February 19, 2018.

already relating to, and differentiating themselves from, other religions.[38] King and Hedges argue that "the traditions we call 'religions' have in fact been encountering and debating with each other for centuries, if not millennia, without any need for modern Western scholars to tell them that they all share some common characteristics."[39] Instead of religion, suggestions of terms to replace religion include "culture," "worldview," "lifeway" (or way of life), and "the sacred." However, many of these terms remain vulnerable to some of the same challenges levied against religion. Regardless of whether the term "religion" is a postcolonial creation of Western European academia, it remains in use across the globe, and when people use it, they most certainly mean something by it. People describe themselves as religious and belonging to, and practicing, and believing in, particular religions. Sociologist José Casanova refers to religion as "an indisputable global social fact" that has become "a discursive reality, both an abstract category as well as a system of classification of reality, used by modern individuals as well as by modern societies across the world, by religious as well as by secular authorities."[40] Casanova points to the "numerous studies [that] have appeared examining the discursive processes through which the categories of 'religion' and 'the secular' have emerged in non-Western cultures," and concludes that the "very fact that the same category of religion is being used globally across cultures and civilizations testifies to the global expansion of the modern secular-religious system of classification of reality that first emerged in the modern Christian West."[41]

As a contested and fluid category, religion is likely to remain under constant construction but not useless. The task of defining the term can be a fruitful exercise when mindful of the likely need for future refining and redefining. Maintaining an ever-provisional definition can still be practical and productive without compromising the tentative, unstable, and fluid nature of the term. Hence, the statement from Brodd's introductory textbook wisely qualifies its definition as a "working definition," always in process, under endless development, and always at the ready to be tailored to particular

---

38 See Paul Hedges, *Controversies in Interreligious Dialogue and the Theology of Religions* (London: SCM, 2010), 74; cited in King and Hedges, "What Is Religion?" 12.

39 King and Hedges, "What Is Religion?" 12.

40 José Casanova, "The Karel Dobbelaere Lecture," *Social Compass* 65, no. 2 (2018): 195.

41 Casanova, "The Karel Dobbelaere Lecture," 192.

contexts and objectives. With such an understanding of religion in mind, McCutcheon proposes replacing the question "What is the study of religion?" with "'Where is the study of religion being practiced, by whom, and for what purposes?' For, depending on its context and the interests that drive it, the study of religion can be very different things."[42] Furthermore, as is the case with the term "interreligious," with King and Hedges, this book recognizes that "'religion' is a term with a particular cultural history, and while many definitions and assumptions with it are problematic, we should not abandon it as it does seem to be meaningful."[43]

In addition to these traditional approaches to the definition of religion (essentialist, functionalist, family resemblance), three approaches to religion are addressed in the forthcoming pages: (1) the emerging interdisciplinary field of interreligious studies (discussed in this chapter), (2) lived religion approaches to the study of religion and interreligious encounters (discussed in chapters 5 and 6), and (3) theological approaches (discussed in chapter 12).

INTERRELIGIOUS STUDIES

Although the emergence of IRS as a recognized academic field is relatively recent, for decades if not centuries scholars have engaged in research, teaching, and activism that would today be considered IRS.[44] As with the term "religion," IRS does not have a universal definition to which all scholars assent. Such definitional malleability may be an asset for IRS as it allows for flexibility and adaptation to various contexts. The aim of this section is to identify common characteristics that mark IRS off from other fields of inquiry.

Interreligious studies at its most basic level investigates the relations and interactions between, among, and within individuals and groups in religiously diverse contexts. Paul Hedges was among the first to propose a succinct definition: IRS's "basic meaning refers to studies involving two or more religious

---

42 McCutcheon, *Studying Religion*, 71.
43 King and Hedges, "What Is Religion?" 14.
44 This section is adapted from Hans Gustafson, "Defining the Academic Field of Interreligious Studies," *Interreligious Studies and Intercultural Theology* 4, no. 2 (2020): 131–54; and Hans Gustafson, "Interreligious and Interfaith Studies in Relation to Religious Studies and Theological Studies," State of Formation, January 6, 2015.

traditions or groups."[45] Scholar-practitioner of IRS Oddbjørn Leirvik, pioneer of the first formal academic program in IRS (at the University of Oslo[46]), maintains that IRS "is something essentially relational in that it focuses on what takes place between religious traditions and their living representatives, on a scale from acute conflict to trustful dialogue."[47] A research team investigating contemporary interreligious encounters in European urban contexts used a practical working definition of "interreligious" to refer to meetings "between people and ideas of different faith traditions."[48] According to Leirvik, the object(s) of study are the very relations and "dynamic encounter between religious (and non-religious) traditions and the space that opens and closes between them."[49] For Eboo Patel, IRS examines the "multiple dimensions of how individuals and groups who orient around religion differently interact with one another, along with the implications of these interactions for communities, civil society, and global politics."[50] Kate McCarthy envisions IRS as "a subdiscipline of religious studies that engages in scholarly and religiously neutral description, multidisciplinary analysis, and theoretical framing of the interactions of religiously different people and groups, including the intersections of religion and secularity."[51] Leirvik, Patel, and McCarthy insist that the study of interreligious relations includes religiously unaffiliated individuals, communities, and spaces. It remains a lively and healthy debate about whether IRS is substantively different from religious studies and, if so, how.

---

45 Paul Hedges, "Interreligious Studies," in *Encyclopedia of Sciences and Religion,* ed. Runehov and Oviedo, 1077. Hedges reiterates this "primary focus [of] interreligious studies [as] encounters or relations" in Paul Hedges, "Interreligious Studies: A New Direction in the Study of Religion?" *Bulletin of the British Association for the Study of Religions* (November 2014): 13.

46 University of Oslo, "Horizon Document for a Planned Program in Interreligious Studies," version 16.10.00 (University of Oslo, Norway: Faculty of Theology, 2000).

47 Leirvik, "Interreligious Studies: A New Academic Discipline?" 37.

48 Julia Ipgrave, Thorsten Knauth, Anna Körs, Dörthe Vieregge, and Marie von der Lippe, eds., *Religion and Dialogue in the City* (Münster: Waxmann, 2018), 11.

49 Leirvik, "Interreligious Studies: A New Academic Discipline?" 36.

50 Eboo Patel, "Toward a Field of Interfaith Studies," *Liberal Education* 99, no. 4 (Winter 2014); quoted in Jeanine Diller, "Toward a Field of Interfaith Studies," in roundtable with Jeanine Diller, Eboo Patel, Jennifer Peace, and Colleen Windham-Hughes, *Journal of Interreligious Studies* 16 (2015), 7–8; also quoted in Eboo Patel and Cassie Meyer, "Teaching Interfaith Leadership," in *Teaching Interfaith Encounters,* ed. Marc A. Pugliese and Alexander Y. Hwang (New York: Oxford University Press, 2017), 300.

51 McCarthy, "(Inter)Religious Studies," 12.

The working theory assumed throughout this book is that IRS's focus on the *interactions* and *relations* between and among religious traditions, persons, communities, and movements is what distinguishes it from (or within) the broader multidisciplinary study of religion. Hence, interreligious studies is an academic field of inquiry that utilizes one or several disciplines and methods to examine encounters and relations historically and today, between, within, and among individuals and communities in religiously diverse contexts.[52] These encounters include episodes of constructive bridgebuilding and destructive conflict, as well as relations between individuals and groups that identify with religious traditions and those that do not identify with a religious or spiritual tradition. IRS can, yet need not, be more complicated and nuanced than this mere definition. Academic scholars, institutions, and programs implement (teach, research, promote) IRS in various ways, with sometimes subtle yet important distinctions. Five common characteristics (family resemblances) emerge among the growing usage of IRS: (1) descriptive, (2) normative, (3) prescriptive, (4) self-implicating, and (5) multi-, inter-, and transdisciplinary.

Descriptive

The student-learning outcomes (SLOs) of the Bachelor level minor program in IRS at Elon University in North Carolina show the field's descriptive nature by articulating what students (and scholars) are expected to do:

1. analyze "the category of religion and the field of interreligious studies, including the histories and theoretical models that inform them";
2. "recognize and appreciate the contours of religious difference both within and between particular traditions";
3. "recognize and explain the ways in which religious traditions and inter-religious encounters are embedded within cultural, political and economic systems";
4. "produce nuanced reflections on ways that religious traditions and religious communities have interacted with other religious traditions and communities throughout history";

---

52 Gustafson, "Introduction," in *Interreligious Studies*, ed. Gustafson, 4.

5. "critique existing models for understanding and facilitating inter-religious encounter";
6. "interact with communities and hear from practitioners" to gain firsthand experience of religious practice and interreligious encounter;
7. "offer constructive suggestions for improving these models."[53]

These SLOs, although descriptive, leave room for and point to normative, pre-scriptive, and self-implicating approaches as well (discussed below). Descriptive empirical analysis, a basic task of any scholar, enables IRS scholars to know and appreciate the history, contexts, and contemporary situations of interreligious encounters. For instance, Scott Daniel Dunbar, reflecting on the place of interreligious dialogue (which for some is a method of interreligious studies) in the study of religion, emphasizes the need for descriptive analysis "because it records and documents the dialogue process for the present and future generations."[54] Dunbar promotes critical approaches with descriptive foundations "not only for documenting the dialogue process but also for par-ticipating in actual dialogue, for it is useful to have a descriptive understanding of another religion before entering into dialogue with one of its followers."[55]

There are differing views about the extent to which the scholar of reli-gion ought to disseminate, promote, safeguard, defend, or control religious practices and beliefs. McCutcheon famously argues scholars are "critics, not caretakers" of religious traditions.[56] Rather, for him, the task of the scholar is to provide the much-needed critical etic[57] perspective that is largely detached

---

53 Amy L. Allocco, Geoffrey D. Clausen, and Brian K. Pennington, "Constructing Interreligious Studies: Thinking Critically about Interfaith Studies and the Interfaith Movement," in *Interreligious/Interfaith Studies*, ed. Patel et al., 40.

54 Scott Daniel Dunbar, "The Place of Interreligious Dialogue in the Academic Study of Religion," *Journal of Ecumenical Studies* 35, no. 3–4 (1998): 462; also cited by Oddbjørn Leirvik, "Interreligious Studies: A Relational Approach to the Study of Religion," *Journal of Interreligious Studies* 13 (February 2014): 16.

55 Dunbar, "The Place of Interreligious Dialogue in the Academic Study of Religion," 457.

56 Russell T. McCutcheon, *Critics Not Caretakers* (Albany: SUNY Press, 2001).

57 "Etic" refers to descriptive accounts that use terms and concepts meaningful first and foremost to scholars or religion, regardless of whether or not religious insiders would recognize or acknowledge them as being meaningful (in contrast to emic accounts that use native terms and concepts meaningful to religious insiders). Hedges, *Understanding Religion*, 47.

from insider confessional perspectives. IRS often also shares this sentiment, although insider perspectives remain welcome as well. The insider/outsider debate or problem[58] remains lively in the study of religion, especially about the appropriate place for insider perspectives. Atalia Omer proposes the role for scholars as "critical caretakers" in the article that asks, "Can a Critic Be a Caretaker Too?" and concludes, "The religion scholar as a critic and a caretaker may offer not only a second-order re-description of religion as a social construct but also a problem-oriented constructive engagement with histories, memories, and theological resources."[59] Insider, outsider, critic, and caretakers roles exist within IRS as well. An insider to IRS might be the scholar-activist who not only investigates interreligious encounters but also participates in interfaith dialogue and engagement movements. She likely has vested interests in not only being critical of interfaith engagement but also seeks solution-oriented constructive knowledge as a caretaker of such activities. As with Elon University's IRS SLOs, the caretaker role extends IRS to normative, prescriptive, and self-implicating aspects as well (discussed below).

IRS requires critical outsider perspectives in addition to, and to serve as a check on, insider voices alone that may unknowingly control the conversation in ways that critical distance might bring.[60] The religious neutrality that scholarly discourse aspires to helps to ground it as an academic field. Hence, some IRS scholars sympathize with McCutcheon's call by echoing that it is not their task to serve as caretakers of religious traditions or interreligious relations.[61] IRS scholars such as Leirvik and McCarthy call attention to the vital distinction between IRS as an academic field and the civic-oriented and activist, grassroots, community-based project to achieve civic pluralism, mutual understanding, peacebuilding, and social cohesion (often referred to as the Interfaith Movement and generically as Interfaith Engagement (IFE) in this book[62]). McCarthy is clear that if IRS "is to be an academic discipline suitable to secular higher education, it must not be construed as an auxiliary

---

58 E.g., see George D. Chryssides and Stephen E. Gregg, *The Insider/Outside Debate* (Sheffield, UK: Equinox, 2020), and Russell T. McCutcheon, ed., *The Insider/Outsider Problem in the Study of Religion* (London: Continuum, 2014).

59 Atalia Omer, "Can a Critic Be a Caretaker Too?" *Journal for the American Academy of Religion* 79, no. 2 (2011): 459 (abstract).

60 Leirvik, "Interreligious Studies: A Relational Approach to the Study of Religion," 17.

61 McCarthy, "(Inter)Religious Studies," 12.

62 The relationship between IRS as an academic field and interfaith engagement (IFE) is explored in greater depth in chapter 8.

of the interfaith movement."[63] In practice, this means that the often-shared concept of civic religious pluralism in IFE requires scholarly examination and that IRS serves as the locus to press the critical and constructive analysis of central theoretical constructs.[64] These constructs include Western civic pluralism and idealism, the universalizing of elite cultures, the almost never-ending incorporation of identities "into configurations of difference that make real difference invisible,"[65] and perpetual "neoliberal projects of the postcolonial nation-state."[66] In other words, as the faculty at Elon University argue, "The academic field of interreligious studies must maintain independence from the interfaith movement in order to critically assess discourses and practices that promote tolerance, pluralism, and respect for diversity."[67] Therefore, the Elon University program envisions IRS serving as a "counterpoint, complement, and correction to the interfaith movement and co-curricular models of interfaith engagement" and, as such, prepares students as scholars "to accomplish three overarching objectives: (1) to analyze the character of interreligious encounter; (2) to think critically about interfaith dialogue; and (3) to historicize diversity, pluralism, and tolerance."[68] For instance, although interfaith practitioners acknowledge their histories of interreligious conflict, oppression, and hatred, "in their effort to cast approved religious traditions in a positive light they are more likely to conclude that, nevertheless, none of our faiths *in their essence* truly promotes hatred and conflict."[69] On the other hand, scholars of religion and IRS, well versed in the pitfalls of essentialism, are "more likely to point out that what Americans like to call 'faiths' have historically been political traditions as much as anything, and that members of so-called 'faith communities' have been interested in asserting political power over others and fostering hatred of those who challenge what they see as their rightful power."[70] As chapter 8 explores, the relationship between IRS as an academic field and interfaith engagement (IFE) is not only complicated, but presents opportunities like the aforementioned example for the two to complement and mutually inform each other.

---

63 McCarthy, "(Inter)Religious Studies," 10.
64 McCarthy, 13
65 McCarthy, 13.
66 Allocco et al., "Constructing Interreligious Studies," 48.
67 Allocco et al., 36–37.
68 Allocco et al., 39.
69 Allocco et al., 41, italics original.
70 Allocco et al., 41–42.

IRS itself is not immune from being critiqued. In fact, it requires and benefits from external critique. For example, Rachel Mikva constructively criticizes IRS, which "has developed a dominant culture, in which progressive religious outlooks may exclude or silence some voices."[71] Such critiques are done in the spirit of caretaking, improving, and building IRS or IFE, which can surface the normative and prescriptive aspects of the field.

Normative and Prescriptive

IRS can adopt normative and prescriptive dimensions. *Normative* claims provide subjective views beyond the assertion of fact, although often grounded in established data. *Prescriptive* claims go a step further by suggesting (or prescribing) a path forward or a course of action.

A *descriptive* claim simply states data	"Relations between and among Jews, Christians, and Muslims took place in medieval Spain."
A *normative* claim provides a subjective view on a subject in a specific context	"Relations between and among Jews, Christians, and Muslims took place in medieval Spain, *where for more than seven centuries [they] lived together in an atmosphere of tolerance, and where literature, science, and the arts flourished.*"[a]
A *prescriptive* claim suggests future course of action	"Encounters between and among Jews, Christians, and Muslims took place in medieval Spain, and contemporary society ought to learn from and replicate it."

[a] Emphasized text is from the title and back cover of María Rosa Menocal, *The Ornament of the World* (New York: Back Bay Books, 2012).

All prescriptive statements contain normative claims, but not all normative statements contain prescriptive courses of action.

Scholars debate over whether scholarship ought to be normative and prescriptive or remain solely in the realm of description. For instance, a team of sociologists doing research on modern interreligious encounters in European urban contexts acknowledge, "while much of the previous research in the field has been conducted by active dialogue participants, the participating researchers in this project agree on an open, non-normative conception of

---

71 Rachel S. Mikva, "Six Issues That Complicate Interreligious Studies and Engagement," in *Interreligious/Interfaith Studies*, ed. Patel et al., 127.

(interreligious) dialogue."[72] Other scholars, however, argue that IRS contains normative agendas. Marianne Moyaert identifies the activist, alongside the scholar and the theologian, as one among three primary academic profiles that contribute to IRS.[73] Hedges maintains that IRS has an "interest in social change, particularly involving social cohesion and religious tolerance in society"[74] and that it "pushes at hegemonic boundaries . . . [which is] often about questioning those who want to keep identities tied down, or else it plays with the boundaries of traditional categories, for instance in exploring dual religious belonging or identity."[75] Jeannine Hill Fletcher shows that IRS strives for "interfaith solidarity," and "as a socially engaged project, interfaith studies might be conceptualized as a discipline dedicated to positively shaping our world by increasing knowledge of diverse faiths and encouraging cooperation among people of different convictions."[76] In other words, not only do IRS scholars examine the many modes and contexts of interreligious relations, but some scholars also inquire about how best to foster "interfaith solidarity," "stimulate change,"[77] and determine whether and how "interreligious dialogue play[s] a role in resolving religious conflicts and healing past injustices."[78]

In support of normative and prescriptive approaches that go beyond collecting data and rigorous observation, Dunbar rhetorically asks and forcefully responds:

Should scholars simply describe the history, sociology, and philosophy of dialogue, or may they promote interreligious dialogue in society? Is it proper for scholars of religion to participate in interreligious dialogue from their own religious convictions, or should they always remain detached and objective? . . . It would be foolish to ignore the need for value-judgments in academic study. It has been said that if we do not know our history we are bound to repeat it. . . . Scholars need to make

---

72 Ipgrave et al., *Religion and Dialogue in the City*, 10.
73 Marianne Moyaert, "The Scholar, the Theologian, and the Activist," in *Interreligious Studies*, ed. Gustafson, 34–42.
74 Hedges, "Interreligious Studies," 1078.
75 Hedges, "Interreligious Studies: A New Direction in the Study of Religion?" 14.
76 Jeannine Hill Fletcher, "The Promising Practice of Antiracist Approaches to Interfaith Studies," in *Interreligious/Interfaith Studies*, ed. Patel et al., 137.
77 Fletcher, "The Promising Practice of Antiracist Approaches to Interfaith Studies," 137.
78 Dunbar, "The Place of Interreligious Dialogue in the Academic Study of Religion," 16.

value-judgments about slavery, Antisemitism, and racism, for example. Fighting racism and Antisemitism are not merely the tasks of others but the tasks of us all, and such vigilance must be continued by every generation. Interreligious dialogue, too, needs to be undertaken perennially as preventative medicine to avoid bloodshed in the name of religion. Scholars must be critical of current religious atrocities as well as atrocities committed in the past. Speaking out against genocide and Antisemitism are tasks within a scholar's duty.[79]

Dunbar's sentiment echoes Elon University's SLO to train students to "offer constructive suggestions for improving these models"[80] and thus invite prescriptive paths forward.[81]

Normative and prescriptive aspects of IRS inform the pronounced applied and practitioner trends in the field, often emerging with the emphasis on professional and vocational skills, traits, and competencies. For instance, Eboo Patel preaches the applied dimension of IRS, which for him and Interfaith America (formerly Interfaith Youth Core) is about "nurturing a cadre of professionals"[82] and interfaith leaders "to make interfaith cooperation the norm in America."[83] Patel envisions a primary goal of IRS is to "recognize the importance of training people who have the knowledge base and skill set needed to engage religious diversity in a way that promotes peace, stability, and cooperation—and to begin offering academic programs that certify such leaders."[84] This vision influences some IRS instructors, such as American professors Wakoh Shannon Hickey and Margarita Suárez, who argue, "Interfaith studies has the explicit goal of promoting pluralism as a social norm."[85] Chapter 14 explores the applied dimension of IRS as practical interfaith wisdom (interreligious phronesis), and chapter 15 touches on the professional application of IRS for leadership. This emerging trend is also captured by Deanna Womack, who imagines "interfaith studies courses would train pre-med students in an interreligious competency that is directly relevant to their field and equip business majors with a skill set for communicating

---

79 Dunbar, 460.
80 Allocco et al., "Constructing Interreligious Studies," 40.
81 Allocco et al., 40.
82 Patel, "Toward a Field of Interfaith Studies."
83 Interfaith Youth Core, "Mission and Programs."
84 Patel, "Toward a Field of Interfaith Studies."
85 Wakoh Shannon Hickey and Margarita M. W. Suárez, "Meeting Others, Seeing Myself," in *Interreligious/Interfaith Studies*, ed. Patel et al., 109.

with diverse clientele."[86] Furthermore, the applied dimensions extend beyond classroom instruction to include continuing education for religious leaders,[87] interreligious leadership training for prison chaplaincy directors,[88] diversity and inclusion competencies in business leadership and professions,[89] and the civic realm of cultivating the contemporary "interreligious city"[90] teeming with urban interreligious encounters,[91] to name a few.

Self-Implicating

Consider the common refrain that "all research is me-search." That is, the scholar is always to some degree implicated in her research, which can impact the questions she asks and the findings she discovers. Leirvik argues, "inter-religious studies should be carried out with the openness to reflect critically on *one's own position* in the spaces between different traditions. When study-ing a separate religion, it has been commonplace in religious studies to claim that you need not—or should not—be implicated yourself in the object of study."[92] In other words, since, for Leirvik, IRS includes the complex spaces "between religion and secularity," it is not possible for the scholar to be situ-ated outside of the field, and, therefore, "it is hard to see how anyone could say that he or she is not part of the field studied. . . . Who is not part of the spaces between religions, cultures, and secularities?"[93] For Hedges, IRS often "recognizes that the researcher, teacher, or student is an agent implicated in negotiations of power[;] for there is no neutral value-free position."[94]

86 Deanna Ferree Womack, "From History of Religions to Interfaith Studies," in *Interreligious/Interfaith Studies*, ed. Eboo et al., 24.

87 Jennifer Howe Peace and Or N. Rose, "The Value of Interreligious Education for Religious Leaders," in *Interreligious/Interfaith Studies*, ed. Patel et al., 170–80.

88 Barbara A. McGraw, "From Prison Religion to Interfaith Leadership for Institu-tional Change," in *Interreligious/Interfaith Studies*, ed. Patel et al., 183–95.

89 Mark E. Hanshaw and Usra Ghazi, "Interfaith Studies and the Professions," in *Interreligious/Interfaith Studies*, ed. Patel et al., 196–208.

90 Heather Miller Rubens, Homayra Ziad, and Benjamin E. Sax, "Towards an Inter-religious City," in *Interreligious/Interfaith Studies*, ed. Patel et al., 209–19.

91 Ipgrave et al., *Religion and Dialogue in the City.*

92 Oddbjørn Leirvik, *Interreligious Studies: A Relational Approach to Religious Activ-ism and the Study of Religion* (New York: Bloomsbury, 2014), 16, italics original.

93 Leirvik, "Interreligious Studies: A New Academic Discipline?" 36.

94 Hedges, "Interreligious Studies: A New Direction in the Study of Religion?" 13.

Hence, Leirvik emphasizes the need for open and critical self-implication in advocating that "interreligious studies can be meaningfully done only in a willingness to reflect critically on one's own position in the space between."[95]

The issue of self-implication recalls the insider–outsider problem raised earlier in the chapter, which seemingly remains eternally present in the study of religion and inquires about the appropriate place of religiously devout scholars of religion. In the case of IRS, the problem more accurately inquires about the place of scholars (regardless of their religious, spiritual, nonreligious, or secular identity), not only in the implementation of their scholarship but also in their relation to interreligious encounter (regardless of whether they actively engage as interfaith activists and practitioners or not). While many IRS scholars welcome engaged activist- or practitioner-research scholarly approaches, McCarthy counsels IRS scholars to continue working "through the insider/outsider problem in a way that emphasizes critical distance."[96] Similarly, without dismissing the importance of the distinction between insider perspectives and outsider theories, Womack urges scholars of IRS to refrain from making an "independent judgment on the reality of a religious tradition but should reflect upon and recognize their own values and biases while also learning from others. Moving beyond the insider–outside dichotomy, this means working to build a common life."[97] IRS often extends beyond the confines of an academic project,[98] blurs the line between scholar and practitioner,[99] and therefore self-implicates the scholar in their research. The agency of the IRS scholar can be considered a defining feature of the field. Leirvik emphasizes the role of scholars as "agents in the spaces between" religions, cultures, and secularities, for they are often significant contributors to power negotiations within and between religious traditions, individuals, and communities.[100]

In 1998, Dunbar proposed an experiential approach to studying interreligious dialogue in the academy. Studying dialogue across religious difference falls within the broad scope of interreligious studies. Although Dunbar acknowledges the approach as "most controversial," it need not be

---

95 Leirvik, "Interreligious Studies: A New Academic Discipline?" 36.
96 McCarthy, "(Inter)Religious Studies," 11.
97 Womack, "From History of Religions to Interfaith Studies," 25.
98 Jennifer Peace, "Toward a Field of Interfaith Studies," in roundtable with Jeanine Diller, Eboo Patel, Jennifer Peace, and Colleen Windham-Hughes, *Journal of Interreligious Studies* 16 (2015): 10.
99 Paul Hedges, "Interreligious Studies: A New Direction in the Study of Religion?" 13.
100 Leirvik, "Interreligious Studies: A New Academic Discipline?" 37.

incompatible with the wider critical academic study of religion. Dunbar's approach beckons the religiously devout scholar to engage in direct encounter as a method of research: "The best way for a scholar to learn about interreligious dialogue, if he or she is religious, is to spend time directly in dialogue and write about it from personal experience."[101]

However, this approach need not be reserved for the religiously devout alone but may be utilized by all IRS scholars. This is especially true if it is the case, as Leirvik suggests, that there is no one who is not part of the spaces between religions, cultures, and secularities. Dunbar continues, "Many scholars are personally engaged in dialogue conferences outside the walls of the university and write about their experiences inside those walls. This is a valid approach."[102] In fact, the belief—outdated to some—in the possibility of an absolutely detached, outside, objective observer has waned.[103] Similarly, Mikva identifies the "promise of interreligious studies is its stress on learning in the presence of the other, weaving the supple cloth of sophisticated study in real relationship."[104] According to Mikva, "interreligious studies and interreligious engagement are interdependent, and they also overlap. Both arenas equip people to navigate a complex multifaith world, and some so equipped to become interfaith leaders."[105] Cultivating the ability to navigate a complex multifaith world—what Womack refers to as "interreligious awareness"[106]— rests squarely within the primary scope of chapter 14 (which examines IRS

---

101 Dunbar, "The Place of Interreligious Dialogue in the Academic Study of Religion," 463.

102 Dunbar, 463.

103 E.g., Gavin Flood argues that research of religion in culture becomes "a dialogical enterprise in which the inquirer is situated within a particular context or narrative tradition, and whose research into narrative traditions, that become the objects of investigation, must be apprehended in a much richer and multi-faceted way. . . . The relationship between the situated observer and situation of observation, becomes dialogical in the sense that the observer is thrown into conversation with people and texts of the object tradition. Rather than the disengaged reason of the social scientist observing, recording and theorizing data, we have a situation in which research is imaged as a 'conversation,' or more accurately 'critical conversation,' in which the interactive nature of research is recognized." Gavin Flood, *Beyond Phenomenology* (London: Cassell, 1999), 143; cited in Leirvik, "Interreligious Studies: A Relational Approach to the Study of Religion," 15.

104 Mikva, "Six Issues That Complicate Interreligious Studies and Engagement," 133.

105 Mikva, 136.

106 Deanna Womack forecasts, "Young people . . . will need to demonstrate interreligious awareness in their private and professional relationships." Womack, "From History of Religions to Interfaith Studies," 25.

for practical interfaith wisdom as interreligious phronesis) and chapter 15 (which situates interreligious phronesis in the context of leadership).

Consider the following "threefold pattern for clarifying the researcher's authorial identity"[107] from Belden Lane, a scholar working in the contemporary study of spirituality:

1. The need to identify openly the authorial self, that is, the writer's own perspective, . . . [which] addresses the problem of the *absent author* whose biases are present but undisclosed.
2. The need to recognize the instructive potential of the authorial self as a bridge figure in providing the reader a deeper understanding of the world of the "other," [which] recognizes the possibilities and difficulties of the *engaged author* whose experience becomes admittedly a part of the analysis.
3. The need subsequently to conceal or deconstruct the authorial self, keeping the researcher's identity in the background so as to focus on the research itself, . . . [which addresses] the problem of the *interfering author* whose subjectivity abandons methodological rigor, risking a dangerous self-indulgence if not a new colonialism with respect to the subject(s) being studied.[108]

Lane's threefold pattern provides a useful template for IRS scholars to locate themselves vis-à-vis the object(s) of their research. Lane shows that the "author's self is always inescapably present" regardless of the scholar's field or discipline, and "to pretend otherwise, out of zealous commitment to the imagined purity of scholarship, is no less dangerous than uncritically inviting the reader into the writer's own private world."[109] Elizabeth Kubek reveals the aspects of self-implication, agency, activism, and self-discovery in IRS that, like feminist studies, are also often present in other multidisciplinary fields and area studies: "the discovery of one's own place within a living narrative of resistance and risk . . . [is a shared] interdisciplinary trait [alongside] focus on a 'problem or issue or intellectual question' rather than on a single body of

---

107 Belden Lane, "Writing in Spirituality as a Self-Implicating Act," in *Exploring Christian Spirituality*, ed. Bruce H. Lescher and Elizabeth Liebert (New York: Paulist Press, 2006), 57.
108 Lane, "Writing in Spirituality as a Self-Implicating Act," 57–58, italics original.
109 Lane, 57.

knowledge."[110] Like feminist studies, religious studies, and other area studies, IRS too is a multi-, inter-, and transdisciplinary field.

Multi-, Inter-, and Transdisciplinary

IRS is *multi*disciplinary because, as the prefix suggests, it includes scholars from a multitude of disciplines, each drawing on their own disciplinary methods, working to address common questions, problems, or themes. However, each scholar will often stay within their discipline, refrain from drawing on other disciplines, and seldom blend disciplines. IRS can be *inter*disciplinary and *trans*disciplinary when scholars integrate their approaches to collaboratively approach a question, problem, or theme with the aim of arriving at a shared synthesized approach or multidimensional conclusion that is dependent on the various disciplinary methods involved. The interdisciplinary process becomes transdisciplinary when it "is at once *between, across* and *beyond* all disciplines"[111] and generates a novel or innovative approach or conclusion, that is, when it *transcends* the traditional boundaries of the disciplines involved to result in something new beyond their sum total.[112] "In interdisciplinary theory, a fieldwork approach is sometimes referred to as 'transdisciplinary' because it allows 'integration . . . of insights generated outside the academy.'"[113] The *trans-* aspect of IRS also raises the question about whether *inter*religious studies, which contains the *inter-* prefix, ought to be more appropriately labeled *trans*religious studies for various reasons relating not only to disciplinary boundaries but also to the fluid and permeable boundaries between religious traditions and identities (a question addressed in chapter 12, especially as it pertains to transreligious theological studies).

Like the general study of religion, IRS draws on several disciplinary methods and approaches to examine "the multiple dimensions of individuals and groups who orient around religion differently interact with one another, along with

---

110 Elizabeth Kubeck, "Common Ground," in *Interreligious/Interfaith Studies*, ed. Patel et al., 28; author's quotations from Allen F. Repko and Rick Szostak, *Interdisciplinary Research*, 3rd ed. (Los Angeles: Sage, 2017), 3–6.

111 Ton Jörg, *New Thinking in Complexity for the Social Sciences and Humanities* (Dordrecht: Springer, 2011), 50; quoting presentation by Mircea Bertea.

112 See Hans Gustafson, "Is Transreligious Theology Unavoidable in Interreligious Theology and Dialogue?" *Open Theology* 2 (2016): 248–60.

113 Kubeck, "Common Ground," 32; author's quotation from Repko and Szostak, *Interdisciplinary Research*, 25.

the implications of [these] for communities, civil society, and global politics."[114] Hence, IRS is multidisciplinary. As IRS has evolved from an "area" of study to a field, Bourdieu's field theory predicts it also can become "a battleground for struggles over academic capital," and thus becomes a contested territory.[115]

IRS is already contested, as various views emerge about its nature and place in the academy. To the question "Is it even a field?" Jeanine Diller argues that its most natural home is within the broader field of Religious Studies (RS).[116] Similarly, McCarthy argues that RS "would seem to be [IRS's] logical disciplinary home."[117] However, Hedges argues that IRS "is a diverse rather than strictly limited field. . . . it is a meeting point of a set of interests and research areas rather than seeking to become a new disciplinary area itself."[118] IRS "is not a self-enclosed discipline nor is it a distinct subject area, rather it is the nexus of a set of interlinked discipline or activities."[119] Patel makes the case for IRS (or interfaith studies) to be more naturally allied with history, political science, and sociology.

- *History* offers "instances where diversity has become coexistence or cooperation."
- *Political science* and theory clarify the questions about "under what political and social conditions can communities who have very different ideas of what is good and lawful on Earth, based on a set of cosmic convictions, live together in the same society?"
- *Sociology* provides data from those "doing empirical work, both ethnographic and quantitative, about how communities who orient differently around religion might get along."[120]

These differing views demonstrate the point that IRS has achieved field status[121] and, what is more, reveal its multidisciplinary nature and manifold

---

114 Patel, "Toward a Field of Interfaith Studies"; cited in Oddbjørn Leirvik, "Area, Field, Discipline," in *Interreligious Studies*, ed. Gustafson, 17.

115 Leirvik, "Area, Field, Discipline," 17 (referencing French social scientist Pierre Bourdieu).

116 Diller, "Toward a Field of Interfaith Studies," 7–8.

117 McCarthy, "(Inter)Religious Studies," 4.

118 Paul Hedges, "Editorial Introduction: Interreligious Studies," *Journal for the Academic Study of Religion* 27, no. 2 (2014): 128.

119 Hedges, "Interreligious Studies: A New Direction in the Study of Religion?" 13.

120 Patel, "Toward a Field of Interfaith Studies."

121 Leirvik, "Area, Field, Discipline," 17.

committed stakeholders. With respect to the role of the researcher, "interreligious studies are by nature interdisciplinary, as the multidimensionality of interreligious relations can be grasped only by a combination of cultural, analytical, legal, social science, religious studies, and theological approaches."[122] Similarly, Kristi Del Vecchio and Noah Silverman identify interdisciplinarity as one among six "principal themes" of IRS curricula because theoretically it "leads to a more holistic accurate approach to interfaith interaction," and practically it "better trains leaders who will work within a wide range of professional sectors."[123]

The majority of IRS scholars come from RS and Theological Studies (TS).[124] McCarthy is among the leading voices on this question, concurring with Diller that IRS is best situated within RS as a subfield:[125] "to locate it in the already multidisciplinary field of religious studies is both apt and problematic."[126] Apt because "religious studies scholars are equipped to address the subject with unique depth and focus"[127] (among other reasons), but problematic because IRS clearly has an "orientation to empathy and engagement," a "boundary [that] will have to be carefully renegotiated" with RS.[128] RS's emphasis on critical scholarship "is, at least on the surface, at odds with the more affective and religion-friendly goals of interfaith and interreligious studies."[129] However, "religion-friendly" does not mean IRS is a theological endeavor despite its often "normative agenda and deep ties to the US interfaith movement whose roots and frameworks are Christian."[130] Leirvik distinguishes IRS from RS and TS due the relational nature of IRS:

---

122 Leirvik, "Interreligious Studies: A New Academic Discipline?" 36.

123 Kristi Del Vecchio and Noah J. Silverman, "Learning from the Field," in *Interreligious/Interfaith Studies*, ed. Patel et al., 52.

124 The significant majority of American scholars involved with the Association of Interreligious/Interfaith Studies (AIIS) and the European Society of Intercultural Theology and Interreligious Studies (ESITIS) come from religious studies and theological studies backgrounds and meet in the "Interreligious and Interfaith Studies Unit" at the annual conference of the American Academy of Religion (AAR) and not the annual conferences for the Association for the Sociology of Religion (ASR), the American Historical Association (AHA), or the American Political Science Association (APSA), to name a few.

125 Diller, "Toward a Field of Interfaith Studies," 7–8.

126 McCarthy, "(Inter)Religious Studies," 3.

127 McCarthy, 12.

128 McCarthy, 9.

129 McCarthy, 8.

130 McCarthy, 2.

In my view, there is something essentially relational with interreligious studies that make them different from religious studies in the conventional sense and from confessional theology. In my understanding, the notion of interreligious studies refers both to the *object* of research and to the *subject* who is carrying out the research (i.e., the researcher and the way in which the research is done).[131]

Does IRS attempt to navigate a middle course between RS and TS, drawing on both RS and TS (and others)? IRS can serve as an "interface between a more traditionally secular Religious Studies discipline, and a more traditional confessional theological discipline."[132] It "bridges the gaps"[133] between RS and TS and "tends to see itself as potentially including both as well as folk from other areas; IRS also has a strong focus or interest (critically and analytically) on such things as interreligious dialogue, relations, and encounters and social cohesion,"[134] which are also of interest to scholars outside RS and TS. In similar fashion, IRS is "an adaptive discipline . . . [that] has the potential to transcend the tension between religious studies and theology with regard to religious confessionalism."[135]

With respect to IRS's relation to theological and dialogical approaches, although IRS "is related to the praxis field of interreligious (or interfaith) dialogue" (e.g., comparative theology), its scope is broader since it goes beyond constructive learning about and from each other's traditions (e.g., dialogue and cooperation) by examining "confrontation and conflict."[136] IRS draws on TS (e.g., confessional approaches with emic claims, comparative theology, intercultural theology, interreligious theology) and RS (secular outsider approaches), but also inquires about public discourse at the levels of grassroots community, geopolitical state, public policy, and institutional and religious leaders. The multilevel possibilities need not obscure the value of IRS. Rather, with the emphasis on the *relations*—between, with, and among

---

131 Leirvik, "Interreligious Studies: A New Academic Discipline?" 36.

132 Hedges, "Interreligious Studies," 1077.

133 Hedges, "Interreligious Studies: A New Direction in the Study of Religion?" 14.

134 Paul Hedges, "Decolonising the Study of Religion (in Relation to the Social and Human Sciences)," *Paul Hedges Weblog*, March 12, 2018.

135 Womack, "From History of Religions to Interfaith Studies," 23. Womack uses the "interfaith studies" and not "interreligious studies".

136 Leirvik, "Interreligious Studies: A New Academic Discipline?" 33.

people and groups that orient around religion differently—IRS can encompass a range of scholarship and methods.

〜   〜   〜

The field of IRS is not new. Scholars have for a long time examined the many ways individuals and groups with various religious and nonreligious identities engage and encounter each another. IRS is a wide-ranging field that only recently has more formally identified itself amidst the flourishing and often turbulent growth of global religious diversity and encounter. As the field continues to evolve and change, and as scholars discover their niches within its manifold, IRS will likely remain intimately indebted and related to the study of religion and its critical resources to interrogate the fluid and contested concept of religion. The remaining chapters of Part I move beyond the concept of religion by examining the global religious landscape, the dynamic nature of religions, the Lived Religion method, and the trend to educate citizenry with a basic religious literacy for a flourishing society.

2

Global Religious Identities

Chapter Outline

I. Global Religious Landscape
    a. *By the Numbers*
    b. *The Religiously Unaffiliated*
II. Religious Identity
    a. *Personal and Social Identities*
    b. *"Forging Solidarities"*
    c. *Authentic Identities*
    d. *It's Complicated*

In 2010, over 83 percent of the world's population identified as religious, and by 2050 it is projected to increase to over 86 percent.[1] Despite the predictions of the 1960s that "God is Dead,"[2] religion remains alive and well for now and the foreseeable future. The study of religion in the academy is flourishing as well. Todd M. Johnson and Brian J. Grim observe, "the increased prominence religion has assumed in academic fields including history, sociology, international relations, and a host of others is one of the unexpected developments of the early twenty-first century."[3] Despite Western secular forces, which

---

    1 Pew Research Center, "The Future of World Religions," April 2, 2015.
    2 Famous *Time* magazine cover that asks, "Is God Dead?" April 8, 1966.
    3 Todd M. Johnson and Brian J. Grim, with Gina A. Bellofatto, *The World's Religions in Figures* (Chichester: Wiley Blackwell, 2013), 1.

remain prominent, religion matters, and global populations continue to religiously identify in various ways. Regardless of whether one is religious or not, or whether one has positive feelings toward it, religion will likely retain its relevance in academic and global life. The datum 86 percent of the world's population identifying as religious is telling but not terribly informative for grasping the global diversity of religious practices, beliefs, and identities. Who identifies with what religions, where, how, and why? What does it mean to express one's religious identity? How are religious identities related to the myriad other ways people identify? Who identifies with religion, and what are some of the ways they identify? Answers to these questions are complicated. This chapter provides an overview of the current global religious landscape by the numbers, with an emphasis on North America, Europe, and the religiously unaffiliated. It examines personal and social dimensions of religious identity with an eye on their complicated dynamic and intersectional nature to "forge solidarities" between and among individuals and groups who orient around religion differently.

GLOBAL RELIGIOUS LANDSCAPE

Engaging religious diversity and studying interreligious relations can begin with the basic questions of who is in the world and how they relate to and identify with religion, and what are the major trends and shifts taking place in global and local religious demographics. Table 2.1 charts the global religious landscape measured in 2010, and its 2050 projections, for the world, North America, and Europe. A brief scan of the data reveals several trends. By the year 2050, the number of Muslims is expected to roughly equal the number of Christians. The percentage of Unaffiliated (which includes atheists, agnostics, and others) is expected to increase in Europe and North America but decline globally. In North America, Jews are expected to decrease in number and percentage, Christians are expected to decrease in percentage (while growing in number at a slower rate), the Unaffiliated are expected to double in number, and Muslims are likely to triple in number. Furthermore, Hindus and those following Folk Religions are forecast to double and Other Religions are expected to triple in percentage. Europe is expected to have fewer Christians and fewer Jews but more Muslims and Unaffiliated (by percentage). Further, Europe is projected to become more religiously diverse with the percentage of Hindus, Buddhists, Other Religions, and Folk Religions all

Table 2.1. Global religious populations.

Religion[a]	2010 % of world (population)	2050 *Projected* % of world (population)	2010 % of North America (population)	2050 *Projected* % of North America (population)	2010 % of Europe (population)	2050 *Projected* % of Europe (population)
Christians	31.4 (2,168,330,000)	31.4 (2,918,070,000)	77.4 (266,630,000)	65.8 (286,710,000)	74.5 (553,280,000)	65.2 (454,090,000)
Muslims	23.2 (1,599,700,000)	29.7 (2,761,480,000)	1.0 (3,480,000)	2.4 (10,350,000)	5.9 (43,470,000)	10.2 (70,870,000)
Unaffiliated	16.4 (1,131,150,000)	13.2 (1,230,340,000)	17.1 (59,040,000)	25.6 (111,340,000)	18.8 (139,890,000)	23.3 (162,320,000)
Hindus	15 (1,032,210,000)	14.9 (1,384,360,000)	0.7 (2,250,000)	1.3 (5,850,000)	0.2 (1,380,000)	0.4 (2,660,000)
Buddhists	7.1 (487,690,000)	5.2 (486,270,000)	1.1 (3,860,000)	1.4 (2,220,000)	0.2 (1,350,000)	0.4 (2,490,000)
Folk Religion	5.9 (404,690,000)	4.8 (449,140,000)	0.3 (1,020,000)	0.6 (2,630,000)	0.1 (870,000)	0.2 (1,590,000)
Other Religions	0.8 (58,150,000)	0.7 (61,450,000)	0.6 (2,200,000)	1.5 (6,540,000)	0.1 (890,000)	0.2 (1,100,000)
Jews	0.2 (13,860,000)	0.2 (16,090,000)	1.8 (6,040,000)	1.4 (5,920,000)	0.2 (1,420,000)	0.2 (1,200,000)

[a] Pew Research Center, "The Future of World Religions."

roughly doubling. India is projected to remain a Hindu majority nation "but also will have the largest Muslim population of any country in the world, surpassing Indonesia."[4] The Christian majority in the United States will drop from three-quarters to nearly two-thirds, and Muslims will overtake Jews as the second largest religion behind Christianity. Drilling deeper into the numbers unveils important details about various religious traditions and global regions.

By the Numbers

Christianity is projected to remain the world's most populous religion, but not by much. Although their numbers will continue to grow—from 2.2 billion in 2010 to 2.9 billion by 2050—Christians will remain roughly 31.4% of the world's population. The United States is projected to remain home to

---

4 Pew Research Center, "The Future of World Religions," 5.

Ranks of unaffiliated are expected to grow due to religious switching			
Religious switching, 2015-2020			
	Switching in	Switching out	Net change
Unaffiliated	12,220,000	4,640,000	+7,570,000
Muslims	1,300,000	880,000	+420,000
Folk religions	760,000	410,000	+350,000
Other religions	370,000	130,000	+240,000
Hindus	30,000	30,000	<10,000
Jews	40,000	80,000	–40,000
Buddhists	470,000	830,000	–370,000
Christians	4,960,000	13,140,000	–8,180,000

Figure 2.1. Pew Research Center, "The Changing Global Religious Landscape," April 5, 2017, 17.

the most Christians, with 11.2% of the world's population in 2010 (and 9.0% in 2050), followed by Brazil. Notably, according to the Pew Research Center (Pew hereafter), "the share of the world's Christian population living in sub-Saharan Africa is expected to grow—from 24% in 2010 to 38% by 2050—while the share living in Europe will continue to fall, from 26% in 2010 to about 16% by 2050."[5] In many regions these changes are largely due to fertility rates; however, "switching," the process by which an individual changes or "switches" religious identity, has a greater impact in certain regions such as North America, Europe, and the Latin American-Caribbean region where "Christians are projected to experience net losses because of religious switching, with most of the switching toward no religious affiliation"[6] (see Figure 2.1).

Muslims around the world, due to young age and high fertility rates, are projected to increase rapidly in number, "growing from about 1.6 billion in 2010 to nearly 2.8 billion in 2050. Muslims are expected to grow twice as fast as the overall global population,"[7] with an increase from 23% of the world's population in 2010 to 30% in 2050. The Asia-Pacific region is projected to remain home to the most Muslims, with approximately 62% in 2010, dropping to 53% by 2050. Indonesia, the country

5 Pew Research Center, 59.
6 Pew Research Center, 67.
7 Pew Research Center, 70.

with the most Muslims with over 13% in 2010, the percentage is expected to drop to 9.3% by 2050, which will place it behind India (expected 11.2%) and Pakistan (expected 9.9%).

The religiously unaffiliated, which includes atheists, agnostics, "nones," and those who report "nothing in particular," are "projected to grow modestly, rising from 1.1 billion in 2010 to a peak of more than 1.2 billion in 2040 and then dropping back slightly."[8] Significantly, the Unaffiliated are concentrated in relatively few countries,[9] and their projected decline is assumed to be largely due to their advanced age and low fertility rate relative to other globally significant religious groups.[10] Pew's data show that "the three largest unaffiliated populations live in China [61.9% of world's unaffiliated population in 2010; 53.9% in 2050], Japan [6.4% of world's unaffiliated population in 2010; 5.9% in 2050], and the United States [4.5% of world's unaffiliated population in 2010; 8.2% in 2050]; there are also significant numbers of religious unaffiliated people in several European countries. All of these areas have older populations and lower fertility rates than the overall global population."[11]

Hindus are expected to retain a stable "share of the world's population over the next four decades, at about 15%,"[12] with India remaining home to over 93% of all Hindus and Nepal a distant second home to 2.3% in 2010 (projected 2.8% in 2050). The United States' Hindu population is expected to increase from 0.2% in 2010 to 0.3% in 2050 (of the world's population), raising the United States from seventh to fifth in the list of top ten countries with the largest Hindu populations.

Buddhists are projected to reach their peak population in 2030 at 511,300,000 (6.1% of world's population) and then decrease to 486,270,000 in 2050 (5.2% of world's population), due to the "Buddhists' ageing population and low fertility rate relative to other religious groups."[13] China is expected to remain home to roughly half of all Buddhists worldwide, decreasing from 50% (2010) to 49.7% (2050). By 2050, the United States is projected to break into the top ten countries with the largest Buddhist populations—the only Western country to do so—with 1.1% of the world's population. According

8 Pew Research Center, 81.
9 Pew Research Center, 85.
10 Pew Research Center, 81.
11 Pew Research Center, 81.
12 Pew Research Center, 92.
13 Pew Research Center, 102.

to Pew, China is also home to 72.7% (2010) of people who identify with Folk Religions, which, defined by Pew for this data, include traditions "closely associated with a particular group of people, ethnicity or tribe. They often have no formal creeds or sacred texts. Examples of folk religions include African traditional religions, Native American religions and Australian aboriginal religions."[14] As a percentage of the world's overall population, Folk Religion representation is expected to decline from 5.9% in 2010 to 4.8%, mostly due to low fertility rates among adherents.

The category Other Religions includes Daoism, Shinto, Sikhism, Zoroastrianism, Wicca, New Religious Movements, Contemporary Paganisms, and others. In 2010, 0.8% of the world's population was identified as Other Religions, which is 58,150,000 people. The category Other Religions is problematic because some of the traditions included are quite large. Sikhism, for instance, is estimated to have between 25 and 30 million followers, which means it makes up roughly half the category, not to mention being two to three times larger than Judaism. Though the majority in the Other Religions category are projected to remain in the Asia-Pacific region (89% in 2010 and 79% expected in 2050) and their growth rate will be slow, some regions will likely have significant growth. In North America, for instance, this group is expected to nearly triple from 4% in 2010 to 11% in 2050 (of the world's population), due, in large part, to North Americans switching into these Other Religions (e.g., Wicca, Asatru, etc.). The United States is expected to become home to the third most in this category by 2050 with 9.4% of the world's Other Religion's population (up from sixth place with 3.3% in 2010). Canada, although a country with a relatively low population, is expected to see a rapid increase in this category and by 2050 is projected to be among the top nine countries.[15]

Jews make up roughly 0.2% of the world's population and are expected to remain so in 2050. Israel recently overtook the United States as home to the most Jews. In 2018, there were nearly nine million Jews in Israel, which is over 44% of the world's Jewish population.[16] While growing in Israel (and in the Middle East–North Africa region), the Jewish population in North America is projected to decline both in number and as a share of the population.

---

14 Pew Research Center, 112.
15 Pew Research Center, 129.
16 TOI Staff, "At 70, Israel's Population Is 8.842 Million, 43% of World Jewry," *Times of Israel*, April 16, 2018.

Although the Jewish population will steadily grow globally, it is projected to decrease in North America and Europe. Likewise, the Jewish percentage of the global population will also decrease in those regions due to immigration of non-Jewish people coupled with an aging Jewish population.[17]

Pew's data report that growth and decline in religious populations are mostly due to what Pew refers to as "natural increase," which is "births minus deaths." Natural increase mutually drives the growth of the two largest religions, Christianity and Islam. According to Pew's data, although "more babies were born to Christian mothers than to members of any other religion in recent years, reflecting Christianity's continued status as the world's largest religious group, . . . this is unlikely to be the case . . . less than 20 years from now [when] the number of babies born to Muslims is expected to modestly exceed births to Christians."[18] In some regions, such as Europe, migration can noticeably influence growth rates. For instance, "Europe has experienced a record influx of asylum seekers fleeing conflicts in Syria and other predominantly Muslim countries,"[19] which prompts some researchers to predict increases of the Muslim population from 4.9% in Europe in 2016 to as high as 14% in 2050. However, "even if migration into Europe were to immediately and permanently stop, the Muslim population of Europe still would be expected to rise from the current level 4.9% to 7.4% by the year 2050. This is because Muslims [in Europe] are younger (by 13 years, on average) and have higher fertility (one child more per woman, on average) than other Europeans."[20] In short, the growing number of Muslims in Europe combined with the shrinking non-Muslim populations in Europe yields an expected "rising *share* of Muslims in Europe's overall population in all scenarios."[21] Similarly, a higher-than-usual rate of switching in North America, usually from Christianity to religiously unaffiliated, influences growth rates as well. The frequency of switching in Europe and North America, reflected in the slower growth rate of Christianity and the rapid growth rate of the religious disaffiliation, raises further questions about one of the fastest growing groups in those regions: the religiously unaffiliated.

---

17 Pew Research Center, "The Future of World Religions," 133–41.

18 Pew Research Center, "The Changing Global Religious Landscape," April 5, 2017, 4.

19 Pew Research Center, "Europe's Growing Muslim Population," November 29, 2017, 4.

20 Pew Research Center, "Europe's Growing Muslim Population," 5.

21 Pew Research Center, 30, italics original.

The Religiously Unaffiliated

Although the percentage of the religiously unaffiliated is projected to decline, their representation in the Western world is expected to continue to increase, especially due to switching and disaffiliation from the tradition in which they were raised to another tradition or to no tradition at all. For instance, in the United States, "it is particularly common for people who grew up as Christians to become unaffiliated, [however] some people who were raised with no religious affiliation also have switched to become Christians."[22] Between 2015 and 2020, Christians are projected to experience the largest losses due to switching. Globally, about 5 million people are expected to become Christians, while 13 million are expected to leave Christianity, with most of these departures joining the ranks of the religiously unaffiliated. The Unaffiliated are projected to add 12 million and lose 4.6 million, for a net gain of 7.6 million, while the projected new changes due to switching for other religious groups are smaller.[23] In the United States, the decline of Christian affiliation "is particularly pronounced among young adults, [but also occurs] among Americans of all ages," race, education, and gender.[24] Roughly one in five of these religiously unaffiliated Americans disaffiliate through switching. Although the unaffiliated identity runs across all categories, the following generalizations can be drawn:

- Religious "nones" now constitute 24% of all college graduates.
- Fewer women than men are religious "nones."
- Although it is low relative to other religious groups, the retention rate of the unaffiliated has increased. . . . And among Millennials [born between 1981–1996], "nones" actually have one of the highest retention rates of all the religious categories.
- The atheist and agnostic share of the "nones" has grown to 31%. Those identifying as "nothing in particular" and describing religion as unimportant in their lives continue to account for 39% of all "nones." But the share identifying as "nothing in particular" while also affirming that religion is either "very" or "somewhat" important to them has fallen to 30% of all "nones."[25]

---

22 Pew Research Center, "The Changing Global Religious Landscape," April 5, 2017, 16.
23 Pew Research Center, 16.
24 Pew Research Center, "America's Changing Religious Landscape," May 12, 2015, 3.
25 Pew Research Center, 14.

Table 2.2. Percent of those who do not believe in God in the United States (atheists).

Year (poll)[a]	%
1944 (Gallup)	4.0
1947 (Gallup)	6.0
1964 (American Piety)	3.0
1994 (GSS)	3.0
2005 (Baylor Survey)	4.0
2007 (Pew)[b]	1.6
2007 (Baylor Survey)	4.0
2014 (Pew)[c]	3.1

[a] All data are from the following unless otherwise noted: Rodney Stark, *What Americans Really Believe* (Waco: Baylor University Press, 2008), 117.
[b] Pew Research Center, "America's Changing Religious Landscape," May 12, 2015, 4.
[c] Pew Research Center, 4.

The category of religiously unaffiliated is broad, diverse, and includes several ideological and theological worldviews and lifestances. It includes those for whom religion remains important, to varying degrees. It includes atheists (those who reject the existence of a God or Gods), agnostics (those who do not know if a God or Gods exist), and those who report their religious identity as "nothing in particular" (which may include SBRN identity: "spiritual but not religious").

The data on the religiously unaffiliated in Europe and North America reveal important distinctions. For instance, even though atheists tend to get much of the attention, they represent a small percentage of this group and of the worldwide population. Table 2.2 shows that polls on the percentage of atheists in the United States predict they represent anywhere from 1.6% to 6% between 1944 and 2014. Other Western nations show similar numbers from 2001 to 2002 for the percentage of those who declare they are "a convinced atheist"; that is, they not only explicitly reject the idea of God(s) but also do not have any spiritual practices, do not belong to a religious community, nor have any spiritual yearnings: Canada (4%), New Zealand (5%), Australia (5%), Great Britain (5%), Sweden (6%), Spain (6%), Germany (7%), and France (14%).[26]

---

26 Rodney Stark, *What Americans Really Believe* (Waco: Baylor University Press, 2008), 118.

The "nones" make up an interesting and complex subgroup within the religiously unaffiliated. In the United States, they constitute approximately one-third of all young adults (born between 1981 and 1996). Elizabeth Drescher's 2016 study on the spiritual lives of America's nones[27] discovered that they reside in relatively similar proportions throughout the United States (with slightly fewer in the southeast) and that fewer are women than men but not by a significant margin. Drescher's data yields a generalized profile of an American None as "younger, urban, white, a bit more likely to be male than female, slightly more than most Americans to have had at least some college education, but no more likely to have completed college or graduate school."[28] The most significant generalization worth consideration is that nones are usually born after 1981. Furthermore, like all religious groups, the religiously unaffiliated and the nones are diverse, complicated, and ought to be understood in their various contexts.[29] For instance, what a European means when she identifies as a Christian may generally be different than what an American means when he identifies as Christian. This is true for all religious identifications and perhaps especially for the very broad category of "unaffiliated." Therefore, chapters 5 and 6 explore the Lived Religion (LR) approach to the study of religion and interreligious relations.

So far, this chapter has presented a bevy of data with some attempt at contextualization. Although a helpful primer, sheer numbers and quantitative data alone are not sufficient for developing an appreciation for how individuals identify with religion. To get deeper into the particulars of religious identity, the remainder of the chapter sketches the intricacies of identity theory within the context of religious identity.

RELIGIOUS IDENTITY

Identity is primarily about relationship. People identify in many ways and are related to others in multiple ways. Identities are formed based on those

---

27 Elizabeth Drescher, *Choosing Our Religion* (New York: Oxford University Press, 2016).

28 Drescher, *Choosing Our Religion*, 20.

29 Chapter 5 explores the particularities of complicated lived religious and nonreligious practices and beliefs of the unaffiliated ("nones") and affiliated ("somes") in North America and Western Europe.

relationships. For instance, my identities include father, son, husband, brother, friend, coworker, teacher, student, neighbor, cousin, colleague, and so on. Identities are also formed based on one's relation to histories, heritage, language (dialect, accent), geographical regions, ethnicity, race, gender, nationality, ancestors, and so on. I identify as an American, Minnesotan male with Scandinavian ancestral roots. These are identities that I hold simultaneously. Since relationships provide the foundation for one's identities,[30] for the purpose of this chapter and book, identity is understood primarily as founded on to whom, and how, an individual is related. That is, identities are ways people begin to articulate who they are in relation to others and to the world. Beliefs, behavior, and belonging are three dominant ways scholars of religion understand how individuals and groups express their religiosity. Beliefs "reveal a person's or group's understanding about the ultimate nature of deities or the universe." Behavior involves "acting a certain way as an individual or in a group, such as through rites, rituals, holidays or daily devotional practices." Belonging affirms "a person's or group's sense of mattering to others may affect the lived experiences of religious individuals and communities."[31]

Identity and self are related, but not the same. Identity refers to the ways individuals define themselves within a society or group and in relation to others.[32] Self refers to the interior capacity of an individual to reflect on their interactions with and impressions of others while also evaluating various modes of beliefs and behavior.[33] In simpler terms, one self has multiple identities. The "self can mobilize many different parts, which are called identities. People take on different identities depending on the social situations in which we find ourselves."[34] For instance, an individual might foreground his identity as respectful and dutiful son when his parents need support and assistance, and his identity as a courageous and relentless combatant when thrust into the

---

30 Paul Hedges and Angela Coco claim that "identity is inherently about relationships.... One's identity is 'always socially located,' that is, built into a network of relationships, issues, and cultural factors." Paul Hedges and Angela Coco, "Belonging, Behaving, Believing, Becoming: Religion and Identity," in *Controversies in Contemporary Religion*, ed. Paul Hedges (Santa Barbara: Praeger, 2014), 163.

31 Benjamin P. Marcus, "Religious Identity Formation," *Religious Freedom Center*.

32 Peter J. Burke and Jan E. Stets, *Identity Theory* (New York: Oxford University Press, 2009), 3.

33 Hedges and Coco, "Belonging, Behaving, Believing, Becoming," 164.

34 Hedges and Coco, 164.

role of militarily solider in the theater of war.[35] The self gives rise to multiple identities and emerges through interactions with society through various identities. Sociologists Peter Burke and Jan Stets recall William James, the well-known American philosopher and psychologist, who theorized in the late nineteenth century about how the self, through interaction with different groups and in different contexts, reflects this diversity in what James referred to as "multiple selves." "Each of these smaller 'selves' within the overall self is called an identity. Thus self as father is an identity, as is self as colleague, self as storekeeper, self as student, and self as any of the other myriad of possibilities corresponding to the various roles one may play"[36] in their personal and social identities in the world.

Personal and Social Identities

Identity theory further distinguishes between personal or individual identities and social or group identities. Personal identity refers to "a set of idiosyncratic traits and personality characteristics"[37] or "a sense of continuity, integration, identification, and differentiation constructed by the person not in relation to a community and its culture but in relation to self and its projects."[38] Social identities, in contrast, are formed in relation to one's memberships of various groups (i.e., one's relations to others within the context of being or not being a member of groups: family, nation, culture, religion, gender, race, ethnicity, etc.). When it comes to religious identities, the personal and social identity categories are helpful. Social religious identity (which may be for many "institutional religious identity") may often be as simple as identifying with a particular tradition or worldview, such as one who claims to be an observant Jew or an agnostic. Personal religious identities are more complicated, since beliefs, behaviors, and modes of belonging

35 "People possess multiple identities because they occupy multiple roles, are members of multiple groups, and claim multiple personal characteristics, yet the meanings of these identities are shared by members of society." Burke and Stets, *Identity Theory*, 3.
36 Burke and Stets, 10.
37 Steven Hitlin, "Values as the Core of Personal Identity," in "Social Identity," ed. Michael A. Hogg and Cecilia L. Ridgeway, special issue, *Social Psychology Quarterly* 66, no. 2 (2003): 121.
38 John P. Hewitt, *Dilemmas of the American Self* (Philadelphia: Temple University Press, 1989), 179; quoted in Hitlin, "Values as the Core of Personal Identity," 121.

ultimately differ from person to person, regardless of their social religious identity. Meredith McGuire observes that "at the level of the individual, religion appears to be a multifaceted, often messy or even contradictory amalgam of beliefs and practices that no particular religious group that an individual belongs to necessarily considers acceptable or important."[39] Although an individual's "personal practices and beliefs" are informed by socialization and interaction within and beyond their religious social group (e.g., their church community), they are determined definitively so.[40] In other words, "group identities may influence, but cannot determine, individual members' personal identities."[41]

Conflating or confusing personal religious identities with social religious identities can result in erecting a major obstacle to constructive interreligious engagement since it can too easily ignore the diversity within and between religious individuals and traditions for the sake of manageable (and facile) comparison.[42] For example, when a conversation is labeled simply as Muslim–Christian dialogue, certain assumptions can be made about what it means to be (and not to be) Muslim and about what it means to be (and not to be) Christian. Relying solely on group identities of Muslim and Christian to frame the dialogue oversimplifies the deeper complexity and messiness of the diverse personal religious identities involved. Furthermore, it risks reducing the complex personal religious identities of the actors involved to caricatures of their group religious identities. This flies in the face of the oft-repeated interfaith maxim that dialogue is not between *religions* but between *persons*. Conversations, at their most fundamental level, take place between and among religious personal identities, not social identities.[43]

39 Meredith B. McGuire, *Lived Religion* (New York: Oxford University Press, 2008), 208.

40 McGuire, *Lived Religion*, 208.

41 McGuire, 209.

42 Various concepts from the remaining sections of this chapter are first introduced in Hans Gustafson "'They're Not Really Christians': Acknowledging Oppression and Violence in Our Traditions for the Sake of Interreligious Understanding," State of Formation, May 27, 2018.

43 Amy-Jill Levine, in reference to Jewish–Christian dialogue, makes this point in *The Misunderstood Jew*: "The conversation will not be between 'church' and 'synagogue' but between Ari and Christine." Levine, *The Misunderstood Jew* (San Francisco: HarperCollins, 2006), 14.

"Forging Solidarities"

Articulating one's religious identity, by its very nature, holds an element of exclusivity in determining who is in and who is out. Identities are often formed in opposition, which is to say they are crafted (implicitly and explicitly) against or in relation to groups with which an individual is not, or does not want to be, associated. Hedges and Coco state, "we often know who we are in relation to what we are not rather than what we actually are."[44] Hence, for cultural theorist Stuart Hall, identities are "more the product of the marking of difference and exclusion than they are the sign of an identical, naturally constituted unity."[45] For example, at a recent American football game in Chicago between the division rivals Minnesota Vikings and Chicago Bears, despite the Vikings winning the game in a blowout victory, in the waning minutes of the game the fans of both teams "forged a solidarity"[46] with one another by joining in a group chant expressing their shared disdain for the more loathed division rival Green Bay Packers.[47] Furthermore, it is not unusual for Viking fans to prefer a Packer loss to a Viking victory.[48] These cases demonstrate how group identification of various groups can be forged around shared outside group nemeses. In other contexts, including professional sports, such group identifications can lead to violent encounters.[49]

---

44 Hedges and Coco, "Belonging, Behaving, Believing, Becoming," 167.

45 Stuart Hall, "Introduction: Who Needs Identity?" in *Questions of Cultural Identity*, ed. Stuart Hall and Paul Du Gay (London: Sage, 1996), 4; quoted in Hedges and Coco, "Belonging, Behaving, Believing, Becoming," 167.

46 See Jeannine Hill Fletcher, "Shifting Identity," *Journal of Feminist Studies in Religion* 19, no. 2 (2003): 5–24.

47 Gabe Henderson (@GabeAHenderson), "I Guess There's One Thing Both #Vikings & #Bears Fans Can Agree On 😂," video included, Twitter, January 8, 2023, 2:24 p.m.

48 E.g., as a born-and-raised lifelong resident of Minnesota, I understand how local *opposition to* the professional American football team in the next state over, the Green Bay Packers, can unify fans of the local Minnesota team, the Minnesota Vikings, more than it can unify shared identity *for* the local team itself. This is evident in the not-so-uncommon local refrain, "It is okay if the Vikings don't win the Superbowl as long as the Packers don't either." In their loathsomeness for the Packers, Viking fans share a kinship, and forge a solidarity, with the fanbase of the Chicago Bears. Hence, at my cousin's wedding in Chicago, a marriage between a Minnesotan groom and Chicago bride, the bride's brother's speech about his new Minnesotan brother-in-law included, "Although he's a Viking fan, at least he's not a Packer fan."

49 "If you support the New York Yankees, you want them to win and therefore their opponents [especially the Boston Red Sox] to lose. On a more extreme level, especially at times in European football, this group identification leads to direct and violent

Jeannine Hill Fletcher draws attention to the "logic of identity," which refers to the "grouping of persons into the various categories of 'the religions' and the assumptions made on the basis of those groupings[,] . . . which too easily erase the diversity and difference within any one community"[50] and dilute the rich internal diversity of a religious tradition by lumping together all Muslims (regardless of whether they identify as Sunni, Shia, etc.) and all Christians (regardless of denominational affiliation or creedal confession). Erasing the diversity and difference within traditions reinforces one of the major obstacles to constructive interreligious encounter today: the over-simplification, essentialization, or reduction of the religious other. On one hand, doing so may serve a constructive end by forging solidarity among those with different identities *within* a religious group (e.g., Protestant Christians with Roman Catholics, Christians with Eastern Orthodox Christians). However, on the other hand, a destructive consequence can be erasure of the diversity and difference that exists *within* religious groups. It can strip individuals of the important elements that distinguish them from each other. Ignoring the rich internal diversity of religions and their varied identities, the application of the logic of identity replaces dialogue between personal identities with dialogue between social identities. It replaces "Pakistani Urdu-speaking Sunni Muslim female"–"Asian American English-speaking Lutheran male" dialogue with "Muslim–Christian" dialogue. As Amy-Jill Levine suggests (see note 43), it replaces Ari-Christine dialogue with Jewish–Christian dialogue. The latter construction based on social identities is not worthless—there may be instances when simpler social categories are more appropriate—however, it is limited.

Authentic Identities

Ignoring the internal diversity of religious traditions and of individual identities can lead to infighting as well as to healthy constructive debate over the strict parameters of a tradition's boundaries. Oversimplifying other traditions, especially one's own tradition, may result in significant

---

confrontation with those who are defined as being outside one's group." Hedges and Coco, "Belonging, Behaving, Believing, Becoming," 167.

50 Fletcher, "Shifting Identity," 14; Fletcher borrows "logic of identity" from Iris Marion Young.

squabbling about who is and who is not allowed in the group. Who gets to be a true Christian, a real Muslim, a genuine Heathen,[51] and so forth? Playing this game may violate Leonard Swidler's well-known fifth rule of interreligious dialogue: "Each participant needs to describe her/himself. For example, only a Muslim can describe what it really means to be an authentic member of the Muslim community."[52] Swidler's rule assumes the benefit of allowing others to identify themselves while still permitting the healthy internal diversity of religious traditions and identities to freely surface (including those deemed by others as corrupt, violent, and oppressive). Raimon Panikkar, Roman Catholic priest and polymathic theologian and philosopher, recalls the story "many years ago in India" about some Christians arguing with "some 'very evolved theologians' who refused to accept them because they were not baptized."[53] The essence of their debate was over what it means to be Christian and whether one needed to be baptized in order to be a real Christian. Their argument arose since there were groups in India declaring their Christian identity without being baptized (a religious rite that many Christian traditions consider essential). Panikkar recounts what, at the time, he believed to be the criteria for being a Christian, "One is a Christian when one sincerely declares oneself to be a Christian and is recognized as such by the community. Nothing more. . . . if a person makes confession in good Christian faith and there is a community that recognizes him as such, there is absolutely no justification for saying that he is not Christian."[54] Panikkar at the time drew on his Christian background to formulate a criterion for determining the authenticity of one's religious identity; however, there is nothing uniquely Christian about it. Panikkar seems to fall within the scope of Swidler's rule by allowing each individual and their immediate community to determine their own religious identities.

---

51 "Heathen" here refers to reconstructed Germanic/Norse Paganism. In *American Heathens*, Jennifer Snook investigates the internal battles waged among American Heathens over who can authentically claim to be "really Heathen."

52 Leonard Swidler, "Dialogue Principles," Dialogue Institute.

53 Raimon Panikkar, *Cultures and Religions in Dialogue*, ed. Milena Carrara Pavan (Maryknoll, NY: Orbis, 2018), 141; talk presented at the Fourth Parliament of the World's Religions (Barcelona, Spain, 2005), originally published as "Hacia una teologia de la liberación," in *Interculturalidad, dialogo y liberació*, ed. H. Kung, J. J. Tamayo-Acosta, and R. Fornet-Betancourt (Pamplona: Verbo Divino, 2005), 61–68.

54 Panikkar, *Cultures and Religions in Dialogue*, 141.

It's Complicated

Identity, at the most basic level, is about relationships. It is about how people are related to other people, communities, viewpoints, beliefs, practices, regions, and ultimately to the world. Individuals have multiple identities because they relate to the world in multiple ways. The increasingly common identity wheel exercise displays several identity categories organized around the hub of the wheel, all of which constitute the self. Categories often include gender, language, education, socioeconomic class, ethnicity/ cultural background, sexual orientation, age, social environment, ability, nationality, geographic origin, religion/worldview/lifeway, practices, family structure, and so on. The exercise often asks participants to reflect on (1) identities they think about most/least often, (2) their own identities they would like to learn more about, (3) identities that have the strongest effect on how they perceive themselves, and (4) identities they perceive as having the greatest effect on how others perceive them. One aim of the exercise is to invite the participant to think about the various identities they carry with them and how, in the context of those perceived identities, they interact with and relate to others and the world. Another aim is to reflect on how various identities intersect to make up their perceived self. Rachel Mikva challenges scholars of interreligious studies (IRS) to take seriously intersectionality, which refers to the "interconnected nature of social categorizations such as race, class, and gender as they apply to a given individual or group, regarded as creating overlapping and interdependent systems of discrimination or disadvantage."[55] Including intersectionality in the conversation about religious identity, Mikva urges scholars to "grapple with the unique ways that aspects of identity combine in our social context. . . . While intersectional analysis runs the risk of multiplying the tensions of identity politics exponentially, it enables participants to encounter each other in their full humanity, with a complex story to tell, still being written."[56] However, Mikva also wisely cautions about the possibility of running the identity politics formula to its logical absurdity, resulting in a view of absolute difference without any grounds for cohesive similarity

---

[55] *Oxford Dictionaries*, s.v. "intersectionality," accessed January 9, 2022, https:// tinyurl.com/2rd3bucz.

[56] Mikva, "Six Issues That Complicate Interreligious Studies and Engagement," in *Interreligious/Interfaith Studies*, ed. Patel et al., 133.

and solidarity. Formulaically basing policy purely on identity alone, and calculated to its absolute climax, can lead to concluding infinite differences between and among all persons. It can lead to deeming every individual as irreconcilably different and dissimilar, which runs the risk of ignoring the common humanity shared among all and working toward social cohesion and cooperation for the common good.[57] Despite the multitude of identity categories (e.g., identity wheel categories listed above), debate continues over which ones are most socially dominant and which ones produce conflict most often. In his well-known "Clash of Civilizations" thesis, Samuel Huntington references George Weigel's observation that the "'unsecularization of the world is one of the dominant social facts of life in the late twentieth century.' The revival of religion. . . . provides a basis for identity and commitment that transcends national boundaries and unites civilizations."[58] Eboo Patel also makes the case for religious identity as one of if not *the* most important identity categories of the twenty-first century,[59] while others, such as Michael Schulson, push back and argue that race remains the more primordial fault line along which conflict generally arises.[60]

---

57 Ursula Baatz argues for scholars of religion to forcefully insist on wresting the term "religion" out of its European roots, which is too focused on belief, belonging (religion a/b), and identity and instead (re)capture an understanding of religion as a transformative way, path, or journey (religion c): "To be able to differentiate between religion *a/b. as a means of identity politics and c. as a path of transformation* might be helpful in a situation where almost all public debates about 'religion' are politically motivated, focusing mostly on religion as 'identity marker' and obscuring the human need for transformation and liberation, which searches for a way and a language." Ursula Baatz, "Territory, Relationship or Path," *Open Theology* 3 (2017): 153, italics original.

58 Samuel P. Huntington, "The Clash of Civilizations?" *Foreign Affairs* 72, no. 3 (Summer 1993): 26.

59 Concerning Huntington's "Clash of Civilizations" thesis, Patel states that Huntington "gets the conclusion wrong, but gets the beginning right, which is religion is a primordial identity and people convene around religion. And I think back to my college years and I think, I am really glad for the robust race, gender, class, sexual orientation conversations. How is it that I went through three years at the University of Illinois and heard religion mentioned five times?" Eboo Patel, "Dynamic Tensions," panel presentation at Symposium on Religion and the Liberal Aims of Higher Education, Boisi Center for Religion and American Public Life, Boston College, November 9, 2012.

60 Michael Schulson writes that some of Patel's writing is "not very intersectional. More specifically, there's something a little artificial about all this interfaith-iness, in that it pulls one element of identity—religious affiliation—to the fore, reads it as a core fulcrum of tension, and then builds an entire process of negotiation and diplomacy around that one identity point. This seems like a narrow way to think about identity. It's

The next two chapters complicate the messy and dynamic nature of religion (chapter 3) and religious identities (chapter 4). A helpful precursor comes from Fletcher and feminist thoughts, which teach that "identities are not constructed on a singular feature (e.g., gender or religion) but that persons are located in multiple spaces and that these aspects of identity are mutually informing."[61] Fletcher recounts the era in North America when this concept surfaced, and feminists of color began arguing that they did not share the same feminist experience as white feminists. Hence, it demonstrated that there are factors other than being a feminist or a woman that shape the way one experiences the world (and the way others experience feminists and women). People are complicated. Hedges and Coco recognize that "whatever self-identity is, despite first-appearances (I am *me* in this body and you are *you* in that body), it is a deeply complex and multifaceted set of relationships."[62] How then ought religious identity be understood? What does it mean to identify as "a Christian?" It depends on who is asked. Drawing on feminist thought, Fletcher speculates about answers from two well-known Christian theologians. American Lutheran George Lindbeck might answer, "my understanding of the world has been thoroughly and uniquely shaped by my association with a particular church or with the Christian story,"[63] and German Roman Catholic Karl Rahner might answer by deeming Christianity "a counter-cultural force binding together all who confess it."[64] However, Lindbeck and Rahner are not the only Christians to confess "I am a Christian." According to Pew's data, there are currently well over two billion Christians in the world, and what they mean when identifying as Christian falls across a wide and diverse spectrum of meanings, beliefs, and practices. Like all religious

---

also a narrow way to think about pluralism, which involves the interaction of all kinds of worldviews. . . . Patel's [book suggested] that religious divisions are now a bigger question for the United States than race. This was wrong in 2007. It is wrong today. Not only does it understate the challenge of the color line. It also overstates the role of faith. Yes, religious ideas are involved in conflict. But they rarely appear alone. The two most virulent forms of religious prejudice in America today—Islamophobia and anti-Semitism—are largely about xenophobia and the construction of Islam and Judaism as racial categories. As I have argued elsewhere, political positions are more divisive than religious positions for many Americans." Schulson, "When Religious Disagreement Seems the Least of Our Problems," Religion Dispatches, December 6, 2016.

61 Fletcher, "Shifting Identity," 14–15.
62 Hedges and Coco, "Belonging, Behaving, Believing, Becoming," 166.
63 Fletcher, "Shifting Identity," 15.
64 Fletcher, 15.

traditions, intra-Christian diversity is great. The way individuals understand and appropriate their religious identities vary widely. Christians come from many backgrounds, cultures, ethnicities, social-economic realities, and political ideologies. They do not all fall in a lockstep agreement on various divisive issues and positions pertaining to economics, social policies, ethics, abortion, ordination of women, same-sex marriage, and so on. Christians also diverge widely on theological positions, with a significant number of Christians embracing practices and beliefs from non-Christian traditions. The Lived Religion approach to the study of religion in the forthcoming chapters illuminates this interesting diversity.

Identity concerns not only how individuals relate to others and the world but also how their various identities relate to each other. An individual's religious identities relate to and inform, and are informed by, their other identities to form their personhood and "self." Recall the many dimensions on the identity wheel cited above: gender, race, culture, language, education, ethnicity, political beliefs, geographic residence, family, friends, age, and so on. Questions about these dimensions—such as whether one is married, has children, the nature of their relationship to one's parents—inform the other various aspects (identities) of an individual's personhood and help form their religious worldview and way of life to various degrees. The Parents Circle–Families Forum (PCFF) is a well-known grassroots organization that seeks reconciliation and sustainable peace by bringing together Palestinian and Israeli families that have lost immediate family members due to the Israeli-Palestinian conflict. The members, mostly parents who have lost children, engage in dialogue and projects and give presentations that support dialogue and reconciliation. Their shared identities as parents bring them together to suffer alongside each other in a spirit of compassionate solidarity. Their parental identities supersede their national, ethnic, and religious identities and allegiances. Having children—having lost children to the same violent conflict—informs their worldview and fosters a sense of empathy that goes beyond any animosity stemming from other conflicting identities between the parents. While chapter 13 examines data concerning the vitality of human relationships to build bridges across religious divides, this chapter recognizes the complexity of identities—religious and otherwise—and acknowledges that, for many, their religious identity can be superseded by other identities they consider more prominent and vital, depending on a given context.

Given that people are complicated, with multiple intersecting identities, an individual cannot exhaustively determine their religious identity without also acknowledging how their religious identity is formed by their other identities. When a person articulates their religious or nonreligious identity, they express important and complicated information about how they experience the world. Their experience is influenced by the many ways they relate to the world. For example, someone might express himself as a North American male with northern European ancestral roots who identifies as a father, son, brother, and husband. Both his parents are deceased, he has a university education, and so on (the list of identities could go on and on). He cannot separate out these various identities of his selfhood and decide to experience the world with only one dimension at a time. If he is a teacher, he cannot step into the classroom and decide to mute all of his identities except for his teacher identity. Although he may be able to do it as an intellectual exercise, in practice all of his identities come to bear on his overall interaction and relation to the world. Hence, his teacher identity in the classroom often draws out his experience of and identity as a father, making reference and analogies to parenting in his instruction. Each individual carries a rich portfolio of identities. When inquiring about someone's religious identity and practices, sociologist Nancy Ammerman asserts it is vital to holistically account for the intersectional nature of their selfhood.[65] For the purpose of cultivating practical wisdom for everyday interreligious solidarity and understanding, a person's rich portfolio of intersecting identities can serve as an asset for "forging solidarity" with and forming bonds across difference (e.g., PCFF cited above).

Religious identity is complicated and shaped by many factors. A Christian born and raised in a Christian-majority society experiences the world differently than a Christian born and raised in a society in which Christians are a small minority. Their religious identities and practices likely take on various aspects from the dominant culture influenced by the majority religion. For instance, Fletcher reflects on her own position as a North American Christian and how her experience of "being a Christian" would be different had she been "born today into the body of a female among the Christian minority in Korea."[66] Like the Korean Christian theologian Chung Hyun Kyung, Fletcher speculates she might "reenvision Christ as a shamanic healer at the intersection

---

65 "An African American Muslim woman in Chicago may be an immigrant, a person of color, a woman, and a Muslim all at once. Understanding her religious practices requires paying attention to the way those things intersect. . . . it makes no sense to talk about any of those things without talking about religion—and vice versa." Nancy Tatom Ammerman, *Studying Lived Religion* (New York: New York University Press, 2021), 17–18.
66 Fletcher, "Shifting Identity," 17.

of Christian and indigenous religious forms, identifying Christ in this way so as to offer a remedy for the healing of brokenness in a postcolonial Asia struggling against poverty, imperials, and sexism."[67] For Fletcher, feminist thought helps destabilize the category of religious identity, which does not destroy it but exposes the incessant fluid nature of identities as ever-changing and dynamic. An individual's religious identity as well, since it intersects and is influenced by other identities, is fluid and prone to ongoing (re)formation over time. The self is a vast web of interconnected dynamic identities that mutually inform and reshape each other. Reminiscent of the Buddhist teaching *anatta* (no-self) and *anicca* (impermanence), the self, understood in this manner, is inexhaustible and impossible to definitively articulate. When understood in this light, for the task of expressing an individual's religious identity, "we can no longer afford a simple designation of 'Christian,' 'Muslim,' or 'Jew.' Instead, each category itself is made up of a collective diversity wherein each individual is a *particular* Christian, a *particular* Muslim, or a *particular* Hindu, with identity features irreducible to the collective."[68]

The Religions in Schools Task Force, an initiative of the American Academy of Religion, states that religions are (1) "not internally homogeneous but diverse," (2) "dynamic and changing as opposed to static and fixed," and (3) "collections of ideas, practices, values, and stories that are all embedded in cultures and not isolated from them."[69] These statements about religions also apply to religious identities, as Fletcher recognizes "identities are not constructed on a singular feature (e.g., gender or religion) but that persons are located in multiple spaces and that these aspects of identity are mutually informing."[70] Generally, people do not identify with any one group alone at the expense of other groups. Furthermore, given the vast internal diversity of groups, people do not align with every internal aspect of the groups to which they belong. People have hybrid and sometimes conflicting identities within the groups to which they belong; however, it does not always mean that they no longer identify with those groups. Rather, it suggests that people can be comfortable with accepting their groups as fragmented. People accept that

---

67 Fletcher, 18, drawing on Chung Hyun Kyung, *Struggle to Be the Sun Again* (Maryknoll, NY: Orbis, 1990).

68 Fletcher, 18, italics original.

69 AAR Religions in Schools Task Force and Diane L. Moore, "Guidelines for Teaching about Religion in K–12 Public Schools in the United States" (American Academy of Religion, 2010), 12–14.

70 Fletcher, "Shifting Identity," 14–15.

groups are not monolithic and contain a certain degree of group incoherence and difference. Intragroup diversity can play a constructive and positive role. Intragroup friendship can lead to reaching across lines of difference to establish intergroup friendship. Put another way, in the context of religion, intrareligious relations can lead to the formation of interreligious relations. As Fletcher observes, "The hybridity of my identity means that although I do not identify completely with any one given category or community, I partially identify with many. The idea of hybrid identities and incomplete identification *within* a category can be embraced as the potential for Christians to forge solidarities *outside* the Christian community."[71]

Identity is about relationships, and people have many relationships. Relationships are complicated, and thus identity is very complicated. What is more, the category of religion, as discussed in the previous chapter, is also rather complicated. Religions are embedded in cultures, shaped by languages, internally diverse, and constantly changing. Likewise, as Richard Jenkins observes, "One's identity—one's identities, indeed, for who we are is always multi-dimensional, singular *and* plural—is never a final or settled matter. Not even death freezes the picture: identity and reputation may be reassessed after death; some identities—sainthood or martyrdom, for example—can only be achieved beyond the grave."[72] The fluid nature of religion and personal religious identities is an increasingly important aspect of how religion manifests in the world. Understanding these fluidities is vital for developing interreligious phronesis or practical wisdom for everyday interreligious encounter and leadership.

---

71 Fletcher, 19.
72 Richard Jenkins, *Social Identity*, 3rd ed. (London: Routledge, 2008), 18; quoted in Hedges and Coco, "Belonging, Behaving, Believing, Becoming," 168.

3

Messy Religion

Chapter Outline

I. Nature of Religion
    a. *Diverse*
    b. *Dynamic*
    c. *Culturally Embedded*
    d. *Linguistically Constructed*

II. Syncretism
    a. *Use of the Term*
    b. *Hard and Soft Syncretism*
    c. *Scholarly Voices*
    d. *Problem and Promise*

Developing practical wisdom for everyday interreligious encounter not only requires a literacy of basic teachings, histories, and practices of the religions but also entails grasping the dynamic nature of religion (this chapter) and the dynamic nature of religious identities (next chapter). Religions are complicated, messy, internally diverse, ever-changing, and evolve with time, culture, language, and circumstance. This is true for an individual's religious identity as well, which, as sociologist Meredith McGuire demonstrates, is "an ever-changing, multi-faceted, often messy—even contradictory—amalgam of beliefs and practices that are not necessarily those religious institutions consider important."[1] This

---

1 McGuire, *Lived Religion*, 4.

chapter introduces the messiness of religion by exploring a fundamental aspect of religions as dynamic, blended, and syncretic. The next chapter explores a fundamental aspect of religious identity in the phenomena of multiple religious orientations (mixing, blending, bricolage, hybridity). Chapter 5 follows with data that show the significant diversity of individuals' religious beliefs, and proposes the Lived Religion (LR) approach to the study of religion as indispensable for scholars of interreligious studies and for practitioners developing practical interfaith wisdom for everyday engagement.

NATURE OF RELIGION

Consider the three fundamental assertions about the nature of religion proposed by the Religions in Schools Task Force, a working group of the American Academy of Religion tasked with producing guidelines for teaching the study of religion in intellectuality sound and appropriate ways for public schools in the United States: "1) religions are not internally homogeneous but diverse, 2) religions are dynamic and changing as opposed to static and fixed, and 3) religions are collections of ideas, practices, values, and stories that are all embedded in cultures and not isolated from them."[2] Religions, at a very basic level, are internally diverse, ever-changing, fluid, and dynamic collections of ideas, practices, and stories embedded in, and influenced by, cultures and languages. Personal religious identities mirror religions in these same ways; that is, a personal religious identity is an internally diverse, ever-changing, fluid, dynamic collection of ideas, beliefs, and stories constructed out of and influenced by culture and language.

Diverse

Not only is there vast diversity and difference *among* religions but *within* religions as well, a point made in the previous chapter. Internal diversity in religions surfaces due to history, ideology, beliefs, practices, social context, language, political contexts, and many other factors. Religions have countless sects, denominations, movements, communities, texts, and traditions.

---

2 AAR Religions in Schools Task Force and Moore, "Guidelines for Teaching about Religion in K–12 Public Schools in the United States," 12–14.

No perfect uniformity exists among practitioners of the same religion. This internal diversity exposes the limits of essentialism (noted in chapter 1) and the inaccuracy of applying monolithic statements to an entire religious group such as "Jews support Israel," "Christians oppose same-sex marriage," "Muslims are from the Middle East," "Hindus are polytheists," "Buddhists are peaceful," and so on. All these comments treat religious individuals uniformly in lockstep with their coreligionists, which is simply and verifiably false.

Dynamic

Religious identities and religions as such are fluid and change over time, a relatively undisputed claim in the scholarship on religion and religious identity. David Bell recognizes that "Religion is part of the many cultural resources [used for identity formation] that are highly relative and prone to changing over time,"[3] and McGuire observes, "[Talal] Asad and many others have demonstrated, not only do religions change over time but also what people understand to be 'religion' changes."[4] Joantine Berghuijs's study on religious identity and hybridity operates on the premise that no single religion is a "unity, but all religions are hybrid and continually change."[5] Simply put, religions are in a constant state of change.

Culturally Embedded

Diane L. Moore makes a fundamental assertion about the nature of religion in that religions are "embedded in cultures and not separable from them."[6] Cultures give rise to and influence, nuance, and shape religious views and practices. Knowing about a religion's embodied culture is necessary for understanding the particularities of that religious tradition. Conversely, knowing

---

3 David M. Bell, "Religious Identity," in *Encyclopedia of Psychology and Religion*, ed. David A. Leeming, Kathryn Madden, and Stanton Marlon (New York: Springer, 2009), 778.

4 McGuire, *Lived Religion*, 5.

5 Joantine Berghuijs, "Multiple Religious Belonging in the Netherlands," *Open Theology* 3 (2017): 20.

6 Diane L. Moore, "Core Principles," Religion and Public Life, Harvard Divinity School.

the deep roots, practices, and beliefs of a religion is necessary for under-standing the culture within which it is embedded. This internal diversity is evident among Catholic communities in the United States in their outward celebrations of St. Patrick's Day and the Feast of All Saints Day in Boston (with many Catholics of Irish ancestry) and Los Angeles (with many Catholics of Mexican, Spanish, and Hispanic ancestry). Irish Catholic celebrations of St. Patrick's Day in Boston look very different from Hispanic Catholic celebra-tions of the Feast of All Saints in Los Angeles. In fact, an outside observer with little knowledge of Catholicism might even conclude that the two groups represent different religions altogether.

Linguistically Constructed

Countless scholars, especially anthropologists and sociologists, maintain that many religious values and norms are linguistically and socially constructed. Paul Hedges and Angela Coco observe how language "is deeply embedded into and helps shape our cultures and values, for it has both 'historical and cultural associations' which relate to the way it provides 'a powerful underpinning of shared connotations.'"[7] Language not only shapes religious worldviews and pathways, but since religion can be a powerful force in the hands of majority groups that control and influence linguistic styles and words, it has the poten-tial to "represent others in ways that identify them as inferior and therefore lacking the necessary attributes to belong to the in-group."[8] Much of what is understood as religion is socially contextual, linguistically constructed, culturally embedded, fluid, and ever-changing. "When we remember that all religious traditions are social—and often seriously contested—constructions," argues McGuire, "then we realize how misleading it is to represent any reli-gious tradition as unitary, unchanging, pure, or authentic."[9] Hence, religions as such and religious identities are formed and exist in a perpetual dynamic state of changing, blending, and innovating.

---

7 Hedges and Coco, "Belonging, Behaving, Believing, Becoming," 176, internal quo-tation from John Edwards, *Language and Identity* (Cambridge: Cambridge University Press, 2009), 55.

8 Hedges and Coco, "Belonging, Behaving, Believing, Becoming," 176.

9 McGuire, *Lived Religion*, 200.

SYNCRETISM

In the context of religions, at the broadest level possible, syncretism "refers neutrally and descriptively to the mixing of religions."[10] Theologians in the majority religion of a given society, who may harbor fear of their tradition intermingling with perceived outside impurities, often use the term pejoratively; that is, syncretism is perceived as "an illicit contamination, a threat or a danger, as taboo, or as a sign of religious decadence."[11] Scholars of religion— and many theologians—are more likely to use the term descriptively or neutrally to simply refer to the reality of how religious traditions are constructed regardless of whether syncretism is good or bad. The aim here is not to rehash or recall the tired, inaccurate, and unfair pitting of theologians against scholars of religion. Many individuals identify as both theologians and scholars of religion, and furthermore, there is a growing number of theologians who embrace—and even encourage—the reality of religious syncretism. Similar to the scholarly argument that contends, "we are all hybrids"[12] and "all humans belong to multiple religions,"[13] most scholars accept the claim that all religions are, and have been, syncretic (to various degrees). The reality is that the history of religion shows that all traditions have syncretic tendencies, and the use of the term has been associated with religion since its ancient Greek origins.[14]

Use of the Term

The word "syncretism" can be traced to an ancient Greek context to refer to the union of two or more people or groups to face a common enemy. Like many contested terms, syncretism's history reveals its change over

---

10 André Droogers, "Syncretism," in *Dialogue and Syncretism*, ed. Jerald Gort, Hendrik Vroom, Rein Fernhout, and Anton Wessels (Grand Rapids, MI: Eerdmans, 1989), 7.

11 Michael Pye, "Syncretism and Ambiguity," *Numen* 18 (1971): 83; also quoted in Perry Schmidt-Leukel, *Transformation by Integration* (London: SCM Press, 2009), 69.

12 Morwenna Griffiths, *Feminisms and the Self* (London: Routledge, 1995), 2; also quoted in Fletcher, "Shifting Identity," 19.

13 J. R. Hustwit, "Empty Selves and Multiple Belonging," *Open Theology* 3 (2017): 111–12.

14 "The history of religion confirms that every religion is in 'essence' syncretistic— there are no pristine origins or essences." Anita Maria Leopold and Jeppe S. Jensen, *Syncretism in Religion* (New York: Routledge, 2004), 5; quoted in Sean McCloud, "Everything Blended," *Implicit Religion* 21, no. 2 (2018): 363.

time from its first known use in Plutarch to refer to the positive joining of military forces on the island of Crete to fend off a common enemy,[15] to Pope Francis's twenty-first-century statement that used the term negatively, which remarked that "true fraternity cannot be lived other than with this attitude of openness to others, which never seeks a conciliatory syncretism."[16] While many theologians and religious leaders use the term with disapproval, most historians of religion use it as a matter of fact referring to the intermingling of disparate religions (regardless of whether the religious practitioners and thought leaders perceive it as problematic). Catholic theologian Raimon Panikkar observes the following four traits of syncretism: "(1) the joining of forces and interests; (2) from people who otherwise were neither united nor friendly to each other; (3) so that, forgetting internal rivalries, they become provisional allies; (4) in order to fight a common enemy or threat."[17] Anthropologists use the term to refer to the coming together of once isolated cultures, and many are likely to affirm anthropologist Charles Stewart's claim that syncretism is "the process by which cultures constitute themselves at any given time."[18] Sociologists define syncretism similarly as "the mixing of elements of two or more cultures into a combination that is different (at least, from the vantage point of the scholar studying these cultures) from any of the donor cultures."[19] This definition nuances the resulting combination of the mixed traditions as something different than (something new from) what previously existed in the donor cultures. Other definitions often lack this nuance by simply referring to "any mixture of two or more religions,"[20] regardless of whether the resulting mixture is different. Michael Pye emphasizes the temporal nature of religions by qualifying syncretism as "the temporary ambiguous coexistence of elements from diverse religious and other contexts within

15 Droogers, "Syncretism," 9.

16 Pope Francis, "Audience with a Delegation of the Emouna Fraternité Alumni Association," oral address, Sala dei Papi of the Apostolic Palace, June 23, 2018.

17 Panikkar, *Cultures and Religions in Dialogue*, 95; originally published in Raimon Panikkar, "Some Notes on Syncretism and Eclecticism," in *Religious Syncretism in Antiquity*, ed. B. A. Pearson (Missoula, MT: Scholars Press, 1975), 47–62.

18 Charles Stewart, "Relocating Syncretism in Social Science Discourse," in *Syncretism in Religion*, ed. Leopold and Jensen, 274; also quoted in McGuire, *Lived Religion*, 190.

19 McGuire, *Lived Religion*, 188.

20 Helmer Ringgren, "The Problems of Syncretism," in *Syncretism*, ed. Sven S. Hartman (Stockholm: Almqvist and Wiksell, 1969), 7; also quoted in Droogers, "Syncretism," 10.

a coherent religious pattern."[21] Cataloging definitions of syncretism could go on, and examples of religious syncretism are endless.

Hard and Soft Syncretism

The process by which several aspects from different religions are brought together to form a novel religious view not found or recognized in any of the donor religions can be considered hard syncretism:

Elements from Religion A + Elements from Religion B = Religion C

Hard syncretism may worry or threaten some religious practitioners, for they may deem the claim of syncretism false because they do not interpret their religion as augmented by, changed from, or a mixture or inheritor of elements from other traditions. Syncretism destabilizes the foundation upon which they may perceive their tradition to be built, and thus they may view it as an assault on the essence and borders of their tradition. The perceived threat can be most obvious when the newly constructed religion or ideology demonstrates blatant oppression and supersession of others, such as Nazi ideology with Christianity.[22]

The process by which elements from two or more traditions are combined with an aim to clarify or enhance the practices, ideas, and concepts already present in one or more of the traditions can be considered soft syncretism:

Elements from Religion A + Elements from Religion B = Religion AB or Religion BA

Soft syncretism is often less threatening to religious practitioners, for there is less of a perceived threat to the essence or core of their traditions. Well-known examples of soft syncretism, which go beyond inculturation or appropriation,[23] could include Thomas Aquinas's use of Aristotle and Greek

---

21 Pye, "Syncretism and Ambiguity," 93; also quoted in Droogers, "Syncretism," 11.

22 Schmidt-Leukel, *Transformation by Integration*, 78.

23 In the context of religious mixing and blending, the term "inculturation" (more often "acculturation") refers to the attempt to make a religion intelligible and accessible in a new culture or context. It can be a form of appropriation. Examples include Japanese Christians participating in the Christian ritual of the Eucharist or Holy Communion by replacing bread and wine with rice and sake. It can also be understood as a dominant oppressive culture or religion strategically taking elements from a local

philosophical language and categories in the articulation of his Christian theology or John Keenan's Mahayana Buddhist philosophy and language to enhance the Christian understanding of Jesus.[24] Scholar of religion and intercultural theology Perry Schmidt-Leukel offers a clear articulation of soft syncretism to explain instances of religious mixing without significant doctrinal or foundational conflict or tension: "If it cannot be excluded that there is truth, goodness, and holiness outside Christianity, then ... the process of receiving and adapting insights and practices from other religions into Christianity cannot *as such* be regarded as a mixing of truth and lie, good and evil, the sacred and the demonic."[25] The Greek philosophical language, metaphysics, and categories became common parlance within Christianity and continue to wield significant theological influence over how Christians understand and articulate their understanding of, and relations between, God, world, and person. It may be argued that Aquinas fundamentally augmented Christianity, and, therefore, his religious mixing with Aristotle is more appropriately hard syncretism. In this light, syncretism can be more properly understood as a continuum of religious mixing along which there exist a range of degrees, from hard to soft.

Scholarly Voices

A prevailing view among scholars of religion is that all religions are, and have been, syncretic and unstable to various degrees in their formations and histories. Interreligious studies scholar Anne Hege Grung argues that all interreligious studies are more appropriately transreligious studies. Transreligious perspectives capture and critically inquire about "the role of fixed religious boundaries ... push questions of representation ... [and] asks about how human differences other than religious diversity are marked and signified" in the encounters and relations between and among

culture and appropriating them in order to convert or assimilate them: for example, non-Native American Christians using Native American symbols and practices in a church or Christian setting for the sole purpose of conversion. A Japanese Christian replacing bread and red wine with rice and sake of their own volition is different than a non-Native American replacing the bread and red wine with the Lakota sacred pipe without consent or consultation with Lakota leaders. Both are forms of inculturation.

24 John P. Keenan, *The Meaning of Christ* (Maryknoll, NY: Orbis Press, 1989).
25 Schmidt-Leukel, *Transformation by Integration*, 78.

religions.[26] In the mid-twentieth century, philosopher of religion Gerard van der Leeuw was among the first to provide an in-depth look at syncretism and concluded that "all religions are syncretic on the grounds that they all combine various forms."[27] Earlier, scholar of religion and theology Hendrik Kraemer recognized "that all religions are syncretistic"[28] regardless of whether they are conscious of it. Scholar of religion Jacques Kamstra later stressed that "syncretism must be seen as a general human trait, and that it is consequently present in all religions, including Christianity."[29] Scholar of religion Robert D. Baird interprets syncretism as "a universal phenomenon; the term is not specific enough to be used for historical research. Borrowing and blending are a normal part of history. In this context, therefore, the term syncretism is superfluous and should be dropped."[30] Religious historian and theologian Kurt Rudolph surveyed the relevant literature on syncretism and determined

that syncretism is becoming a relatively value-free concept which, however, is still in need of a clear typology, and which has not yet been defined satisfactorily, except in terms of dynamic nature. Syncretism is generally seen as the mixing of religions, and it is widely accepted that no religion, expect the most isolated, is free of syncretism, both in respect to its origin and to its subsequent history.[31]

More recently, scholar of interreligious studies and comparative theology Paul Hedges, echoing the scholars noted above, writes, "it is increasingly clear from the history of religions that all religion is syncretic. Every religion has, even at its elite levels, learnt, borrowed, adapted, or modified the texts, beliefs,

---

26 Anne Hege Grung, "Interreligious or Transreligious?" in *Interreligious Studies*, ed. Gustafson, 59.

27 Droogers, "Syncretism," 9; reference to Gerardus van der Leeuw, *Phänomenologie der Religion* (Tübingen: Mohr, 1965), 692.

28 Droogers, "Syncretism," 9; reference to Hendrik Kraemer, *De Wortelen van het Syncretisme* (The Hague, The Netherlands: Boekencentrum, 1937), 7.

29 Droogers, "Syncretism," 10; reference to Jacques H. Kamstra, *Synkretisme* (Leiden: Brill, 1970), 23.

30 Droogers, "Syncretism," 11; reference to Robert D. Baird, *Category Formation and the History of Religion* (The Hague and Paris: Mouton, 1971), 142–52.

31 Droogers, "Syncretism," 12; reference to Kurt Rudolph, "Synkretismus vom Theologischen Scheltwort zum religionswissenshaftlichen Begriff," in *Humanitas Religiosa* (Stockholm: Almqvist and Wiksell, 1979), 193–212.

practices, or customs of another religion."[32] Comparative religion scholar Peter van der Veer concurs, "indeed every religion is syncretistic, since it constantly draws upon heterogeneous elements to the extent that it is often impossible for historians to unravel what comes from where."[33] Panikkar similarly reckons syncretism "a fundamental factual, often practical attitude. . . . It is a natural attitude that happens, comes into being, and influences cultures and religions by virtue of a natural human interaction on the plane of life and history—for good or for bad."[34] Philosopher of religion J. R. Hustwit bluntly states, "the fact of the matter is that all religions have appropriated once-foreign beliefs and practices."[35] Religion scholar Sean McCloud correspondingly instructs to "remain attentive to the historical fact that all cultural activities and social movements—whether we call them religious or not—are always already combinations of pre-existing elements."[36] Theologian Monica Coleman contextualizes such sentiment in the observation,

There are no pure cultures. Religions are embedded in who we are and our cultures; and there can be no encounter—however brief or long-term, voluntary or violent—that does not change who and how we are who and what we are. . . . All religions—and cultures, for that matter—are syncretic. The historical development and current practice of all religious traditions are syncretic. The idea that we live in discrete religious traditions and communities is fallacious for most everyone.[37]

Sociologist Meredith McGuire incisively summarizes the spirit of these scholarly voices: "the key point is that all religions are necessarily syncretic and continually changing, as people try to make sense of their changing

32 Paul Hedges, "Multiple Religious Belonging after Religion," *Open Theology* 3 (2017): 55.

33 Peter van der Veer, "Syncretism, Multiculturalism, and the Discourse of Tolerance," in *Syncretism/Anti-Syncretism*, ed. Charles Stewart and Rosalind Shaw (London: Routledge, 1994), 208; also quoted in Schmidt-Leukel, *Transformation by Integration*, 67; also quoted in Perry Schmidt-Leukel, *Religious Pluralism and Interreligious Theology* (Maryknoll, NY: Orbis, 2017), 234.

34 Panikkar, *Cultures and Religions in Dialogue*, 98; originally published as Panikkar, "Some Notes on Syncretism and Eclecticism."

35 Hustwit, "Empty Selves and Multiple Belonging," 112.

36 Sean McCloud, "Everything Blended," *Implicit Religion* 21, no. 2 (2018): 378.

37 Monica A. Coleman, "The Womb Circle," *Practical Matters* 4 (Spring 2011): 9; also quoted in Rachel A. Heath, "Multiple Religious Belonging and Theologies of Multiplicity," *Journal of Interreligious Studies* 21 (October 2017): 33.

social worlds, including their cultures with which they come in contact."[38] In fact, syncretism is so basic and foundational to religion that anthropologists Rosalind Shaw and Charles Stewart argue—with McGuire's support—that it would make more sense to analyze *anti*syncretism.[39] McGuire concludes, "all cultural groups are fundamentally syncretic, but not all have attitudes or social movements against the syncretism of others."[40] Despite the scholarly establishment of syncretism as a basic fact of all religious traditions' formation and continual development, caution still remains—often from religious leaders and practitioners—about whether and to what degree it should be embraced as a positive influence.

Problem and Promise

Many Western theologians, particularly from Christianity and Islam, traditionally express suspicion of syncretism, perceiving it as a corruption of truth, superficial, uncommitted, inconsistent, and dangerously subject to the whims of individuals.[41] Cultural anthropologist André Droogers refers to this understanding of syncretism as *subjective*, which "includes an evaluation of such intermingling from the point of view of one of the religions involved. As a rule, the mixing of religions is condemned in this evaluation as violating the essence of the belief system."[42] Even though living religions are in a constant state of flux and change, as Panikkar observes, "often the despised heretics of yesterday are the recognized prophets of tomorrow."[43] In fact, Panikkar maintains,

practically all religious traditions of the world present typical examples of syncretistic phenomena, not only in the past but also in the present. This

---

38 McGuire, *Lived Religion*, 192.
39 Rosalind Shaw and Charles Stewart, "Introduction," in *Syncretism/Anti-Syncretism*, ed. Stewart and Shaw, 1; quoted in McGuire, *Lived Religion*, 190.
40 McGuire, *Lived Religion*, 190.
41 See Schmidt-Leukel, "In Defence of Syncretism," in *Transformation by Integration*, 70; Berghuijs, "Multiple Religious Belonging in the Netherlands," 21.
42 Droogers, "Syncretism," 7.
43 Panikkar, *Cultures and Religions in Dialogue*, 47; originally published in Raimon Panikkar, "Religious Identity and Pluralism," in *A Dome of Many Colors*, ed. A. Sharma and K. M. Dugan (Harrisburg, PA: Trinity International Press, 1999), 23–47.

has led historians of religions to have another view of syncretism with the view put forward by mainly Christian theologians, who tended to link syncretism with the dilution of Christianity and loss of its uniqueness and purity, so that any interaction or intercourse with the non-Christian world would be considered pollution, if not simply idolatry.[44]

Not all Christian and Muslim theologians and religious leaders deem syncretism scandalous nor something to be avoided. German theologian Perry Schmidt-Leukel, defending syncretism from a Christian perspective, confesses, "I do not see any problems with syncretism as such. All great religions are, after all, the product of syncretistic processes."[45] Moreover, in an effort to "contribute to a more open-minded, less fearful and indeed constructive theological approach to the phenomenon of syncretism,"[46] Schmidt-Leukel makes the case for syncretism not as a superficial smorgasbord of personal beliefs chosen at one's whim, but rather argues that "an integrative, syncretistic effort can thus be an act of true commitment to God"[47] because religious practitioners take seriously the claims of religious worldviews and lifeways of others. Advocating for "interreligious theology," Schmidt-Leukel argues that "if theology wants to be taken seriously on a global level, it can simply no longer afford to neglect the contributions that relate to the same subject area but come from other religious traditions."[48] Schmidt-Leukel envisions the future of all theology as interreligious: "I think it is one of the major tasks of future theology—and now I am speaking not only of Christian theology—to find out to what extent the religious traditions of the world share different though nevertheless incompatible insights."[49] The claim is that theologians who fail to recognize contributions from traditions outside their own are no different than those who ignore the scientific community when doing theology in the context of the physical and natural world (e.g., ignoring the geophysical age of the planet and cosmos, or what it means to be human from biological, psychological, and evolutionary perspectives). Theologians who pontificate on the age of the earth based purely on ancient texts are bound

---

44 Panikkar, *Cultures and Religions in Dialogue*, 95; originally published in Panikkar, "Some Notes on Syncretism and Eclecticism," 47–62.
45 Schmidt-Leukel, *Religious Pluralism and Interreligious Theology*, 138.
46 Schmidt-Leukel, *Transformation by Integration*, 69.
47 Schmidt-Leukel, 80.
48 Schmidt-Leukel, *Religious Pluralism and Interreligious Theology*, 139.
49 Schmidt-Leukel, *Transformation by Integration*, 84.

to be dismissed as religious zealots, as sloppy, or as incredibly naive for their ignorance or dismissal of the overwhelming data generated by the geophysical sciences. On the other hand, theologians who welcome and engage voices and data from outside their tradition as authoritative contributions to their work are more likely to be taken seriously by religious and nonreligious audiences. The claim is that the same is or will be the case for the doing of interreligious theology, which takes seriously the voices of other traditions as partners in conversation.

North American theologian Michelle Voss Roberts identifies the root of syncretism's prefix *syn* (Greek), which means "together" as in to "to bring together in a significant manner," and argues that syncretism "should not be a feared adulteration of an original purity, for it reflects the intersectionality of all human identity."[50] Looking ahead, Droogers forecasts, "syncretistic views, though often already part and parcel of world religions, are gaining momentum."[51] Furthermore, McGuire and others argue that those who oppose, condemn, or try to control syncretism do so because they perceive it as threatening to something they might lose. When syncretic innovative religions are expressed, practiced, and recognized as genuine and legitimate expressions of religious traditions, it is often those in power and with control that become uneasy, for they may feel threatened by voices that challenge their perceived authentic status as legitimated by their religious institution and society.

Theologians are not alone in their dismissal of syncretism. Scholars of religion also fail, as McGuire recognizes, "to acknowledge that the boundaries separating recognized religions from those religions considered suspect—as syncretic—are themselves political, serving to privilege certain religions—including scholars' own religion or those of their society's dominant classes and ethnic groups."[52] Droogers echoes this in his analysis of the various responses to syncretism. Resistance to syncretism is largely tied to power, especially by individuals and corporate bodies that represent recognized and "official" religions controlled by clerical authority. For them,

---

50 Michelle Voss Roberts, "Religious Belonging and the Multiple," *Journal of Feminist Studies in Religion* 26, no. 1 (Spring 2010): 58.

51 André Droogers, "The Future of New Worldview Studies," in *Methods for the Study of Religious Change*, ed. André Droogers and Anton van Harskamp (Sheffield, UK: Equinox, 2014), 170.

52 McGuire, *Lived Religion*, 190.

Syncretists are always the others. They may be lay people but can also be members of the lower clergy. When the social context involves cultural plurality, the power struggle may be not just between clergy and laity, or higher and lower clergy, but between different cultures. Official religion, whether imported or indigenous, almost always acts as a dominant cultural factor. . . . Syncretism, then, may be viewed as an expression of protest, against clerical *and* secular authorities.[53]

Religious syncretism among religious traditions mirrors individuals' multiple religious identities. They both clearly challenge "the orthodoxies guarded by the gatekeepers of religious traditions."[54]

To expose these power dynamics, and given the universality and commonality of syncretism among all religions and religious practitioners, it is helpful to reframe the conversation. Instead of focusing on syncretism, Shaw and Stewart argue that focus ought to be more on antisyncretism, the rarer of the two phenomena. Centering antisyncretism as the problem can make more sense, especially given "that the antisyncretist impulse is closely linked with the claim of essentialism and the privileging of one's own religion, race, language, or national identity."[55] Privileging these categories need not be cause for major concern; rather, the concern arises when one of them is privileged above all else at the expense of those outside the group in a manner that marginalizes and oppresses. McGuire takes issue with the way many "scholars of religion have treated the antisyncretic position as somehow normative."[56] The concern is, "Uncritically accepting any group's identity claims leads to failed comprehension of how group identities (whether antisyncretic or highly syncretic) are developed, changed, and maintained in the context of modern and increasingly globalized societies."[57] Individual and group religious identities are too diverse, dynamic, and complex to be uncritically accepted outside their embedded contexts.

Schmidt-Leukel's "Defence of Syncretism" argues that individuals moved by aspects of religious traditions other than their own ultimately have little to no choice but to take those aspects seriously. The popular American Showtime

53 Droogers, "Syncretism," 16, italics original.
54 Roberts, "Religious Belonging and the Multiple," 44.
55 McGuire, *Lived Religion*, 207.
56 McGuire, 208.
57 McGuire, 208.

television series *Homeland* that aired between 2011 and 2020 depicts the aftermath of a United States Marine Corps sniper, held prisoner of war for eight years by al-Qaeda, during which time he was tortured but ultimately "converted" to Islam. Upon his rescue and integration back into his life in the United States, when confronted with the question of how and why he could take up the religion of his captors and torturers, his responses (or sometimes lack thereof) demonstrate more of a calling or some transcendent pull from beyond which he had no choice but to accept. Although a fictional and rather fantastic example of religious "conversion," it bears marks of reality by demonstrating how many individuals articulate their call to take up elements of traditions other than their own or "convert" to another tradition. Schmidt-Leukel reflects,

> If in the process of inter-religious encounter someone recognizes in some non-Christian religion what he or she understands as a sign of divine truth, as a manifestation of something good and holy, if someone hears the "voice of God" in and through some element of a non-Christian religion, he or she is not entitled to reject this. From a spiritual perspective there is not a choice. . . . They will have no choice but to integrate the truth as recognized in the other with the truth as known from their own tradition. A lack of genuine commitment, a lack of serious commitment to God, would be to ignore, deny or resist God's voice—independent of where and how it has been heard.[58]

For Schmidt-Leukel, this openness need not be understood as a lack of commitment to one's home tradition but rather a genuine act of true commitment and openness to the divine or transcendent.

Upon his return to the West, after having spent a third of his life in India, Raimon Panikkar observed, "I left a Christian, I found myself as a Hindū, and I return back as a Buddhist, without having ceased to be a Christian."[59] Far from shedding his Christian identity or developing an eclectic mix of three religions or a doctrinal synthesis of a new religion, he discovers his threefold religious identity analogous to three great rivers, dynamic and fluid, with many smaller streams flowing into them. "Each river, like each personal religion, is fed by the small rivulets of our personal biographies."[60] Given an

---

58 Schmidt-Leukel, *Transformation by Integration*, 79–80.
59 Panikkar, *Cultures and Religions in Dialogue*, 48.
60 Panikkar, 48.

individual's social, historical, and geophysical location, they may take up and take in various contexts and cultures around them. Panikkar reflects, "When meandering through a Christian territory I feel Christian, but some who know other lands tend to call me a Hindū or a Buddhist. And vice versa: When my life flows in a Hindū milieu, some call me a 'pukka'[61] Hindū and others a 'dangerous' Christian."[62] Far from producing a new religious tradition, one that combines all three into some super religion, Panikkar considers his multireligious identity "singing basically a single melody in three tones."[63]

Panikkar's complicated religious identity illustrates the potential for individuals to simultaneously orient around and practice multiple religious traditions, an increasingly common phenomenon and central concern of the next chapter.

---

61 पक्का (Hindi): genuine, excellent, appropriate.

62 Panikkar, *Cultures and Religions in Dialogue*, 48.

63 Panikkar, 49; Panikkar reflects, "I am a Christian whom Christ has led to sit at the feet of the great masters of Hinduism and Buddhism and become also their disciple. It is my being a Hindū-Buddhist-Christian. . . . This allows me to declare myself a bona fide Christian and also a Hindū, a Buddhist, and a scholar. . . . I am a Hindū whose karma has led him to encounter Christ and a Buddhist whose personal effort has led him to similar result regarding the two other traditions. . . . In short, I discover myself a Christian-Buddhist-Hindū. . . . What, then, is my religion? Do I not belong simultaneously to the three? Or are they not rather harmoniously transformed in me? Are not all the waters of the Bhāgirathī, Alaknanda, Gomati, Yamunā, Ghaghra, Son, Assi, Varuna, all waters of the Ganges, once they reach a certain point? I could have said Negro, Japurá, Jurqá, Purus, Madeira, and Tapajós, all waters of the Amazon. At a certain moment in life the river is only one, be it carrying waters from Wisconsin, Illinois, Des Moines, Missouri, Arkansas, Minnesota, or Mississippi" (51–52).

4

Multiple Religious Orientations

Chapter Outline

I. Multiple Religious Orientations
II. Religious Blending
    a. *Bricolage*
    b. *Hybridity*
    c. *Assemblage*

Like the nature of religion itself, religious identities can be messy and dynamic as expressed through various modes and manifestations of the phenomena of multiple religious orientations, including bricolage, hybridity, and assemblage. Data from various Lived Religion studies bear this out by showing the complicated nature of individuals' religious identities and practices. For instance, a significant number of American Christians report "believing in" ghosts, reincarnation, and astrology (to name a few nontraditional Christian beliefs). The study of Lived Religion, without ignoring the official traditional teachings of a religion, strives to understand more fully how people practice their traditions. It pays attention to practices (e.g., yoga) and beliefs (e.g., reincarnation) of individual practitioners regardless of whether they are found in authoritative historical or official teachings and texts. Contemporary scholarship recognizes the self as made up of multiple identities, which change and switch over time in various situations, contexts, and among societal factors. A fundamental aspect of identity theory suggests that people assume several identities throughout a lifetime while enacting

several simultaneously.[1] An individual strategically employs multiple identities from a quiver of those they have been socialized into and learned on
their own, exercising them in various contexts.[2] The human person "is a
pluralistic being."[3] How an individual portrays their self can vary given the
context: e.g., job interview versus informal social gathering with childhood
friends versus a family meal versus happy hour with colleagues and business
associates and so on. According to Steven Hitlin's sociology of psychology,
"identity theory holds that individuals are a compilation of discrete identities, often tied to their social roles, which become salient as situations call
for them."[4] This understanding of the self, informed by current scholarship
on identity theory, frames this chapter's exploration of multiple orientations
(MROs) under the categories multiple religious identity (MRI), multiple
religious belonging (MRB), multiple religious participation (MRP), and
other phenomena of religious blending such as religious bricolage, hybridity, and assemblage.

MULTIPLE RELIGIOUS ORIENTATIONS

MROs refer to the many ways individuals and groups live out multiple
religious traditions at once. Proposed by philosopher of religion Jeanine
Diller, MRO encompasses several common patterns "that span the
gamut from no participation in any religion to multiple ways of
participating in multiple religions."[5] MRI, MRB, and MRP fall under
the umbrella of MRO. MRI, more specific than MRO, refers to the phenomenon of individuals explicitly identifying simultaneously with two

---

1 Peter J. Burke and Jan E. Stets, *Identity Theory* (New York: Oxford University Press, 2009), 131.

2 André Droogers, "The World of Worldviews," in *Methods for the Study of Religious Change*, ed. Droogers and Harskamp, 37.

3 Panikkar, *Cultures and Religions in Dialogue*, 17; originally published as Raimon Panikkar, "The Myth of Pluralism," *CrossCurrents* 29 (Summer 1979): 197–230.

4 Hitlin, "Values as the Core of Personal Identity," 121, citing Sheldon Stryker, *Symbolic Interactionism* (Menlo Park, CA: Benjamin/Cummings, 1980) and Sheldon Stryker and Peter J. Burke, "The Past, Present, and Future of an Identity Theory," *Social Psychology Quarterly* 63 (2000): 284–97.

5 Jeanine Diller, "Multiple Religious Orientation," *Open Theology* 3 (2017): 344.

or more religious traditions. Likewise, MRB and MRP respectively refer to the phenomena of individuals belonging to and participating in or practicing two or more religious traditions or communities.

Scholarship is growing on MROs. Embracing the inherent multiplicity of the individual advocated by contemporary identity theory, several scholars endorse the view that MROs ought to be understood as the default position (not SROs, or single religious orientations) and not as the outlier.[6] Philosopher of religion J. R. Hustwit argues that "ontologically speaking, every person always already belongs to more than one religion because every religious tradition is an amalgam of earlier traditions. There is nothing new about multiple religious belonging. It is nearly unremarkable."[7] Hustwit's reasoning is straightforward:

1. since "all religions have assimilated content from at least one other religion," and
2. "all humans belong to at least one religion" (assuming that non-religion, dis- or unaffiliation count as religious orientations, and belonging does not entail "cognizance or agreement" but can be unconscious),
3. then it follows that "all humans belong to multiple religions" especially since "the fact of the matter is that all religions have appropriated once-foreign beliefs and practices."[8]

Hustwit's logic for the reality of MRO as an ontological condition of all individuals ties directly to the claim made in the previous chapter that all religions are syncretic; that is, all religions mix, combine, and appropriate elements that were once foreign to them. The premise of this chapter is that all individuals are already religiously multiple to some degree (whether they are aware of it or not) and that their religious identities are constantly in a state of dynamic change and formation as they live and interact with other individuals, groups, and the world.[9]

---

6 McGuire, *Lived Religion*, 186; Catherine Cornille, "The Dynamics of Multiple Belonging," in *Many Mansions?* ed. Catherine Cornille (Maryknoll, NY: Orbis Books, 2002), 1–2.

7 Hustwit, "Empty Selves and Multiple Belonging," 108.

8 Hustwit, 111–12.

9 McGuire, *Lived Religion*, 209.

Assuming this premise is true—that all individuals are already religiously multiple to varying degrees—does not mean that all are necessarily conscious of or intentional about it. Consider the distinctions within the MRO category: MRI versus MRB versus MRP.[10] Since more exhaustive treatments of MRO modalities exist,[11] the aim here is to flesh out the major contours of MRO and how they relate to religious identity, the nature of lived religions in the contemporary world, and for developing interreligious studies for practical everyday wisdom.

Although everyone may have multiple identities—and multiple religious orientations according to Hustwit's logic above—the claim here is not that all people are multiple religious belongers or participants. In fact, explicit MRB and MRI seem to be rare. MRI, narrower than MRO, names a greater commitment to two or more religious traditions, practices, and beliefs. It

---

10 Proposed in Hans Gustafson, "Descandalizing Multiple Religious Identity with Help from Nicholas Black Elk and His Spirituality," *Journal of Ecumenical Studies* 51, no. 1 (Winter 2016): 80–113. Multiple religious participation is also used in John Berthong, *The Divine Deli* (Maryknoll, NY: Orbis, 1999), 35, and John Thatamanil, "We Are All Multiple," paper presented at the American Academy of Religion (Baltimore, MD, November 25, 2013), among others.

11 Jeanine Diller offers eight forms of "Multiple Religious Orientations": (1) seeking, (2) multiple religious curiosity, (3) hybrid identity without belonging, (4) open single belonging, (5) single belonging with crossing over, (6) hybrid identity with belonging, (7) double belonging, and (8) beyond belonging. Diller also identifies four other religious orientations in addition to multiple; they are (1) nonreligiosity, (2) light religiosity, (3) single identity without belonging, and (4) single belonging. Diller, "Multiple Religious Orientation," 338–53.

Steve Bruce proposes six modalities of multiple religious phenomena: (1) multiple religious belonging, (2) universalistic reinterpretation of multiple religions, (3) multiple religious association, (4) multiple religious interest, (5) ancillary religious respect, and (6) secular respect for all religions. Steve Bruce, "Multiple Religious Belonging," *Open Theology* 3 (2017): 611–12.

Rose Drew looks at six different "kinds and degrees" of multiple religious participation: (1) "cultural identity and particular religious functions," (2) "dual religious upbringing," (3) "occasional ritual participation," (4) "adoption of particular practices or ideas," (5) "contemporary bricolage religiosity," and (6) "inculturation and interreligious dialogue." Rose Drew, "Christian and Hindu, Jewish and Buddhist," in *Controversies in Contemporary Religion*, ed. Hedges, 248–51; also referenced in Hedges, "Multiple Religious Belonging after Religion," 50.

Michelle Voss Roberts identifies three models that "reflect scholarship on the confluence of religious traditions." They are (1) The Great Pioneers (focusing on "the dogmatic reflections of religious elites" and doctrinal synthesis), (2) Popular Practice (focusing on practices and "popular ritual participation" among the general masses and laity), and (3) The Hybrid (focusing on the intersection of "hybrid identities of communities on the borders of traditions and cultures)." Roberts, "Religious Belonging and the Multiple," 46–52.

manifests in several ways, including MRB and MRP. MRI contrasts with SRI (single religious identity). Likewise, MRB and MRP contrast with SRB (single religious belonging) and SRP (single religious participation). These categories, like religion and religious identity as such, are fluid and overlap to various degrees. MRI may be construed as broad enough to encompass both MRB and MRP, while MRO remains broader still as the master umbrella category.[12] MRI includes the MRPer who participates semi-regularly in other traditions but does not confessionally belong to them. This might be a Christian who regularly practices Zen mediation or draws inspiration from non-Christian spiritual texts, yet only explicitly belongs to Christianity. Michelle Voss Roberts observes, "It is not uncommon for Christians who attend church on Sunday to be found studying kabbalah, practicing yoga, or visiting a traditional healer during the week, without thereby ceasing to belong to the Christian community."[13] In Roberts's example, such a Christian remains an SRBer but also an MRPer. Belonging in SRB and MRB is stricter and more rigorous than participation in SRP and MRP. Belonging entails more than being infrequent to regular participation, and for this reason (among others), MRB often captures the most attention from scholars. It is also often the most challenged.

Unlike MRP, MRB includes a more rigorous level of commitment and belief. While one might practice or participate in something with less commitment, adherence, or belief, belonging, as Steve Bruce argues, holds a more central place for belief. Bruce argues, "any enduring belonging to any religious collectivity will result in us believing things we would not believe were we not associated with that collectivity."[14] MRP, on the other hand, need not necessarily require strict belief or commitment. An individual may discover great benefit in Buddhist mediation practice but also be reluctant to identify as a "belonger." They may not desire, or be able, to maintain any worldview or all-encompassing way of life that aligns with traditional Buddhist belonging. Furthermore, they may not wish, or be able, to commit to or join a Buddhist community (to whatever degree that might entail).

While true MRB remains rare, MRP, given its broad parameters, is more widespread. Participation need not require belonging or hard-and-fast commitment to a tradition or community. Similar to hybridity (discussed below), MRP allows flexibility for multiple religious orientations and identifications.

---

12 See Diller, "Multiple Religious Orientation," 338–53.
13 Roberts, "Religious Belonging and the Multiple," 43.
14 Steve Bruce, "Multiple Religious Belonging," *Open Theology* 3 (2017): 43.

With MRP understood more broadly as proposed here, the reported figure of 23 percent of the Dutch population engaging in MRP (not MRB) seems likely. Though the Dutch study's category of MRB is too broad (or confused with MRP), the researchers nuance it by identifying a number of useful "modalities, bonding styles, mobilities, and motivations."[15] Such nuance is needed in order to more precisely clarify the ways in which people simultaneously orient around multiple religious traditions, worldviews, and lifeways. The term "belonging" often muddies the waters and can needlessly complicate matters. Roberts insightfully destabilizes belonging, a term she argues is about ownership, and asks, "Is ownership the most fitting description of engagement with religious traditions?"[16] In Roberts's estimation, no

> ownership falls short [because it] . . . does not adequately mirror the agency involved in the intense theological reflection, flexible ritual practices, and dynamic self-understandings of the persons and communities [often associated with MRI] . . . The idea that persons belong to institutions, or that traditions of thought and practice belong to anyone, echoes with the ideology that women and subordinate men "belong" to fathers, husbands, and masters.[17]

Accordingly, Roberts argues for the more flexible term "identity" over "belonging." In related fashion, Paul Hedges raises the issue of using the category of belonging in non-Western contexts, especially in the Chinese context, as potentially problematic. Instead, Hedges proposes "the terminology of Strategic Religious Participation in a Shared Religious Landscape is more useful"[18] because it provides more space for participants to make suitable choices that are meaningful for them within a Chinese religious landscape (or "religious ecology"). This context is understood, in large part, by its residents as a Shared Religious Landscape in which traditions are "not composed of hermetically sealed borders of mutually exclusive religious belief-based territories."[19] Lessons from the Chinese landscape and the general acceptance of religious

---

15 Joantine Berghuijs, Hans Schilderman, André von der Braak, and Manuela Kalsky, "Exploring Single and Multiple Religious Belonging," *Journal of Empirical Theology* 31 (2018): 22–23.
16 Roberts, "Religious Belonging and the Multiple," 54.
17 Roberts, 55.
18 Hedges, "Multiple Religious Belonging after Religion," 62.
19 Hedges, 63.

traditions as fluid movements with porous borders can be applied to other contexts. The dominant religious traditions of non-Chinese and non-Asian contexts may allow for a "shared religious landscape" in which individuals can participate in multiple traditions in ways that are individually suitable and meaningful.

Several issues and questions surface in the conversation about multiple religious identities. Hedges and others refer to the reality of MRO as a "phenomenon" because it exists and people find the language useful in articulating their religious orientation, identity, belonging, and participation.[20] Despite whether official religious teaching embraces or recognizes MRO, the lived religious lives and practices of everyday people make evident the existence of MROs. In other words, MRO is not just a conversation about identity (MRI), but is something that people do (MRB and MRP). Yet, as Hedges observes, MRO is also very much a discourse.[21] It manifests often enough—MRP in particular—that it may be that SROs ought to receive the greater share of interrogation, not MROs. Berghuijs and colleagues argue that "from an empirical perspective, there is every reason to assume that religious commitment does not always imply fixed and lasting combinations of belonging and believing."[22] From a speculative and theoretical perspective as well, intuitively there is little reason to assume that the religious commitments of individuals remain fixed. People are in a constant state of change. They continually learn, reflect, and revise beliefs, views, and practices, including the manner in which they conduct their daily lives, use technology, understand the natural world through scientific discoveries, and so on. Likewise, with religious practices and beliefs, people constantly rethink worldviews and revise their childhood beliefs in light of their everyday experience and interaction with the world. Perhaps then it is not the phenomena of MROs that should be so hotly debated, but the phenomena of SROs.

Scholars who investigate MRO raise similar challenges to defining the category of religion in the context of MRO. Roberts suggests it is "modern definitions of *religion* [that] are partly responsible for perceptions of multiple commitments as problematic."[23] There is likely more resistance to MROs in Western traditions. Negative connotations are cast upon MROs out of

---

20 Hedges, 51.
21 Hedges, 51.
22 Berghuijs et al., "Exploring Single and Multiple Religious Belonging," 19.
23 Roberts, "Religious Belonging and the Multiple," 46, italics original.

the perception that they dilute, scandalize, or pervert the purity of traditions as originally intended. This aversion is due in part to the problematic
understanding of religion perpetuated by predominately Western Christian
(Protestant) perspectives that conceive of religions as internally coherent
systems that primarily emphasize belief in the divine and function as pure,
unchanging, tightly bound monoliths. Such an approach to religion produces
false assumptions and, as Hedges argues in the context of MRO, is problematic
because it (1) understands religions to be "bounded territories of belonging,"
(2) places too much emphasis on "believing in a set of principles," and (3)
assumes religions operate with an internal coherence.[24] All three are problematic because they are not true for most religions.

Claim (1) asserts that religions are bounded territories of belonging, and
thus "each religion, therefore, is a distinct and discrete unit to which sole
allegiance is required."[25] If this is true, then MRO becomes more problematic.
However, the reality is that religions have messy and blurry borders. Likewise,
"the border line between culture and religion is often not fixed,"[26] and there
is no shortage of examples to demonstrate this. Ursula Baatz argues that
religion as a Western concept falls short when discussing MRO, and for this
reason Baatz suggests that terms such as "path" or "way" are more accurate in
describing religious identity, which, like religion, is more properly understood
as a dynamic journey as opposed to a static mode of being.[27]

Leonard Swidler, well-known "pioneer and peacemaker"[28] of interreligious
dialogue, routinely advocates for the use of "way" over "religion," with the
reminder that "Most of the great world religions have at their center the idea
and term 'the Way,' rather than the Western term 'religion.'"[29] In fact, as

---

24 Hedges, "Multiple Religious Belonging after Religion," 53–54.
25 Hedges, 54.
26 Hedges, 55.
27 "The metaphor of a 'way' or a journey is used in all traditions: in the Indian traditions it is *mārga*; in Christianity the trias of *via purgativa, via illuminativa, via unitiva*;
'journey' in the Sufi traditions is a frequently used metaphor; also metaphors of ascent
and descent in Jewish mysticism use the image of a 'way' or a 'journey', and *dào* in the
Chinese traditions." Baatz, "Territory, Relationship or Path," 159.
28 Harold Kasimow, "Leonard Swilder," *Journal of Ecumenical Studies* 50, no. 1
(Winter 2015): 37–41.
29 Leonard Swidler, *Dialogue for Interreligious Understanding* (New York: Palgrave
Macmillan, 2014), 73. Swidler identifies terms within the major world religions that suggest "the Way," and contextually situates them within their respective traditions to show
their advantage over the term "religion." These terms are: Hebrew *Halacha* (Judaism),

Rose Drew points out, "in contrast to the West, there are Asian societies in which multiple religious identities have long been the norm and are more a matter of cultural identity than personal choice."[30] It may only be a matter of perception that in the West religious identities are single (not multiple) neatly and tightly bound territories of belonging. The lived reality of religion in the West bears more similarity to non-Western contexts than is generally acknowledged.

Claim (2) asserts that religion places too much emphasis on "believing in a set of principles." Scholars have long argued that religions in West emphasize belief or doctrinal confession above all else, and this is likely due to the Protestant Christian bias that informs the constructed definition of religion. The argument is that since many of the early scholars of religion were European Protestant Christians, their understanding of religion was informed by their Protestantism, which places significant emphasis on belief and doctrinal confession. About religion, Roberts argues that "the definition most restrictive in terms of multiple belonging reduces religion to doctrinal systems, 'fixed presuppositions' that can then be rationally adjudicated 'by citation of the creeds or other [official] documents.'"[31] As Western scholars began learning about traditions outside of Europe, it became evident that not all emphasize belief or an intellectual assent to a set of principles. If the Western emphasis on theological belief and intellectual assent is the norm for religious observance, then it becomes more difficult to adhere to two or more at the same time (especially when their doctrines conflict). However, if belief in doctrines is of less importance, and practices, ritual, and communal belonging count for more, then adhering simultaneously to multiple traditions with conflicting doctrines becomes less problematic.

Claim (3) asserts that religions operate with an internal coherence. However, as McGuire's research shows, "At the level of the individual, religion is not fixed, unitary, or even necessarily coherent. Rather, each person's religious practices and the stories they use to make sense of their lives are continually

New Testament Greek *Hodos* (Christianity), Arabic *shari'a* (Islam), Sanskrit *Marga* (Hinduism), Pali *Magga* (Buddhism), Chinese Dao (Chinese traditions), and Shinto's *To*.

30 Drew, "Christian and Hindu, Jewish and Buddhist," 248.

31 Roberts, "Religious Belonging and the Multiple," 53; internal quotations from Joseph S. O'Leary, "Toward a Buddhist Interpretation of Christian Truth," in *Many Mansions?*, ed. Cornille, 30.

adapting, expanding or receding, and ever changing."[32] Identities, which includes religious orientations, are fluid. Borders of religions and religious orientations are generally porous and ever shifting, not just in non-Western traditions but in Western traditions as well. For many people, their religion and religious orientation extend far beyond mere belief or assent to a set of principles. Furthermore, they often hold beliefs that do not always systematically and internally cohere. Religions and religious orientations are complicated, and precision is needed for understanding them. For these reasons, among others, the Lived Religion approach, explored in the next chapter, enjoys increasing popularity among scholars. For it offers a method for investigating the complicated multiple religious orientations that blend religions.

RELIGIOUS BLENDING

MROs as phenomena do not arise out of thin air, nor are they simple. Religious mixing occurs in a several ways. As discussed above, one reason for MROs stems from the reality that religions as such are conglomerates and amalgams of several other traditions. Not only are religions themselves internally diverse, but so too are personal religious identities. The diversity of individuals' own internal religious nature, metaphorically speaking, mirrors the internal diversity found within religious traditions. This relationship is demonstrated in Perry Schmidt-Leukel's fractal theory of religious diversity: "The nucleus of the theory is that the diversity we observe *among* the religions globally is mirrored in the diversity that we find *within* each of the major religious traditions. And that we can also discern some patterns of this diversity—or elements thereof—*within the religious orientation of individual persons*."[33] The implications of this theory are profound, multifaceted, and continually show up in the ways individuals are led to investigate not only religiously diverse traditions other than their own but also the religious diversity within their own selfhood.[34] Religious mixing takes on several modes, such as bricolage, hybridity, and assemblage, among others.

---

32 McGuire, *Lived Religion*, 210.
33 Perry Schmidt-Leukel, "A Fractal Interpretation of Religious Diversity," in *New Paths for Interreligious Theology*, ed. Alan Race and Paul Knitter (Maryknoll, NY: Orbis Books, 2019), 1, italics original.
34 See section "Bridges," chapter 10.

Bricolage

As a general concept, bricolage refers to "a social practice by which an individual constructs a creative assembly by eclectically pasting together seemingly disparate, preexisting bits and pieces of meaning and practice."[35] Bricolage is a form of MRP in that while individuals do engage in various practices from multiple religions, they seldom commit wholly and exclusively to one tradition. This distinguishes it from MRB and perhaps MRI altogether. Engaging in borrowed practices and entertaining borrowed ideas from, and occasional participation in, traditions other than one's own does not constitute MRB since there is no "rootedness in any tradition."[36] However, bricolage is most certainly a form of MRO. With an emphasis on the individual over any one tradition or practice, bricolage, seen as patchwork religiosity, is sometimes labeled (fairly or not) "New Age" in the West or "believing without belonging,"[37] in which "individuals draw selectively on ideas and practices from a range of traditions without being immersed in or committed to *any*."[38] Examples include practicing yoga without commitment to a wider Hindu worldview, practicing various Buddhist meditation techniques without adhering to Buddhist teachings, or non-Jews practicing various teachings of Kabbalistic mysticism, among countless others. Bricolage is a broad category that most often refers to religious mixing on the scale of the individual. Religious *hybridity*, then, "is often a result of the practice of bricolage, because individuals' blended elements can become culturally shared elements for future individual or group synthesis."[39]

Hybridity

Religious hybridity occurs at a more basic level within the individual than bricolage since, as Morwenna Griffiths argues, "we are all hybrids."[40] That is,

35 McGuire, *Lived Religion*, 195; quotation references Claude Lévi-Strauss, *The Savage Mind* (Chicago: University of Chicago Press, 1966), 16–33.
36 Drew, "Christian and Hindu, Jewish and Buddhist," 265.
37 Catherine Cornille, "Multiple Religious Belonging and Christian Identity," *The Santa Clara Lecture* (2011): 4, cited in Drew, "Christian and Hindu, Jewish and Buddhist," 250.
38 Drew, "Christian and Hindu, Jewish and Buddhist," 250, italics original.
39 McGuire, *Lived Religion*, 195.
40 Griffiths, *Feminisms and the Self*, 2; also quoted in Fletcher, "Shifting Identity," 19.

individuals take on multiple intersecting identities. However, at the collective level hybridity can surface for several reasons. Hybridity as such "in fact describes all religious subjects insofar as gender, age, race/ethnicity, education, employment, and sexual orientation intersect with religious identity. Every subject negotiates many identity markers alongside religious commitment.... Hybridity happens to all of us."[41] Collective hybridity—that is, the communal blending of religions with other religions and other cultures—is a phenomenon found throughout history. For instance, the necessity of hybridity for survival: "religious hybridity was necessary, especially for any religion existing outside its foundational culture."[42] Christians in early Christian churches in Antioch, Rome, and Corinth maintained preexisting cultural understandings that informed and directed their everyday lives precisely in order to practice Christianity in their everyday lives. These included "kinship systems, social class structures, languages, gender norms, . . . what they ate or what clothing they wore, and how they provided livings for their families."[43] Consider the well-known "peaceful conversion"[44] of the Icelanders in 1000 CE. Two groups of religious rivals (Christians who followed Christ and "pagans" who followed the Norse Gods) were set against one another in what could have become a bloody conflict, but which ended up being an underwhelming and uneventful affair. Archeologist Jesse Byock reports, "When a major warlike encounter appeared imminent, a typical Iceland scenario developed: mediators intervened, and the dispute, which was treated as a feud ripe for settlement, was submitted to arbitration."[45] The thirteenth-century text *Njal's Saga* stylistically recounts the decision for the island's residents to embrace Christianity. The decision was surprisingly and decisively swayed by an argument made by the non-Christian ("pagan" or "heathen") public legal speaker Thorgeir Thorkelson, who made the case for Christianity based purely on, it seems, a desire to maintain peace, social cohesion, and lawfulness. Thorgeir states,

It appears to me that our affairs will reach an impasse if we don't all have the same law, for if the law is split asunder, so also will peace be split asunder, and we cannot live with that. Now I want to ask the heathens and the Christians whether they are willing to accept the law I

---

41 Roberts, "Religious Belonging and the Multiple," 52.
42 McGuire, *Lived Religion*, 191.
43 McGuire, 191.
44 Jesse L. Byock, *Viking Age Iceland* (London: Penguin, 2001), chap. 16.
45 Byock, *Viking Age Iceland*, 300.

proclaim. . . . This will be the foundation of our law, that all men in this land are to be Christians and believe in one God—Father, Son, and Holy Spirit—and give up all worship of false idols, the exposure of children, and the eating of horse meat. Three years outlawry will be the penalty for open violations, but if these things are practiced in secrete [sic] there shall be no punishment.[46]

The communal "conversion" still allowed the private practice of preexisting non-Christian or "heathen" ways that went without punishment if done in stealth. Though abolished later, these practices included "idol-worship" (devotion to non-Christian Norse deities), "exposure of children [to perish]" (a form of aborting newborns), and "eating horse meat" (for surviving in a rugged region with a scarce food supply). The mechanism of "conversion" presented opportunities for blending and hybridity.

In the same context, Helgi "Magri (the Lean)" Eyvindarason and his wife Þórunn "Hyrna" Ketilsdóttir, two of the first settlers to Iceland in the ninth century, exhibit this predisposition for religious blending on an individual level. The thirteenth-century text *Landnámabók*, or "Book of Settlements," which contains a detailed description of the Icelandic settlement, tells of Helgi the Lean, who

> went to Iceland with his wife and children and his son-in-law. . . . Helgi's faith was very much mixed: he believed in Christ but invoked Thor when it came to voyages and difficult times. When Helgi sighted Iceland, he consulted Thor as to where he should put in, and the oracle guided him north of the island. . . . Helgi believed in Christ and called his home after him.[47]

Helgi built his farmstead and named the place Kristnes, meaning Christ-ness, located 12 kilometers outside present-day Akureyri. As Christianity spread throughout Europe in the centuries that followed, McGuire argues, it was the expanding development of, in part, the cult of saints, in which "the cults of various saints were identified with local holy sites, such as wells, caves, mountains, and stones, in every region," that "enabled Christianity to absorb

---

46 *Njal's Saga*, trans. Robert Cook (London: Penguin, 2001), 181 (§105).
47 *Landnámabók (The Book of Settlements)*, trans. Herman Pálsson and Paul Edwards (Winnipeg: University of Winnipeg Press, 1972, reprinted 2006), 97 (§ 218).

and transform pre-Christian, pagan elements of indigenous cultures."[48] The enduring remnants of pre-Christian European elements in contemporary Western Christian cultures persist, especially during the Christian Christmas and Easter holy days, both of which incorporate significant elements from pre-Christian European Germanic and Nordic traditions.[49]

There are countless instances of religious mixing, and sometimes they involve traditions that seem irreconcilable but nonetheless are mixed through the form of assemblage.

Assemblage

"Assemblage" (to assemble) refers to the collection of parts into an internally organized and purposeful system. Anthropologist Marloes Janson's research relies on the concept of *assemblage* in the examination of "Chrislam" in Lagos, Nigeria. Chrislam refers to "a series of religious movements that emerged in Nigeria's former capital, Lagos, in the 1970s: the mixing of Christian and Muslim beliefs and practices."[50] Instead of employing the language of syncretism to understand Chrislam, Janson argues that assemblage theory is better suited, especially when understood in a manner defined by Collier and Ong. They define assemblage as "the product of multiple determinations that are not reducible to a single logic. . . . It does not always involve new forms, but forms that are shifting, in formation, or at stake. . . . [It is] heterogeneous,

---

48 McGuire, *Lived Religion*, 192.

49 The name "Easter" has connections to the Germanic goddess Ēostre (*Ostara*), the Germanic/Nordic goddess of spring, fertility, and rebirth. The symbolic colors of pink and green, and the hare, all connected to Ēostre, are familiar to Christians. Another example comes from "the pre-Christian Celtic religion of the British Isles [having] identified specific hilltops, mountains, and springs as sacred sites. Many of these, for instance literally thousands of holy wells, were then identified with specific, locally venerated Christian saints and continued to serve as sacred sites (for healing, protection, and fertility for example) as they had in pre-Christian times. Likewise, pre-Christian calendrical rituals, such as those for winter and summer solstices, were given Christian meanings: the winter solstice (which was celebrated by the Roman sun cult of late antiquity on December 25, according to the pre-Christian Julian calendar) became the date for celebrating Jesus' nativity (i.e., Christmas), and the summer solstice (i.e., Midsummer's Night's Eve) became the Feast of St. John, celebrated with bonfires and fire wheels, symbolic of the sun." McGuire, *Lived Religion*, 192.

50 Marloes Janson, "Unity through Diversity," *Africa* 86, no. 4 (2016): 646.

contingent, unstable, partial, and situated."[51] Janson's ethnographic work on Chrislamists observes that the "underlying idea in Chrislam's assemblage of Christianity and Islam is that to be a Christian or Muslim alone is not enough to guarantee success in this world and the hereafter; therefore, Chrislam worshippers participate in Christian as well as Muslim practices, appropriating the perceived powers of both."[52] Furthermore, Janson demonstrates how the concept of assemblage, in the context of Chrislam, "provides a rationale for scrutinizing the very concept of syncretism and offers an alternative analytical case for understanding its mode of religious pluralism"[53] insofar as it produces new ways to understand religious mixing not only from an outsider's perspective but also in a manner that aligns "with the way in which its worshippers perceive their religiosity."[54] Syncretism falls short to describe Chrislam in this context since syncretism is often associated with the attempt to harmonize, or bring into coherence, two distinct traditions. This does not fit the case of Chrislam in Lagos since "Chrislamists do not strive to harmonize Christianity and Islam, and they are not bothered by ontological contradictions between the two traditions."[55] Hence, assemblage, referring to a "product of multiple determinations that are not reducible to a single logic,"[56] fits this unique mixing of Islam and Christianity. Janson contends that "assemblage as a conceptual model helps us understand Chrislam as a heterogeneous and unstable arrangement of practices that are not reducible to a single logic."[57] Therefore, it can show how misleading it is to understand the category of religion as a heterogeneous and unstable arrangement of beliefs and practices that follow a coherent and internal system of logic. Rather, as Janson discovers, assemblage helps shift attention "towards a perspective that focuses on how religious practitioners actually 'live' religion in their daily lives, and on ambiguities, inconsistencies, aspirations and double standards as the constitutive moments in their lived religiosity."[58]

---

51 Stephen J. Collier and Aihwa Ong, "Global Assemblages, Anthropological Problems," in *Global Assemblages*, ed. Stephen J. Collier and Aihwa Ong (Malden, MA: Blackwell, 2005), 12; quoted in Janson, "Unity through Diversity," 648.

52 Janson, "Unity through Diversity," 672 (abstract).

53 Janson, 672 (abstract).

54 Janson, 672 (abstract).

55 Janson, 667.

56 Collier and Ong, "Global Assemblages, Anthropological Problems," 12; quoted in Janson, "Unity through Diversity," 648.

57 Janson, "Unity through Diversity," 667.

58 Janson, 667.

The point here is not only that "we are all hybrids,"[59] but, as asserted in the previous chapter, "all religions are necessarily syncretic and continually changing, as people try to make sense of their changing social worlds, including their cultures with which they come in contact."[60] Given the overwhelming dynamic complexity and particularity of religions and religious orientations, the scholar of religion requires the agility to adopt new methods and approaches. Continually retooling their methods and instruments, scholars sharpen their focus and precision to investigate religious orientations, identities, practices, and traditions. Interreligious Studies examines relations between and among various communities and individuals. Investigating the depths and nuances of these complex relations uncovers the phenomena, and their importance, of mixed, hybrid, blended, and syncretic identities, practices, and traditions (and the contexts from which they arose). Going deeper into the particularities of the lived reality and contexts of these relations and practices is the focus of the next two chapters on the Lived Religion (LR) approach to the study of religion (chapter 5) and its value for Interreligious Studies (chapter 6).

---

59 Griffiths, *Feminisms and the Self*, 2; also quoted in Fletcher, "Shifting Identity," 19.
60 McGuire, *Lived Religion*, 192.

5

Lived Religion

Chapter Outline

I. Lived Religion Approach
   a. *Kindred Approaches*
   b. *Benefit of Lived Religion*
II. The United States and Western Europe
   a. *The Data*
   b. *Practices and Blending*

In the 2013 Paul Hanly Furfey Lecture, delivered to the Association for the Sociology of Religion in New York, sociologist Nancy T. Ammerman drew on the popular *Where's Waldo?* children's books that depict busy scenes of human intersection and landscape for the reader to search for Waldo, adorned in his iconic red and white striped attire, like a needle in a haystack. Ammerman argues that a Lived Religion approach (LR hereafter) to the study of religion is akin to searching for Waldo, the everyday person amidst the busy world. Using Waldo as a metaphor for everyday religion, Ammerman endorses the LR approach, which "instead of starting from official organizations and formal membership, [it] begins with everyday practice; instead of taking the experts and official theology as definitive, [Ammerman joins] the lived religion scholars in arguing that we need a broader lens that includes but goes beyond those things."[1] This chapter is

---

1 Nancy T. Ammerman, "2013 Paul Hanly Furfey Lecture," *Sociology of Religion* 75, no. 2 (2014): 190.

grounded in the spirit endorsed by Ammerman that the scholar of religion—and for this book the scholar-practitioner seeking practical wisdom for everyday interreligious encounter—is well served by the tools and methods of LR. The LR method is introduced alongside significant data about the lived religious reality of the global population (especially as it pertains to multiple religious orientations). The next chapter contends that the scholar of interreligious studies, as well as the scholar-practitioner-leader with the desire to understand religion in the contemporary world, benefits from LR by more accurately understanding the relations between, among, and within the living religious (and nonreligious) traditions, communities, and individuals.

LIVED RELIGION APPROACH

The LR approach to the study of religion is relatively new, with roots in the "popular religion" approach, trendy in the 1960s and 1970s, which focuses on the religious beliefs and practices of the masses (the populous) opposed to official teachings and doctrines of institutional religious bodies and texts.[2] For instance, the study of popular religion often focuses on "festivals and shrines, ritual healing practices, and stories of miracles."[3] It examines religion as it happens on the margins away from, or in response to, more orthodox modes. LR is not the same as popular religion.[4] Although LR occurs on margins, it also happens within orthodox religious institutions. However, LR is not an alternative to the official or institutionalized forms of religion often taught in the so-called "World Religions paradigm."[5] Rather, LR is "a different way of looking at them. Lived religion explores the way in which individuals, and communities, live out these religious traditions in their everyday lives, the way in which religion interacts with work, with family, with other elements of identity, with relations within the community

---

2 David D. Hall, "Lived Religion," in *Encyclopedia of Religion in America*, ed. Charles H. Lippy and Peter W. Williams (Washington, DC: CQ Press, 2010), 1282.

3 Ammerman, "2013 Paul Hanly Furfey Lecture," 190.

4 Ammerman, 190.

5 Lower-level undergraduate courses, often electives, "continue for the most part to teach religions according to a model that is subjective (biased) and unempirical (based on essentialisms rather than ethnographic and historical data), referred to as the World Religions paradigm." Owen, "The World Religions Paradigm," 253–54.

and beyond."[6] As such, LR is much broader, more flexible, and more complex than standard textbook (often essentialized) versions of religion or the official religious orthodoxy of religion as preached by authoritative religious leaders.

Popular religion is nonetheless important for LR, since "in general, studies of popular religion have made us wary of assuming that what institutions or leaders wanted was how laypeople behaved."[7] There is often a difference between, on the one hand, what religions teach and preach through official documents and creeds, and, on the other hand, what people actually practice and believe in their everyday lives. Hence, it should come as no surprise that the LR method is sometimes referred to as "religion as lived" to juxtapose it with "religion as preached." LR primarily investigates, Meredith McGuire contends, "how religion and spirituality are practiced, and expressed by ordinary people (rather than official spokespersons) in the context of their everyday lives."[8] It distinguishes the actual lived religion of individuals as it is carried out "on-the-ground" from the more official or institutionally pre-scribed understanding of religious practices and beliefs. Popular religion and LR are both more interested in the former (without rejecting the importance of the latter). Historian of religion Robert Orsi champions the LR approach:

the study of lived religion directs attention to institutions *and* rituals, practice *and* theology, things *and* ideas. . . . The key questions concern what people *do* with religious idioms, how they use them, what they make of themselves and their world with them, and how, in turn, men, women, and children are fundamentally shaped by the worlds they are making as they make these worlds.[9]

Not only does LR listen to how people express themselves religiously, it also observes the "material, embodied aspects of religion as they occur in everyday life," which "means looking wherever and however we find people invoking a sacred presence."[10] Hence, the task for students of LR is to seek out the "lived" aspects in the actions and decisions "made by individuals,

6 Martin D. Stringer, "Lived Religion and Difficult Conversations" (Birmingham Conversations of the Faith, Neighbors, Changemakers Collaboration, 2015), 4.
7 Hall, "Lived Religion," 1286.
8 McGuire, *Lived Religion*, 12.
9 Robert A. Orsi, "Is the Study of Lived Religion Irrelevant to the World We Live In?" *Journal for the Scientific Study of Religion* 42, no. 2 (2003): 172, italics original.
10 Ammerman, "2013 Paul Hanly Furfey Lecture," 190–91.

not by institutions."[11] In short, instead of focusing on "religion-as-preached" in community, LR examines "religion-as-lived" by each individual's "often-mundane practices for remembering, sharing, and creatively assembling their most vital religious narratives."[12] LR approaches to the study of religion are increasingly vital not only for a proper understanding of how particular individuals and groups live out their religious identities in the everyday world but also for interreligious studies that explore how individuals and groups interact within and between others with various religious identities.

Kindred Approaches

Students of the LR approach are served well by having familiarity with similar approaches, such as studies of popular religion (mentioned above), material religion, vernacular religion, and the contemporary study of spirituality. All focus on the lived, material, embodied, and experiential dimensions of religion as it is carried out by particular individuals and communities in particular places and at particular times. Since these approaches pay serious attention to the complex nature of religion, they are important for understanding the complicated nature of religious traditions and identities. The LR approaches focus on the particularities and intricacies of religion and not only demonstrate an effort to "get it right"—that is, to understand what is really going on at the individual level and "on the ground"—but also honor the nuanced manner in which religion manifests in communities and individuals. Hence, importantly, these methods tend to naturally avoid drawing generalizations, stereotypes, and misconceptions that portray essentialized forms of religion.

Material religion focuses on the material nature of religion, which includes physical objects, images, artwork, buildings, spaces, clothing, actions, embodied practices, scents, and sounds. It assumes "that things, their use, their valuation, and their appeal are not something *added* to a religion, but rather inextricable from it."[13] The spirit of material religion embraces the idea that

---

11 Hall, "Lived Religion," 1283.

12 Meredith B. McGuire, "Embodied Practices," in *Everyday Religion*, ed. Nancy Ammerman (New York: Oxford University Press, 2008), 187; also quoted in Hall, "Lived Religion," 1283.

13 Brigit Meyer, David Morgan, Crispin Paine, and S. Brent Plate, "The Origin and Mission of Material Religion," *Religion* 40 (2010): 209, italics original.

"whether treasure or refuse, objects bear traces that yield valuable material evidence, sometimes almost the only evidence we have of the everyday lives of devotees."[14] Consider the definition of material religion articulated by some of its leading scholars today:

The material study of religion concentrates on what bodies and things do, on the practices that put them to work, on the epistemological and aesthetic paradigms that organize the bodily experience of things, hierarchizing sensations and media, all within the network of relations that make the sacred a social reality. What then does it mean to study the material culture of religions? It means to focus one's investigation on the evidence and insights offered by *bodies*,[15] *things*,[16] *places*,[17] and *practices.*[18,19]

The study of vernacular religion investigates the way religion shows up in a people's (folk's)[20] vernacular, which refers to "a way of communicating,

---

14 Meyer et al., "The Origin and Mission of Material Religion," 208–9.

15 In addition to being corporeal and fleshy vehicles for presence, practice, mindfulness, cognition, and emotion, "bodies are the medium of social experience, the gateway to the social bodies to which individuals belong, with which they identify, through which they feel and perceive themselves, others, and the divine." Meyer et al., 209.

16 In addition to being objects that are subject to the body's manipulation and comprehension, things "are also agencies within themselves, either as other bodies, or as the extension or completion of a body, or as the presence or symbol of a social body." Meyer et al., 209.

17 "Places are the fit between bodies and things, sites for their organization into theatres for the performance of self. And places are the flesh of social bodies, where people go to find themselves part of something larger." Meyer et al., 209.

18 "Practices are bodies, things, and places put to work, put on display, put into circulation, exchanged and hoarded, heard, smelled, fondled, destroyed. Practices are ways of activating bodies, things, and places, recognizing in their interrelations a presence or voice or power that engages humans and their institutions and communities." Meyer et al., 209.

19 Meyer et al., 209, italics added.

20 The study of *folk religion* shares a kindred spirit with lived religion approaches, especially vernacular religion. Folk religion refers to the religion of "the people" (*Das Volk*). In the broad scope of the study of religion, folk religion refers to "the appropriation of religious beliefs and practices at a popular level. This may occur as much in urban as in rural environments, and may also be the way in which individuals or groups belonging to mainstream religions practise their religion: it may be at considerable variance from what is officially supposed to be the case, and is thus also referred to as non-official religion." "Folk Religion," in *The Concise Oxford Dictionary of World Religions*, ed. John Bowker (Oxford: Oxford University Press, 2000).

thinking, behaving within, and conforming to, a particular cultural circumstance."[21] The field of vernacular religion largely draws on the concept of vernacular employed in architecture. Vernacular architecture is "concerned with domestic and functional rather than public or monumental buildings";[22] from "commercial buildings in American Chinatowns to seasonal communities in Idaho, from linoleum flooring in middle-class kitchens to garrets housing urban slaves, from farmsteads to urban tenements, vernacular architecture and its settings shape everyday life."[23] The study of vernacular architecture examines the ways in which "buildings, towns, and landscapes, [charged with dense cultural meanings that speak to both makers and users] comport behavior, shape identity, orchestrate ritual, and negotiate social relationships."[24] Likewise, the study of vernacular religion is

by definition, religion as it is lived: as human beings encounter, understand, interpret, and practice it. . . . [It] involves an interdisciplinary approach to the study of religious lives of individuals with special attention to the process of religious belief, the verbal, behavioral, and material expressions of religious belief, and the ultimate object of religious belief.[25]

The above definition of religion emphasizes belief, which invites critics who argue this definition reveals its Protestant Christian bias. Nonetheless, belief can be replaced with practice or lifeway to broaden the understanding of religion beyond cognitive ascent or belief.

The contemporary study of spirituality, although more aligned with theological and confessional approaches, emphasizes the study of lived religious experience in the world as reported by individuals and communities. Its object of study is the particular (e.g., particular experience of a particular person or community in a particular place at a particular time). Specifically, the content of the contemporary study of spirituality concerns the lived religious practice or experience of an individual or group. Scholar of spirituality

---

21 Leonard Norman Primiano, "Vernacular Religion and the Search for Method in Religious Folklife," *Western Folklore* 54, no. 1 (1995): 42.

22 *Oxford Dictionaries*, s.v. "vernacular," last accessed July 13, 2018, en. oxforddictionaries.com/definition/vernacular.

23 "Call for Papers," Vernacular Architecture Forum (website).

24 "Call for Papers."

25 Primiano, "Vernacular Religion and the Search for Method in Religious Folklife," 44.

Philip Sheldrake describes the contemporary study of spirituality as "the study of 'felt experience' and 'lived practice' in ways that, while not detached from theological tradition, overflow the boundaries that positivist theology tends to set."[26] Whereas the contemporary study of spirituality is more often attached to a confessional commitment or theological tradition and focuses on individuals' experience of the sacred, LR is more often detached from any confessional commitments or theological traditions and focuses on how individuals and groups practice their religions in the everyday world (which includes their experiences of the sacred or transcendent).

Benefit of Lived Religion

Robert Orsi maintains that "'religion' cannot be neatly separated from the other practices of everyday life, from the ways that human beings work on the landscape, for example, or dispose of corpses, or arrange for the security of their offspring."[27] Therefore, scholars of LR claim that the LR approach is optimal for the study of religion because it meets "men and women at this daily task, in all the spaces of their experience."[28] Since LR refers to the "study of how particular people, in particular places and times, live in, with, through, and against the religious idioms available to them in culture," its methodology favors empirical and phenomenological investigation "concerned with what people *do* with religious practice, [and] what they make with it of themselves and their worlds."[29] LR scholars assume "religious practice is polysemous and that it is constituted—assembled—by cultural bricolage."[30] Thus, they remain open to the complicated nature of religion and the ways people take on various religious identities. Orsi argues it is with such a disposition and understanding of religion that LR scholars propose "that to study lived religion entails a fundamental rethinking of what religion is and what it means to be religious."[31]

---

26 Philip Sheldrake, "Spirituality and Its Critical Methodology," in *Exploring Christian Spirituality*, ed. Lescher and Liebert, 15; cited in Hans Gustafson, *Finding All Things in God* (Eugene, OR: Pickwick, 2016), 8.

27 Robert Orsi, "Everyday Miracles," in *Lived Religion in America*, ed. David D. Hall (Princeton, NJ: Princeton University Press, 1997), 6–7.

28 Orsi, "Everyday Miracles," 7.

29 Orsi, 7, italics original.

30 Orsi, 7.

31 Orsi, 7.

LR provides the study of religion with the necessary nuance to the dynamic nature of religion and religious identity discussed in the two previous chapters. Sociologist of religion Danièle Hervieu-Léger concurs by claiming that what the scholar of LR investigates—that is, "lived" religion—"is, by definition, fluid, mobile, and incompletely structured."[32] Orsi adds that "the analytical nature of religious studies, organized as it still is around a series of fixed, mutually exclusive, and stable polar opposites, must be reconfigured in order to make sense of religion as lived experience. A new vocabulary is demanded to discuss such phenomena, a language as hybrid and tensile as the realities it seeks to describe."[33] The benefits of the LR approach lie in its nimble ability to make sense of complicated religious identities as multiple and by giving voice to everyday people who may otherwise be overshadowed by institutional and powerful voices. LR is especially useful for empirically investigating religion, for empiricism relies on precision of measurement and observation (to the extent that such a thing is possible with religion). Furthermore, LR can excavate beneath monolithic explanations of religions and expose any assumed essentialist tendencies.

McGuire teaches that since religions and religious identities are messy and complicated, and because lived religious aspects serve as the primary objects of study for LR, one of the main findings of LR shows that "because religion-as-lived is based more on such religious practices than on religious ideas or beliefs, it is not necessarily logically coherent. Rather, it requires a practical coherence," which is to say, "it needs to make sense in one's everyday life, and it needs to be effective, to 'work,' in the sense of accomplishing some desired end (such as healing, improving one's relationship with a loved one, or harvesting enough food to last the winter)."[34] In other words, perhaps from a systematic perspective seeking perfect logical coherence between and among religious beliefs and practices, the religions of others as lived seem woefully illogical, contradictory, and incoherent. However, such internal coherence is of little concern, challenge, or problem for many religious practitioners. Ammerman's vision of "studying lived religion simply means watching people do religious things, even when what they are doing seems fragmentary and doesn't fit neatly with other things they

---

32 Danièle Hervieu-Léger, "'What Scripture Tells Me,'" in *Lived Religion in America*, 22.

33 Orsi, "Everyday Miracles," 11.

34 McGuire, *Lived Religion*, 16.

do."[35] For instance, recall the *assemblage* of "Chrislam" discussed in the previous chapter. Chrislamists combine (assemble) elements of Christianity and Islam with, what seems to be, less emphasis on coherence and logic. However, they do so with the conviction that "to be a Christian or Muslim alone is not enough to guarantee success in this world and the hereafter; therefore, Chrislam worshippers participate in Christian as well as Muslim practices, appropriating the perceived powers of both."[36] Consider the remarks of Catholic theologian and priest Michael J. Himes about the everyday practices and beliefs of American Catholics:

> The Trinity doesn't make much difference to people. I have often remarked to students that if I and my fellow preachers mounted our pulpits some Sunday and announced that we had a letter from the Vatican saying that there are not three Persons but four, most people in the pews would simply groan. "Oh, when will these changes stop?" But to most of them it would cause no problem other than having to think about how to fit the fourth one in when making the sign of the cross.[37]

Though Himes is expressing his concern for the state of contemporary American Catholicism (they either do not understand, take seriously, or care about the doctrine of the Trinity), McGuire's logic of religion-as-lived is affirmed. Though the doctrine of the Trinity may not matter nor be understood by many Catholics, and perhaps it could be drastically changed on a whim as Himes half-jokingly suggests, the point is that the main challenge for adding a fourth person of the Trinity wouldn't be logical theological coherence. It would be more about the practical matter of signing the cross. McGuire candidly asks whether "we are mistaken in our expectation of cognitive consistency between individuals' religion, as intuitionally framed, and a person's actual religion, as lived."[38] McGuire's ethnographic research supports Himes's intuition. For most, internal logical coherence is not terribly important when it comes to religious beliefs and practices. McGuire reports, "after nearly forty years of talking to people about their individual religions, I have the impression that

---

35 Ammerman, *Studying Lived Religion*, 19.
36 Janson, "Unity through Diversity," 672 (abstract).
37 Michael Himes, "Living Conversation," *Conversations on Jesuit Higher Education* 8 (October 1995): 3.
38 McGuire, *Lived Religion*, 15.

only a small and unrepresentative proportion struggle to achieve tight consistence among their wide-ranging beliefs, perceptions, experiences, values, practices, and actions."[39] In other words, it may simply be that many, perhaps most, people are comfortable living with multiple tensions and internal inconsistencies between and among their many religious beliefs, practices, and experiences.

However, the LR approach does not disregard, ignore, or deem inauthentic the institutionalized and official practices and beliefs of religion. "Official religion and what religious organizations promote as 'religious' are surely part of the picture."[40] However, "by emphasizing individuals' practices in everyday life . . . [LR gets] closer to understanding religion in all its complexity and diversity."[41] Developing interreligious practical wisdom for everyday living and leadership requires understanding religion and religious orientations in their full complexity and diversity. To this end, the LR approach is invaluably essential.

THE UNITED STATES AND WESTERN EUROPE

The empirical investigation of religion emphasizes the examination of particularities, yet it does not rule out making universal (general) claims based on the particular empirical data. Recall the previous chapter's focus on the dynamic and fluid nature of religious orientations and identities. When the focus is on lived religion, more perspective is gained on how individuals draw from their religious and cultural resources to form complex identities and commitments.[42] This section presents data, mined from relevant empirical studies, that show the complexity of religious (and nonreligious) orientations. While the previous chapter theoretically examined the dynamic nature of religious orientations and identities, this section outlines the empirical reality of the complicated and dynamic nature of religious orientations and identities. It begins with an examination of religion as lived in the United States and Western Europe, and concludes with data on lived religious practices and blending.

---

39 McGuire, 16.
40 McGuire, 16.
41 McGuire, 16.
42 McGuire, *Lived Religion*, 187.

The Data

The 2016 study "Religion in Everyday Life," completed by the Pew Research Center, examines the everyday lived religious practices of Americans. It uncovers several findings about what it means to be religious in America. It shows that Americans "who are highly religious are more engaged with their extended families, more likely to volunteer, more involved in their communities and generally happier with the way things are going in their lives."[43] Those considered "highly religious" self-report to "pray daily and attend religious services at least once a week."[44] All other respondents are deemed "not highly religious." The study shows bias toward prayer and attending services as determinate practices for what it means to be highly religious. When asked what is essential for being Christian, according to American Christians, "believing in God tops the list, with fully 86% saying belief in God is 'essential' to their Christian identity."[45] Other significant responses include "being grateful for what you have" (71%), "forgiving those who have wronged you" (69%), "being honest at all times" (67%), and "praying regularly" (63%). Notice "attending religious services" was mentioned by only 35%.[46] These numbers vary among the particular Christian denominations.[47]

What do Americans mean when they say they believe in God? It cannot be assumed they all have the same idea of God. Even though 80% of Americans believe in God, only a slim majority of Americans (56%) say they believe in God "as described in the Bible." Of the 19% who respond "no" to the question of whether they believe in God, 9% still "do believe in some higher power/spiritual force."[48] At the end of the day, only 10% of Americans do not believe in any higher power, God (or Gods), or a spiritual force. Even among the nones and religiously unaffiliated (who make up approximately 23% of all Americans), 15% believe in the God of the Bible and 53% believe in a higher power or spiritual force. Thus, a total of 70% of religious nones believe in the

43 Pew Research Center, "Religion in Everyday Life," April 12, 2016, 4.
44 Pew Research Center, "Religion in Everyday Life," 4.
45 Pew Research Center, 7.
46 Pew Research Center, 7.
47 Pew Research Center, 34.
48 Pew Research Center, "When Americans Say They Believe in God, What Do They Mean?" April 25, 2018, 4–5.

biblical God or some other higher power or spiritual force.[49] According to the Understanding Unbelief project, which details interim findings about atheists and agnostics in six countries,[50] a significant minority of atheists and agnostics reject "the existence of supernatural beings/phenomena."[51] This underscores the point that not all—in fact, a significant minority of—atheists and agnostics discount belief in a higher power.

Among American Jews, a total of 89% believe in God or a higher power; however, only 33% of American Jews believe in the God as described in the Bible, while 56% believe in a different higher power of some kind.[52] Among American Christians, the dominant concept of God reflects a fairly classical Western Christian theistic understanding:[53] 93% believe God is all-loving, 87% believe God is all-knowing (omniscient), 78% believe God is all-powerful (omnipotent), and 74% believe God is all three: all-loving, omniscient, and omnipotent. The percentage who believe God is all three is higher among historically Black Protestants (91%) and Protestant Evangelicals (87%) than among Catholics (61%).[54] For American Jews, the dominant concept of God is, understandably, less influenced by Classical Western thought: 70% believe God is all-loving (compared to 93% among Christians), 49% believe God is all-knowing (compared to 87% among Christians), 39% believe God is all-powerful (compared to 78% among Christians), and only 30% believe God is all three (compared to 74% among Christians).[55] When asked whether they talk to God (or a higher power), 74% of all Americans said yes, 90% of

---

49 Pew Research Center, "When Americans Say They Believe in God, What Do They Mean?" 11.

50 Brazil, China, Denmark, Japan, the United Kingdom, and the United States.

51 This does not necessarily mean that this group believes in "God," however. Stephen Bullivant, Miguel Farias, Jonathan Lanman, and Lois Lee, "Understanding Unbelief: Atheists and Agnostics around the World" (2019), 15.

52 Pew Research Center, "When Americans Say They Believe in God, What Do They Mean?" 23.

53 A classical theistic account of God draws on the thought of Plato, Aristotle, Plotinus, Augustine, St. Anselm, Maimonides, Averroes, Thomas Aquinas, and others. It upholds classical attributes of God such as incorporeality (God has no physical body), simplicity (God has no parts and is indivisible), unity (there is only one God), eternity (God is eternal and beyond time), immutability (God does not change), omnipotence (God is all-powerful), omniscience (God is all-knowing), impassibility (God does not suffer nor is affected by the world), and goodness (God is all-good).

54 Pew Research Center, "When Americans Say They Believe in God, What Do They Mean?" 12.

55 Pew Research Center, 24–25.

American Christians said yes, and 63% of American Jews said yes; however, 65% of the religious nones also said yes. When asked whether God (or a higher power) talks directly to them, the numbers were much lower, with only 28% of all Americans saying yes; 35% of Christians said yes, only 9% of Jews said yes, and, perhaps surprisingly, 21% of nones also said yes.[56]

Concerning the authority and influence that religious leaders have on Americans, the data reveal that most Americans rely on their own conscience and research when making major life decisions. "When asked where they look for guidance when making major life decisions, Americans overall say they rely more on their own research than on direction from experts. Fully eight-in-ten Americans say they rely 'a lot' on their own research when making major decisions,"[57] while only 15% rely a lot on "advice from religious leaders." When it comes to American Catholics, the difference between lived religious belief and practices versus official teachings is pronounced. "Three-quarters of Catholics say they look to their own conscience 'a great deal' for guidance on difficult moral questions. Far fewer Catholics say they look a great deal to the Catholic Church's teachings (21%), the Bible (15%) or the pope (11%) for guidance on difficult moral questions."[58] These tendencies are revealed in Figure 5.1, which shows majority swaths of Catholics in the United States parting ways in their lived religious practice with their tradition's teaching.

Rodney Stark's research on *What Americans Really Believe* reveals the diversity within American Christian communities and offers a snapshot of the lived religious reality of American religion. Stark finds that 57% of American Protestant Christians and 81% of Roman Catholic Americans believe it is "completely true" that Jesus was born of a virgin, and only 44% of American Protestant Christians and 47% of Roman Catholic Americans "definitely" believe Jesus will return to earth someday.[59] Forty percent of Protestants and 36% of Roman Catholics are "absolutely sure there is a devil," and 50% of Protestants and 48% of Roman Catholics are "absolutely sure there is life beyond death."[60] Interestingly, when asked whether Satan and heaven absolutely exist: 52% of "liberal" Protestants (labeled liberal by

---

56 Pew Research Center, 27.
57 Pew Research Center, "Religion in Everyday Life," 11.
58 Pew Research Center, 11.
59 Stark, *What Americans Really Believe*, 4.
60 Stark, 6.

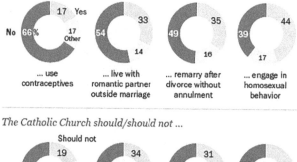

Fewer Than Half of Catholics Say Homosexual Behavior, Remarriage Without Annulment, Cohabitation, Contraception Are Sins

Do you personally think it is a sin to ...

... use contraceptives
... live with romantic partner outside marriage
... remarry after divorce without annulment
... engage in homosexual behavior

The Catholic Church should/should not ...

... allow Catholics to use birth control
... allow cohabiting Catholics to receive Communion
... allow those remarried without annulment to receive Communion
... recognize marriages of gay and lesbian couples

Source: Pew Research Center Survey of U.S. Catholics and Family Life, May 5–June 7, 2015. "Other" includes those saying "don't know" and those who do not believe in sin.

PEW RESEARCH CENTER

Figure 5.1. Tendencies among American Catholics.

denominational affiliation[61]), 88% of "conservative" Protestants (labeled conservative by denominational affiliation[62]), 52% of Roman Catholics, and 8% of Jews believe Satan absolutely exists; 66% of "liberal" Protestants, 92% of "conservative" Protestants, 69% of Roman Catholics, and 27% of Jews believe heaven absolutely exists.[63] These data quantitatively show not only the lived reality of religious individuals as diverse within and between

---

61 Includes Unitarian, United Church of Christ, Episcopalian, Methodist, Presbyterian, Lutheran, and others.

62 Includes Church of God in Christ, Pentecostal, Baptist, Assemblies of God, and others.

63 Stark, *What Americans Really Believe*, 8.

religions, but divergent from static and monolithic concepts of their traditions that are reduced to official teachings and doctrines.

Predictably, almost all "highly religious" Americans report thanking God for something in the past week (99%) and asking God for help (98%), but surprisingly the "not highly religious" Americans also, in large part, report thanking God for something in the past week (68%) and asking God for help (55%). Most Americans, religious or otherwise, respond positively to the language of God in the context of gratitude and petition. What is more, the group with the highest percentage reporting to have been "angry with God" in the past week is also the "highly religious" (10%).[64] An insight gleaned from this shows that the concept of God is alive and well in the contemporary American populous, especially among American Christians. In fact, for all major religious traditions analyzed in the 2016 Pew study on "Religion in Everyday Life" (Evangelical Protestants, Mainline Protestants, historically Black Protestants, and Catholics), "belief in God is the highest-ranking item seen as essential to Christian identity,"[65] whereas for most American Jews belief in God is not essential to Jewish identity. Rather "remembering the Holocaust" (73%) and "leading an ethical life" (69%) are the top two reported essentials of what being Jewish means.[66] Overall, the American populous is fairly religious when measured by standards of religious commitment. Most retain some degree of appreciation for the concept of God and commitment to religious practices. Even Americans who fall into the broad categories of unaffiliated, none, or "not highly religious" are still somewhat religious. In fact, "American 'nones' are as religious as—or even more religious than—self-identifying Christians in several European countries, including France, Germany and the UK,"[67] and "Americans, overall, are considerably more religious than Western Europeans."[68] For example, 20% of Americans who identify as "religiously unaffiliated" report that they "pray daily," compared with 11% of Western Europeans who identify as Christian. Likewise, whereas 13% of Americans who identify as "religiously unaffiliated" say "religion is very important in their lives," only 11% of Western Europeans who identity

---

64 Pew Research Center, "Religion in Everyday Life," 31.

65 Pew Research Center, 39.

66 Pew Research Center, "A Portrait of Jewish Americans," October 1, 2013, 14.

67 Neha Sahgal, "10 Key Findings about Religion in Western Europe," Pew Research Center, May 29, 2018.

68 Pew Research Center, "Being Christian in Western Europe," May 29, 2018, 47.

as Christian say, "religion is very important in their lives." These contrasting data prompt important questions about religious self-identification, especially about what it means to be Christian, in Western Europe.

The 2018 Pew study on "Being Christian in Western Europe" demonstrates the broad nature of religious labels. It shows that what it means to be Christian varies widely. Despite popular American impressions, Western Europe remains predominately Christian. In fact, approximately the same percentage of Western Europeans and Americans identify as Christian (71%).[69] However, differences emerge when their religious practices are examined. It is increasingly common for people to identify as (1) "spiritual but not religious" (SBNR), while some may identify as (2) "religious but not spiritual" (RBNS). Still others identify as (3) "both religious and spiritual" (BRS) or (4) "neither religious nor spiritual" (NRNS). These four categories are measured in the 2018 Pew study on being Christian in Western Europe. In the study, religion generally refers to identifying with a particular tradition, regularly attending religious services, praying daily, and believing in God or some other higher power. Spirituality refers to "beliefs or feelings about supernatural phenomena, such as life after death, the existence of a soul apart from the human body, and the presence of spiritual energy in physical things such as mountains, trees or crystals."[70] In the United States, 48% say they are BRS compared with approximately 24% of Western Europeans. Only 6% of Americans say they are RBNS compared with about 15% of Western Europeans, and 27% of Americans identify as SBNR compared with only 11% of Western Europeans. The greatest chasms between the two regions surface with those who identify as NRNS: 18% of Americans and 53% of Europeans.[71] Accordingly, not only are Western Europeans generally less "religious" than Americans, but they are also generally less "spiritual."

The emergence and growth of the religiously unaffiliated (a category that includes atheists, agnostics, and "nothing in particular") constitutes a growing percentage of the population (a substantial or significant minority), and thus their lived religious beliefs and practices are essential when examining religion in the West. The Netherlands (48%), Norway (43%), and Sweden (42%) have the highest percentage of the unaffiliated, while Portugal (15%), Ireland (15%), and Italy (15%) have the lowest.[72] Unlike the nones in the United

---

69 Pew Research Center, 6.
70 Pew Research Center, 119.
71 Pew Research Center, 49.
72 Pew Research Center, 39.

States, the majority of nones in Western Europe do not believe in God or some other higher power or spiritual force; however, a substantial minority do hold some spiritual beliefs (approximately 28% compared with 70% in the United States).[73] When Western European religiously unaffiliated are asked whether they agree "they have a soul as a well as a physical body," the majority who agree also have some belief in God, higher power, or spiritual force (about 74%). Yet, predictably, among the religious unaffiliated with no belief in God, higher power, or spiritual force, agreement is much lower (about 29%).[74] These data show the complicated reality of the lived religious diversity among those who do not affiliate with religion, and how regional contexts can shape can influence these trends.

Despite having similar percentages of Christians (71%) and religiously unaffiliated (approximately 24%), the United States and Western Europe differ in religious practice and the perceived importance that religion plays in their lives. Put simply, "Western Europeans are less religious than Americans"[75] when religiosity, as understood by Pew, is measured by whether an individual prays daily, believes in God, attends religious services, and deems religion important in their life. However, there is no uniform agreement about what constitutes appropriate metrics for measuring religiosity given the contested nature of the concept of religion. Fifty-three percent of Americans agree that "religion is very important in their lives," compared with 11% of Western Europeans. Among Christians, 68% of American Christians agree, while only 14% of Western European Christians agree. Even 13% of American religious unaffiliated agree, compared to 1% of Western European religiously unaffiliated. Similar patterns emerge in responses to questions about attending religious services on a monthly basis, praying daily, and belief in God with certainty. As stated above, "in fact, by some of these standard measures of religious commitment, American nones are as religious as—or even more religious than—Christians in several European countries, including France, Germany and the UK."[76] For instance, a higher percentage of American religiously unaffiliated report praying daily (20%) and believing in God with certainty (27%) than Western European Christians do (18% and 23%, respectively).[77]

---

73 Pew Research Center, 43.
74 Pew Research Center, 44.
75 Pew Research Center, 47.
76 Pew Research Center, 47.
77 Pew Research Center, 47.

Not only is it valuable to have a sense of the global quantitative landscape of religion, because it provides context for comparative work between and among regions and groups, but data like these also provide a useful foundation from which to generate questions about the more complicated particularities of the lived reality of religion for individuals and groups.

What it means to be religious and/or spiritual is unclear without an adequate inquiry into the specific beliefs and practices of individuals (an aim of the LR approach). A deeper analysis of Western Europe and the United States reveals that only 15% (median) of Western Europeans believe in God with absolute certainly and 58% (median) say they still believe in God (just not with absolute certainty).[78] These figures do not differ drastically from the United States, where 63% believe in God with absolute certainty. Twenty-seven percent (median) of Western Europeans believe in God as described in the Bible (56% in the United States), 38% (median) believe in some other higher power or spiritual force (24% in the United States), and 26% (median) do not believe in any higher power (10% in the United States).[79] However, as the previous chapters argued, belief in God is not the best measure of an individual's religiosity. For the study of LR, questions about belief in God need not be as high on the list of concerns as the lived practices, blending, and experiences of religion in the everyday hustle of life.

Practices and Blending

Having a sense of how individuals and groups perform and blend various religious practices can be just as valuable for LR and for measuring religiosity as having a sense of religious beliefs, if not more so. Religious practices can include giving money to religious organizations, which 24% (median) of Western Europeans do. Other practices include wearing or carrying religious symbols (17% median), fasting during holy times (12% median), and trying to persuade others to adopt their religious views (8% median).[80] The empirical data on religious blending and sharing in beliefs and practices support the identity theory offered in the previous chapter that individuals' religious orientations are complicated, fluid, and multiple. Sean McCloud claims that

---

78 Pew Research Center, 95.
79 Pew Research Center, 107.
80 Pew Research Center, 104.

"while many scholars still rely on conceptions of religion that entail coherent traditions neatly bound by institutions and textual dogma, the practices of Americans reveal that individuals pick and combine cultural materials from a variety of sources."[81] For instance, 24% of Americans and 26% (median) of Western Europeans consider yoga a spiritual practice (not just exercise), and many of them (perhaps most) are Christians. Twenty percent of American Protestant Christians and 28% of American Catholic Christians consider yoga a spiritual practice. Similar patterns emerge with other beliefs[82] such as reincarnation (24% in the United States, 20% in Western Europe), astrology (25% in the United States, 23% in Western Europe), the "evil eye" or casting curses (16% in the United States, 16% in Western Europe), and spiritual energy in physical things (26% in the United States, 23% in Western Europe).[83] Furthermore, 19% (median) of Western Europeans practice meditation and 13% (median) consult a horoscope or tarot cards.[84] In the United States, 29% report being in touch with the deceased, 18% report experiencing ghosts, and 15% consult fortunetellers.[85] Stark and the 2008 Baylor survey on religion find that, among Americans who identify as religious (majority Christians who report devoted institutional and religiously sanctioned practices, membership, and doctrines), 50% believe ghosts exist, 44% believe extraterrestrials exist, 63% believe in psychic phenomena such as "ESP,"[86] and among all Americans, 53% agree that dreams can sometimes foretell the future and 37% agree places can be haunted.[87] Scholarly debate exists over whether such blending of religious practices in America is truly "nothing new."[88] McCloud argues that "combinativity, syncretism, and bricolage were part of the American landscape from the first contacts between Europeans and Native Americans, and likely long before that," and such "picking, mixing, and combining religious and cultural materials is a constant in American religious history."[89] These

---

81 McCloud, "Everything Blended," 363.
82 Pew Research Center, "Eastern, New Age Beliefs Widespread," December 2009, 8; "Being Christian in Western Europe," 135.
83 Pew Research Center, "Eastern, New Age Beliefs Widespread," 8; "Being Christian in Western Europe," 135.
84 Pew Research Center, "Being Christian in Western Europe," 135.
85 Pew Research Center, "Eastern, New Age Beliefs Widespread," 10.
86 Stark, *What Americans Really Believe*, 91.
87 Stark, 126.
88 McCloud, "Everything Blended," 367.
89 McCloud, 367.

data demonstrate that significantly sized groups routinely blend practices and beliefs from a diverse set of traditions and concretely show why it is incomplete and misguided to conceptualize religions (practices, beliefs, etc.) as bounded, internally coherent wholes with sealed borders.

The 2013 Pew study on American Jews shows that Jews also often combine traditions, especially when they marry non-Jews (particularly Christians). For example, 32% of American Jews reported having a Christmas tree in their home the year prior. This number soars to 71% among Jews married to non-Jews. Jews in their thirties and forties are the most likely among all Jews to have a Christmas tree at 40%. Jews married to non-Jews in their child-raising years (thirties and forties), likely with young children, are very likely to have a Christmas tree in their homes. Since the mid-1990s, over 50% of all married American Jews have married a non-Jewish partner (hence the Jewish intermarriage rate of 58% between the years 2005 and 2013[90]). However, it is mistaken to assume Jews in interfaith marriages identify with both their tradition and their partner's tradition. Nor should it be assumed the couple is raising their children as both Jewish and Christian. Rather, the data simply show a wide practice of MRP, but not belonging (MRB). This may be partly evident in the relatively low percentage of American Jews that report attending non-Jewish religious services the year prior, which is just 15%.[91]

Empirical data about the lived religious reality of MRB are still slim. A substantial 2017–18 study in the Netherlands[92] found that "MRB is present among at least 23% of the population in varying combinations and intensities."[93] To generate such a high percentage of MRB, a rather broad range of MRB combinations and intensities is needed. In fact, the range is so broad in the study that, by most measures, many scholars who study MRB may reject many of the combinations as authentic instances of MRB.[94] Among them is Steve Bruce,

---

90 Pew Research Center, "A Portrait of Jewish Americans," 9.
91 Pew Research Center, 80.
92 Berghuijs et al., "Exploring Single and Multiple Religious Belonging," 18–48.
93 Berghuijs, "Multiple Religious Belonging in the Netherlands," 19.
94 Language concerning MRO (MRI, MRB, MRP) is not used uniformly and consistently by all scholars. The Netherlands study uses a very broad understanding of MRB defined as "the variety of ways in which individuals are connected to one or more religious traditions, by combining elements (texts, beliefs, practices, or other) from one or more traditions in their lives. [MRB] is defined as combining elements from more than one religious tradition in one's life." Berghuijs et al., "Exploring Single and Multiple

who points out "the very generous way" the Netherlands study defines MRB, which, Bruce contends, "inflates the figures for those who would normally be described in those terms."[95] Such a broad interpretation of MRB "allows an estimate of the numbers of people in the West who are religious that is vastly greater than those produced by more conventional ways of estimating the popularity of religious sentiment such as counts of religious activities redolent of religious belief (such as church-going), counts of the use of religion for rites of passage, or conventional attitude surveys."[96] For instance, applying the Netherlands study's parameters to the US context, all American Jews who regularly put up Christmas trees in their home could be deemed to be practicing MRB, which tends to run contrary to the usual manner in which the label is applied. Alternatively, if MRB refers to simultaneous observant commitment to two or more religions then the percentage of Dutch labeled as MRB drops from 23% to 3%. Bruce contends, "when one looks closely at just *what* is present, one gets a rather different picture. When asked the direct question, only 3 percent identify as adherents of two or more religions . . . if we apply a conventional understanding of the notion of 'belonging,' MRB is revealed to be extremely unpopular."[97]

Although Bruce's criticisms are well founded and not to be ignored, the Netherlands study yields telling data about how people, in this case the Dutch combine, blend, and share religious traditions. One of Bruce's central criticisms of the study is that it does not really measure MRB since it stretches the definition of MRB too far beyond its usual parameters.

Religious Belonging," 21. This definition of MRB is closer to the broader category of MRO, proposed in the previous chapter, which can be appropriately applied to the 23% of the Dutch population that "combines elements of different religious traditions in their lives." Berghuijs et al., 20. The Dutch study's understanding of MRB "ranges from people who are intensely involved in two religions and who are members of two religious communities, to 'unaffiliated spirituals' who combine elements from different religious traditions, without joining a religious community, and everything in between, for instance Christians who practice Zen meditation." Berghuijs et al., 21. With all of these possibilities included, 23% seems accurate. This does not mean that 23% belong to two or more religious traditions. Belonging is a much more involved and committed position than combining elements from various religions. However, when the respondents in the study were asked the question directly about adhering to two or more religions, only 3% respond that they do. This 3% is likely closer to the reality of the percentage of MRBers·
95 Bruce, "Multiple Religious Belonging," 607.
96 Bruce, 603.
97 Bruce, 607, italics original.

This criticism is addressed by nuancing the language and dropping the category of MRB in place of other categories proposed previously: MRI, MRO, and/or MRP. The researchers in the Netherlands study helpfully distinguish between several dimensions of MRB (modalities, bonding styles, mobilities, and motivations), which contribute to the conception of such a broad interpretation of MRB to begin with. Although the study's conclusion of 23% of Dutch qualifying as MRB is suspect in the conventional sense of MRB, it is clarified by shifting the language from MRB to MRP (with MRP referring to *participation* in one or more religious traditions without the condition of confession, commitment, or belonging). MRP more accurately describes the Netherlands study's interpretation of MRB, which it defines as "the variety of ways in which individuals are connected to one or more religious traditions, by combining elements (texts, beliefs, practices, or other) from one or more traditions in their lives. [MRB] is defined as combining elements from more than one religious tradition in one's life."[98]

If 23% of the Dutch population engages in MRP, not MRB, then it more closely correlates with the figures in other Western regions. For instance, as the study shows,

26% of the inhabitants of former West-Germany and 13% of former East-Germany draw from different religious traditions.... About one in four American adults (24%) indicate that they attend services of at least one faith other than their own, and roughly one-in-ten (12%) say they participate in the services of two or more faiths in addition to their own, aside from weddings and funerals.[99]

The Netherlands study confirms the prevalence of multiple religious blending, hybridity, and sharing (all instances of MRP). The study's empirical method is invaluable for examining the depths and degrees to which people combine and blend religious practices, beliefs, and traditions.

This chapter demonstrates the method and value of the LR approach for investigating and understanding the complexity of religion, religious

---

98 Berghuijs et al., "Exploring Single and Multiple Religious Belonging," 21.
99 Berghuijs et al., 20; data from US from Pew Research Center, "Eastern, New Age Beliefs Widespread."

practices, and religious orientations. As the data show, the lived reality of people's religious lives is often more complicated than explanations offered by brief essentialized textbook descriptions or quantitative tables of religious populations. The next chapter argues for the value of the LR approach and its indispensability for interreligious studies and for developing practical interreligious wisdom for everyday living.

6

Lived Interreligious Encounter

Chapter Outline

I. Value for Interreligious Studies
   a. *Overcoming Essentialisms and Stereotypes*
   b. *Dangerous Religious Ideas and Self-Critical Faith*
   c. *Self-Implication and Porous Borders*
II. Encountering Religious Difference
   a. *Challenging the Powerful*
   b. *LR for Interfaith Dialogue*
   c. *Reflexivity, Secularization, and Multiple Religious Orientation*
III. Putting a Human Face on Religion

The previous chapter asserted the value of the Lived Religion approach (LR hereafter) for understanding the complex nature of religion and religious orientations. This chapter argues for the value of LR for interreligious studies (IRS)[1] and for interfaith engagement (IFE). By examining complicated contexts and particularities, LR helps overcome the major obstacle of essentialism that reduces religious traditions, practices, communities, and orientations to monolithic misconceptions and stereotypes. Several benefits of LR for IRS emerge. (1) It helps challenge and balance the powerful, (2)

---

1 Portions of this chapter are inspired by and adapted from Hans Gustafson, "Vitality of Lived Religion Approaches," in *Interreligious Studies*, ed. Gustafson, 91–97.

it opens constructive inroads to dialogue, and (3) it reveals the need for religious reflexivity, especially in Western contexts of increasing seculariza-tion and multiple religious orientations (MRO). The chapter concludes by looking ahead to the remainder of the book and offers a brief word on the relationship between LR and developing practical interreligious wisdom for everyday leadership.

VALUE FOR INTERRELIGIOUS STUDIES

A common refrain in the interfaith world preaches that interreligious engage-ment is not between -*isms*, but is between people. It is not between Judaism and Buddhism, for example; rather, it is between Jews and Buddhists. The benefit of LR for interreligious studies is manifold. It exposes essentialisms and stereotypes, reveals misconceptions and dangerous religious ideas, and constructively implicates scholars in their research.

Overcoming Essentialisms and Stereotypes

A major obstacle to constructive interreligious encounter surfaces in the over-simplification of others or rigidly reducing the religious orientations of others to static monolithic versions of their tradition. Appling the LR approach not only prevents ignorance of the rich internal diversity of religious traditions but also exposes the rich internal diversity of the individuals themselves and the many ways they construct their identities. McGuire argues that "by overemphasizing religious organizations and official versions of religion as definitive, sociologists and other scholars of religion may have failed to notice the extent of within-group diversity due to individuals' selection, adaptation, and amalgamation of elements in their lived religions."[2] The LR approach emerges as a necessity for properly investigating the dynamic nature of reli-gious orientations and practices, for it avoids reducing individuals' religion to an essentialized textbook version. McGuire instructively asserts, "when we no longer assume that individuals' religions can be equated with their religious affiliation or encompassed by their membership in a religious organization,

---

2 McGuire, *Lived Religion*, 210.

then we realize that we must ask [new and] different questions,"[3] many of which can be generated from interreligious studies.

Ignorance of the vast internal diversity within religions often generates and reinforces misconceptions and stereotypes, many of which are hateful, and some of which are harmful and precursors to violence. Interreligious studies (IRS) and interfaith engagement (IFE) activities often entail implicit (and sometimes explicit) attempts to categorize religious individuals for the sake of comparison and conversation. When an encounter or dialogue is labeled Muslim–Christian, assumptions are sometimes made about what it means to be Muslim and about what it means to be Christian (even if the people involved in the dialogue self-identify as Muslim and Christian, respectively). Such encounters can also advance assumptions about what being Muslim or Christian does not entail. Yet labeling the dialogue "Muslim–Christian" conveys something about the encounter, despite its inadequacy. If constructive interreligious understanding involves acknowledging the internal diversity of one's tradition, then instead of shying away from and ignoring oppressive and violent tendencies within their own traditions, scholars and practitioners alike can apply an LR approach to tackle difference head on. Doing so not only illuminates *intra*religious difference and understanding but *inter*religious difference and understanding as well.[4] The LR approach steps beyond the superficialities of equating religious practitioners solely with their traditions by digging beneath the surface to probe the complexity of the traditions and, more importantly, the sophistication with which religion is lived out at personal individual levels. Since the LR approach involves "observing *social* practices, the particularities of the people and places will always be central to the story."[5] Not only is the LR approach promising for IRS, but it holds practical implications for practitioners involved in IFE.

Robert Orsi, in his keynote address to the Society for the Scientific Study of Religion in Salt Lake City in 2002, questions whether the study of LR is relevant for the contemporary world. Orsi inquires, "What is the cash value or real-world payoff of this way of thinking about religion?"[6] What difference does it make whether we know how every person who identifies as a Christian or a Muslim practices their traditions in their own unique and idiosyncratic

---

3 McGuire, 210.
4 See Gustafson, "'They're Not Really Christians.'"
5 Ammerman, *Studying Lived Religion*, 54, italics original.
6 Orsi, "Is the Study of Lived Religion Irrelevant to the World We Live In?" 170.

ways? Is there a greater benefit and practical purpose for understanding Christianity and Islam on a broader level, especially in a world that produces religious fanatics who hate, oppress, and terrorize others in the name of their religion? Orsi's address came one year after two airplanes were deliberately flown into New York City's World Trade Center towers on September 11, 2001, by men allegedly motivated by their religion. Orsi recognizes that, at the time, there was pressure "to define a normative 'Islam' in contradistinction from whatever it was that motivated the men who flew their planes into the towers who, we were told (by the President of the United States among others), did not represent 'real' Islam."[7] A public discussion in the United States ensued on the nature and definition of "real Islam." Orsi recounts the popular narratives. There is the "good Islam—which we recognized as like ourselves," that is, the Islam that conforms to contemporary Western American modern secular values. And there is "a bad distorted something else that existed in Middle Eastern lands but had nothing to do with Islam and was our enemy, and once so designated, we lost any interest in this other thing except to bring it within the range of our weapons."[8] The debate asked whether the Qur'an endorses violence, and this conversation was disturbingly removed from the diverse experiences, histories, practices, and interpretations of Muslims around the globe. Orsi laments,

All this talk about "Islam" proceeding at such a remove from history and practice served only to obscure (and so also to protect Americans from) a clear view of lived experience in Islamic countries, from the complexity of political and religious realities there, and most of all from any understanding of the role of the United States in that region. It is precisely against this that a lived religion approach sets itself.[9]

Sociologist Cawo Abdi's article "Where Is My Islam?" published on CNN. com attempts to "reclaim Islam" from groups like ISIS[10] and Boko Haram[11]

---

7 Orsi, 171.

8 Orsi, 171.

9 Orsi, 171.

10 ISIS refers to the Islamic State of Iraq and Syria, and is also known as ISIL (Islamic State of Iraq and the Levant), "Daish," and "Daesh." A militant terrorist organization, ISIS gained global notoriety in 2014 after successfully pushing Iraqi forces out of strategic cities in Western Iraq.

11 Boko Haram refers to the Islamic State in West Africa (ISWA). A militant terrorist organization, Boko Haram, is based in northeastern Nigeria and is aligned with ISIS.

without denouncing these groups' claims to identify as Muslims. Rather, Abdi remarks the "groups executing these atrocities represent an extreme in their readings of Islam."[12] Abdi cleverly illustrates the power and dynamism of Islam to rise above and foster other (nonviolent) readings of Islam beyond the oversimplified narratives dominated by terror groups and extremists often presented in major media. Dismissing ISIS and Boko Haram as not "really Muslim" is not dissimilar to deeming the Nazi party as not "really religious," the Ku Klux Klan as not "really Christian," or the 9/11 bombers as not "really Muslim." These groups claim(ed) a religious identity. An unnuanced essentialized view of Islam (or Islams), or any religious tradition, leads to binary constructions removed from their very complicated lived contexts.

Politicians and journalists, often with good intentions, revoke any genuine religious identity from those who perpetrate violent and hateful acts in the name of their tradition. Stephen Gregg contends that the LR approach "is absent when we look at media discourse, political discourse and, crucially, the interdisciplinary discourse when it approaches the study of religion in different contexts."[13] Gregg offers an example from political discourse demonstrating the practical need for an LR approach: a British parliamentarian urging Parliament "to use the term Daesh instead of ISIS when it was talking about the terrorist group in Syria and Iraq . . . on the grounds that he didn't want the word Islam, or anything Islamic, linked with a terrorist organization,"[14] which is reasonable from a community relations point of view. Gregg's concern with this, however, is not that it avoids any "deep analysis of ISIS" because "this really isn't the time or the place for that," but that it can imply that "anyone that commits a violent act, in the name of religion, isn't a *real* Muslim."[15] Analogous situations include, "if we're thinking of suicide bombings in Sri Lanka in the Civil War—they're not *real* Buddhists; or sexual abuse by clergy

---

According to the Associated Press, they are responsible for killing 20,000 people and forcing 2.3 million from their homes over a six-year insurgency. "Nigeria's Boko Haram Kills 49 in Suicide Bombings," *Washington Post*, November 18, 2015.

12 Cawo Abdi, "Where Is My Islam?" CNN.com, August 24, 2015.

13 Stephen Gregg, "The British Association for the Study of Religions (BASR) and the Impact of Religious Studies," panel with Steve Sutcliffe, Stephen Gregg, Christopher Cotter, Suzanne Owen, and David Robertson, *The Religious Studies Project* (podcast audio), March 12, 2018.

14 Gregg, "The British Association for the Study of Religions (BASR) and the Impact of Religious Studies."

15 Gregg.

isn't something that a *real* Christian would do."[16] Scholars of religion will readily point out the problematic reductionism and essentialism at work here since, as Gregg notices, it "takes away the everyday experience of people that I hope you disagree with in the name of religion, but they are doing so in the name of religion."[17] In other words, particular religious identities are being boiled down to (over)simplified caricatures. An LR approach effectively complicates religious traditions and, more importantly, the religious lives and practices of everyone who orients around their tradition, and often in complex and different ways.

Hesitancy to acknowledge that sometimes violent groups are inspired by their religious traditions is likely well intentioned and done out of respect for the nonviolent majority in those traditions. However, without such recognition, it becomes more challenging to raise awareness, and remind the world, of the destructive potential that lurks within the human person to harness religious zeal for hateful and destructive purposes. The LR approach serves as a powerful tool to expose to the world the complexity of religious beliefs, behaviors, and belongings in all their messiness (sometimes disturbing and other times inspiring) to better combat the oppressive, hateful, and violent factions (as marginal as they may be). Furthermore, exposing this messiness also reveals the heartening and encouraging movements of religion, which often combat those violent tendencies. Operating from a more informed position yields greater potential to inquire about methods appropriate for combating the violent tendencies that come from within and without one's own religious tradition. Furthermore, in the example offered by Stephen Prothero, failing to recognize the religiosity of Nazis, terrorists, racists, hate groups, and the like is "terrifying" since it allows those within those traditions to "absolve themselves of any responsibility for reckoning with the dark side of their tradition[s]."[18] Admirably and effectively, Abdi critically combats this foreign dark side of her own tradition and its dangerous ideas. Abdi embodies the spirit and sentiment put forth by scholar of Jewish and interreligious studies Rachel S. Mikva that "all religious ideas are dangerous, and self-critical faith is essential."[19]

---

16 Gregg.
17 Gregg.
18 Prothero, *God Is Not One*, 10.
19 Rachel S. Mikva, *Dangerous Religious Ideas* (Boston: Beacon Press, 2020), 6.

Dangerous Religious Ideas and Self-Critical Faith[20]

Harm, hate, and violence are perpetrated in the name of religion. Despite being the minority view at the margins of these traditions, religious hate and violence often receive the most media attention. It is true that "much violence ostensibly committed in the name of religion can be analyzed as political, social, or economic; . . . [but] this is not to say that religions are let off the hook, as they can provide a justifying ideology."[21] Several scholars and religious practitioners advocate for publicly acknowledging these tendencies in their own traditions. Mikva points out how concepts of God can be used to support various and opposing positions on gun control, reproductive rights, tax policy, marriage, and much else.[22] Likewise, scripture and authoritative holy texts are used to justify and condemn slavery, LGBTQ+ rights, and scientific knowledge.[23] This includes Christians acknowledging the history of antisemitic Christian theologies that blames Jews for killing Jesus and justifies racist antisemitism (e.g., the "German Christian" movement that sought to reconcile Christianity with Nazi ideology). Christians that fight this hateful tendency of Christianity to spawn antisemitic views might deem such an interpretation a perversion, a misunderstanding, or simply incorrect. The argument scholars make is that it is more effective to acknowledge that these hate groups are inspired by Christianity instead of ignoring them, refusing to acknowledge them as serious, or rejecting them as not "real Christians." Acknowledging such tendencies allows Christians to set about the hard work of countering this narrative.[24]

Shira Lander, rabbi and professor of Jewish Studies, instructively articulates this point:

---

20 Section title inspired by Rachel S. Mikva's book *Dangerous Religious Ideas*.
21 Hedges, *Understanding Religion*, 357.
22 Mikva, *Dangerous Religious Ideas*, 4.
23 Mikva, 4.
24 This is not an argument for why one should insist those in other traditions condemn the violence in their own traditions. Rather, as Todd Green argues, revealed in the subtitle of his book *Presumed Guilty*, "We Shouldn't Ask Muslims to Condemn Terrorism." Green, *Presumed Guilty: Why We Shouldn't Ask Muslims to Condemn Terrorism* (Minneapolis: Fortress Press, 2018). To insist that our Muslim friends, neighbors, and colleagues need to constantly condemn violence every time it occurs only exhibits an offensive lack of trust. Instead, the argument here is a call to avoid dismissing the violent and oppressive tendencies that lurk within one's own traditions.

Rather than dismissing the radical or fundamentalist wings of religion as "hijacking" the faith and distancing ourselves from them by denying any relationship between our own version of religion and that of religious fanatics, we need to take full responsibility for the harmful elements within our traditions without fear that those who oppose us will use our words against us.[25]

Drawing on her Jewish tradition, Lander explains, "rather than dismissing and condemning these folks as lunatics and radicals, my own tradition requires that I sit down and begin a conversation with them, or at least their allies and supporters, articulated as 'seeking peace and pursu[ing] it' (Ps 34:15: *bakkesh shalom v'rodfehu*)."[26] Although it may not always be reasonable to sit down for a conversation with ISIS or the Nazi party, it might be reasonable to converse with their nonviolent supporters and sympathizers.

The LR approach and the examples above raise questions about religious orientation, namely: What does it mean to be religious? What does it mean to be Christian? Who gets to be Jewish? Who decides who is and who is not a Muslim? An LR approach, among others, takes these questions seriously. Chapters three and four explored the dynamic and messy nature of religions and religious orientations, thereby alluding to these concerns raised by LR. Not only does LR establish a solid framework for understanding religious orientations and identities, but it is also a productive approach to the general study of religion, interreligious studies, and for community-based interfaith engagement activities that aim for interreligious understanding. Marianne Moyaert admits that although textbook pedagogy in the classroom remains "highly valuable, but [it is] still too remote from lived religion, which often revolves around particular religious practices. That is why," argues Moyaert, "as interreligious educators, we should develop methods that encourage students to move beyond texts and to participate in various religious practices."[27] In addition to examining the relations between and among religious leaders, institutions, and authorities, LR takes seriously the encounter between and among the ordinary everyday practitioner living out their complicated

---

25 Shira Lander, "The Role of the Religious Voice in the Twenty-First Century—A Jewish Perspective," in *Religious Identity and Renewal in the Twenty-First Century*, ed. Simone Sinn and Michael Reid Trice (Leipzig: Evangelische Verlagsanstalt, 2015), 88.

26 Lander, "The Role of the Religious Voice in the Twenty-First Century," 88.

27 Marianne Moyaert, "On the Role of Ritual in Interfaith Education," *Religious Education* 113, no. 1 (2018): 59.

religious traditions in religiously diverse contexts. In so doing, LR provides a useful platform from which stereotypes and misconceptions can be countered, and authorities can be checked, limited, and decentered when necessary.

By taking the time to examine the particularities of people's lived religious practices and beliefs, the scholar quickly realizes that one cannot simply equate an individual's lived religion with the official version from sacred texts, doctrines, and religious authorities. By complicating religion, by exposing the messiness that exists not only within religious traditions but within an individual's religious identity, the major barrier to constructive interreligious encounter—reducing or oversimplifying religions to the official version without recognizing the internal diversity—can be acknowledged and overcome. The LR approach exhorts scholars to ask new questions in the study of religion. Many of these questions are interreligious questions since they involve the relations between, among, and within religious communities and individuals.

Self-Implication and Porous Borders

The LR approach beckons the scholar into their research. Like IRS, LR can be a self-implicating exercise. Unsurprisingly, a field that primarily examines the lives and relations between and among people with deeply held religious convictions is likely to make demands on the researchers and their relationship to the object of study. Orsi confirms, "the study of lived religion risks the exposure of the researcher. His or her most deeply held existential orientations and moral values are on display with an obviousness not found in earlier ethnographic or, especially, historical accounts. . . . The existential implication of the study of lived religion is this: we can no longer constitute the objects of our study as other";[28] especially since the objects of study are often not objects at all but living breathing [human] subjects related to the researcher. "Lived Religion refers not only to religion as lived by others but also to life as lived by those who approach others' everyday experience to learn about culture and history; it refers, in other words, to the conjuncture of two lived worlds in the study of religion."[29] In this way, the LR approach serves as a well-positioned and indispensable methodological ally for IRS.

---

28 Orsi, "Everyday Miracles," 18.
29 Orsi, 18.

What is more, LR aids in the exposure of the porous border between IRS as an academic field (which includes LR as one of its primary methods) and the wider, more activist and normative, community-based "interfaith movement" or interfaith engagement (IFE). The opening chapter suggested that IRS scholars more or less embrace this distinction and share Kate McCarthy's proposition that if IRS "is to be an academic discipline suitable to secular higher education, it must not be construed as an auxiliary of the interfaith movement."[30] This sentiment is evident in the guideline from Elon University's interreligious studies program that states the "academic field of interreligious studies must maintain independence from the interfaith movement in order to critically assess discourses and practices that promote tolerance, pluralism, and respect for diversity."[31] However, IRS and IFE are not unrelated (see chapter 8). They can operate together and share similar characteristics. IRS can be a resource for IFE, serving as a "counterpoint, complement, and correction to the interfaith movement."[32] Many IRS scholars themselves already engage in IFE where their "deeply held existential orientations and moral values are on display."[33] Their IRS scholarship informs their IFE, while their IFE informs their IRS scholarship. Just as Orsi claims of the LR scholar, the IRS scholar too has little choice but to be implicated in their research. Therefore, the LR approach not only serves the academic field of IRS, but also serves the wider interfaith movement engaging in IFE aimed at constructive interreligious understanding.

ENCOUNTERING RELIGIOUS DIFFERENCE

Several beneficial implications result from an LR approach to studying interreligious encounter. First, LR helps to balance power and challenge religious authority, especially when power and authority abuse, marginalize, and oppress. Second, intentional focus on individuals' religious experience in interreligious dialogue aids in overcoming barriers to dialogue such as stereotyping and essentializing. Third, an LR approach to the increased frequency

---

30 McCarthy, "(Inter)Religious Studies," 10.
31 Amy L. Allocco, Geoffrey D. Clausen, and Brian K. Pennington, "Constructing Interreligious Studies," in *Interreligious/Interfaith Studies*, ed. Patel et al., 36–37.
32 Allocco et al., "Constructing Interreligious Studies," 39.
33 Orsi, "Everyday Miracles," 18.

of individuals' encounter with religious diversity (stemming from increased global religious diversity) sheds light on the rise of multiple religious orientations (MROs) and religious disaffiliation. Specifically, it helps address the question of whether increased levels of religious reflexivity, due to more frequent encounters with religious difference, helps account for secularization, MROs, and disaffiliation in the West.

Challenging the Powerful

By focusing on the everyday religious experience of individuals, not just on authoritative or official teachings of religions as preached by official spokespeople and leaders, LR aids in decentering power (i.e., control, influence, authority, resource) and amplifying the voice of the laity. McGuire raises this issue in the context of the Long Reformation,[34] a period during which "Western Christian churches attempted to centralize the authority by which diverse religious beliefs and practices would be judged as acceptable for Christian faith and practice."[35] Religious authorities, in this case Christian clerics, claimed that "they were the sole arbiters of the authentic Christian tradition" and therefore "denounced syncretism and individual bricolage because they involved unauthorized uses of elements of the authorized tradition." As such, "the kinds of playful hybridity that characterized much popular religious expression" were treated "as downright subversive—and indeed, they sometimes were."[36] In other words, those with power and authority often determine the rules of the game and set the parameters of a tradition. Multiple religious orientations and practices, including modes of blending, bricolage, hybridity, and syncretism, remain controversial within many Western traditions. "Today, as in medieval and early modern contests, religious hybridity raises the issue of authority."[37]

---

34 Historians of religion speak of the "Long Reformation" to refer generally to the long period of the European Christian reformations "that started somewhere in the Late Middle Ages and continued until at least 1650, but perhaps even to 1700 or 1750." Per Ingesman, "Introduction," in "The 'Long Reformation' in Nordic Historical Research," report ed. Per Ingesman on behalf of Head of the Nordic Reformation History Working Group and prepared for discussion at the 28th Congress of Nordic Historians in Joensuu, Finland (August 14–17, 2014), 7.
35 McGuire, *Lived Religion*, 199.
36 McGuire, 199.
37 McGuire, 200.

McGuire asks, "Who has the authority to articulate a religious group's core tradition?"[38] The Long Reformation demonstrates the power of religious and political authorities to centralize authority and "wrest authority from laypeople by greatly reducing the local and particularistic religious practices that had allowed nonauthorized laypersons immediate access to the sacred."[39] Religious authorities had the power and ability to establish rigid borders that determined what was (and was not) religiously allowed. LR helps to (re)balance this power by giving voice to the laity as well. This can be especially beneficial for inter-religious contexts. Cultural anthropologist André Droogers argues

for a rehabilitation of lay people in religious matters. Their religion is as important a field for study of religion as is erudite religion. Lay people are active meaning-makers, despite the official clerical dominance. . . . The participation of the laity in a possible interreligious dialogue should be advocated, as they may represent the hidden face of a religion. The clergy of a religion should not monopolize the dialogue. . . . At the level of the common believers, a different dialogue should be stimulated. Since syncretism creates commonness, more than diversion, this dialogue may even be more promising than the official, between clerical authorities.[40]

Droogers calls on large and powerful Christian organizations such as the World Council of Churches to employ this tactic. If they want to defend "the interests of the voiceless, then this should also be put into effect in questions of dialogue, transforming the voiceless into spokesmen."[41] By amplifying the voice of the everyday religious experience of ordinary individuals and by surfacing previously unheard marginalized groups and individuals, LR generates insights into particular realties of interreligious relations and serves interreligious studies.

LR for Interfaith Dialogue

Martin Stringer researches people in Birmingham by listening and talking to individuals about the way they understand religious diversity and its

---

38 McGuire, 200.
39 McGuire, 200.
40 Droogers, "Syncretism," 22.
41 Droogers, 22.

values.[42] At the inaugural "Birmingham Conversations" in 2014, Stringer was asked to conduct a study on the question "What would happen if, instead of engaging in interreligious dialogue through the medium of doctrine, rituals, scriptures and so on, we asked people to talk about how their religion affected their everyday lives within the city of Birmingham?"[43] The Birmingham Conversations project brings people together with various religious orientations for deep and "difficult conversations" about their faith traditions and public life. Stringer's case study on this group, which met over a six-month period, demonstrates the power of focusing on lived religious experience to overcome some of the main barriers to constructive interreligious encounter.

Using the LR method, Stringer observed what happens when dialogue begins with the way people actually use religion "on a day-to-day basis rather than starting with the traditions based in belief, ritual, scripture, and philosophy."[44] Stringer intuited that interreligious conversations "had the potential to open up a whole new way of thinking about the relationship between various religious traditions and, perhaps more importantly, the people of Birmingham who came from these different traditions."[45] Although the majority of the case-study data exceed the length and scope of this chapter, three observations are worth noticing.

First, by focusing on lived religious experience, Stringer observed, the dialogue group more easily overcame the major obstacle of oversimplifying the religious identities of the others or reducing (essentializing) the others' traditions to a monolithic Wikipedia version (learned from the internet, hearsay, and other media). The group more easily overcame "the tendency to treat other religions, and other communities, as single undifferentiated entities."[46] This tendency was first evident when participants referred to traditions other than their own with assumptions that ascribed the same practices and beliefs to all its practitioners. In most instances, participants referred to the collective with examples of unfavorable practice (e.g., many "treated Muslims as a single entity, as all sharing common features and all culpable for the bad actions of a few").[47] Although participants tended "to talk in terms

---

42 Martin D. Stringer, "Professor Martin Stringer."
43 Stringer, "Lived Religion and Difficult Conversations," 2.
44 Stringer, 4.
45 Stringer, 4.
46 Stringer, 6.
47 Stringer, 6.

of collectives . . . when talking about religion,"[48] through conversation that focused on the particularities of each individual's lived religious experience, the group gradually recognized when they slipped into this kind of language, acknowledged "immediately what they were doing,"[49] and apologized. While their language did not change drastically going forward—that is, they kept slipping into this way of reducing the other to the collective—the group became more aware of it, which is a significant step toward recognizing the internal complexity and dynamic nature of religious traditions and, more importantly, the complicated and dynamic nature of individual religious orientations. Such a process helps extinguish harmful, hateful, and inaccurate stereotypes and misconceptions.

Second, the study confirmed the importance and power of storytelling as a primary tool for interreligious communication. Stringer states, "Much of the communication was in the form of stories, whether individual narratives of experiences that people had had in the past, stories of others from within the tradition who had suffered, or stories that were part of the heritage of the community is a whole."[50] Since religious experience frequently involves deep personal emotion (often of "resentment and suffering"[51]), and since LR focuses on personal experience, the evocation of emotion in storytelling is of little surprise. The power and centrality of storytelling—that is, conveying stories of self—for effective interfaith engagement (and especially for leadership[52]) is well documented and confirmed in Stringer's case study. It suggests "that lived religion, the day to day expression of religious life as recounted by those involved in the conversation, was something that was best expressed through experience and emotion, primarily in the form of anecdote or story."[53] Personal storytelling provides space for nuance and complexity that the recitation of and reflection on religious doctrine, scripture, and history do not. Through personal storytelling, participants are able to distinguish their religion-as-lived from their religion-as-preached. The LR method for dialogue and engagement values storytelling. Stringer confirms that "listening to these stories, and respecting those who told

---

48 Stringer, 7.
49 Stringer, 6.
50 Stringer, 9.
51 Stringer, 9.
52 See chapters 14 and 15.
53 Stringer, "Lived Religion and Difficult Conversations," 9.

them and the central force of the stories, was an important lesson from the conversations."[54]

Third, in the groups' focus on "'lived religion' and people's everyday experiences," to Stringer's surprise, "the language used to express feelings and interrelations tended not to be that of religion."[55] The group seldom used religious language. Instead of language orientated around prayer, scripture, and God (which were nonetheless present), the most common idea shared among the group was "friendship."[56] Stringer's observation about the prominence of friendship parallels evidence about effective and sustainable methods for bridging religious difference. For the case study's group, "relationships, friendship, sharing, hospitality, companionship, all of these were expressed both as important resources available from within the religious traditions, but also seen as necessary for future dialogue."[57] To establish genuine and appreciative respect of others and their traditions, and religious identities, groups like these often conclude that friendship, which is strong and long lasting, is needed over mere tolerance, which is fragile and inherently rooted in begrudgingly accepting something of significant difference and ultimate disagreement. Stringer's case study on the benefit of focusing on lived everyday religious experience previews the promising potential and power of interreligious encounter for developing interreligious *phronesis*.

Reflexivity, Secularization, and Multiple Religious Orientation

The concept of reflexivity in social theory refers generally to an individual's ability to continually (re)examine themselves (thoughts, feelings, motives for acting, etc.) in any given situation. *Religious* reflexivity "points to a deliberative and problem-solving dynamic that is a distinctive and unavoidable element of contemporary religious selves."[58] Gerardo Martí argues that since "reflexivity is involved in any attempt by individuals to live out/construct/ produce/engage/negotiate their religious selves in everyday settings,"[59] and

---

54 Stringer, 10.
55 Stringer, 11.
56 See chapter 13.
57 Stringer, "Lived Religion and Difficult Conversations," 11.
58 Gerardo Martí, "Religious Reflexivity," *Sociology of Religion* 76, no. 1 (2015): 3.
59 Martí, "Religious Reflexivity," 2.

since religious "pluralism[60] is not merely an ideology but an empirical fact,"[61] then "religious reflexivity urges us to search out new logics guiding religious performances and points toward new approaches for legitimating thought and behavior."[62] Therefore, religious reflexivity, as a "sustained mode of human action necessitated by encounter with novel situations,"[63] may contribute to the increased phenomena of multiple religious orientation (MOR) and multiple religious identity (MRI) in the contemporary West since daily encounter with religious diversity (novel situations) is also increasing for most people. With increasing religious diversity, does religious reflexivity help account for the ways people recognize and maneuver "the broader realm of moral imperatives that confront individuals as they selectively consider how to honor and navigate a variety of core concerns"?[64] Put simply, does increased encounter with religious difference increase internal reflection and reflexivity about one's own religious orientation, and thus lead to an increase in the ways people religiously orient and identify? Martí concludes, "a crucial quality of future religious virtuosi will lie in their ability to accommodate the varied pressures of modern society. More specifically, those who craft a sustained—even elegant—capacity for consistent, legitimated, and reflexively responsive religious behavior will most readily attain the highest levels of religious prestige and influence."[65] It may be that those who are able to maintain a self-legitimated form of MRO, to some degree, will be more likely to sustain their religious orientation in our future world's religious environment.

Does the concept of religious reflexivity help explain the rise of MRO in the West when considered in tandem with the argument that increased religious difference in the modern world need not stifle religious identity and innovation, but rather encourages it? Martí contends, "The continual encounter with difference and novelty—pluralism and cleavage—makes individualized reflexivity a constant and distinctive feature of contemporary society."[66]

---

60 Martí uses "pluralism" to refer to the empirical reality of religious diversity in the world. Martí is referring neither to Diana Eck's "civic pluralism" (engagement with religious diversity) nor to theological pluralism in Alan Race's threefold typology of soteriological and epistemological theologies of religions (see chapter 11).

61 Martí, "Religious Reflexivity," 10.

62 Martí, 10.

63 Martí, 10.

64 Martí, 10.

65 Martí, 11.

66 Martí, 4.

Increased religious diversity offers a growing menu of options for and with which individuals must confront and grapple. "Everyday people are (constantly, aggressively) confronted with options, spurring deliberation, demanding religious reflexivity,"[67] and with the erosion of religious authority in the West (due to decreased trust in institutions and increased religious disaffiliation) "individuals have little choice but to rely on themselves."[68] Various scholars are sympathetic to the argument that increased encounter with religious difference and diversity promotes increased MRO. Rose Drew maintains that "greater knowledge of other religious traditions and growing interreligious interaction is increasingly yielding multiple religious identities that challenge"[69] monolithic and mutually exclusive religious identities. The logic is intuitive: the more options people are confronted with, the more difficult it is for them to choose only one among many, and thus they discern ways to combine, blend, orient, and identify with multiple religious options at the same time. In short, the question is whether an increase in religious diversity results in an increase of MRO.

Intuitive as the argument may be, not all scholars are convinced. Steve Bruce insists that before any conclusions are rigidly drawn, the "secularization thesis" must be considered. The secularization thesis (discussed in chapter 11), often traced to sociologist C. Wright Mills in 1959, hypothesizes that religion will become extinct and that humans will "inevitably overcome the need to be religious."[70] For Bruce, if the thesis is taken seriously, then the prevalence of MRO and MRB (multiple religious belonging) ought to be reconsidered since the thesis supposes, "diversity undermines the certainty with which people can hold their beliefs."[71] Without denying the possibility that encounter with difference promotes MRB, Bruce argues that the history of, and data from, Western countries clearly show a correlation between religiosity and diversity in that (1) "the most religious societies in the West are the most religiously homogeneous (e.g., Poland, Ireland, Greece)"[72] and (2) "that almost every Western society has become more religiously diverse since 1900 and they have become less

---

67 Martí, 4.
68 Martí, 5.
69 Drew, "Christian and Hindu, Jewish and Buddhist," 247.
70 Russell T. McCutcheon, "What Is the Future of 'Religion'?" in *Religion in 5 Minutes*, ed. Hughes and McCutcheon, 305.
71 Bruce, "Multiple Religious Belonging," 603.
72 Bruce, 609.

religious."[73] In other words, the data seem to show that the more religiously diverse a society, the less religious it tends to be. Therefore, if the claim is that MRO is on the rise (as some studies and scholars argue), then "the proposition that diversity weakens religious sentiment is rebutted."[74] The phenomena of MRO and MRB do not negate secularization, "religious people"[75] might argue. Rather, Bruce suggests "the social scientist should see it instead as an *expression* of secularization,"[76] which "is accompanied by a proliferation (not a decline) in the number and variety of religions on offer."[77] MRO is an expression of secularization because: (1) the fact that MRO even exists as a live option demonstrates the weakening of "once-hegemonic religious organizations"[78] that are no longer powerful enough to subdue and stamp it out as dangerous and heretical (i.e., people are free to openly profess or dabble in MRO without fear of being oppressed); and (2) MRO's emphasis on the "individual's right to decide what he or she will believe" demonstrates "the general rise in consumerist orientation that is the death of historic faiths."[79] Bruce's claim is that secularization, contrary to opposing or resisting MRO, is what makes MRO an option in the first place. Although, as Bruce points, unlike MRO, the number of people in the West who claim intentional MRB is very small, around 3 percent or less, hence Bruce's conclusion that although "secularization permits us MRB; it also ensures that few of us will take up the opportunity."[80]

---

73 Bruce, 609.
74 Bruce, 609.
75 Bruce, 610.
76 Bruce, 610, italics original.
77 Bruce, 610.
78 Bruce, 610.
79 Bruce, 610.
80 Bruce, 610. Conceivably, secularization contributes to both the rise of MRO (and perhaps MRB as well), but it also stimulates religious disaffiliation since "nothing in particular" becomes a live option as well. Freedom *of* religion, a mark of the modern secular multicultural Western liberal democracy, also permits freedom *from* religion. The continual encounter with increased religious difference provides opportunities for individuals "of every conceivable background [to] open up new religious freedoms for themselves. They recast pre-existing religious world-views and develop composite religious identities in the various stages of their personal spiritual journey." Ulrich Beck, *A God of One's Own* (Cambridge: Polity Press, 2010), 140; quoted in Martí, "Religious Reflexivity," 7. And, with decreased confidence in, or the need for guidance from, official religious authorities and doctrines, more in the West, it seems, are turning to alternative sources (e.g., other traditions, friends, family, themselves) to complement traditional sources (e.g., religious teachers, clerics, institutions, texts, doctrines). In this way, secularization (not to be confused with secularism or secularity; see chapter 11) refers to "the loss of

PUTTING A HUMAN FACE ON RELIGION

This book is about interreligious studies and developing practical interfaith wisdom for everyday encounters. It is about developing the leadership virtue of being aware of potential tensions and opportunities in (inter)religiously complex situations and having the skill, resources, and knowledge to do something constructive about them through thoughtful action, leadership, and motivation of others. Leaders are not only big-picture people who dwell on the overall outcomes (the macro) or the bottom line, but they also pay attention to the details (the micro). An effective leader knows well that she ignores the minutiae at her own peril. In the day-to-day tasks of managing and leading others, effective leaders are sensitive to the diversity and complexity of the religious practices, worldviews, and cultures evident in the groups and individuals they lead. Effective leaders appreciate the power of personal conviction, ideology, and principle among their team members. They know what is important to and what motivates them. This includes understanding and appreciating others' core religious convictions and practices. Effective leaders are not only interested in generating "buy-in" from others, but they ultimately aim at motivating others to act. The effective leader, at the end of the day, is interested in spurring groups and individuals toward common actions and goals.

Leading in (inter)religiously complex situations requires more than the textbook versions of the team members' religious traditions. Rather, a leader equipped with the practical knowledge of the lived religious experiences and practices of those they lead is more likely to flourish. Developing everyday practical interfaith wisdom for the contemporary world involves getting beyond the textbook and into the complicated world of individuals' messy religious lives. Scholar of religion and comparative theologian Marianne Moyaert contends, "Interreligious learning is experiential learning not focused

---

influence in society that religion has suffered" by being relegated "to a separate sector of society, or more precisely, to the private and individual sphere." Droogers, "The World of Worldviews," 31. Secularization involves dechurching or deinstitutionalization, which means that although an increasing number of people "no longer go to temple, synagogue, church or mosque . . . they still consider themselves to be religious. They no longer let the institution or its clergy influence their decisions about how to organize their life." Droogers, 31. It is not yet clear how secularization forces relate to interreligious encounter and contribute to or detract from increasing MRO. Questions of religious pluralism(s) and secularism(s) are explored in chapter 11.

on textbook knowledge about different religious traditions, but rather on promoting interreligious literacy. The goal is to equip students with the necessary competencies to address religious diversity. Interreligious learning is focused on giving religions a human face."[81] Part II of this book explores the utility of interreligious studies for interfaith engagement by, above all, putting a human face on religion.

---

81 Moyaert, "On the Role of Ritual in Interfaith Education," 59.

7

(Inter)Religious Literacy

Chapter Outline

I. Defining Religious Literacy

II. Value of Religious Literacy

III. Interreligious Literacy

IV. Is (Inter)Religious Literacy Sufficient?

The term "literacy" refers generally to "competence or knowledge in a speci-fied area" and more specifically to the "ability to read and write."[1] Someone who is literate in a given field is familiar with its relevant literature. The literacy rate of a particular population or region often refers to the percent of the population with the ability to read and write, which in this case is the ability to "grasp the meaning of any piece of writing addressed to the general reader."[2] Applied to the context of religion, literacy refers to competence or knowledge in the area of religion. This basic definition is not often disputed; however, what precisely qualifies as competence or knowledge (practical, theoretical, or otherwise)—and hence what constitutes religious literacy—is contested among scholars and educators.[3] This chapter sketches various approaches to and definitions of religious literacy, especially in the context

---

1 *Oxford Dictionaries*, s.v. "literacy."

2 E. D. Hirsch, *Cultural Literacy* (New York: Vintage Books, 1988), 12.

3 Martha Shaw, "Towards a Religiously Literate Curriculum," *Journal of Beliefs and Values* 41, no. 2 (2020): 150; Johannes C. Wolfhart, "'Religious Literacy': Some

of the contemporary religious literacy movement (RLM),[4] wrestles with the challenge to measure the value of religious literacy, proposes a way beyond religious literacy to interreligious literacy, and concludes by recognizing the limits of religious literacy.[5]

DEFINING RELIGIOUS LITERACY

With E. D. Hirsch's 1988 book, *Cultural Literacy: What Every American Needs to Know*, in mind, scholar of religion Stephen Prothero in 2007 published the *New York Times*-bestseller *Religious Literacy: What Every American Needs to Know—and Doesn't*, in which he states a religiously literate person has "the ability to understand and use in one's day-to-day life the basic building blocks of religious traditions—their key terms, symbols, doctrines, practices, sayings, characters, metaphors, and narratives."[6] Akin to Hirsch, Prothero offers the following premises: (1) understanding religion is necessary for understanding the world and to make responsible decisions, (2) a society, culture, or civilization cannot function properly without an educated citizenry, and (3) understanding religion is a significant part of understanding the world. Therefore, Prothero argues, society ought to strive to promote a general understanding of religion that is, if it is interested in functioning properly. Prothero states, "I am convinced that one needs to know something about the world's religions in order to be truly educated. . . . The argument is that you need religious literacy in order to be an effective citizen."[7] Literacy refers to having a basic competency in a particular language. Likewise, for Prothero, just as there are several languages and several religions, there are several religious literacies (Christian literacy, Jewish literacy, and so on). No one in the world speaks every language, and no one knows everything about every religion. Complete religious literacy is impossible, as Leonard Swidler's frequent refrain explains: "Nobody knows

---

Considerations and Reservations," *Method and Theory in the Study of Religion* (published online ahead of print 2022): 6.

4 Religious literacy movement is similar to what Johannes C. Wolfhart refers to as the "religious literacy paradigm." Wolfhart, "'Religious Literacy,'" 4.

5 This chapter expands significantly on Hans Gustafson, "What Does It Mean to Be (Inter)Religiously Literate," State of Formation, April 27, 2018.

6 Stephen Prothero, *Religious Literacy* (New York: HarperOne, 2007), 15.

7 Prothero, *Religious Literacy*, 11.

everything about anything."[8] One person simply cannot know everything about every religion in all contexts, and to place such an expectation on those striving for basic religious literacy is unrealistic, impractical, and unhelpful. This section on defining religious literacy traces the general progression of the contemporary scholarly conversation about what it means to be religiously literate. Major voices include Stephen Prothero, Douglas Jacobsen and Rhonda Hustedt Jacobsen, Adam Dinham, Diane L. Moore, the American Academy of Religion, and Benjamin P. Marcus. Their thought leadership on the definition of religious literacy has implications for understanding the baseline requirements for proper civic responsibility and global citizenship, university education, professional service and workplace conduct, and social cohesion, to name a few.

Being literate in a religious tradition entails knowing its basic beliefs, texts, practices, and history. For Americans, Prothero argues for the importance of Christian literacy not because he thinks Christianity is more valuable, more important, and more truthful than other religions (which he does not claim), but rather because (1) most academic departments of religion at public colleges and universities in the United States (which educate roughly 75% of all American college undergraduates) no longer teach about Christianity; (2) a majority of Americans identify as religious and specifically as Christian (in fact, Prothero claims the United States is "the world's most Christian Country"); and (3) in American "corridors of power," Christianity has dominated and continues to dominate (by which he means that most congress people, governors, and elected officials have all been Christians (so far)).[9] Thus, in order to understand US politics and history, an individual needs to understand how Christianity motivates voters and the elected officials as they create policy and enact legislation. There is no shortage of examples of this, and Prothero mentions several. For instance, political speeches, legal documents, and laws contain biblical or Christian references such as the Golden Rule, the Promised Land, Armageddon, and the Apocalypse. Bible passages are often quoted by high-ranking officials. During President George W. Bush's administration, President Bush quoted the Gospel of Matthew countless times in articulating the so-called War on Terror. On several occasions, President G. W. Bush preached "you're either with us or you're with the enemy," a play

---

8 Leonard Swidler, "Nobody Knows Everything about Anything!" *Journal of Ecumenical Studies* 45 (Spring 2010): 2.

9 Prothero, *Religious Literacy*, 16.

on Matthew 12:30, which states, "whoever is not with me is against me," a phrase recognized by the biblically literate. Prothero's rhetorical argument is that Americans, regardless of whether they identify as Christian, need to know this stuff (and they do not know this stuff anymore, his book argues).

Prothero advocates for more than just Christian or biblical literacy. He directly states that "Christian literacy is not enough"[10]; rather, given the nature of the interconnected and globalized world, Americans need to enhance their literacy of other religions in order to understand and responsibly navigate world affairs. Does having a religious literacy of Tibetan Buddhism help to understand more fully foreign policy on Tibet? Does having a religious literacy of Judaism and Islam help to more comprehensively understand the Israeli–Palestinian conflict? US secretary of state John Kerry seems to think so, given his 2013 remark, "if I went back to college today, I think I would probably major in comparative religion, because that's how integrated it is in everything that we are working on and deciding and thinking about in life today" (a quote unsurprisingly featured on countless webpages of Religious Studies departments).[11] Kerry apparently found his own lack of religious literacy beyond the Christian traditions insufficient for his global work in international relations, conflict management, and peacekeeping.

Douglas Jacobsen (scholar of religion) and Rhonda Hustedt Jacobsen (scholar of psychology) devote a chapter to religious literacy in their 2012 book *No Longer Invisible: Religion in University Education*. Like Prothero, who recalls a passing comment from a European colleague who observes that American college students "are very religious but they know next to nothing about religion,"[12] the Jacobsens assert that "America is one of the most religious nations in the world, and perhaps paradoxically, Americans are also, as a whole, remarkably illiterate about religion."[13] They argue that the

---

10 Prothero, 16.

11 John Kerry, "Speech," August 7, 2013. In 2015, John Kerry wrote: "One of the most interesting challenges we face in global diplomacy today is the need to fully understand and engage the great impact that a wide range of religious traditions have on foreign affairs. I often say that if I headed back to college today, I would major in comparative religions rather than political science. That is because religious actors and institutions are playing an influential role in every region of the world and on nearly every issue central to US foreign policy." "John Kerry: 'We Ignore the Global Impact of Religion at Our Peril,'" *America Magazine*, September 2, 2015.

12 Prothero, *Religious Literacy*, 1.

13 Douglas Jacobsen and Rhonda Hustedt Jacobsen, *No Longer Invisible* (New York: Oxford University Press, 2012), 59.

objective of religious literacy is to foster "the ability to observe, understand, and intelligently discuss different expressions of religion as they actually exist in the world."[14] The Jacobsens' standard for religious literacy exceeds Prothero's proposal since, in their view, Prothero's understanding (1) focuses too much on facts (doctrines and texts), (2) does not go far enough beyond focusing only on knowledge and beliefs of the world's religions, and (3) his "dictionary of religious literacy" too heavily favors Christianity, with over 58 percent of entries devoted to Christianity.[15] The Jacobsens acknowledge, as with other literacies, religious literacy has degrees that range across a spectrum.[16] Religious literacy does not require exhaustive knowledge of everything about every religion.

Adam Dinham and Stephen H. Jones published a 2010 analysis on "Religious Literacy Leadership in Higher Education" to help institutions of higher education (primarily in the United Kingdom). Dinham and Jones define religious literacy as "having the knowledge and skills to recognize religious faith as a legitimate and important area for public attention, a degree of general knowledge about at least some religious traditions, and an awareness of and ability to find out about others."[17] An important aspect of this definition is the "ability to find out." Religious literacy is not only about procuring basic knowledge, but more importantly it is about having the competency to find the proper knowledge should a situation call for it. Barbara McGraw echoes this point in her 2017 article about interfaith leadership: "Religious literacy is not about knowing every religion—which is impossible—but being well-informed enough generally to know what one needs to find out to be effectively literate for the situation at hand."[18] Eboo Patel refers to the ability to recognize what one does not know and the ability to find as "building a radar screen for religious diversity."[19] Developing interreligious *phronesis* (or practical interfaith wisdom for everyday use) refers to sensing that religion might influence various contexts, ranging

---

14 Jacobsen and Jacobsen, *No Longer Invisible*, 70.

15 Jacobsen and Jacobsen, 64.

16 Jacobsen and Jacobsen, 71.

17 Adam Dinham and Stephen H. Jones, "Religious Literacy Leadership in Higher Education."

18 Barbara A. McGraw, "Toward a Framework for Interfaith Leadership," *Engaging Pedagogies in Catholic Higher Education* (EPiCHE) 3, no. 1, *Interfaith Opportunities for Catholic Higher Education* (2017): 6.

19 Eboo Patel, *Interfaith Leadership* (Boston: Beacon Press, 2016), 135.

from how teachers accommodate a religiously diverse classroom by recognizing when some students may be absent due to religious observance
obligations, to business negotiations involving cultural norms and customs
that are rooted deeply in religious traditions,[20] to administering health
care to patients with religiously diverse worldviews about the human body,
medicine, end-of-life care, and death, to effective group leadership with a
team made up of diverse cultural and religious modes of communication
and leader–follower styles, and so on.

Diane L. Moore is the director of the formerly named Religious Literacy
Project (RLP) (now named Religion and Public Life (RPL)) at Harvard University. For Moore and the RLP/RPL, religious literacy "entails the ability to
discern and analyze the fundamental intersections of religion and social/
political/cultural life through multiple lenses."[21] Therefore, a religiously literate person will possess:

1. a basic understanding of the history, central texts (where applica-
    ble), beliefs, practices, and contemporary manifestations of several
    of the world's religious traditions as they arose out of and continue
    to be shaped by particular social, historical, and cultural contexts,
    [and]
2. the ability to discern and explore the religious dimensions of
    political, social, and cultural expressions across time and place.[22]

These two identify the understanding of (1), and the ability to navigate (2), a
religiously diverse and intersectional world in which religion is historically
and contemporarily embedded in multiple dimensions of civic life.

---

20 Paul Lambert, Assistant Dean at Georgetown University's McDonough School of
Business and Senior Business Fellow at the Religious Freedom & Business Foundation,
argues, "In the context of business, religious literacy is familiarity with, and understanding
of, religious influences on people. At the core, business is all about people: it is people who
are making your product and it is people you're bringing these products to in the market
place. If you want to be successful in creating your product and running a business, you
need to understand the primary things that influence people. Religious literacy is about
understanding those influences. You don't have to be a scholar of religious studies to be
religiously literate. But you do need to make an effort to understand." "An Interview with
Paul Lambert," The Fletcher Forum of World Affairs, November 17, 2017.
21 Diane L. Moore, "What Is Religious Literacy?" Harvard Divinity School Religious
Literacy Project.
22 Moore, "What Is Religious Literacy?"

For those seeking to create welcoming workplaces for religiously diverse workforces, a religiously literate manager or supervisor ought to have a sense of the various religious traditions of their team and clientele. Deborah Levine argues that training "should not aim for a Kumbaya moment in which world peace is achieved. Rather, the training should be designed to achieve two major objectives: 1.) Improve service [to] customers and clients 2.) Improve relationships with diverse markets."[23] Further, Levine identifies five themes central to religious diversity training: "1.) Sacred Space, 2.) Sacred Time, 3.) Sacred Language, 4.) Death, and 5.) Sacred Food."[24] Each theme includes "a matrix of terminology, religious practices, and taboos for more than a dozen faith traditions."[25] Levine's vision of effective training emphasizes these five categories insofar as they apply to practical concrete situations such as to "avoid scheduling mistakes, plan the food for celebrations and gifts, [and to market] to a cultural community that is known to embrace a specific religion"[26] to name a few. Effective religious diversity training includes not only a basic religious literacy of the traditions of the work team and their clientele but also opportunities to converse about their lived religious obligations and observances, especially those that may pose burdens in the workplace and require strategizing ahead of time to determine the best ways to minimize those burdens and impact.

Acknowledging the complex and fluid nature of the concept of religious literacy (hence several definitions coexist), Adam Dinham and Matthew Francis in their 2016 edited volume, *Religious Literacy in Policy and Practice*, assert that religious literacy, at the most basic level, begins with an understanding that "religion or belief pervade as majority, normal and mainstream, whatever one's own position or stance."[27] Furthermore, a basic grasp of religious literacy "requires a willingness to recognize it as relevant,"[28] thus it contains an inherent normative claim on its own positive value. Among the many articles in the volume, two are particularly relevant for this chapter in their direct attempts to define religious literacy. James Conroy's chapter defines religious literacy as "engagement with religious language and its import. . . .

---

23 Deborah J. Levine, "The Why and How of Religious Diversity Training," *Huffington Post*, December 29, 2015.
24 Levine, "The Why and How of Religious Diversity Training."
25 Levine.
26 Levine.
27 Dinham and Francis, "Religious Literacy," 11.
28 Dinham and Francis, 11.

It also embodies the capacity to locate particular ideas within their historical, ethical, epistemological and social context."[29] Michael Barnes and Jonathan D. Smith, in their chapter, give religious literacy a confessional, positive, and an almost spiritually endowed energy. They define it as *lokahi*, a Hawaiian concept that means "harmony through diversity." Their understanding of religious literacy as *lokahi* stands out, they believe, in its increased emphasis on "the face-to-face encounter of individuals and communities of all faiths and beliefs, their presence having been accepted."[30] They envision religious literacy as knowledge gained through mutual-relational disclosure. "Rather than knowing *about*, *lokahi* stresses knowing *with* and *from* positive inter-action with religious diversity—both that discerned within myself and that disclosed in my respectful and honest endeavors to value and to promote a harmonious society."[31] Recognizing the challenge of pinning down the definition of religious literacy, Dinham and Francis argue that it ought to be understood, as "a stretchy, fluid concept that is variously configured and applied in terms of the context in which it happens," and as such "is very much how it should be."[32]

The American Academy of Religion (AAR), the largest association of scholars of religious and theological studies in the world, completed a five-year project (2016–2021) to establish "religious literacy guidelines for college students."[33] Under the direction of Eugene V. Gallagher and Diane L. Moore, the project sought to identify "the knowledge and skills related to religion that every associate's or bachelor's degree recipient should gain."[34] This includes, the project argued, "a basic understanding of how religion affects human life" and "some critical understanding about the ways in which religion shapes human behavior."[35] Arguing for the value of religious

---

29 James C. Conroy, "Religious Illiteracy in School Religious Education," in *Religious Literacy in Policy and Practice*, ed. Adam Dinham and Matthew Francis (Bristol: Policy Press, 2016), 169.

30 Michael Barnes and Jonathan D. Smith, "Religious Literacy as *Lokahi*," in *Religious Literacy in Policy and Practice*, ed. Dinham and Francis, 88.

31 Barnes and Smith, "Religious Literacy as *Lokahi*," 88, italics original.

32 Adam Dinham and Matthew Francis, "Religious Literacies," in *Religious Literacy in Policy and Practice*, ed. Dinham and Francis, 257.

33 American Academy of Religion, "Religious Literacy Guidelines for College Students."

34 American Academy of Religion.

35 American Academy of Religion, "AAR Guidelines," draft 3.1, authors: Eugene V. Gallagher, Diane L. Moore, Amir Hussain, Cherie Hughes, Eugene Lowe, Margaret

literacy for the academic disciplines and preprofessional programs, the project offered an ambitious definition of religious literacy by stressing five abilities:

1. Discern accurate and credible knowledge about diverse religious traditions and expressions.
2. Describe the internal diversity of at least one religious tradition.
3. Describe how religions have shaped the experiences and histories of individuals, communities, nations, and regions.
4. Describe how religious expressions make use of cultural languages and artistic representations of their times and contexts, and therefore are historically embedded.
5. Distinguish confessional or prescriptive statements from descriptive or analytical statements.[36]

According to the AAR, every graduate of two- and four-year undergraduate degree programs ought to have these five abilities to be considered religiously literate.

Benjamin P. Marcus argues that "religious fluency requires far more than knowledge of beliefs because religious identities are not necessarily belief-based."[37] In other words, the religiously fluent person needs to know more than the dictionary or textbook versions of the various religious traditions. Rather, in order to communicate about and with people from diverse religious traditions and identities, the religiously literate individual ought to be equipped with a sense of the complicated, nuanced, and messy realities of lived religion. Marcus suggests, "Just as knowledge of the textbook vocabulary or formal grammar of a language does not ensure a fluent conversation, familiarity with certain religious concepts and terms does not necessarily signal an ability to understand religiously or lived religious experience."[38] Marcus captures the necessity of engaging lived religion—or religion as lived—for optimal and practical religious literacy.[39]

Lowe, Brian Pennington, and Martha Reineke, distributed at the American Academy of Religion annual conference (Boston, November 18, 2017), 2.

36 American Academy of Religion, "AAR Guidelines," 2, 4.

37 Benjamin P. Marcus, "Religious Literacy in American Education," in *The Oxford Handbook of Religion and American Education*, ed. Michael D. Waggoner and Nathan C. Walker (New York: Oxford University Press, 2018), 60.

38 Marcus, "Religious Literacy in American Education," 61.

39 Marcus, 65.

Arguments for the value of religious literacy as a good to be pursued and developed rest largely on intuition, what Johannes C. Wolfhart refers to as "the rhetorical calculus of *incalculable social value*, especially in the guise of 'civic competency,'"[40] or what Maria Chiara Giorda deems "wishful thinking"[41] for which there is no evidence. Despite the impressive aforementioned thought leaders (Prothero, Moore, etc.) and the AAR's helpful proposed criteria for religious literacy, the value of religious literacy and the means by which to promote, measure, and teach it are not self-evident.

VALUE OF RELIGIOUS LITERACY

It is one question to ask what religious literacy means, and it is another to ask whether religious literacy is of any value. Diana Eck, founder and director of the Pluralism Project at Harvard University, makes the case for the necessity of religious literacy for global citizenry.

We cannot live in a world in which our economies and markets are global, our political awareness is global, our business relationships take us to every continent, and the Internet connects us with colleagues half a world away and yet live on Friday, or Saturday, or Sunday with ideas of God that are essentially provincial, imagining that somehow the one we call God has been primarily concerned with us and our tribe. No one would dream of operating in the business or political world with ideas about Russia, India, or China that were formed fifty, a hundred or five hundred years ago.[42]

Religious literacy has practical value for conducting meaningful business and geopolitical relations in an increasingly globalized world (and hence an increasingly religiously diverse world).

Barbara A. McGraw, founder and director of the Center for Engaged Religious Pluralism at Saint Mary's College of California, builds on Eck's call

---

40 Wolfhart, "'Religious Literacy,'" 3, italics original.

41 Maria Chiara Giorda, "Different Illiteracies for Different Countries," in *Religious Literacy, Law and History*, ed. A. Melloni and F. Cadeddu (Abingdon: Routledge, 2019), 42; cited in Wolfhart, "'Religious Literacy,'" 18.

42 Diana L. Eck, *A New Religious America* (San Francisco: HarperCollins, 2001), 24.

above for the value of religious literacy, especially for professionals. McGraw recognizes that due to the incessant and unavoidable intercultural and inter-religious contact today,

> Professionals can unwittingly contribute to conflict by ignoring their constituents', colleagues', clients', and partners' religion, spiritual, or non-faith orientations. This, then, can undermine society-at-large when the matters involve decision-making with wide effects, such as in judi-cial or government public policy arenas. Consequently, professionals in various sectors (healthcare, law, business, education, government service and public policy) are beginning to recognize the need to address the religious dimensions of their work.[43]

The 2010 analysis on "Religious Literacy Leadership in Higher Educa-tion" reported that in the United Kingdom, "Jewish and Muslim figures in particular cite misinformation as the single biggest barrier to developing amicable relations between members of those religious traditions and the secular mainstream."[44] Common examples include misconceptions about antisemitism (failing to recognize Palestinian Muslims who are also Semites), *jihad* (equating the term solely with terrorism), and *shari'a* (deeming it a fixed body of civic law). The analysis argues that inculcating religious literacy among the citizenry could alleviate these misconceptions and work toward building bridges. The study also recognized that although "many people want greater religious literacy—government, people of faith, civic bodies and others—primarily because they see it as a mechanism for building bridges between different groups of people, . . . the idea is underdeveloped, and people want it for many different, and sometimes conflicting reasons."[45] These include:

- the desire to be understood and to understand;
- as a basis for interfaith conversation and sometimes proselytization;
- to engage better in public partnerships and community initiatives;
- to maintain or strengthen a particular cultural language; or
- out of sheer curiosity and interest.[46]

---

43 McGraw, "Toward a Framework for Interfaith Leadership," 2.
44 Dinham and Jones, "Religious Literacy Leadership in Higher Education," 5.
45 Dinham and Jones, 5.
46 Dinham and Jones, 5.

Two or more of these might conflict at a given time. Above all, the study contends the purpose of religious literacy is to work toward social cohesion. Its purpose is to "avoid stereotypes, respect and learn from others and build good relations across difference," and hence it is best understood as "a civic endeavor rather than a theological or religious one, and seeks to support a strong, cohesive multifaith society, which is inclusive of people from all faith traditions and none in a context that is largely suspicious and anxious about religion and belief."[47] According to the study, the overall aim of religious literacy is "to inform intelligent, thoughtful and rooted approaches to religious faith that countervail unhelpful knee-jerk reactions based on fear and stereotype."[48]

Dinham and Francis suggest that since "religion and belief are everywhere,"[49] there is a need for the ability to talk about religion. It does not help that many (in the West) were raised in a generation that was taught to avoid speaking about religion and politics in polite company. Furthermore, "decades of relativistic, non-confessional religious education (RE) in schools, and a shift in welfare from churches to states, have left religious language out of public talk for at least a generation."[50] In short, they argue, people have lost the ability to speak meaningfully about religion, especially in public. When religion does come up in conversation, it is often "muddled" and "mired with anxieties about extremism or sex, and frequently leading to knee-jerk reactions, which tend to focus on issues such as the wearing of the veil or forced marriage."[51] Dinham and Francis do not argue for a return to confessional religious education in schools. Rather, they insist on developing meaningful ways people can discuss religion intelligently and thoughtfully. They report that "the problem is not people's willingness to have the conversation [about religion]; it is their ability to do so."[52] Despite the stable increase year-over-year of the religiously unaffiliated, people's interest in religion remains steady. Dinham and Francis challenge "the assumption that religion is a private matter"[53] alone, independent of secular and public significance—and thus

---

47 Dinham and Jones, 6.
48 Dinham and Jones, 6.
49 Dinham and Francis, "Religious Literacy," 4.
50 Dinham and Francis, 4.
51 Dinham and Francis, 4.
52 Dinham and Francis, 6.
53 Dinham and Francis, 6.

undeserving of a prominent place in public discourse. They conclude that the "world was never simply religious nor simply secular, but has always been complexly both,"[54] and therefore call for a return of religion (and thus religious literacy) in public discourse.

With regard to the practical implementation of reforms and working toward greater religious literacy within a society, in addition to the AAR's guidelines,[55] Stephen Prothero identifies four ways to cultivate religious literacy: at the individual level, in religious congregations, in the media, and in educational institutions. *Individuals* can study religion, read religious texts, and meet religious people on their own. *Religious congregations* (churches, synagogues, mosques, temples, etc.) can step up education programs and "go back to teaching the basics" of their own tradition since the data show that most Americans, regardless of religious affiliation, do not know the basics. *The media* report daily on religion, but often get it wrong, grossly oversimplify it, or naively assume their readers know the basics. Journalists can improve by increasing their own religious literacy, recognizing the vast internal diversity of all religious traditions (especially in the United States), and by relying on scholars of religion when necessary. Educational institutions, both public and private, secular and religious, can incorporate basic religious literacy into their K–12 and higher education curriculum alongside reading, writing, and arithmetic.[56] This is the basic thrust of Prothero's prescription to treat America's religious illiteracy.

Prothero is not alone in the call for increased religious literacy for people of all ages. The authors of the introductory article to a special issue in the journal of *Religion and Education* titled "Religious Literacy across the Professions" deem it "the responsibility of public schools to offer constitutionally friendly courses about religion and to apply religious literacy principles across the curriculum."[57] Their plea for increased religious literacy extends beyond students[58] to professionals and civic leaders in service of the common good. They maintain that "it is also the civic duty of every profession to promote religious literacy as a civic competency. Professionals play a unique role

---

54 Dinham and Francis, 6.

55 American Academy of Religion, "AAR Guidelines," 2, 4.

56 Prothero, *Religious Literacy*, 20–22.

57 Nathan C. Walker, W. Y. Alice Chan, and H. Bruce McEver, "Religious Literacy," *Religion & Education* 48, no. 1 (2021): abstract.

58 Kate E. Soules and Sabrina Jafralie, "Religious Literacy in Teacher Education," *Religion & Education* 48, no. 1 (2021): 37–56.

in cultivating religious literacy in business,[59] journalism,[60] social media,[61] healthcare,[62] and law."[63,64] The rationale for the trending energy in the current Religious Literacy Movement (RLM) often rests on the intuition that the more citizens know about the religious and cultural traditions present in their community, the more they will (1) avoid conflict due to ignorance, stereotypes, and misconceptions and (2) work toward greater and more effective social cohesion. American legal scholar Jay Wexler recognizes "the relationship between understanding and tolerance makes intuitive sense"[65] and cites the United Nations Educational, Scientific and Cultural Organization's (UNESCO) website, which "endeavours to build tolerance through education,"[66] the idea being that the more knowledge an individual has about another group or concept, the more likely they will tolerate it. However, Wexler acknowledges the "speculative" nature of this argument and admits "whether a populace better educated about religion will be a more tolerant one is ultimately an empirical question that nobody knows the answer to for sure."[67] In other words, there is not yet enough evidence for whether it is indeed the case that greater religious literacy leads to greater tolerance of diverse religious orientations.

As several scholars point out, despite the rhetorical power of these intuitions,[68] there are not yet sufficient data to show that greater religious literacy leads to these outcomes. Wolfhart raises questions about the

---

59 Brian J. Grim, "Religious Literacy and Diversity for Business," in *Reimagining Faith and Management*, ed. Edwina Pio, Robert Kilpatrick, and Timothy Pratt (New York: Routledge, 2021), 236–50.

60 Michael Wakelin and Nick Spencer, "Religious Literacy and the Media," in *Religious Literacy in Policy and Practice*, ed. Dinham and Francis, 227–36.

61 Andrew M. Henry, "Religious Literacy in Social Media," *Religion & Education* 48, no. 1 (2021): 89–101.

62 W. Y. Alice Chan and Jessica Sitek, "Religious Literacy in Healthcare," *Religion & Education* 48, no. 1 (2021): 102–20.

63 Amarnath Amarasingam, Hicham Tiflati, and Nathan C. Walker, "Religious Literacy in Law," *Religion & Education* 48, no. 1 (2021): 121–40.

64 Walker et al., "Religious Literacy," abstract.

65 Jay Wexler, *Our Non-Christian Nation* (Stanford, CA: Redwood Press, 2020), 165.

66 United Nations Educational, Scientific and Cultural Organization, "International Day of Tolerance."

67 Wexler, *Our Non-Christian Nation*, 165.

68 According to Wolfhart, "In the multi-disciplinary humanities subfield of Religious Studies, dire predictions of the social costs of ignorance of (or indifference to) our specialty are widely presented as self-evident truths." Wolfhart, "'Religious Literacy,'" 3.

evidentiary basis of the claims and expectations made by RLM advocates that religious literacy provides "diverse collective and social benefits, including pro-social effects in situations of increasing religious diversity, inoculation against radicalization, general violence aversion, and peace-making."[69] Even Prothero, a leading champion of religious literacy, admits it "is not the panacea some advocates of interreligious dialogue imagine it to be."[70] These credible concerns are addressed below, prior to which *inter*religious literacy is defined and distinguished from religious literacy.

INTERRELIGIOUS LITERACY

Some scholars distinguish between *religious* literacy and *interreligious* literacy, the latter emphasizing knowledge, abilities, and competencies for engaging and navigating contexts that involve interactions and relations between and among diverse religious perspectives. Other scholars include interreligious literacy under the umbrella of religious literacy. While both religious and interreligious literacy emphasize knowledge, skills, and competencies about religious traditions and diversity, interreligious literacy has a special focus on the relations and interactions between and among diverse religious perspectives. Eboo Patel advocates for moving beyond the "objective, neutral, 'just the basics' approach"[71] of religious literacy, and instead preaches the need to develop an "appreciative knowledge" of religions that "actively seeks out the beautiful, the admirable, and the life giving rather than the deficits, the problems, and the ugliness."[72] This appreciative approach echoes Krister Stendahl's famous call to always leave room for "Holy Envy."[73] "Appreciative knowledge" and "Holy Envy" push basic religious literacy into the arena of interreligious literacy. Patel identifies three main parts of appreciative

---

69 Wolfhart, 2.
70 Prothero, *Religious Literacy*, 18.
71 Patel, *Interfaith Leadership*, 112.
72 Patel, 113.
73 Stendahl describes Holy Envy as moments "when we recognize something in another tradition that is beautiful but is not in ours, nor should we grab it or claim it. . . . Holy envy rejoices in the beauty of others." Krister Stendahl, "From God's Perspective We Are All Minorities," *Journal of Religious Pluralism* 2 (1993). See Hans Gustafson, "Suppressing the Mosquitoes' Coughs," in *Learning from Other Religious Traditions*, ed. Hans Gustafson (New York: Palgrave MacMillan, 2018), 1–12.

knowledge: "recognizing the contributions of other traditions, having sympathetic understanding of the distinctive history and commitments of other traditions, and developing ways of working with and serving other communities."[74] While many approaches to religious literacy strive for a basic descriptive understanding of religious traditions, interreligious literacy adds an element of normative appreciation for those traditions.

Barbara McGraw argues more is needed beyond basic religious literacy:

> although it is certainly a worthy endeavor for those aspiring to be interfaith leaders to gain basic knowledge of world religions, that knowledge is not enough. For example, learning the basics of Islam—even of its two main branches, Sunni and Shi'a—is a good start. However, knowing that will not be enough to understand its many variants, including Hanafi, Maliki, Ismali, Kharijite, and Sufi.[75]

McGraw's concern is assumed and addressed by the AAR's second "ability" (above), which calls for graduates with religious literacy to be able to "describe the internal diversity of at least on religious tradition" (i.e., a student who recognizes the internal diversity of one tradition will assume it of other traditions). McGraw extends this concern beyond the so-called "major world religions" and beyond those confined to an American context:

> Similarly, learning the basics of world religions will not be enough to comprehend the many variants of Native American spiritualities, Neopagan religions, or New Age spiritualities. The vastness of religious diversity is not, of course, unique to the United States. It is a global phenomenon. For example, India and Africa include much religious diversity, even when one or two religions are dominant.[76]

Barnes and Smith's definition of religious literacy as *lokahi* rests "not so much on religious as on *inter*religious literacy" because it is rooted in "active encounter" and protects against "any reductionist account of religion, instead seeing diversity as the fundamental 'DNA' of religious identity and religious communities."[77] Interreligious literacy as *lokahi* emphasizes "the face-to-face

---

74 Patel, *Interfaith Leadership*, 114.
75 McGraw, "Toward a Framework for Interfaith Leadership," 5–6.
76 McGraw, 6.
77 Barnes and Smith, "Religious Literacy as *Lokahi*," 88, italics original.

encounter of individuals and communities of all faiths and beliefs";[78] it puts human faces on religion in the most intimate manner—face to face—through encounter between and among individuals and groups with various messy fluid religious identities and ways of living.

Only a handful of scholars explicitly define interreligious literacy and distinguish it from religious literacy. Scholar of religion and comparative theologian Marianne Moyaert frames interreligious literacy in the context of teaching religious literacy and recognizes that "minimal religious literacy is a basic condition of effective citizenship. Thus, one of the primary goals of religious education is to tackle the problem of religious literacy by ameliorating the knowledge people have about other religious traditions."[79] Certainly religious literacy advances the constructive project of breaking down barriers between religious communities and individuals, but the question remains to what degree. Advocates for intentional interreligious learning (which aims at interreligious literacy) perhaps share the concern of religious literacy skeptics (e.g., Wolfhart) that little evidence is available to enthrone religious literacy as the cure to all religious conflicts that ail societies. With focus on the *inter* of interreligious, Moyaert sets interreligious literacy apart:

> Beyond overcoming religious prejudices, interreligious learning or learning from religious others fosters and enhances interreligious literacy, the ability to sensitively and effectively relate across religious differences. This is an expertise that focuses on the cultivation of the "inter," which as [Martin] Buber (1952) rightly pointed out is always interpersonal; it is learning from different religions by engaging in a reciprocal encounter with people who belong to and identify with these different traditions.[80]

It is precisely this concern to combat harmful religious stereotyping (which can lead to violence) that the crucial distinction of "inter" (in interreligious literacy) can make. For Moyaert, "If a lack of (inter)religious literacy correlates with stereotyped understanding of religious difference, interreligious competency correlates with the capacity to handle ambiguity, nuance, and a variety of perspectives."[81] In addition to the trendy language of "skills and competencies" in modern pedagogy, including for instructors of interreligious

---

78 Barnes and Smith, 88.
79 Moyaert, "On the Role of Ritual in Interfaith Education," 50.
80 Moyaert, 51.
81 Moyaert, 54.

literacy, Moyaert speculates whether "it would also make more sense to move from talk about interreligious literacy to discussions about interreligious sensibility, thereby making clear at once that the whole person, with all his senses, is involved in this process."[82] This sentiment dovetails with the common impulse in the field of interreligious studies for teaching and research that emphasize (1) lived interreligious encounter between, among, and within individuals and communities while (2) retaining space for the importance of virtues related to *empathy, leadership*, and *grit* among others.[83] Moyaert argues for the necessity of experiential encounter for effective interreligious learning, which is "not focused on textbook knowledge about different religious traditions, but rather on promoting interreligious literacy. The goal is to equip students with the necessary competencies to address religious diversity."[84] This outlook is not unique to Moyaert and scholars of religion. Tone Lindheim, scholar of cross-cultural management, workplace diversity, inclusion, and leadership studies, advocates for the necessity of professionals to develop religious literacy as a job skill and competency in the workplace through "diversity management practices" that encourage "conversational spaces for religion."[85] More to the point, "developing religious literacy using conversational spaces in the workplace, requires everyday religion to enter the conversational space."[86] Religious identity and interreligious literacy are not optional add-ons or adjuncts (nonessential components) to workplace diversity, inclusion, and leadership; rather, they play a central role alongside

---

82 Moyaert, 56.

83 See Patel, *Interfaith Leadership*; Catherine Cornille, "Interreligious Empathy," in *Interreligious Studies*, ed. Gustafson, 223–27; Catherine Cornille, "Empathy and Otherness in Interreligious Dialogue," in *Dynamics of Difference*, ed. Ulrich Schmiedel and James Matarazzo (New York: Continuum/T&T Clark, 2014), 221–30; Catherine Cornille, "Conditions for Interreligious Dialogue," in *The Wiley-Blackwell Companion to Inter-Religious Dialogue*, ed. Catherine Cornille (Hoboken, NJ: Wiley, 2013), 26–28; Catherine Cornille, *The Im-Possibility of Interreligious Dialogue* (New York: Crossroad Publishing, 2008), 137–76; Catherine Cornille, "Empathy and Inter-Religious Imagination," *Religion and the Arts* 12, no. 1–3 (2008): 102–18, also published in *Traversing the Heart*, ed. Richard Kearney and Eileen Rizo-Patron (Leiden: Brill, 2009), 107–21; and Stephanie L. Varnon-Hughes, *Interfaith Grit* (Eugene, OR: Wipf & Stock, 2018).

84 Moyaert, "On the Role of Ritual in Interfaith Education," 59.

85 Tone Lindheim, "Developing Religious Literacy through Conversational Spaces for Religion in the Workplace," *Nordic Journal of Religion and Society* 33, no. 1 (2020): abstract.

86 Lindheim, "Developing Religious Literacy through Conversational Spaces for Religion in the Workplace," 19.

other core identities that influence the way individuals and groups interact, communicate, and perceive the world.

Methodologies and pedagogies like those advocated by Moyaert and Lindheim place significant emphasis on lived interreligious encounter. Inherent in the concept of religious and interreligious literacy is the capacity to know that religion can influence particular contexts. Moreover, and a central concern of this book, (inter)religious literacy is a significant component to the leadership virtue of having the awareness to discern and learn whether and how religion influences a situation, and having the wherewithal to do something about it while bringing others along in a manner that serves the common public good. The religiously literate person has basic knowledge about the ways religion shapes human behavior; the interreligiously literate person has the practical everyday wisdom to recognize and navigate potentially interreligiously complex situations, with an eye to producing effective and constructive outcomes. Put simply, (inter)religious literacy assumes the ability to communicate within and across religions in concrete contexts and includes the "know how"—the practical wisdom (*phronesis*)—and ability to communicate and lead in everyday situations.

IS (INTER)RELIGIOUS LITERACY SUFFICIENT?

This book is about interreligious *phronesis* (IP), or practical interfaith wisdom for everyday encounter. This inherently includes basic interreligious literacy, which assumes religious literacy. Are basic religious and interreligious literacy enough, or is more needed? Enough for what? Is more needed for what? It is unrealistic and unnecessary to prescribe all to earn advanced academic degrees in the study of religion, and it is not clear whether advanced academic degrees alone would contribute to the development of IP or lead to some of the promised benefits religious literacy proponents advocate for, such as "saving the world,"[87] social improvement and progress, a cure to societal ills, "inoculation against radicalization, general violence aversion, and peace-making."[88]

The call to integrate basic religious literacy into core curricula for K–12+ education seems an intuitive way to combat religious misinformation,

---

87 Diana Eck, Diane Moore, Eboo Patel, and Mara Willard, "Religious Literacy," Harvard Divinity School YouTube Channel, November 13, 2013.
88 Wolfhart, "'Religious Literacy,'" 2.

stereotyping, xenophobia, and similar hate-ridden and oppressive responses to religious diversity that ail society. However, some scholars argue there is a dearth of hard and definitive data on whether religious literacy education makes people more tolerant and respectful across religious divisions. Wolfhart contends there remains "a paucity of empirical evidence for the material, social or societal benefits widely ascribed to enhanced religious literacy."[89] Tenzan Eaghll challenges the "cliché" (or false platitude) that "learning about religion leads to tolerance."[90] Similarly, Bengt-Ove Andreassen points out that "it is not a given that knowledge about religions automatically leads to understanding, respect and/or tolerance [and] ... that there is no causality in knowledge about religions leading to understanding 'the other' or tolerance."[91] The call for more research to measure the efficacy of religious literacy to form attitudes is warranted. Such studies have emerged,[92] but "much more measurement and evaluation needs to be done."[93] The contemporary Religious Literacy Movement (RLM), a phrase coined here for the purpose of this chapter, implicitly includes those who advocate for the value of basic religious literacy as part of a standard education for the citizenry. Scholars continue to raise questions about the inherent and self-evident value of religious literacy: Does religious literacy really lead to peace, tolerance, justice, and social cohesion, or is this just a myth (the "literacy myth")? Can religious literacy become too similar to moral religious education with an objective to form moral and tolerant citizens, and thus become a kind of covert theological enterprise?

---

89 Wolfhart, 23.

90 Tenzan Eaghll, "Learning about Religion Leads to Tolerance," in *Stereotyping Religion*, ed. Bard Stoddard and Craig Martin (London: Bloomsbury, 2017), 113–30.

91 Bengt-Ove Andreassen, "'Knowledge about Religions' and Analytical Skills in Religious Education," *Religion, Education, and the Challenges of Contemporary Societies* 9, no. 4 (2019): 77, citing Marie von der Lippe and S. Undheim, "Why Common Compulsory RE in School?" in *Religion i skolen: Didaktiske perspektiver på religions- og livssynsfaget*, ed. Marie von der Lippe and S. Undheim (Oslo: Universitetsforlaget, 2017), 14–15.

92 See Emile Lester and Patrick S. Roberts, *Learning about World Religions in Public Schools* (Nashville: First Amendment Center, 2006); Emile Lester and Patrick S. Roberts, "Learning about World Religions in Modesto, California," *Politics and Religion* 4, no. 2 (2011): 264–88; Siebren Miedema, "A Plea for Inclusive Worldview Education in All Schools," in *Vir Christelike Wetenskap* 77, no. 1 (2012): 1–7; W. Y. Alice Chan, *Teaching Religious Literacy to Combat Religious Bullying* (New York: Routledge, 2021); Linda K. Wertheimer, *Faith Ed* (Boston: Beacon Press, 2015); and Lauren Kerby, "Teaching for Tolerance," *Colgate Academic Review* 6 (2012): art. 7.

93 Walker et al., "Religious Literacy," 8.

Scholars debate the primary purpose of the academic study of religion and the value of religious literacy. Among the first scholars to advocate for the value of religious education in nonreligious (secular) settings was religion scholar Ninian Smart who, according to Eaghll, proclaimed it is "through a thorough study of religious diversity we learn tolerance and mutual understanding, [as well as] empathy and compassion."[94] Smart's view that a primary goal of the study of religion is to work toward a better world dovetails with the spirit that often surfaces in the contemporary RLM. Eaghll concludes that "the cliché of religious education emerges when it is assumed that the goal of the study of religion is to improve tolerance and understanding about religion, rather than an analysis of its use and function in society."[95] The concern is with aligning the goal of religious literacy too closely with any normative aims, which may make it, for some scholars, more of a civic, political, or theological project than an academic pursuit of knowledge. Scholar of religion Daniel Enstedt also questions the normative and ethical thrust of religious literacy advocates who suggest it helps form morally responsible, respectful, and tolerant citizens. Enstedt asks whether doing so is a form of nonconfessional religious training, and asks whether "non-confessional religious education [has] simply taken over the moral and ethical imperatives from the previous confessional education?"[96] Scholar of religion Suzanne Owen also worries that understanding the point of religious education this way risks blurring "the boundaries between religious education and moral education"[97] and therefore advocates for the separation of "religious education into two subjects, moral philosophy and religious studies, based on a cultural studies approach."[98] Enstedt and Owen argue that while religious literacy education ought to teach about religion, any normative moral and personal development ought to more appropriately take place in philosophical or moral reasoning education (or nonacademic religious training outside formal education).

---

94 Eaghll, "Learning about Religion Leads to Tolerance," 124.

95 Eaghll, 129.

96 Daniel Enstedt. "Religious Literacy in Non-Confessional Religious Education and Religious Studies in Sweden," *Journal of Humanities and Social Science Education* 1 (2022): 41.

97 Enstedt, "Religious Literacy in Non-Confessional Religious Education and Religious Studies in Sweden," 44.

98 Owen, "The World Religions Paradigm," 266.

Although the concerns raised here by Eaghll, Enstedt, and Owen ought not be ignored by advocates of religious literacy, they are also not wholly applicable to the contemporary RLM, which is primarily concerned with teaching *about* religion and how it often functions as a powerful force in the world, and therefore deserves respect precisely so that religious conflicts, violence, and oppression can be properly understood and confronted in their historical and contemporary contexts. In other words, although religious literacy is a good first step in knowing about religion, it is not a panacea.[99] If religious literacy advocates can agree that it is primarily about building basic knowledge and not about forming attitudes, then it ought to be appropriately included in the development of interreligious phronesis.[100]

The critical caution of not overpromising on the value of religious literacy is warranted, and it aligns with Patel's advocacy for the need for more than an "objective, neutral, 'just the basics' approach"[101] to knowing religion. Stendahl's famous suggestion to leave room for "Holy Envy" similarly suggests that mere knowledge is not enough. Likewise, the growing number of scholars championing the cultivation of empathy[102] in pedagogy and scholarship exposes the limits of knowledge for knowledge's sake. "In sum," Wolfhart argues, "language linking 'religious *il*literacy' . . . to injustice, violence, and social disorder and religious literacy to peace, justice, and social order, enjoys both currency within the academy and beyond. . . . [Put similarly,] knowing about religion makes people nicer; not knowing about religion makes them nasty."[103] This is the "literacy myth,"[104] which assumes increased literacy leads to social improvements or progress. To be sure, knowledge is necessary and foundational. However, with Patel, Stendahl, and other empathy advocates, this book—on the development of practical interfaith wisdom for everyday

---

99 Prothero, *Religious Literacy*, 18.

100 This corresponds to the position of sociologist of religion Jenn Lindsay that "Rather than emphasizing a change in *attitude* first, we argue a different strategy for improving intercultural and interreligious competence: *knowledge* of other cultures must come prior to the development of skills to interact with them, thereby paving the way, finally, for the area of competence most deep-seated in cognition and the most resistant to change: the attitude." Lindsay, "Growing Interreligious and Intercultural Competence in the Classroom," 22, italics original.

101 Patel, *Interfaith Leadership*, 112.

102 See note 83.

103 Wolfhart, "'Religious Literacy,'" 5, 15, italics original.

104 Harvey J. Graff, *The Literacy Myth* (New York: Academic Press, 1979); referenced in Wolfhart, "Religious Literacy."

encounter—heeds the literacy myth by calling for the need for more beyond basic knowledge of religion(s).

Encounter—especially face-to-face engagement—and interreligious *phronesis* push religious literacy into the territory of interreligious literacy. Given the emphasis that interreligious literacy and interreligious *phronesis* place on person-to-person encounter, as Moyaert argues, it should be no surprise to the reader that chapters 3 through 6 forcefully affirmed the value of lived religion approaches to the study of religion and interreligious studies (and ultimately for the development of interreligious *phronesis*). The end of this chapter marks the shift from Part I to Part II, from knowledge to encounter, from understanding religion to interreligious understanding, from interreligious studies (IRS) to interfaith engagement (IFE). The next chapter—Spider Silk, the Rock Climber, and Rocky Balboa's Broken Nose—is an interstitial transitional intermezzo between Part I and Part II that examines the relationship between IRS and IFE.

Intermezzo

IRS & IFE

8

Spider Silk, the Rock Climber, and Rocky Balboa's Broken Nose[1]

"You see nothing. . . . You got the heart but you ain't got the tools . . .," says Mickey to Rocky, followed by a hard slap to Rocky's face like a Zen master to his student. "You didn't even see that comin, did ya?"[2]

—Mickey Goldmill

Chapter Outline

I.   Three Vignettes

II. Interfaith Engagement (IFE)

III. Reconciling Mickey (IRS) and Rocky (IFE)

IV. Normative and Reflexive Turns

V.   Scholar-Practitioner Model

This chapter marks the book's transition from interreligious studies (IRS) to interfaith engagement (IRE) by opening with three vignettes to illustrate their relationship. IRS and IFE are briefly distinguished from one another

---

1 This chapter is adapted, revised, and extended from Hans Gustafson, "Sparring with Spider Silk," in *The Georgetown Companion to Interreligious Studies*, ed. Lucinda Mosher (Washington, DC: Georgetown University Press, 2022), 32–40.

2 Mickey Goldmill (character), *Rocky II* (Chartoff-Winkler Productions, 1979).

followed by an examination of analogous academic fields and attempts to reconcile them with their practitioner-based counterparts. The questions answered in this chapter include: How do the general twentieth-century normative and reflexive turns in academia—especially the relation between the study of religion and theological studies—bear on wrestling with the relation between IRS and IFE? Above all, is it possible to distinguish between IRS and IFE and situate them in a mutually beneficial relationship to one another?

THREE VIGNETTES

Rocky Balboa's Broken Nose: In the iconic Sylvester Stallone movie *Rocky*, the central character, Rocky Balboa, a tough underdog blue-collar "everyman" boxer from an Italian neighborhood of Philadelphia, routinely brags about never breaking his nose despite being "busted up" all over after boxing matches. Early in the film, Rocky tells Adrian, his romantic interest, "the thing I'm proud of is I been in over sixty fights an' never had a busted nose—Bent an' twisted an' bitten but never broke. . . . That's rare." His trainer, Mickey Goldmill, a gruff no-nonsense "old-school" trainer, even chides Rocky by saying, "You got heart, but you fight like a god-damn ape. The only thing special about you is ya never got your nose busted—well, leave it that way, nice and pretty, and what's left of your mind. . . . Hey kid, did ya ever think about retirin'? . . . You think about it." In the spirit of the Rocky mythos, in the final boxing match of the film—the climax—against Apollo Creed, Rocky gets his nose broken in the first round. Mickey sits Rocky down in his corner and bluntly says, "Your nose is broken." Rocky retorts, "How's it look?" to which Mickey snaps back, "ah, it's an improvement!" Rocky gets pummeled for fourteen grueling rounds only to emerge victorious at the end. The final fight in each *Rocky* film follows this familiar script: he'd get the hell beat out of him for most of the fight only to triumph the heroic victor in the end through sheer downright hard work, grit, and determination not to lose. Whatever technical skill and athleticism Rocky lacked was made up for by hard work and his stubbornness simply to not lose.

Spider Silk: Consider the longstanding adage that "spider silk is stronger than steel" (by weight, that is). This has been confirmed time and again, including on the popular TV series *Myth Busters Jr.* on the Science Channel[3]—so it must be true! Almost as strong as Kevlar, the strongest human-produced polymer, spider silk is finer than human hair, retains its strengths in extreme cold (below −40°C) when others become very brittle, and yet still remains very elastic, sticky, and unbroken after being stretched two to four times its natural resting length.[4] Like Rocky Balboa, spider silk heroically "punches above its weight,"[5] can take a beating, and can even be "bent an' twisted an' bitten but never broke . . . [but] that's rare." Like Rocky and his nose, however, spider silk can indeed break if stretched too far.

Rocky and spider silk are tough, robust, and resilient. The quality of being robust entails strength, health, sturdiness, and the ability to "withstand or overcome adverse conditions."[6] Rahuldeep Singh Gill defines resilience in a person as

the ability of an individual to adapt to and overcome harmful stimuli in healthy ways that lead to good outcomes. Resilience is an elasticity and sponginess. Resilient people can bounce back from traumatic events. They bend, but they do not break. They absorb. They retain. They have the ability to take in others' viewpoints.[7]

Nassim Nicholas Taleb, the provocative Lebanese American writer, may agree that spider silk, but especially Rocky, is "antifragile," a word Taleb coined to refer to the opposite of fragile. Antifragile things are those which "thrive and

---

3 *Myth Busters Jr.*, "Episode 8: Bug Special," Science Channel, February 6, 2018.

4 Vivienne Li, "Spider Silk," The Molecule of the Month (website), University of Bristol.

5 The popular idiom means "to perform, achieve, or do something at a level that is considered beyond one's abilities, talents, or personal attributes." *The Free Dictionary*, "punch above your weight," accessed June, 28, 2019.

6 *Oxford English Dictionary*, s.v. "robust," last accessed July 6, 2019, https://www.lexico.com/en/definition/robust.

7 Rahuldeep Singh Gill, "From Safe Spaces to Resilient Places," *Journal of College and Character* 18, no. 3 (2017): 204, citing David Scott Yeager and Carol S. Dweck, "Mindsets That Promote Resilience," *Educational Psychologist* 47, no. 4 (2012): 302–14.

grow when exposed to volatility, randomness, disorder, and stressors and love adventure, risk, and uncertainty."[8] Taleb contends antifragility is different from, and often preferred to, robustness and resiliency (but not always), since the robust and "the resilient resists shocks and stays the same; [whereas] the antifragile gets better."[9] Rocky only gets stronger as his fights wear on and his body wears down. The antifragile thrives on chaos, uncertainty, and "grows from disorder, . . . [whereas] the robust doesn't care too much."[10] "Antifragile" is perhaps another way to state Ernest Hemingway's famous observation in *A Farewell to Arms*: "The world breaks everyone and afterward many are strong at the broken places."[11]

Taleb offers several examples (e.g., from Greek mythology to business to medicine to biology and so on), categorized as fragile, robust, and anti-fragile. The guiding example comes from Greek mythology depicting the fragile as the "Sword of Damocles" (it hangs by a single horsehair, which eventually breaks, over Damocles' head), Phoenix as the robust (whenever it is destroyed it is reborn from its own ashes), and the multiheaded serpent-like creature Hydra as the antifragile (each time one of its heads is cut off, two new ones regenerate). The horsehair is fragile because it breaks, the Phoenix is robust because it always rises again, but the Hydra is antifragile because it grows stronger each time it is destroyed (and thus prefers chaotic encounter).

The Rock Climber: There are countless examples of antifragility in the world. Obvious examples include athletic training (breaking down muscle and punishing the body) to become stronger and faster, and healthcare practices that subject the body to low doses of risk and harm (e.g., medicine, vaccines, chemical and radiation therapy) to help it overcome disease. The documentary film *The Dawn Wall* features Tommy Caldwell, considered by many the greatest rock climber in the history of the sport. Passing him on the street, he wouldn't likely stand out with his average height, size, and muscle mass. There is nothing average about his life story. At the age of twenty-two, he and his fellow climbers were taken hostage for six

8 Nassim Nicholas Taleb, *Antifragile* (New York: Random House, 2012), 3.
9 Taleb, *Antifragile*, 3.
10 Taleb, 20.
11 Ernest Hemingway, *A Farewell to Arms* (New York: Scribner, 1929, 2014), 317.

days by Islamist rebels in Kyrgyzstan. Deprived of adequate food and water, they were marched around the rugged mountainous terrain of the region, witnessed shootouts with the local military, and observed some of their captors get shot and killed. Teetering on the edge of desperation, with no end in sight, Caldwell took an opportunity to shove their lone captor off a cliff, killing him and allowing his party to safely escape back home to the United States. The next year, working with his father's table saw, Caldwell sawed off most of his left index finger, a seemingly essential appendage for a professional rock climber. Not only did Caldwell keep climbing, but he excelled as a climber, successfully completing routes no one had before, including himself. When exposed to stress, volatility, and disorder, Caldwell grew stronger. Not only did he resist the turbulent and traumatic shocks of life, he improved—as the title of his *National Geographic* lecture demonstrates: "How Becoming a Hostage and Losing a Finger Made Him a Better Climber."[12] After being a hostage and losing a finger, Caldwell's story captures the essence of the human capacity to rise above adversity and exhibit antifragility. He reflects,

it like lit this fire inside of me. And I started, sort of, approaching climbing with everything I had. I went back to try and climb this climb called the Salathé Wall in a day, which is something I had failed on right before we had gone to Kyrgyzstan and before I had chopped off my finger. And it was like my test. And so . . . just about a year after I'd chopped off my finger, I successfully climbed the Salathé Wall in a day. And it was like this works; like I actually acquired these tools through these hard experiences that are gonna like . . . they're kinda like the key to making me excel in this world of big wall climbing which was kind of everything to me at this point.[13]

Caldwell successfully applied this antifragile method to his climbing career. However, as Taleb acknowledges, antifragility is not always

---

12 Tommy Caldwell, "How Becoming a Hostage and Losing a Finger Made Him a Better Climber," *National Geographic*, June 25, 2017.
13 Caldwell, "How Becoming a Hostage and Losing a Finger Made Him a Better Climber."

optimal.[14] Rocky, Caldwell, and spider silk are robust, resilient, and perhaps even antifragile. Despite being robust and resilient, they will eventually break under enough stress. Rocky, no doubt, is antifragile in the boxing ring, for it wasn't until he busted up his nose that he was able to reach the next level and become the champ. Although Rocky may not have realized this—after all, he was rather proud of his unscathed nose being all "nice and pretty"—Mickey knew the whole time. Mickey had a sense of that antifragile wisdom in his toolkit. While Micky criticized Rocky's pretty nose and pride, he was proud of his own busted-up nose. Micky preaches to Rocky,

> what ya need is a manager. A manager, listen to me. I know, because I've been in this racket for fifty years . . . I've seen it all, all of it. Ya know what I've done? . . . I have done it all . . . I've got twenty-one stitches over this left eye. I've got thirty-four stitches over this eye. Do ya know that I had my nose busted seventeen times?

What Caldwell discovered as the power of adversity as a tool for antifragile improvement, Mickey sagely already knew: for Rocky to reach new heights, he too would have to break his nose.

INTERFAITH ENGAGEMENT (IFE)

What do spider silk, Tommy Caldwell, and Rocky's nose have to do with developing interreligious *phronesis* and the relationship between interreligious studies (IRS) and interfaith engagement (IFE)? Ought IFE become like Rocky and enter the chaos and wisdom of its sparring partner IRS (represented by Mickey) and strive for spider-silk-like resilience and possibly Caldwell-like and Rocky-like antifragility? As a verb, "to spar" refers to "make the motions of boxing without landing heavy blows, as a form of training."[15] It can also mean to "argue with someone without marked hostility."[16] As a noun, "spar"

---

14 Suffering, adversity, and stress for their own sake should not be glorified nor used to justify unjust and oppressive suffering of individuals or communities.

15 *Oxford English Dictionary*, s.v. "spar," last accessed July 2, 2019, https://www.lexico.com/en/definition/spar.

16 *Oxford English Dictionary*, s.v. "spar."

can refer to a close friend[17] (e.g., "Finn was Tom's spar and he didn't want to let him down").[18] The relationship between IRS and IFE can be understood as that of sparring partners exchanging critically constructive and chaotic blows for mutual benefit with the aim to make the other stronger and more resilient. This chapter examines the intersection between IRS as an academic field of critical inquiry and the civic project of IFE and considers their relation, from the perspective of IRS, as analogous to "sparring with spider silk" akin to delivering friendly punches to sharpen one's teammate, a tough and malleable fighter like Rocky. From the perspective of IFE, the relation may yield welcome antifragile benefits that help develop immunity through adversity. The three opening vignettes illustrate the spirit of this relationship. This section provides brief definitions of IRS and IFE, and the next section gleans insight from analogous academic fields in relation to the normative commitments of their practical-activist counterparts. Normative commitments and reflexive attitudes in Religious Studies and Theological Studies are examined insofar as they lend insights into wrestling with and bridging the tensions and relations between IRS and IFE. Above all, this chapter inquires about properly situating IRS and IFE in relationship to one another in a manner of mutual benefit. To that end, the chapter concludes by endorsing the scholar-practitioner model as a *via media* between IRS and IFE.

Interreligious Studies (IRS), treated at length in the opening chapter and situated in relation to the broader multidisciplinary study of religion, refers to the academic field that investigates the relations and interactions between, among, and within individuals and groups in religiously diverse contexts. Depending on the institutional context within which it is carried out, IRS utilizes various methods and approaches (e.g., critical, practitioner, normative-activist). Furthermore, scholars of IRS hold a variety

---

17 *Oxford English Dictionary*, s.v. "spar."
18 Rock climber Tommy Caldwell's recent book *The Push* (and accompanying film *The Dawn Wall*) documents his quest to be the first to conquer Yosemite's "Dawn Wall," identified by many as the hardest free climb in the world. His narrative situates his drive to conquer it as a result of emerging from a personally painful divorce (showcasing again his antifragile tendency to grow stronger in the face of adversity). Interestingly, in his quest to conquer the climb, there is a point at which he has the opportunity to complete the climb without his climbing partner Kevin Jorgenson, who had struggled to complete a crucial section. Growing tired and weak amidst their nineteen-day historic climb, Caldwell resolves to turn back, sacrifice his own goal, in order to spur (spar) on his friend Jorgenson. Caldwell resolved to not complete the climb without Jorgenson also completing it.

of commitments and identities that inform their methods, approaches, norms, and goals.[19] Interfaith Engagement (IFE), which includes interfaith dialogue and cooperation, refers to the spirit of the normatively committed and agenda-driven so-called "interfaith movement,"[20] which, according to American interfaith pioneer and leader Donald "Bud" Heckman, is mostly understood as "a fluid network of people and organizations working to advance tolerance, understanding and genuine respect for the religious 'other' (plural) and the positive appropriation of religious diversity."[21] For Patrice Brodeur and Eboo Patel, two well-known North American practitioners and thought leaders in the interfaith movement (especially among young people), "a movement is a group of people committed to making an idea a reality. The idea of the interfaith youth movement is that young people from different backgrounds can come together to build better understanding and cooperation for the common good of humanity as a whole."[22]

---

19 Chapter 1 identifies five common characteristics or Wittgensteinian "family resemblances" emerging among the scholarly approaches of IRS scholars: (1) descriptive, (2) normative, (3) prescriptive, (4) self-implicating, and (5) multi-, inter-, and transdisciplinary.

20 "Movement" used here refers "to an activity that can spread horizontally by using particular, known methods, without necessarily depending either on charismatic leaders or on material support or authority from one or a few centers." Kusumita P. Pedersen, "The Interfaith Movement," *Journal of Ecumenical Studies* 41, no. 1 (2004): 77. For an overview and history of the modern interfaith movement, see John Fahy and Jan-Jonathan Bock, "Introduction," in *The Interfaith Movement*, ed. John Fahy and Jan-Jonathan Bock (London: Routledge, 2019), 4–10; Paul D. Numrich, "Epilogue," in *The Interfaith Movement*, ed. Fahy and Bock, 219–23; and Leonard Swidler, "The History of Inter-Religious Dialogue," in *The Wiley-Blackwell Companion to Inter-Religious Dialogue*, 3–19.

21 Donald Heckman, "Why the 'Interfaith Movement' Must Rebrand," *Huffington Post*, March 11, 2013. In the edited volume *InterActive Faith*, Heckman proposes a "Taxonomy of Interfaith," that identifies eighteen categories which "almost all interfaith organizations fit into." They are chaplaincies, ad-hoc groups, congregationally based organizations, resource agencies, interfaith offices or agencies (within one faith tradition), dialogue groups, interfaith ministries/seminaries, for-profit groups, media groups, national and international organizations, chapters of national and international organizations, umbrella organizations, religious leaders/clergy groups, retreat/conference centers, social issue(s) and action groups, women's groups, student/youth groups, and other. Heckman, "Appendix A," in *InterActive Faith*, ed. Donald Heckman with Rori Picker Neiss (Woodstock, VT: SkyLight Paths Publishing, 2008), 223–29.

22 Patrice Brodeur and Eboo Patel, "Introduction," in *Building the Interfaith Youth Movement*, ed. Eboo Patel and Patrice Brodeur (Lanham, MD: Rowman & Littlefield, 2006), 5.

According to Diana Eck, a movement, and the interfaith movement in particular, is not a single organization but "constituted by a multiform energy moving in the same direction, producing powerful currents, gradually reshaping the landscape."[23] The interfaith movement's "common energy and commitment [aims] to improve relations between people and different religions."[24] Its energy manifests in grassroots community organizations made up of individuals, religious communities, and secular nonprofits; it takes place on university campuses[25] in student groups and often among Student Affairs professionals[26] as well as within campus ministry offices and by chaplaincy professionals; and it is also carried out through the work of foundations, NGOs, and groups focused on public and international spaces, in airports and hospitals, in prisons, and in the military, to name a few. Paul Numrich contends the nature of the modern interfaith movement, like other social movements, "is decentralised, disparate, fluid and fragmented."[27] John Fahy and Jan-Jonathan Bock describe the movement's disparateness as "tens of thousands of initiatives and transnational networks that span the globe," and as such "might be best understood as a 'religiously engaged social movement,'"[28] a 'religiously based social

---

23 Diana L. Eck, "Preface," in *Building the Interfaith Youth Movement*, ed. Patel and Brodeur, ix.

24 Pluralism Project, "America's Growing Interfaith Structure."

25 E.g., the Campus Ministry office of Georgetown University, a Jesuit-Catholic institution in Washington, DC, espouses, "One of the core values of Georgetown is Interreligious Understanding, a commitment to be in community with and learn from those of various religious backgrounds. The Office of Campus Ministry allows for students to engage in these practices through various interfaith events and series." Georgetown University, "Interfaith Programs and Services," Campus Ministry (website).

26 Kathleen Goodman, Mary Ellen Giess, and Eboo Patel, in a "handbook" for Student Affairs professionals, capture the normative and activist spirit of the interfaith movement and its emphasis on personal formation, leadership, and changemaking. They recognize that college and university "campuses have the opportunity to be laboratories and launching pads for a new kind of ethic and a new kind of leader. In the 1980s and 1990s, student affairs staffs led the way by advocating for multiculturalism. The movement changed higher education and the United States. It is time to include religious identity in that mix." Kathleen Goodman et al., "Introduction," in *Educating about Religious Diversity and Interfaith Engagement*, ed. Kathleen Goodman, Mary Ellen Giess, and Eboo Patel (Sterling, VA: Stylus Publishing, 2019), 4.

27 Numrich, "Epilogue," 219.

28 Kenneth Wald, Adam Silverman, and Kevin Fridy, "Making Sense of Religion in Political Life," *Annual Review of Political Science* 8 (2005): 121–34; cited in Fahy and Bock, "Introduction," 14.

movement,'[29] or perhaps a 'religious social movement.'"[30,31] However, nonreligious, secular, and religiously unaffiliated actors are increasingly involved as participants and leaders in the interfaith movement. Fahy and Bock point out, as these descriptions show, that "the interfaith movement is often understood to be a 'religious' rather than a social or political phenomenon."[32] However, they, along with several other scholars, suggest "that the interfaith movement is best understood as a socio-political phenomenon, within which religious actors and institutions occupy a privileged place."[33] Fahy and Bock claim that "in its essence, then, the interfaith movement can be described as an expansive collective of religious people who are committed to improving relations between two or more religious traditions."[34] However, there are a growing number of nonreligious actors involved in the interfaith movement committed to improving relations between two or more religious and nonreligious worldviews and ways of life.

The Interfaith Movement's activities often involve actors explicitly advocating for public policies on the local, national, and international levels. They also include building better local relations between and among people "who orient around religion differently."[35] A key thread running through these groups in the movement is their shared normative-activist vision for fostering positive and constructive engagement across lines of religious difference. In other words, as with other movements (e.g., human rights movements, environmental movements), the Interfaith Movement has an agenda and is not shy about it. It aims to make the world a more peaceful and just place and works toward greater harmonious social cohesion, to the extent that such a thing is possible, on various levels and in various locales. Kusumita Pedersen identifies three main nonmutually exclusive motives for interfaith work: "(1) to live together harmoniously, mitigate tensions, and resolve conflict; (2) to engage a 'common task'; and (3) to search for truth and understanding

---

29 Elizabeth Hutchinson, "Spirituality, Religion, and Progressive Social Movements," *Journal of Religion and Spirituality in Social Work: Social Thought* 31, no. 1–2 (2012): 105–27; cited in Fahy and Bock, "Introduction," 14.

30 Heather Gregg, "Three Theories of Religious Activism and Violence," *Terrorism and Political Violence* 28, no. 2 (2016): 338–60; cited in Fahy and Bock, "Introduction," 14.

31 Fahy and Bock, "Introduction," 14.

32 Fahy and Bock, 3.

33 Fahy and Bock, 4.

34 Fahy and Bock, 17.

35 Phrase made popular by Eboo Patel and the Interfaith Youth Core (Chicago, USA).

in the context of religious plurality."[36] In similar fashion, Anna Halafoff distinguishes four aims: "developing understanding of diverse faiths and of the nature of reality; challenging exclusivity and normalising pluralism; addressing global risks and injustices; and creating multi-actor peacebuilding networks for common security."[37]

This chapter asks about the distinction and relation between IRS and IFE. Kate McCarthy argues for a clear separation between the two: if IRS "is to be an academic discipline suitable to secular higher education, it must not be construed as an auxiliary of the interfaith movement."[38] With McCarthy, the faculty from Elon University (North Carolina, USA) who created an Interreligious Studies minor reason, "The academic field of interreligious studies must maintain independence from the interfaith movement in order to critically assess discourses and practices that promote tolerance, pluralism, and respect for diversity."[39] Should it be a concern if the efforts of the interfaith movement to foster interreligious understanding, tolerance, peacemaking, and civic pluralism become too easily confused and conflated with scholarship? IRS and IFE are related, to be sure, but at what point can a line be drawn between the two? Some scholars contend that the separation between the two is more intimate. Theologian Jeannine Hill Fletcher's 2020 article "Scholarship as Activism" encourages IRS scholars to consider adopting methods of scholar-activism inspired by Max Horkheimer and Critical Theory in response to contemporary currents running through the geopolitical landscape. Fletcher writes, "Through this lens, the question for the emergent field of Interreligious Studies is whether and how scholars 'form a dynamic unity with the oppressed class' and commit themselves to be a force to 'stimulate change' within our concrete historical situation."[40] In similar fashion, Marianne Moyaert claims that "the so-called interfaith movement" (carried out by "activist bridge-builders") is one of three primary contexts that contributes to the rise of IRS. The other two contexts are religious studies

36 Pedersen, "The Interfaith Movement," 75.
37 Anna Halafoff, *The Multifaith Movement* (Dordrecht: Springer, 2013), 51; cited in Fahy and Bock, "Introduction," 17.
38 McCarthy, "(Inter)Religious Studies," 10.
39 Amy L. Allocco et al., "Constructing Interreligious Studies," in *Interreligious/Interfaith Studies*, ed. Patel et al., 36–37.
40 Jeannine Hill Fletcher, "Scholarship as Activism," in *Interreligious Studies*, ed. Gustafson, 250; quoting Max Horkheimer, "Traditional and Critical Theory (1937)," in *Critical Theory*, ed. M. O'Connell (New York: Continuum Press, 1999), 215.

(carried out by IRS scholars) and theology (carried out by theologians). How-ever, Moyaert argues for the deconstruction of the disciplinary boundaries between these three.[41] The reality is that not only are IRS and IFE intimately related in their practical implementation, but many (probably most) IRS scholars also promote and engage in concrete IFE activities.

RECONCILING MICKEY (IRS) AND ROCKY (IFE)

Like Mickey and Rocky, IRS and IFE can be situated in a mutually beneficial way. Models exist from other academic fields that may serve as models for their relationship. Although they share some common aims and character-istics, IRS and IFE can be properly distinguished from one another. While IRS maintains a core impulse to generate knowledge and critically investi-gate and assess interreligious relations, it also embraces various aspects of the normative-activist orientation of IFE. Likewise, IFE can be open to the external critique of IRS while remaining passionately devoted to its core aim to foster understanding between, among, and within communities and individuals with various religious identities and to civically advance local, global, and glocal communities toward a more harmonious social cohesion.

The question of an academic field's relation to practice and normative commitments outside the walls of the academy is not new. IRS scholars can look to similar relations in other academic fields. The faculty from Elon University wonder whether the "distinction between the interfaith move-ment as an action- and engagement-oriented *civic project* and interreligious studies as a *curricular project and academic field*" is similar to the "relation-ship between social programs of poverty alleviation and the discipline of sociology."[42] A more direct analogy likens the distinction between IFE as a civic project and IRS as an academic field to the relationship between envi-ronmentalism that seeks protection and flourishing of the environment to Environmental Studies, which investigates issues relating to the environment using scientific, social scientific, and humanistic tools of inquiry.[43] Whereas a

---

41 Moyaert, "The Scholar, the Theologian, and the Activist," in *Interreligious Studies,* ed. Gustafson, 34–42.

42 Allocco et al., "Constructing Interreligious Studies," 38, italics original.

43 National Center for Educational Statistics, "Environmental Studies," CIP 03.0103 (CIP 2000), Classification of Instructional Programs.

civic project promotes constructive society-building in ways that serve common public goods, such as safety, social cohesion, understanding, security, public health, and environment to name a few, a curricular project promotes academic learning objectives around knowledge acquisition and generation, skill-building, and practical understanding. The more established academic fields of various ethnic studies (Jewish Studies, Black Studies), Peace Studies, and Sustainability Studies lend insight for understanding the relation of IRS to IFE.[44] These fields have traveled the path of self-identification insofar as they have wrestled with their relationship to closely aligned normative movements outside academia. The scholar-practitioner model, common in education, clinical psychology, and medical professional programs, offers a unique perspective on the relation of IRS to IFE. Furthermore, the enduring distinction between the critically inclined field of Religious Studies and the confessionally inclined field of Theological Studies offers analogous lessons for understanding the relationship of IRS to IFE.

Jewish Studies: In 1976, David R. Blumenthal asked, "Where does 'Jewish Studies' Belong"[45] within the academy? By identifying Jewish Studies as a "data-field"[46] that employs methods that are decidedly not "Jewish" (e.g., philological, comparative literature, sociological, and history-of-religions methods),[47] Blumenthal complicates the question by likening the field to various traditional Jewish modes of learning such as Talmud Torah. He sees three ways Jewish Studies and Talmud Torah are continuous with one another: (1) their "critical spirit of inquiry," (2) their ability to "extract methods and techniques from the surrounding culture and to apply them to the study of the Jews and their literary traditions," and (3) their

---

44 A further example is Rachel S. Mikva's insight about what IRS can learn from the development and evolution of Women's Studies (now Gender Studies). Mikva observes that "the fields share a critical mix of theory and praxis, a commitment to seek understanding across lines of difference, contemporary relevance, and intersectional and interdisciplinary complexity." Rachel S. Mikva, "Reflections in the Waves," *Journal of Ecumenical Studies* 53, no. 4 (2018): abstract, 461.

45 David R. Blumenthal, "Where Does 'Jewish Studies' Belong?" *Journal of the American Academy of Religion* 44, no. 3 (1976): 535–46.

46 Blumenthal, "Where Does 'Jewish Studies' Belong?" 535.

47 Blumenthal, 535.

shared normative approach to their subject.[48] Blumenthal cites
nineteenth-century scholars in Jewish Studies who saw "the aim of
research into Jewish literature was scholarship, public recognition
of Jewish rights, and 'the winning of the favor of those in power and
the good will of sensible men.'"[49] Others, through scholarship in
Jewish Studies, sought to "create a world-view that justifies Jewish
identity, [and] to create the grounding for a normative description
of Jewishness."[50] In fact, Blumenthal recognizes that the same might
be stated for many ethnic studies, which show their tendentious
character by arguing that "learning should serve the purpose of
identity-formation."[51] Does IRS, in its relation to IFE, share similar impulses expressed by Blumenthal's understanding of Jewish
studies? A cursory scan of course syllabi in IRS, especially in the
United States, reveals the themes of identity formation, leadership development, and practice.[52] However, Blumenthal keenly
recognizes how Jewish Studies differs from Talmud Torah and
does not share identical aims. Similarly, just because there is some
resonance between IRS and IFE it does not mean that they share
identical aims and goals.

Black Studies scholars Henry Louis Gates Jr. and Manning Marable
assert that "in truth, the ideal of wholly disinterested scholarship—
in any field of research—will probably remain an elusive one. . . . The
ideal of knowledge for its own sake—what Robert Nisbet once called
'academic dogma'—may be unfashionable, and even unrealizable;
but it should command our respect all the same. For it remains the
basic rationale of the university."[53] Such sentiment quells in part any
concern IRS scholars may have about their pursuit of "pure" scholarship and generation of knowledge remaining uncontaminated

---

48 Blumenthal, 538–39.
49 Blumenthal, 540; citing Nahum A. Glatzer, "The Beginnings of Modern Jewish
Studies," in *Studies in Nineteenth-Century Jewish Intellectual History*, ed. Alexander
Altmann (Cambridge, MA: Harvard University Press, 1964), 39.
50 Blumenthal, "Where Does 'Jewish Studies' Belong?" 540.
51 Blumenthal, 540.
52 Trina Janiec Jones and Cassie Meyer, "Interfaith and Interreligious Pedagogies,"
Journal of Interreligious Studies 36 (2022): 9–34.
53 Henry Louis Gates Jr. and Manning Marable, "A Debate on Activism in Black
Studies," in *Companion to African-American Studies*, ed. Jane Anna Gordon and Lewis
Gordon (Oxford: Wiley Blackwell, 2006), 97.

SPIDER SILK, THE ROCK CLIMBER, AND ROCKY BALBOA'S BROKEN NOSE

by political or activist agendas, which, although commendable, is probably ultimately impossible. Gates and Marable acknowledge,

as the academic field [of Black Studies] has become institutionalized, black America continues to suffer massive inequities that are the legacy of historical racism. . . . Unfortunately, many of our conventional traditional modes of analysis simply fail to engage the vexing nature of these class differentials. "People don't care that you know," a street slogan has it, "until they know that you care." But genuine progress will depend not just on caring more, but knowing more.[54]

Scholars and students of IRS can learn from this call to balance passion, care, and devotion to a normative agenda with the critical study and knowledge generation about, within, and beyond the agenda. IRS and IFE have the potential to mutually cooperate in complementary, yet distinct, ways in pursuit of genuine progress that responds to shared aims and goals. Gates and Marable recognize the need to balance descriptive knowledge generation with prescriptive action. Although Black Studies scholarship richly describes "the contours of black life and history, examining the reality of the black experience from the point of view of black people themselves,"[55] it also challenges and corrects racist stereotypes and assumptions about "black genetic or cultural inferiority that unfortunately still exist within much white scholarship."[56] Gates and Marable explain that Black Studies remains prescriptive and is integral to combatting racism and empowering Black people.[57] Similarly, IRS scholars align with IFE activists in combating antisemitic and anti-Muslim currents around the globe, including the growing tendency to racialize religious identities and groups.

Gates's and Marable's vision of Black Studies challenges IRS scholars to reflect on the relation of IRS scholarship to IFE activism. In restating the historical development of Black Studies, they stress that "both theoretical and practical connections between scholarship

---

54 Gates and Marable, "A Debate on Activism in Black Studies," 97–98.
55 Gates and Marable, 99.
56 Gates and Marable, 99.
57 Gates and Marable, 99.

and social change" originally formed the heart of the field. However, they lament the reality that today several Black Studies departments no longer yoke the two under one roof. "The function of Black Studies scholarship should be more than the celebration of heritage and self-esteem; it must utilize history and culture as tools through which an oppressed people can transform their lives and the entire society. Scholars have an obligation not just to interpret but to act."[58] Here the question is not whether IRS ought to be equated to Black Studies in its focus on assisting a historically oppressed people. The question is whether IRS's relation to IFE is similar to Black Studies' relation to the promotion of equity and liberation of Black Americans and can contribute to the transformation of lives and society for the betterment of all. Inviting scholars to "jump into the fray" of normative action toward civic outcomes, to "commit themselves to be a force to 'stimulate change' within our concrete historical situation,"[59] and to have "skin in the game" takes IRS beyond a field dedicated solely to descriptive analysis and knowledge generation. Why not "jump into the fray," asks scholar of Africana political thought Jane Anna Gordon, who argues the "attempt to rid science of explicit human commitments and projects promises to reduce the validity of the work as genuine science, masking, as it seeks to make the procedure transparent, the substance of what is actually being tested and proven."[60] In Gordon's view, genuine "humanistic social science calls and commands that one jump into the fray,"[61] like the critically attuned gadfly incessantly reminding the world "that things could be otherwise and that what we choose, we must choose reflectively."[62] In *Skin in the Game*, Nassim Nicholas Taleb argues that having skin in the game is not only required for fairness, efficiency, and risk management, but is necessary to properly

---

58 Gates and Marable, 99.
59 Fletcher, "Scholarship as Activism," 250.
60 Jane Anna Gordon, "Some Reflections on Challenges Posed to Social Scientific Method by the Study of Race," in *Companion to African-American Studies*, ed. Gordon and Gordon, 282.
61 Gordon, "Some Reflections on Challenges Posed to Social Scientific Method by the Study of Race," 301.
62 Gordon, 302.

and accurately understand the world.[63] Having skin in the game refers to sharing a vested interest (both the benefits and the harms) of a joint venture. Rock climbers like Caldwell literally have skin in the game by cutting, scraping, and rubbing their fingers and hands against the rock, which builds up strong resilient calluses that help them become better climbers. This idea is not new and echoes clinical psychologist Wendy Mogel's well-known 2001 book *The Blessing of a Skinned Knee*, that teaches "when we treat our children's lives like we're cruise ship directors who must get them to their destination—adulthood—smoothly, without their feeling even the slightest bump or wave, we're depriving them."[64] The implication is that learning to walk or ride a bike entails failure and skinned knees, blessings without which children will not properly understand, or be prepared for, the world ahead. Although there may be drawbacks of jumping into the fray and having skin in the game, such as the scholar becoming closely aligned with their object of study in ways that may blind them, these drawbacks can be outweighed by the benefit of producing a necessary and more accurate understanding of the world.

Peace Studies is a multidisciplinary field, often with normative and political commitments,[65] that investigates the origins, resolution, and prevention of international and intergroup conflicts[66] without shying away from promoting peace and justice as civic norms. The website for the Justice and Peace Studies program at the University of St. Thomas (Minnesota, USA) states, "'Everybody talks about the weather but nobody does anything about it.' Likewise,

---

63 Nassim Nicholas Taleb, *Skin in the Game* (New York: Random House, 2018), 3.
64 Wendy Mogel, *The Blessing of a Skinned Knee* (New York: Scribner, 2001), 91.
65 "As a discipline, Justice and Peace Studies and similar programs are nonpartisan but unapologetically political, inquiring about how power operates in systems, institutions, and among populaces. Commonly articulated goals of Peace Studies include ending or preventing wars; resolving entrenched conflicts without violence; building peaceable societies that are just, sustainable, and equitable; and addressing the root causes of many social, political, and economic problems." Mike Klein, Amy Finnegan, and Jack Nelson-Pallmeyer, "Circle of Praxis Pedagogy for Peace Studies," *Peace Review: A Journal of Social Justice* 30, no. 3 (2018): 273–74.
66 National Center for Educational Statistics, "Peace Studies and Conflict Studies," CIP 30.0501 (CIP 2020), Classification of Instructional Programs.

everybody knows of violence and injustice in the world, along with racial inequity, tension between religions, climate change, and on and on. But what can we do about it? Is there hope? . . . unlike the weather, we can do something."[67] Rooted in a pedagogical model of engaged learning and framed by "The Circle of Praxis," the program encourages students to be involved "in real-life situations of injustice, poverty and social conflict. . . . [and connect] with community organizations" to work "towards greater justice and a more peaceful world."[68] Without losing sight of the primary aim of pursuing knowledge, the program contends that "new perspectives and knowledge aren't worth much, however, unless we act on what we are learning."[69]

With roots in twentieth-century Latin American liberation movements, the Circle of Praxis is a philosophical model for pedagogy and research that follows an iterative four-stage process of insertion, descriptive analysis, normative analysis, and action planning. "Woven together in an iterative process of action and reflection, the Circle of Praxis guides transformative education toward both personal agency and structural change to promote justice and peace."[70] *Insertion* is the scholarly immersion in which the researcher begins, not at the level of concept or theory, but "in direct or indirect encounters with people who are oppressed or marginalized from the dominant power structures, struggling to survive, and overcoming the brutalities of unjust social systems."[71] Put simply, insertion is about "being there"[72] in the encounter to listen, learn, and observe while challenging and reframing one's own limited experiences and inadequate inherited worldviews.[73] *Descriptive analysis*, which refers to the "rigorous academic efforts that seek to expose and understand

---

67 University of St. Thomas, "Justice and Peace Studies Homepage."
68 University of St. Thomas.
69 University of St. Thomas.
70 Klein et al., "Circle of Praxis Pedagogy for Peace Studies," 270.
71 Klein et al., 272.
72 "Being There" is appropriately the title of an important volume on anthropological and ethnographic methods of "fieldwork encounters and the making of truth." John Borneman and Abdellah Hammoudi, eds., *Being There* (Berkeley: University of California Press, 2009).
73 Klein et al., "Circle of Praxis Pedagogy for Peace Studies," 272.

causal factors and unjust systems,"[74] uses social scientific methods and tools to record and articulate data from the insertion stage. *Normative analysis* (1) considers any assumptions and judgments produced in the learning process, (2) recognizes the reality of human suffering and oppression (and the many forms it takes and implications stemming from it), and (3) proposes policies with the potential to promote greater peace and justice—all of which often depend on reevaluating and shifting values.[75] Klein and colleagues confess that normative analysis "invites us to unleash our imaginations to envision alternative futures and to see ourselves as participants in a vital process of reshaping our world."[76] *Action planning* asks scholars to serve as change agents by holding them accountable for the knowledge gained in the process. "While critical consciousness is the explicit educational goal, a more just and peaceful world is the practical goal of Justice and Peace Studies."[77] The Circle of Praxis, modeled by Peace Studies, can be a model for the relation between IRS and IFE. The fourth step—*Action planning*—is particularly relevant. As "the component of the Circle of Praxis that extends peace studies into peacebuilding,"[78] action planning appeals to the scholar-practitioner model and analogously extends IRS into IFE. The Circle of Praxis does not end with *action planning* but calls for the ongoing iterative return to *insertion, descriptive analysis*, and so on. For Peace Studies, the "Circle of Praxis is iterative and continuous, moving us toward ever more effective and ethical learning and action to promote justice and peace."[79] The Circle of Praxis offers IRS a potential model to realize its normative commitments, should they be accepted, of promoting a more harmonious and socially cohesive world across religious differences.

Sustainability Studies, an emerging field often closely allied with Environmental Studies, centers the "concept of sustainability from an interdisciplinary perspective" and includes "sustainable

---

74 Klein et al., 273.
75 Klein et al., 274–75.
76 Klein et al., 274–75.
77 Klein et al., 275.
78 Klein et al., 276–77.
79 Klein et al., 277.

development, environmental policies, ethics, ecology, landscape architecture, city and regional planning, economics, natural resources, sociology, and anthropology."[80] Sustainability discourse is multidisciplinary with a normative aim to maintain beneficial rates or levels of growth while avoiding harmful depletion of resources (natural, economic, or otherwise). Jens Jetzkowitz describes the field as "all the efforts to preserve the conditions that make it possible for societies to exist in the future."[81] Analogously, IFE as interfaith discourse aims at preserving, or creating, the conditions that make it possible for societies to exist in relative peace now and in the future. According to Jetzkowitz, the social sciences are central to Sustainability Studies because they "provide knowledge about observable regularities and structures within societies" and keep "the question of how human coexistence can be best organized in the future" at the core of their research aims.[82] Assuming a scholar-practitioner or scholar-activist model, Jetzkowitz rhetorically inquires, "Why is it such a problem for the social sciences to get seriously involved in sustainability discourse?"[83] It need not be a problem for IRS, a multidisciplinary field that draws on social scientific and humanistic methods, to get seriously involved with IFE. Sustainability Studies' relation to professionals, practitioners, and policymakers who strive to create a more sustainable civilization offers a model for IRS to engage interfaith practitioners who strive to create more socially cohesive and civically religiously plural and diverse societies. It is possible for IRS as an academic field to be rigorously engaged with interfaith discourse without collapsing into IFE.

The list of analogous fields and their relations to their normative counterparts goes on. Consider any study of an -ism to the -ism itself.

IRS : IFE :: study of X*ism* : practice of X*ism*

---

80 National Center for Educational Statistics, "Sustainability Studies," CIP 30.3301 (CIP 2000), Classification of Instructional Programs.
81 Jens Jetzkowitz, *Co-Evolution of Nature and Society* (Cham, Switzerland: Palgrave Macmillan, 2019), 5.
82 Jetzkowitz, *Co-Evolution of Nature and Society*, 29.
83 Jetzkowitz, 29.

Some analogies logically resonate with IRS:IFE, while others do not. Consider the study of secularism versus promoting secularism (or being secular), the study of communism versus promoting communism (or being a communist), the study of racism versus being racist, the study of terrorism versus terrorizing, the study of peace versus promoting peace, and so on. One need not be a secularist to be a scholar of secularism, Islamophobic to study Islamophobia, Christian to study Christianity, or British to study British literature. For the scholar, there is a tension between the benefits and drawbacks that come from both (1) having the critical distance that comes from *not* personally identifying with or practicing the object of their study and (2) jumping into the fray with skin in the game and the intimate experience of an insider to the object of study. IRS is not the first field to wrestle with this tension, its relation to other fields and practices, and the normative and reflexive turns that come along the way.

NORMATIVE AND REFLEXIVE TURNS

Acknowledging normative, reflexive, and self-implicating commitments in their research and pedagogy, IRS scholars are not only able to maintain more transparency between their scholarship and IFE but also more likely to avoid unnecessary misunderstandings and expectations between them. Chapter 1 introduced the multidisciplinary academic study of religion, a broad field under which IRS can be properly situated as a subfield (according to some IRS scholars). The present chapter addresses the relation of IRS to the normative commitments of IFE. "Normative" here refers to making claims about or having commitments to explicit or assumed ways one *ought* to act or think.[84] When a scholar brackets or puts aside their normative commitments, to the extent such a thing is possible, they attempt to avoid allowing their personal commitments (whether they be religious, political, ideological, etc.) to influence the questions they ask, the way they analyze their findings, or critique their objects of study. Normative claims are unavoidable in most disciplines, especially the study of religion. It is unnecessary to try to avoid them altogether; rather, it is more helpful to beware of the normative claims

---

84 Thomas A. Lewis, "The Inevitability of Normativity in the Study of Religion," in *Theology and Religious Studies in Higher Education: Global Perspectives*, ed. Darlene L. Bird and Simon G. Smith (London: Continuum, 2009), 88.

and offer justification for them.[85] For an IRS scholar to hold and justify an interfaith commitment might entail the acknowledgment of an obligation to promote scholarship that produces actionable data and generating knowledge that informs policies and practices contributing to making religiously diverse societies more peaceful, socially cohesive, and free.

Recent scholarship, especially in the social sciences and humanities, has given way to a so-called "normative turn," which suggests that "all scholarship is value laden" within which "philosophical and ideological assumptions" constantly play a role.[86] Scholars increasingly suggest too much is made of the distinction between normative and descriptive approaches. Such a distinction may ultimately be illusory anyway. Normativity is inherently embedded "in all studies that investigate empirical dimensions of religion, values and society."[87] Scholars can be "aware of *what* normativity is at work, and *how* it is at work"[88] by reflecting on why they want to undertake a particular research question, what their assumptions are, and what their opinions or *normative* beliefs about what ought to be the case (the norm or normal view) are. For instance, if a researcher investigates how various religious individuals and communities responded to the COVID-19 pandemic that began in 2020, then the researcher's normative response articulates what they personally believe ought to be the appropriate ways others should have or would have responded in their respective contexts. The researcher's normative response is value-based, rooted in a personal perspective, and states what "should" be the case.

---

85 Lewis, "The Inevitability of Normativity in the Study of Religion," 88.

86 Travis Warren Cooper, "Taxonomy Construction and the Normative Turn in Religious Studies," *Religions* 8, no. 12: 270 (2017): 10.

87 Jan-Olav Henriksen, "Normative Dimensions in Empirical Research on Religion, Values, and Society," in *Difficult Normativity: Normative Dimensions in Research on Religion and Theology*, ed. Jan-Olav Henriksen (Frankfurt am Main: Peter Lang, 2011), 12–13; cited in Tone Stangeland Kaufman, "Normativity as Pitfall or Ally?" *Ecclesial Practices* 2 (2015): 92.

88 Henriksen, "Normative Dimensions in Empirical Research on Religion, Values, and Society," 15, italics original; cited in Kaufman, "Normativity as Pitfall or Ally?" 92. Henriksen identifies various types of normativity inherent in empirical, and especially theological, research. These include "research design, research ethics, the social context of the study, theological normativities, epistemology, institutional and political normative positions, and the normativity of the scholar undertaking the research." Kaufman adds, "the normativity of practices conducted in the field of study." Kaufman, "Normativity as Pitfall or Ally?" 92.

Sociologist Gerardo Martí's cautious optimism about the recent movement of theologians doing ethnographic work offers insight into how normative commitments can impact scholarship. Since "theologians may not yet adequately recognize the hazards involved" with doing ethnographic research without being aware of their normative commitments, their "insights generated by participant observation are constantly at risk of personal presumptions and variously asserted 'truths,' especially when researchers enter the field of observation with strongly held convictions and compelling worldviews."[89] Martí's concern may ultimately apply to all ethnographers of religion, including IRS scholars, and not just the theologians, since a predominately Western–Protestant–Christian concept of religion is often imposed or asserted in the overall arch of many ethnographic projects from their beginnings. Being aware of one's own normative biases can help avoid certain biases, personal presumptions, and variously asserted truths hazardously risking original insights generated from field work. Furthermore, Martí provides considerations for scholars, especially theologians, "toward becoming sensitized and self-reflexive about how theology may work within the researcher . . . [by asking]: What does the researcher impose conceptually as a theological framework in making sense of empirical observations?"[90] Being self-reflexive refers to recognizing how one's own context and background influence the ways they generate knowledge, ask questions, and interpret data.[91] Reflexive scholars recognize that being academically neutral—that is, having no normative commitments—"is no longer a feasible defence for refusing to discuss one's own agenda and perspective," but instead foregrounds their authorial self and "autobiographical confession," Paul Hedges argues, as "a useful part of academic work to position any author and their prejudices and expectations."[92] The scholar does this by acknowledging and analyzing her own presence, experiences, situatedness, and positions relative to, and

---

89 Gerardo Martí, "Found Theologies versus Imposed Theologies," *Ecclesial Practices* 3 (2016): 159.

90 Martí, "Found Theologies versus Imposed Theologies," 167. The considerations are (1) the potentially dominating influence of "metaphysical" beliefs, (2) the challenge of revealing empirical dynamics versus reinforcing theological convictions, (3) the shallow use of theories and concepts from sociology/anthropology/psychology to advance a preferred theology, (4) the danger of theological systems overdetermining expectations for social life, and (5) the focus on ideal cases with front-loaded assumptions (167–71).

91 Hedges, "Encounters with Ultimacy?" 363.

92 Hedges, 363.

alongside, the analysis of the people she studies. In the process, her research will likely alter her view, which becomes a part, albeit a minor part, of the research process itself.[93]

For many, the debate over whether scholars ought to set aside their ethical, normative, and other commitments seems fleeting. Acknowledging one's commitments, accepting normativity and reflexivity as allies,[94] and concluding that doing so is "inevitable in the study of religion"[95] and probably in most academic fields. Nonetheless, the quest for objectivity—even if pure objectivity is unattainable—need not be pushed to the wayside. A certain degree of distance and separation from one's object of study seems appropriate and sometimes necessary. The question raised here is whether (and how) scholars can critically practice reflexivity, as Kaufman concludes, "changing the tacit and implicit normativity of the researcher from a pitfall to an ally, and ultimately, enabling the researcher to see and produce a better account of the field studied."[96] The self-reflective scholar challenges her own normative assumptions. For instance, Gaille Cannella's and Yvonna Lincoln's following questions serve as a constructively self-critical preresearch thought exercise:

Whose knowledge is this? Why (as a researcher) do I choose to construct this problem? What assumptions are hidden within my research practices? How could this work produce exclusions? What do I do as I encounter those unexpected exclusions or oppressions that result from the work? What is my privilege (or power position) in this research? How am I subtly re-inscribing my own universals and/or discrediting others?[97]

Approaching academia as normative and in a reflexive manner may help scholars strengthen their research insofar as they become more aware, to the extent it is possible, of various blind spots, biases, and assumptions. It should hardly be controversial for IRS scholars to maintain normative, reflexive, and autobiographical (self-implicating) commitments in their research and

---

93 Ammerman, *Studying Lived Religion*, 210–11.
94 Kaufman, "Normativity as Pitfall or Ally?" 91–107.
95 Lewis, "The Inevitability of Normativity in the Study of Religion," 88.
96 Kaufman, "Normativity as Pitfall or Ally?" 107.
97 Gaille S. Cannella and Yvonna S. Lincoln, "Predatory vs. Dialogic Ethics," *Qualitative Inquiry* 13, no. 3 (2007): 316; quoted in Aisha-Nusrat Ahmad, Maik Fielitz, Johanna Leinius, and Gianna Magdalena Schlichte, "Introduction," in *Knowledge, Normativity and Power in Academia*, ed. Aisha-Nusrat Ahmad, Maik Fielitz, Johanna Leinius, and Gianna Magdalena Schlichte (Frankfurt: Campus Verlag, 2018), 16.

pedagogy to not only maintain transparent relations between IRS and IFE, but to avoid unnecessary misunderstandings and expectations between them as well.

❥ ❥ ❥

The function of IRS is to critically assess IFE. IRS serves as a "counterpoint, complement, and correction to the interfaith movement and co-curricular models of interfaith engagement."[98] IRS challenges IFE by asking, "Who benefits from interreligious harmony and interfaith cooperation? What values, communities, or interests are empowered by it and which are marginalized?"[99] A healthy academic field, if interested in ensuring its future, "must work to identify and deconstruct its assumptions."[100] Hence IRS can and should self-critique its own deficiencies as an academic field. However, students should be able to "offer constructive suggestions for improving these models."[101] Notice that the orientation of the academic field to the lived practice is that of trainer to fighter. IRS, as a trainer, sparring partner, or coach, strategically and critically (de) constructs the athlete, fighter, or performer not as an exercise worthy of pursuit in its own right, but with the aim to improve and strengthen their craft and efficacy. This sentiment is present in the humanities and social sciences, and also across the well-worn and tired debate between religious studies and theology.

---

98 Allocco et al., "Constructing Interreligious Studies," 39.

99 Allocco et al., 47.

100 Allocco et al., 47. The authors offer several critiques of IRS and IFE worth analyzing: "that it suppresses and stigmatizes conflict; that it naturalizes and normativizes a bland and interiorized spirituality; that it provides domestic cover for racist and imperialist projects abroad; that it makes the world safe for global capital; that the logic of the incorporation of difference on which it is based is part and parcel of the imperialist US project; that it co-opts difference for its own purposes and manufactures hegemonic depictions of minority difference; that it compels an accommodation to Protestant secularism; that it foregrounds projects of identity recognition over analysis of material sources of conflict; and that it normalizes US-style pluralism and thereby advances American exceptionalism." Allocco et al., 47.

101 Elon University, "Interreligious Studies Minor" (website). For instance, an IRS scholar or student might assess IFE by identifying excluded groups and individuals. Consider Grove Harris's "examination of Pagan inclusion in and exclusion from the interfaith movement highlights the need for tolerance and engagement beyond tolerance, within and among religious traditions." Grove Harris, "Pagan Involvement in the Interfaith Movement," *CrossCurrents* 55, no. 1, "Current Issues in Interfaith Work" (Spring 2005): 67.

IRS could be to IFE as Mickey Goldmill is to Rocky Balboa. IRS could be the critical friendly spar that spurs IFE on in an effort to improve it, strengthen it, make it more resilient and more aware of its blind spots and shortcomings. IRS could create the proper conditions to cultivate antifragility and growth in IFE while at the same time learning in, and about, the process. The Mickey : Rocky :: IRS : IFE analogy reveals that IRS, like most or all academic fields, has normative commitments. It also suggests IRS has mutually aligned interests with IFE. In other words, IRS has "skin in the game." Just as Mickey unapologetically desires Rocky to become the champ, and as Peace Studies is "unapologetically political,"[102] IRS too, it seems, is often unapologetically political, practice-oriented, activist, and agenda-driven toward promoting and establishing certain norms around religious diversity, civic pluralism, and interreligious relations. Mickey does not bracket his desire for Rocky to become the champ. Indeed, it is his very job and aim to train Rocky to be the champ. In addition to producing knowledge about the complex nature of interreligious relations, IRS can serve as IFE's grump and gruff sparring partner, trainer, coach, and critical advocate who leverages its knowledge and experience to push IFE to become more flexible, resilient, antifragile, and spider-silk-like. IRS can be IFE's greatest advocate by providing the resources, encouragement, and honest critical care that is necessary for flourishing.

SCHOLAR-PRACTITIONER MODEL

Many scholars of IRS who teach and do research about interreligious relations are also IFE practitioners who promote constructive avenues toward understanding and bridgebuilding in religiously diverse societies. In other words, they are both scholar and practitioner, both coach and fighter, both Mickey and Rocky. In 2006, Eboo Patel and Patrice Brodeur wrote prophetically about "scholar-practitioners in the emerging academic field of interfaith studies."[103] In 2013, Patel identified the "strong practitioner dimension" as the central thread uniting the prominent academic disciplines of IRS: "Scholars in these areas ask and pursue critical research questions, but they also create

---

102 Klein et al., "Circle of Praxis Pedagogy for Peace Studies," 273.
103 Patrice Brodeur and Eboo Patel, "Introduction," in *Building the Interfaith Youth Movement*, ed. Patel and Brodeur, 6.

programs of study that shape leaders who 'do' in their areas."[104] In 2020, Patel articulated a "civic approach" to IRS (or "interfaith studies"), emphasizing "the significance of research, teaching, and practice for what [he] calls civic interfaith leadership."[105] A civic approach emphasizes ways in which the field benefits, and prepares individuals to address, issues of common public concern. Civic interfaith leadership includes the knowledge and ability to create and organize social spaces and processes that contribute positively to people with various religious identities sharing in common society.[106]

Similar to the scholar-practitioners (or researcher-practitioner or scientist-clinician) popular in public health, medicine, clinical psychology, social work, and educational leadership fields, IRS scholar-practitioners value both theory and practical application and act as "boundary spanners" moving back and forth between academy and community, between IRS and IFE in mutually informing and beneficial ways for scholar and practitioner audiences.[107] Like the health-related fields, the field of educational leadership embraces echoes of the Circle of Praxis and includes a scholar-practitioner model in which "Knowledge gained through research and observation leads to the construction of new knowledge. Incorporating this new insight into daily professional practice connects the observation of the scholar with the implementation of the practitioner."[108] IRS scholar-practitioners gain knowledge through research about, observation of, and participation in activities and contexts involving interreligious encounter. The data and insights generated not only inform new directions for research but also contribute to the preparation of individuals with knowledge and ability to create and organize social spaces and processes that contribute positively to people with various religious identities sharing in common society to address issues of common public concern. In other words, the scholar-practitioner model not only advances the field of IRS but also promotes the civic goals of IFE.

---

104 Patel, "Toward a Field of Interfaith Studies."

105 Patel, "A Civic Approach to Interfaith Studies," in *Interreligious Studies*, ed. Gustafson, 30.

106 Patel, *Interfaith Leadership*, 11.

107 L. Shakiyla Smith and Natalie Wilkins, "Mind the Gap," *Journal of Public Health Management and Practice* 24, no. 1 (2018): S7.

108 K. Hampton, "Transforming School and Society," *Scholar-Practitioner Quarterly* 4, no. 2 (2009): 190; cited in Charles Lowery, "The Scholar-Practitioner Ideal," *Journal of School Leadership* 26 (February 2016): 49.

As a model that builds knowledge in relation to theory *and* practice, the scholar-practitioner aligns with *phronesis* (practical wisdom for everyday encounter); in the context of religious diversity, it algins particularly well with the development of interreligious *phronesis* (IP). Bridging the healthy tension between the critical scholarship of IRS and the practice of constructive IFE, the scholar-practitioner approach resonates with the spirit of the Circle of Praxis's commencement point "in direct or indirect encounters with people"[109] and Gordon's call for scholars to "jump into the fray"—to have "skin in the game"—to gain a more accurate understanding of the world. With Fletcher, it challenges scholars to become activists that "commit themselves to be a force to 'stimulate change' within our concrete historical situation."[110]

Ought IRS scholars consider the mutual benefit of friendly sparring relations with IFE practitioners? Doing so would challenge IRS scholars to become "boundary spanners" and "knowledge brokers"[111] operating in the liminal spaces between the illusory ideal of pure scholarship and the heroic role of selfless interfaith leader and practitioner. Many IRS scholars and IFE practitioners consider themselves scholar-practitioners operating in the middle. Most will appropriately privilege either the scholar or practitioner identity of their vocation. Not only does sparring occur *inter*personally between IRS scholars and IFE practitioners, but also on a deeper *intra*personal level within one's own self. The traditional wisdom of intrapersonal sparring is commonplace in literature, philosophy, and religious and spiritual traditions. Some *midrashim* wonder whether the man with whom Jacob famously wrestled in the Hebrew Bible (Gen 32:24) was Jacob himself. A common interpretation of the *Bhagavad Gita* understands the dialogue between Arjuna and Krishna as an internal struggle that takes place with one person's own inner self. A critique of *The Brothers Karamazov* interprets the novel as Dostoevsky working out his own interior identity in a fictional autobiography with the four sparring brothers representing different identities of the author himself. As the Hebrew Bible, the author of the *Bhagavad Gita*, and Dostoevsky may

---

109 Klein et al., "Circle of Praxis Pedagogy for Peace Studies," 272.

110 Fletcher, "Scholarship as Activism," 250. Many IRS scholars engage in IFE and may consider themselves scholar-practitioners or scholar-activists. In 2016, sociologist Anna Halafoff revealed, "[I] have been conducting research on interfaith relations for 10 years now, so I'm a scholar-practitioner, or 'scholar-activist.'" Berkley Center for Religion, Peace, and World Affairs, "A Discussion with Anna Halafoff," Georgetown University, September 22, 2016.

111 Smith and Wilkins, "Mind the Gap," 3.

attest, in the quest for spider-silk-like strength, resilience, and growth, it is perhaps one's own self that serves as the most evenly matched and worthy adversary for sparring. IRS and IFE are intimately related and poised to remain in a mutually beneficial relationship. The reality is that most IRS scholars also either engage in or support meaningful IFE activities and goals. An aim of IRS in relation to IFE is to be the friendly spar to build up IFE's spider-silk-like tendencies beyond resilience to become antifragile so that, like when Rocky Balboa breaks his nose or when the rock climber builds up calluses against the abrasive rock, it grows stronger, reaches new heights, and achieves its civic goals.

Part II

Interfaith Engagement (IFE)

9

The "Interfaith" Lexicon

Chapter Outline

I. Interfaith or Interreligious?

II. (inter)Worldview and (inter)Lifeway

"'Interfaith is so seventies," a senior scholar grumbled at a recent conference on interfaith studies. His rhetorical protest declares the term "interfaith" to no longer be adequate for a religiously diverse landscape that covers ground well beyond the Abrahamic traditions. Perhaps he shares Donald Heckman's feeling that "the 'Interfaith Movement' must rebrand."[1] The challenge of language eventually surfaces at most gatherings (conferences, symposia, etc.) that focus on the theory and practice of interfaith engagement. Common complaints target the labels of interfaith, multifaith, interreligious, and so forth. Concerns and questions include what language and terms are most appropriate, precise, inclusive, and useful for interfaith engagement and the academic field that studies it. This chapter does not put these questions to rest. Rather, this chapter lays bare the many ways scholars and practitioners refer to IFE, especially with an eye to overarching terms such as "interfaith," "interreligious," "worldview," and "lifeway." What may seem a rather insignificant investigation—after all, what does one silly little word matter?—turns out to have practical implications for how encounters are perceived both within and beyond the groups and individuals involved.

---

1 Donald Heckman, "Why the 'Interfaith Movement' Must Rebrand," *Huffington Post*, March 11, 2013.

Part II of this book focuses primarily on interfaith engagement (IFE), beginning with this chapter on language. Despite some difference in opinion over the prefix *inter-* (e.g., some argue *trans-* is more appropriate, as discussed below), most often discussion centers on the word(s) that come(s) after *inter-* such as *inter*faith, *inter*religious, *inter*spiritual, and so on. This chapter also discusses the terms "worldview" and "lifeway" (i.e., way of life or lifestance), which are increasingly used. Finally, this chapter considers the merits of these terms when applied to the contexts of interfaith engagement and interreligious studies.

INTERFAITH OR INTERRELIGIOUS?[2]

The two most commonly used terms in IFE are "interfaith" and "interreligious."[3] Many use them interchangeably, while others distinguish one from the other. Some use interfaith to refer to the normative and activist-orientated movement to bring about constructive relations between and among religious communities and individuals for the common good, betterment, and general social cohesion of society and use interreligious more simply as an adjective—divorced from any normative commitments—to describe encounters between religious communities and individuals, whether they are characterized by constructive cooperation or destructive conflict.

---

2 This section is adapted and extended from Hans Gustafson, "'Interfaith' Is So 1970s!" State of Formation, April 12, 2018.

3 The term "ecumenical" is sometimes used (mostly by Christian-centric communities) to connote interfaith relations between two or more religions. However, it "technically refers to relations between and among Christian churches." Pedersen, "The Interfaith Movement," 77. Some scholars suggest that "interreligious" is more common in Europe and "interfaith" is preferred in the United States. Others suggest that "interfaith" is used more often by activists while "interreligious" is used by scholars. Inger Furseth observes that "interreligious" is more common among Catholics and "interfaith" is more common among Protestants. Furseth, "The Return of Religion in the Public Sphere?" *Institutional Change in the Public Sphere*, ed. Fredrik Engelstad, Hakon Larsen, Jon Rogstad, and Kari Steen-Johnsen. (Warsaw: De Gruyter Open, 2017), 225n. While these tendencies may be accurate, it is less clear whether these distinctions are helpful. In Europe, "interreligious" is used in the academic society European Society for Intercultural Theology and Interreligious Studies (ESITIS), while in the United States, the academic group at the American Academy of Religion uses both in the "Interreligious and Interfaith Studies Unit." The Association for Interreligious/Interfaith Studies (AIIS), the North American counterpart to ESITIS, also uses both.

Less often, interfaith (and *much less* often interreligious) is used to refer to an effort to create novel syncretic religions that draw on elements of many religions. When used this way, the *inter-* prefix probably connotes a certain degree of integration of beliefs and practices.[4]

"Faith" and "religion" become important since the two most dominant terms—interfaith and interreligious—assume them. But do all religious traditions have a concept of faith? Probably not. Does the term "interfaith" privilege traditions like Christianity that hold a central place for faith? Probably. Does the term "faith" presume that a religion has concepts relating to the divine, sacred, God, Gods, or something in which to have faith? Perhaps, but not necessarily. Does "faith" alienate nontheist positions (such as many Buddhists)? It probably can.[5] These questions are among the most common when the language of "interfaith" is discussed. The terms "religion" and "religious" (in "interreligious"), on the other hand, are not free from these language problems either.

By emphasizing religion, the term "interreligious" can be perceived to refer to relations exclusively or primarily between organized and institutionalized religions or high-level religious leaders (e.g., rabbis, priests, political leaders, and so forth). This can be problematic for the increasing number of people—especially young people—who shun institutionalized religion yet still embrace spirituality (hence the popular label "spiritual-but-not-religious" or SBNR). "Interfaith," however, may sound a little less stuffy and formal and a bit more open, relational, intimate, accessible, and spiritual to these younger groups. After all, it is the Interfaith Movement, not the Inter*religious* Movement. Likewise, it seems that "interfaith" is more often used by students and staff in Student Affairs, campus ministry, chaplaincy, and spiritual life offices in higher education contexts.

Consider the growing number of young people who identify as spiritual-but-not-religious, religiously unaffiliated, nonreligious, without faith, or with traditions that explicitly reject religious labels such as secular humanism, the nones, and nothing in particular (presented in Part I). The contemporary

---

4 Rachel S. Mikva seemingly uses "interspirituality" in this more syncretic manner in "Reflections in the Waves," 475.

5 "How about the 'question guy,' [who] answers his own questions? . . . Hey guess what, I'm not impressed. Those are not hard questions. . . . Do I find [that guy] irritating? Yes. Yes, I do." Kevin Nealon, "Kevin Nealon: Now Hear Me Out!" stand-up comedy (Vivendi Entertainment, 2009).

Interfaith Movement and academic field of IRS generally welcome and include these groups under the overarching rubric of interfaith/interreligious encounter, despite these two terms being ill-suited for the religiously unaffiliated. To address this concern, Eboo Patel and the organization Interfaith America (formerly Interfaith Youth Core) popularized the language of describing interfaith cooperation as including "people who orient around religion differently,"[6] which cleverly places religion at the center and includes space for all possible orientations (including nonreligious).

The concept of religion is complex, confusing, and potentially problematic (discussed in chapter 1). The definition of the term "religion" is not clear. Faith is often defined as belief in the sacred, supernatural, or ultimate reality beyond verification or proof; it also refers to putting trust in someone or something (as George Michael sings, "gotta have faith"). Consider Wilfred Cantwell Smith's well-known view of faith as a "human activity . . . a quiet confidence and joy which enables one to feel at home in the universe and to find meaning in the world and in one's life, a meaning which is profound and ultimate and is stable no matter what happens to oneself at the level of immediate event."[7] Faith in this sense contrasts with belief, which for Smith is "the holding of certain ideas. Some might even see it as the intellect's translation (even reduction?) of transcendence into ostensible terms; the conceptualization in certain terms of the vision that, metaphorically, one has seen."[8] With Smith's account of "faith" in mind, inter*faith* becomes broad enough to include traditions that do not hold a central place for the more traditional belief-centered idea of faith. Smith is among those who declare the concept of religion a creation of modern Christian Europe. In place of religion, Smith identifies the traditions as "cumulative" and multiple modes of expressing "faith."[9] For Smith, "faith" is universal and, as Tomoko Masuzawa interprets him, what religion "really is,"[10] and therefore suggests the term "religion" ought to be abandoned and replaced by "faith."

In *Faith and Belief*, as the title suggests, Smith distinguishes faith and belief by embracing the former for the latter. Faith refers to an individual's total

---

6 "Interfaith Cooperation," Interfaith Youth Core (website), n.d.

7 Wilfred Cantwell Smith, *Faith and Belief* (Oxford: Oneworld, 1998), 12; also quoted in James L. Fredericks, *Faith among Faiths* (New York: Paulist, 1999), 81–82.

8 Smith, *Faith and Belief*, 12; also quoted in Fredericks, *Faith among Faiths*, 81–82.

9 Mikva, "Reflections in the Waves," 469–70.

10 Tomoko Masuzawa, "The Production of 'Religion' and the Task of the Scholar," *Culture and Religion* 1, no. 1 (2000): 125; cited in Russel T. McCutcheon, "Religion, Ire, and Dangerous Things," *Journal of the American Academy of Religion* 72, no. 1 (2004): 177.

orientation and response to the world, others, and oneself.[11] Belief, on the other hand, refers to upholding certain ideas while attempting to articulate "that reality which faith apprehends."[12] Faith and belief are often conflated in the West because "it is characteristic of Western Christianity that it has linked belief and faith 'more closely, more deliberately, more emphatically, than . . . any other group.'"[13] Smith's contention that faith functions as a "foundational category for all religious life, and, indeed, for all human life"[14] carries implications—for better and for worse—for the study of religions and interreligious relations.

Despite Smith's universal vision of faith, the term can be problematic for non-Christian and especially for non-Abrahamic traditions. Buddhist scholar Abe Masao praises Smith's effort to cast faith as "a spiritual orientation of the personality, a capacity to live at a more than mundane level, and man's relation to transcendence that appears constant throughout human history";[15] however, he cautiously inquires "whether we should take 'faith' as the foundational category."[16] Ultimately, Masao concludes, from a Buddhist perspective, the term "faith" is inadequate to "comprehend the whole process of man's history of religion" since it does not sufficiently "recognize the existence of the religion of self-awakening which is not easily commensurable with the religion of faith." Interestingly, Masao counter-proposes "Boundless Openness" (a reinterpretation and generalization of the Buddhist notion of Śūnyatā or "emptiness").[17] Smith's view of faith as the foundational category for all human life appeals to some because it seemingly opens various new horizons. By emphasizing a common ground to all human life—a religious common ground—Smith's "faith" may function as an entryway into interreligious encounter and dialogue.[18] However, the same questions

---

11 Wilfred Cantwell Smith, *Towards a World Theology* (Philadelphia: Westminster Press, 1981), 113–14.

12 R. W. L. Moberly, "Knowing God and Knowing about God," *Scottish Journal of Theology* 64, no. 4 (2012): 408.

13 Moberly, "Knowing God and Knowing about God," 408–9, internal quotations Smith, *Faith and Belief*, 12, 205.

14 Smith, *Towards a World Theology*, 125.

15 Abe Masao, "Faith and Self-Awakening," *The Eastern Buddhist* 31, no. 1 (1998): 14.

16 Masao, "Faith and Self-Awakening," 14.

17 Masao, 24.

18 Kenneth Cracknell argues, "the reason dialogue can take place at all lies in the fact that faith is ubiquitous." Kenneth Cracknell, "'We Talking about Us': Wilfred Cantwell Smith's Relevance to Theology without Walls," *Journal of Ecumenical Studies* 51, no. 4 (2016): 519.

and concerns may also be raised for Masao's proposal of Boundless Openness as a foundational category in place of faith. Given the inevitable pitfall of all language, the task may be less of determining the perfect terms but more of discerning the least inadequate ones.

Regardless of one's position on Smith's view of "faith" (or another view of faith for that matter), the concern remains that using "interfaith" as an umbrella term can unfairly privilege or emphasize faith or belief at the expense of other central aspects of religion such as practice, ritual, community, relations, and so on. Other terms used in place of interfaith include *multifaith, interspiritual, interbelief, transreligious,* and *intercultural.*

Multifaith appears as often as interfaith and interreligious. Unlike interfaith and interreligious, *multifaith*—with the prefix *multi* (not *inter*)—more generally does not assume any interactions or relations between and among religious people or traditions. A multifaith center often functions as a venue where people of various traditions can gather and practice their traditions independently of one another (despite possibly being alongside one another). Airports and hospitals have multifaith (sometimes called interfaith) chapels with this purpose in mind. The US Air Force describes their architecturally stunning Cadet Chapel in Colorado Springs (USA) as "an all-faith center of worship for cadets [that] includes Protestant, Catholic, Jewish and Buddhist chapels, an All-Faiths Room, and a Falcon Circle, each with its own entrance. The Chapel is capable of holding services in all rooms at one time."[19] The Cadet Chapel allows individuals and groups to practice their traditions simultaneously and independently from one another in the same space, exemplifying the multifaith approach. The All-Faiths room may be used by traditions without a room dedicated to their tradition or perhaps used for interreligious co-mingling.[20] Those with more "theologically exclusivist views" (see chapter 12) may perceive that the term "multifaith" allows more freedom (than interfaith) for their tradition to stand on its own, apart from other traditions, while not ignoring or minimizing differences among religions. Yet others—though rarely—may interpret multifaith to refer to the practice of multiple traditions simultaneously and thus, for them, risks stripping them down to a lowest common denominator without recognizing differences.

---

19 United States Air Force, "Cadet Chapel."

20 For critical analysis of multifaith spaces, see Ryszard Bobrowicz, "Keeping Religion in the Closet," doctoral diss., Lund University, Sweden, 2022.

Interspiritual and *interbelief* may be used to emphasize either experience (spirituality) or belief. In Minnesota, there is a community dialogue group named Inter-Belief Conversation Café, which focuses on "questions of beliefs as they affect our world." It seems this group makes the deliberate decision to emphasize beliefs (over practice and experience) as underscored in their name. Maybe they want to avoid the problems of the term "faith" and hence use interbelief over interfaith. However, focusing on belief, they similarly risk implicitly privileging traditions for which beliefs play a prominent role (e.g., American Protestant traditions). Centering *interspiritual* dialogue runs the same risk (opportunity?) by featuring spiritual experience over belief and thus privileging traditions for which spirituality plays a prominent role. Although interspiritual conversation may appeal more to the spiritual-but-not-religious crowd, it may be less attractive to skeptics of spirituality in general or perceived as confused by those who rhetorically ask, "How can one be spiritual without religion?"[21] Needless to say, all language is imperfect. Interspiritual and interbelief are nonetheless useful for *more clearly distinguishing between* cognitive belief and lived experience. Furthermore, they help make the case—should one be so inclined—for reserving the broader terms of "interfaith" and "interreligious" as umbrella terms under which various emphases can be made, such as spirituality, belief, practice, community, ideology,[22] and so on.

Transreligious, with the prefix *trans-*, emphasizes the fluid and unstable nature of religions as incessantly evolving, dynamic, and (re) negotiated within, beyond, and between individuals and communities. *Trans-* connotes an element of novel (newness), a going beyond, a surpassing, a *trans*cendence. By destabilizing the oft-perceived fixed boundaries between religious traditions, transreligious approaches recognize the unfixed porous borders of religions that spill over into one another. Furthermore, a transreligious approach complicates the internal and intersectional religious

---

21 For context on the label "Spiritual but not Religious," see King and Hedges, "What Is Religion?" 22–24.

22 Leonard Swidler's well-known "Dialogue Decalogue" references *interideological* dialogue, which makes space for nonreligious worldviews such as Marxism, atheism, and secular humanism. Using interideological in tandem with interreligious, Swidler broadens the dialogue circle to include worldviews and lifeways of ultimacy beyond those of traditional major religions or those with a central tenet of transcendence or the sacred. Swidler, "Dialogue Principles," italics original.

identities that make up individual persons.[23] Religions are "collections of ideas, practices, values, and stories that are all embedded in cultures and not isolated from them."[24] The encounters and relations that take place between and among individuals and communities who orient around religion are more complicated than rigid encounters of different religious practices, ideas, and beliefs. Since religions are embedded in cultures, interreligious encounters are inherently intercultural and intracultural as well. There is a growing trend, albeit small, in the contemporary academic study of religion to move beyond the language of "religion" and "religious" studies toward world-view studies. This trend is less evident in the Interfaith Movement among community-building organizers and activists and among the various state and governmental affairs programs. However, there is a growing tendency to adopt language that recognizes secular (nonreligious) worldviews and life-ways. Hence, the well-worn words of interfaith, interreligious, and religious diversity are increasingly complemented with religious, spiritual and secular (RSS) identities. The terms "interfaith" and "interreligious" remain dominant in the field; however, several others are beginning to be used more frequently. Among those are worldview and lifeway.

(INTER)WORLDVIEW AND (INTER)LIFEWAY

To assuage the justified criticism leveled against the Western construction and imposition of the term "religion," some scholars of religion opt for the term "worldview," while others use "lifeway" or "way of life." Sometimes, they are used together—"worldviews and lifeways"—or with the term "religion": "religions, worldviews, and lifeways." This section explores the rationale for using worldview and lifeway, and their implications for IRS and IFE.

---

23 Anne Hege Grung raises "questions of representation: How are the participants in the dialogues regarded as representatives, and who decides the accepted param-eters of religious representation? Do participants represent official versions of their traditions on behalf of a larger group, are they representing themselves as an individual believer, or a combination of the two? Lastly, a 'trans-religious' perspective asks about how human differences other than religious diversity are marked and signified in the dialogues." Grung, "Interreligious or Transreligious," in *Interreligious Studies*, ed. Gustafson, 58–65.

24 AAR Religions in Schools Task Force and Moore, "Guidelines for Teaching about Religion in K–12 Public Schools in the United States" (American Academy of Religion, 2010), 14.

André Droogers and Ann Taves, among others, advocate for the contemporary move to "worldview" language over "religion." They contend that religion is "a sub-category of the term worldview, by which we mean that religion needs to be viewed as part of a larger field in which people struggle for and with meaning."[25] In fact, Droogers describes "worldview as a category that is derived from an even wider concept: culture."[26] "Religion," "secular," "ideology," and "spirituality" (none of which are mutually exclusive nor independent in the makeup of an individual's identity) function as subcategories of religion. Thus, worldviews (religious, spiritual, or secular) emerge as important components of an individual's cultural markers and personal inventories. Comparable to culture, worldview refers to both a human capacity and the result of exercising that competence humans hold to make meaning of the world.[27] Worldviews, as attempts at meaning-making, are nourished by experience, reason, behavior, and emotion.[28]

Critics of the move to "worldview" argue the term privileges the cognitive apprehension of reality over affective, practical, material, and psychomotor responses to and in the world. Droogers recognizes that "'worldview' has not only a visual/sensory connotation, as in a view or observation, but also a cerebral, cognitive bias, with an emphasis on ideas, beliefs and reflection (another visual term)."[29] As a visual term, "worldview" has a tendency to conjure up physical images or scenery (e.g., scenic outlook or viewpoint) in an individual's mind. Philosopher of religion J. R. Hustwit observes that "Thinkers who describe religions as worldviews are sometimes accused of a cognitivist bias, reducing religions to nothing more than propositional beliefs.

---

25 Droogers, "Introduction," in *Methods for the Study of Religious Change*, ed. Droogers and van Harskamp, 2.

26 Droogers, "The World of Worldviews," in *Methods for the Study of Religious Change*, ed. Droogers and van Harskamp, 18.

27 Droogers, "The World of Worldviews," 21–22.

28 Ellen Hijmans and Adri Smaling propose the following basic and ultimate questions humans ask about themselves and their world, and therefore contribute to their worldview: (1) What is considered beautiful (aesthetics)?; (2) What is morally good behavior (ethics)?; (3) Why do humans live and die (ontology)?; (4) What can we know to be true (epistemology)?; and (5) How do we as individuals and communities distinguish ourselves from others as authentic human beings (identity)? Ellen Hijmans and Adri Smaling, "Over de relatie tussen kwalitatief onderzoek en levensbeschouwing," in *Kwalitatief onderzoek en levensbeschouwing*, ed. Adrei Smaling and Ellen Hijmans (Amsterdam: Boom, 1997), 17; also cited in Droogers, "The World of Worldviews," 22.

29 Droogers, "The World of Worldviews," 30.

But a worldview shapes more than just truth claims. Worldview precedes ratiocination. So while it is necessary to explain what religious people think, worldviews also shape what religious people value, what they do, and how they feel."[30] As a cerebral term with cognitive bias, "worldview" can privilege the realm of the individual's mind, beliefs, and intellectual assent to truth. Taves, Asprem, and Ihm, in their study on worldviews, acknowledge this bias. They argue "'worldview' and 'worldview dynamics' are appropriately discussed at the level of persons, groups, and human interactions and that sense making is an inherently multi-level *cognitive process* that provides a framework for understanding the mechanisms we rely on to generate worldviews."[31] Therefore, they define a worldview as a cognitive process of questioning and revising information relevant to the following domains ("BQs" or "big questions") that "define and govern a way of life":

1. ontology (what exists, what is real?),
2. epistemology (how do we know what is true?),
3. axiology (what is the good that we should strive for?),
4. praxeology (what actions should we take?), and
5. cosmology (where do we come from and where are we going?).[32]

Taves and colleagues situate and distinguish worldview in relation to "way of life" and "world-making" in that worldviews characterize the human capacity to create "transcendental social worlds, that is, worlds that go beyond face-to-face transactions."[33] All humans have a way of life, even if some or most

---

30 Hustwit, "Empty Selves and Multiple Belonging," 109n.

31 Ann Taves, Egil Asprem, and Elliot Ihm, "Psychology, Meaning Making and the Study of Worldviews," *Psychology of Religion and Spirituality* 10, no. 3 (2018): 208, italics original.

32 Taves et al., "Psychology, Meaning Making and the Study of Worldviews," 208.

33 Taves et al., 208. The authors acknowledge that their definition of worldview may be limited to humans. However, they also recognize that other nonhuman organisms respond to the world in ways that exhibit "world-and-self modeling capacities [that] enact implicit answers to some of the BQs." They define a "way of life" as that which "designates the organisms' habitual patterns or interaction with affordances in its world," and as such may correspond to implicit approaches (answers) to the big questions. However, even though an organism may be capable of enacting a way of life (or lifeway)—that is, despite living in a manner that corresponds to implicit answers to the big questions—not all are capable of a worldview. Taves and colleagues "contend that all beings capable of leveraging natural affordances have a way of life and thus generate implicit answers to at least some of the BQs, [but they] do not think that all organisms have a worldview." In other

of it is implicitly grounded in actions and beliefs they take for granted.[34] A worldview entails not only the cognitive thinking ability to ask but also the ability to propose answers to, the Big Questions in life.[35]

Limiting the category of worldview to social animals (humans), Taves and colleagues propose a threefold schema of overlapping modes of world-view expression: *enacted, articulated,* and *memorized* (textualized). *Enacted* worldviews are implicit and carried out in practice, often in response to challenges posed by one's environment. *Articulated* worldviews, expressed through language, may not always cohere with enacted worldviews (i.e., the way one *acts* is not always logically consistent with the way they *express* their worldview). *Memorized* or textualized worldviews draw on oral and textual narratives.[36] This threefold schema lends a structure for conceptualizing the ways humans manifest their worldviews. Furthermore, as Taves and colleagues intend, distinguishing between the three modes "highlights the extent to which people (and peoples) may develop world models without reflecting on the fact that they are doing so."[37] Finally, and perhaps most helpful, it suggests that the human manifestation of worldviews (enacted, articulated, and memorized) is ultimately a process of implicit and explicit sense-making or meaning-making.

The category of religion is inadequate. It fails to capture worldviews that attempt to make sense of the world but fall outside traditional religion. Such worldviews are often (and awkwardly) referred to as "nonreligious" or (less awkwardly) as "secular." These terms—nonreligious and secular—as Taves points out, "helpfully expands our focus beyond atheism or 'non-belief,' but both terms are still defined in opposition to religion." Hence, the need for "worldview," an "overarching third term that encompasses both."[38] In other words, religions have worldviews,[39] but the category of religion is not broad enough to capture

---

words, the category of lifeway (or way of life)—even if often implicit in an organism—is the "larger, more encompassing concept. Taves et al., "Psychology, Meaning Making and the Study of Worldviews," 208–9.

34 Taves, "Finding and Articulating Meaning in Secular Experience," 17.

35 Taves et al., "Psychology, Meaning Making and the Study of Worldviews," 209, italics original.

36 Taves et al., 210.

37 Taves et al., 210.

38 Taves, "Finding and Articulating Meaning in Secular Experience," 14.

39 As Taves recognizes, several influential scholars of religion, such as Ninian Smart and Mark Juergensmeyer, have proposed the study of religion as worldviews, while still

all attempts (worldviews) to make ultimate sense of the world. The category of worldview, on the other hand, "is designed to accommodate everyone."[40]

To simplify: Lifeway serves as the master umbrella category under which worldview is situated. Within worldview there are explicit and implicit religious, secular, and spiritual worldviews. Taves proposes the following series of questions under three categories for an individual to articulate, discuss, reflect on, compare, and develop their worldview in the context of everyday lived experience and meaning-making:[41]

Worldview-Sense of Meaning

- Do you have answers to the "big questions" (BQs)?
- If so, how do you answer them?
- Do you consider your answers religious, spiritual, or neither?
- If you don't think much about the BQs, how would you describe your way of life?
- What is most important to you?
- Do you have a general sense of meaning or purpose in life?
- If so, how would you describe it?
- If not, is this something that troubles you? If so, when has it been an issue?

Lived Experience

- What is it like for you to hold this worldview or more generally live life as you do?
- When, if at all, does it come to mind? Why?
- Are there times when you consciously draw upon it? If so, when?

Experiences

- What experiences have you had that stood out for you in some way? Why did they stand out?

---

others advocate replacing the study of religion with the more general study of worldviews. Taves, "Finding and Articulating Meaning in Secular Experience," 16.

40 Taves, 18.
41 Taves, 21.

- Were the experiences linked to particular situations or practices or did they arise seemingly spontaneously?
- How did you understand the experience?
- If its meaning wasn't immediately obvious, did you later figure it out? If so, how?[42]

Taves's prompts provide significant nuance and complexity to the task of an individual seeking to understand their meaning-making in the world and in a manner broad enough to encompass religious and nonreligious worldviews. In the quest for a broad category that gets beyond the limitations of religion and encompasses everyone, "worldview"

> is the most plausible option because it is already in widespread popular and scholarly use, can be defined in terms of BQs without privileging religion, and can be melded with the generic meaning systems framework, which, when grounded in an evolutionary perspective allows us to consider unconscious meaning making processes, implicit worldviews, and worldview dynamics as they are expressed in everyday life of humans under both ordinary and exceptional conditions.[43]

The question of whether an individual enacts, articulates, and memorizes their way of life through an explicit or implicit worldview is not always clear, for the distinction between a worldview and way of life is blurry, although not problematic.

Consider the well-known story, recounted by Mircea Eliade in his journals, of an American philosopher inquiring of Hirai, a Japanese Shinto priest, about Shinto theology. The philosopher remarks to the priest, "'I see temples, I attend the ceremonials, the dances, I admire the costumes and the courtesy of the priest—but I don't see any theology implied by Shintoism.' Hirai reflected a second and answered: 'We have no theology. We dance.'"[44] Hirai's dancing may be interpreted simply as an unreflexive way of life, or, alternatively, the dancing may reflect an implicit enacted worldview that addresses BQs such that which is real (ontology), true (epistemology), good (axiology, ethics),

---

42 Taves, 21.
43 Ann Taves, "What Is Nonreligion?" *Secularism and Nonreligion* 7, no. 9 (2018): 4.
44 Mircea Eliade, *No Souvenirs* (New York: Harper & Row, 1977), 31; also cited in Gustafson, *Finding All Things in God*, 4.

to which actions ought to aim (praxeology), and how to be oriented in the world (cosmology). The priest's rejection of theology implicit in the dancing is, perhaps, the point. The priest's rejection of theology (a cognitive activity), together with the pure and powerful act of dancing (an embodied practice), profoundly enacts and articulates a worldview unto itself. This may be similar to the well-known Zen story or *kōan* that depicts a disciple asking the master, "What is enlightenment?" to which the master responds, "Before enlightenment, chop wood, carry water. After enlightenment, chop wood, carry water." The worldview is expressed in the very negation of the cognitive process and in the embrace of the action.

Scholar of interfaith, biblical, and Jewish studies, Russell C. D. Arnold, similar to Taves's threefold reflection exercise, proposes an even broader reflection exercise with prompts that get beyond "worldview" to "way of life." Similar to the popular "identity wheel," in which the category of religion usually appears alongside several other identity markers (e.g., culture, language, race, age, etc.), and in order to complicate religious identity in a manner that includes everyone (including secular and nonreligious identities), Arnold proposes the "Way of Life" wheel, which aims not only "to break free from the overly representational religious identity paradigm and adopt an intersectional approach" but also "to foster deep reflection and dialogue about the complex constellation of experiences that shape how we live in the world."[45] The "Way of Life" wheel includes twelve categorized spokes: "1) Beliefs about god(s), 2) Justice/Social Action, 3) Beauty/Wonder, 4) Beliefs of Human Nature, 5) Peoplehood/Ethnic Ties, 6) Holidays/Celebrations, 7) Sexuality/Gender, 8) Beliefs about Death/Afterlife, 9) Moral Values, 10) Ritual Practices, 11) Community Associations, and 12) Reflective Practices."[46] By spending "time with each category, reflecting on experiences, ideas, texts, or other sources that shape their relationship with that category,"[47] the individual is invited into a deeper process of understanding their ultimate meaning-making in the world.

Taves's move to replace religious studies with worldview studies is appropriate given the academic locus of her work. However, in nonacademic spaces—in public, civic, semipublic, and community spaces—there is likely need for the broader term of "lifeway," which assumes worldview. This language is catching

---

45 Russell C. D. Arnold, "Complicating Religious Identity," in *Interreligious Studies*, ed. Gustafson, 186.

46 Arnold, "Complicating Religious Identity," 186–87.

47 Arnold, 187.

on. The Council for Religious and Life Stance Communities (STL) in Norway combines religion and life-stance language. "Life stance," (*Livssyns*) instead of "lifeway," perhaps steers a middle way between worldview and lifeway (more accurately *life-view*), especially since "stance," like "view," connotes more deliberate or explicit adoption of certain positions, postures, and practices. The term "lifestance" may accommodate more people; however, its critics might nonetheless insist its emphasis on stance privileges the same cognitive approaches that "worldview" does.

For IRS and IFE, the language of worldviews and lifeways is slowly gaining traction as the concept of religion is increasingly contested as problematic. Several of the concerns addressed in this chapter show up in community interfaith organizations as they wrestle with the various ways to be more inclusive. Some combine terms, such as "religious, secular, and spiritual identities"[48] or "Religious and Life Stance Communities." Others use the following succinct phrase to acknowledge the complexity of religious orientation: "people who orient around religion differently."[49] Some add the prefix inter- to terms and replace -faith or -religious with -worldview or -lifeway, such as a recent major study that used "interworldview" to describe close relationships and friendships across religious and worldview differences.[50] Language is not perfect. Perhaps this is for the best. Incessant disagreement and discomfort over ill-fitting language may constructively prod interlocutors to continually reevaluate and examine its utility and appropriateness. While it seems "worldviews" and "lifeways" are on the horizon, "faith" is continually retooled for more precise uses.

---

48 Convergence on Campus, "Mission Statement."
49 Interfaith Youth Core, "Interfaith Cooperation."
50 Alyssa N. Rockenbach, Tara D. Hudson, Matthew J. Mayhew, Benjamin P. Correia-Harker, Shauna Morin, and Associates, "Friendships Matter" (Chicago: Interfaith Youth Core, 2019).

10

Encountering Religious Diversity

Chapter Outline

I. *The Sneetches and Other Stories*
II. Patel's B-Words
III. The Dignity of Difference
IV. Beyond the Bubble and Babel

As more regions of the world grow increasingly religiously diverse and secular—that is, more religious traditions are represented while simultaneously more people are disaffiliated with religion—individuals, communities, and nations face challenges and opportunities in the ways they respond. Responses—micro (personal) and macro (collective)—range from entrenching in tribalism and erecting barriers to outsiders, to building bubbles of assimilation, to building bridges of understanding and cooperation, and to everything in between. This chapter maps various responses to diversity in the context of religious difference and encounter. After a journey through the beloved Dr. Suess's *The Sneetches and Other Stories*, this chapter introduces Eboo Patel's analysis of common human responses to diversity (the B-words) and Raimon Panikkar's five stages of intercultural encounter. Then it considers Jonathan Sack's "Dignity of Difference" approach to religious diversity as a response to tribalism and universalism. Finally, in anticipation of the next chapter, it reflects on religious pluralism and the secular in interreligious encounter and transformation.

THE SNEETCHES AND OTHER STORIES

"Dr. Seuss" (Theodor Seuss Geisel),[1] in his popular four-story collection *The Sneetches and Other Stories*, illustrates common responses to, and concerns about, engaging difference. The feature story—"The Sneetches"—depicts two types of Sneetches: Star-Belly Sneetches and Plain-Belly Sneetches. The former proclaimed their superiority over the latter by shunning them and excluding them from social activities. When the opportunistic Sylvester McMonkey McBean ("the Fix-It-Up Chappie") arrives with his enterprising "Star-Off" and "Star-On" machines, the story becomes interesting. Plain-Bellies pay McBean three dollars each for a trip through the Star-On machine to have stars imprinted on their bellies. Not to be fooled, the original Star-Bellies remind the newly starred Sneetches of their original superiority and pay McBean to remove their stars. Of course, the newly tattooed Star-Bellies accordingly follow suit and pay McBean again to remove their new Stars in a continued effort to be like the snooty Sneetches who were now Plain Bellied. McBean's hustle continues in entertaining fashion as all the Sneetches spend their day going from the Star-On to the Star-Off until they run out of money. The chuckling McBean rides off with cartoonish piles of cash spilling off his vehicle. The story concludes with a lesson about how all the Sneetches became enlightened on that day by forgetting about stars and realizing there is no difference between a Star-Belly and a Plain-Belly. The Sneetches learned that day to amend their response to difference by looking past superficial differences and find common ground.

The second story—"The Zax"—introduces two Zax (fictional Dr. Suess characters) traveling through the prairie of Prax, "a North-Going Zax" and

---

1 The Art of Dr. Seuss Collection acknowledges that "while the vast majority of the works he produced are positive and inspiring, Ted Geisel also drew a handful of early images, which are disturbing. These racially stereotypical drawings were hurtful then and are still hurtful today." The *Collection* also acknowledges that "Dr. Seuss's later works show an evolution of values and beliefs. Those who knew him believe that if he were alive today he would have jumped at the chance to be a part of the country's evolving dialogue about diversity and inclusion." The Art of Dr. Seuss Collection, "Dr. Seuss' Use of Racist Images." About reckoning with potential troubling narratives and actions of a source's past—such as Geisel's disturbing early images—I am inspired by Eboo Patel's engagement with the sordid narratives and accusations of Aziz Ansari and Leon Wieseltier, about which Patel acknowledges, "Where their work is useful, we should engage with it, as I do here. And where their behavior crosses lines of decency and causes pain, we should note it, as I am doing now." Eboo Patel, *Out of Many Faiths* (Princeton, NJ: Princeton University Press, 2018), 190n5.

a "South-Going Zax," that meet face to face and stubbornly refuse to step one foot to the side to allow the other to pass. The North-Going Zax proudly brags he's prepared to stand still for fifty-nine days, while the South-Going Zax retorts he'd never budge for fifty-nine years. The stubbornness of the Zaxes to budge in the least to the west or the east paralyzes them indefinitely as the world develops around them, with bustling freeways around and over them. The story of the Zax teaches the potential futility of responding to difference by putting up barriers with obstinate inflexibility.

The third story—"Too Many Daves"—introduces Mrs. McCave, a mother of twenty-three sons, all named Dave. Needless to say, a household of twenty-three sons with the same name causes confusion. Mrs. McCave reflects on how she wished she had given them all unique names, and the story concludes, "But she didn't do it. And now it's too late." The short story of Mrs. McCave, who named all twenty-three of her sons Dave, perhaps in an effort to blur the differences and make things easier and equal, only created greater headaches and confusion.

The final story—"What Was I Scared Of?"—depicts a first-person account of a cautious character who encoutners an empty pair of green pants with nobody inside them. The character encounters the scary pants time and again in unexpected places (around the corner and almost knocking the character over) and doing unexpected activities (e.g., riding a bicycle, rowing a boat). The story climaxes when the character must run an errand "to pick a peck of Snide." In reaching inside the Snide Bush, the character frightfully feels his hand touch something, the pair of empty green pants with nobody inside them. Standing face to face with the empty pants, with fear for life, the character witnesses the pants beginning to cry and realizes they were just as scared as he. The final scene of the story shows the character consoling the pants as a newfound friend, and all it took was building a small bridge of understanding by standing face to face with the previously faceless pair of green pants with nobody inside them.

As Dr. Seuss's fables depict, everyone—young and old—can relate to encountering difference and diversity on several levels. Not only are several regions of the world becoming more religiously diverse, in both number and percentage of worldviews represented, but the number of people reporting interior religious diversity, such as multiple religious orientations, is also increasing. Although secularization has not progressed with the pace or trajectory once predicted by many sociologists of religion, secular discourse continues to grow and influence most societies. Individuals, communities, and nations can respond in several ways to the concurrent forces of pluralization and secularization. Like the Sneetches, they can tribally distance themselves from outsiders. Like the Zax, with perceived opposing views, they can stubbornly dig their heels in, lock horns, refuse to budge, and blind themselves from potential practical solutions. Like Mrs. McCave, they may impractically insist on assimilative uniformity to flatten or ignore unique differences. They can also stumble around in debilitating fear or go out of their way to avoid face-to-face encounters with others who seem different, like the mysterious pair of green pants with nobody inside them.

PATEL'S B-WORDS

In the book *Interfaith Leadership*, Eboo Patel sketches four common human responses to diversity and difference in general: *bunkers, barriers, bludgeons,* and *bridges*.[2] There is a fifth B-word response: *blurring* lines or borders between, among, and within traditions. These five responses are not mutually exclusive nor occur in progression. Developing any leadership virtue entails continual growth in deeper understanding of oneself. This includes becoming self-aware of how one responds to difference and diversity in various contexts. Knowing one's faults and strengths, among other things, although perhaps interesting, helps one to better harness their talents and skills (while avoiding and curtailing faults) for more effective future action in the pursuit of personal and social flourishing. This section introduces the five B-word responses to diversity and explains how individuals and groups manifest them in contexts of religious diversity and interreligious encounter.

Bunkers: People retreat to bunkers by sheltering themselves from the outside world. Bunkering aims for complete separation or self-isolation. Quite literally, a bunker is a fortified structure (concrete, steel) designed as protection from harmful advancing military, dangerous storms, or deadly diseases. Bunkers as such are not problematic. They are often advantageous for the wise person seeking to avoid danger. The desire to bunker can be effective for self-preservation, and it may even be embedded into the human instinct. Individuals tend to avoid situations, experiences, animals, and other people that they are afraid of or simply do not know (e.g., many instinctually leap backwards upon encountering a snake). Robert Putnam's research discovered that "people

2 Patel, *Interfaith Leadership*, 63.

living in ethnically diverse settings appear to 'hunker down'—that is, to pull in like a turtle"[3] and "the higher the diversity, the more people distrust their neighbors."[4] Not only may hunkering down be a default survival tactic for humans for self-preservation, but it can also weaken a community's fabric by sowing greater distrust. Patel explains that people in bunkers may have little or no interest in others and in engaging diversity. Bunkers can be erected out of fear, disinterest, distrust, and perhaps even contempt for those who are different. People in bunkers may or may not believe they have something to learn from those who are different than them, but the danger or fear is too great a risk to venture beyond the bunker to find out. Bunkers function as intended: they prevent people from encountering others. Raimon Panikkar suggests that intercultural encounter progresses through five stages, the first of which is *isolation and ignorance*, in which "every culture lives within its own context, and the problem of interculturality[5] does not even arise,"[6] presumably since there is no contact with, or knowledge of, the other to begin with. *Denial* is the first "way" of Milton J. Bennett's well-known Developmental Model of Intercultural Sensitivity (DMIS), a continuum framework to analyze how people experience and engage cultural difference. In this stage, a person *denies* the reality of difference to begin with. They "experience psychological and/or physical isolation from cultural difference . . . [and] are disinterested or perhaps even hostilely dismissive of"[7] communication and interaction across cultural and other forms of difference. The *bunker* response is akin to denial, isolation, separation, and ignorance.

Barriers: "People who build barriers are interested in proudly proclaiming the righteousness of their identity and loudly denouncing other identities.

---

3 Robert Putnam, *"E Pluribus Unum," Scandinavian Political Studies* 30, no. 2 (June 2007): 159; cited in Patel, *Out of Many Faiths*, 18.

4 Patel, *Out of Many Faiths*, 18.

5 Interculturality, for Panikkar, refers to actively engaging in dialogue across, between, among, and within cultures but also invites participants to investigate the depths and foundations of the various cultures. Panikkar, *Cultures and Religions in Dialogue*, 124; first appeared as "Tres grandes interpretaciones de la interculturalidad," in *Interculturality, Gender, and Education*, ed. Raul Fornet-Betancourt (Frankfurt am Main and London: Iko, 2004), 277–44.

6 Panikkar, *Cultures and Religions in Dialogue*, 165; first appeared in *Pace e Interculturalitá*, ed. Milena Carrara Pavan (Milan: Jaca Book, 2002, reprinted 2006).

7 Milton J. Bennett, "The Developmental Model of Intercultural Sensitivity," IDRInstitute (2014). For the DMIS model applied to interfaith awareness, see Deanna Ferree Womack, *Neighbors* (Louisville, KY: Westminster John Knox Press, 2020), 118–20.

They amplify differences and disagreements in a manner that is scornful of others,"[8] writes Patel. Unlike bunker builders who hunker down, barrier builders do not necessarily seal themselves off from the outside world altogether. Rather, when they do venture out into the world, they establish strategic defenses (obstacles, shields, walls) to minimize, polarize, or combat difference. The second way on Bennett's DMIS continuum is *defense*, in which difference is perceived in a polarizing tribal manner that organizes cultures into "'us and them,' where typically the 'us' is superior and the 'them' is inferior."[9] Barriers serve the same defensive function as bunkers. When people build barriers, they might simply avoid contact with others altogether out of a belief that there is little to nothing to learn or gain from them. Panikkar's second stage of intercultural encounter, *indifference and contempt*, parallels barrier building: "when contact becomes inevitable, the first reaction is to think that the *other* culture has nothing to do with us; at most it is regarded as a harmless rival."[10]

Upon seeing the spooky pair of green pants with nobody inside them in a rowboat, Dr. Suess's character retreats in fear and hides away for two nights straight. Similarly, in the Sneetches, the Star-Bellies exclude the Plain-Bellies in all of their social gatherings and keep separation from them year after year. People frequently erect barriers between themselves and others to avoid engaging difference of any kind. For instance, imagine someone avoiding their second cousin at a large family gathering to prevent an uncomfortable political haranguing or argument. To make sure this doesn't happen, he cleverly keeps a distance from his second cousin throughout the gathering by putting strategic barriers in place (e.g., running to the toilet, making a phone call, etc.). This hypothetical example of avoiding contact with the second cousin is more-or-less harmless, but one might imagine a scenario in which harm—psychological or otherwise—is not unthinkable. An individual may perceive their encounter with difference to be harmful, ugly, and evil. Patel captures such an attitude that can often motivate one to build barriers: one might think, "In a world of different paths, I am on the one that is good and right. Everyone else is walking a road that is ugly and evil."[11] Recall the two

---

8 Patel, *Interfaith Leadership*, 63.
9 Bennett, "The Developmental Model of Intercultural Sensitivity."
10 Panikkar, *Cultures and Religions in Dialogue*, 165, italics original; first appeared in *Pace e Interculturalitá*.
11 Patel, *Interfaith Leadership*, 63.

clashing Zax refusing to ever budge an inch. At times, everyone exhibits Zax-like attitudes in the face of difference. More alarming, the world holds no shortage of instances of people responding to diversity, religious or otherwise, not only like the stubbornly defensive Zax but, worse, in bludgeoning acts of violence and hate.

Bludgeons: When individuals bludgeon in the face of difference, according to Patel, they "are violently antagonistic toward people who are different. [They are willing] to use physical force to dominate those who are different. It's not 'my way or the highway'; it's my way or get beat over the head.'"[12] Of all the B-words, *bludgeoning* requires the least description and explanation, given how commonly antagonistic and violent acts occur in the world. Patel uses another B-word to drive home the bluntness of this response to difference: "bombs." It can entail using one's resources, authority, advantage, and ideology to attack others. Unlike bunker and barrier responses, which avoid contact and engagement with difference, bludgeoning responses actively seek out encounter in order to attack, sometimes in violent ways. Such a response does not perceive the other as a harmless rival unworthy of one's time, attention, or worry. Rather, as with the barrier response, the bludgeon response perceives the other as a threat against which to defend. However, unlike the barrier response, the bludgeon response goes on the offense to actively attack the perceived threat. Such a response corresponds to Panikkar's third stage of intercultural encounter of *condemnation and conquest*. In this stage, "if the relationship becomes more stable and lasting, the *other* culture begins to be seen as a threat to react against and, if possible, suppress."[13] Patel acknowledges the bludgeon response "is rare in contemporary American life. Muslim extremists like Al-Qaeda, the Islamic State, and the Taliban are the most common examples in our era of religious groups who respond to diversity with a bludgeon."[14] Yet there remains the threat and disturbing trend of religiously motivated attacks on synagogues, mosques, churches, and other visibly religious spaces, communities, and individuals.

Blurring: Minimizing, ignoring, dismissing, and indifference[15] to evident differences within, between, and among traditions can problematically erase,

---

12 Patel, 64.
13 Panikkar, *Cultures and Religions in Dialogue*, 165, italics original; first appeared in *Pace e Interculturalità*.
14 Patel, *Interfaith Leadership*, 64.
15 Interfaith Youth Core "Module 2.2. Models of Religious Diversity" (video).

conflate, and *blur* any distinctions between them. Patel also refers to this as a *blasé attitude*[16] toward difference, which can result in "simply losing identity altogether."[17] In the story of Mrs. McCave, who had twenty-three sons and named them all Dave, the author reminds the reader this wasn't a smart thing to do because when she calls one son Dave to come into the house, all twenty-three Daves scamper forth. Mrs. McCave may have good intentions, but ultimately having good intentions not only doesn't count for much but can also be harmful.[18] A response that blurs boundaries between traditions is often done with good intentions and without malice or contempt. One might do it out of mere indifference to the other, which may be a nuanced *barrier* to avoid contact with difference. More often, a blurring response is likely done out of ignorance, lack of information, or unfamiliarity. An individual may simply want to get along and considers engaging difference too great of a risk to jeopardizing that getting along. For the sake of amiable coexistence, minimization and tolerance of difference become the dominant modes of engagement. Panikkar identifies this response as the fourth stage of intercultural encounter: *coexistence and communication*, in which one realizes that "victory [over other cultures] is never total, and the cultures discover that they have to tolerate each other. The *other* culture thus becomes a challenge or an oddity,"[19] but one that can be tolerated (the limits of tolerance are discussed in the next chapter). The third way on Bennett's DMIS continuum is *minimization*, in which individuals reduce the need for barriers or defense by "stressing cross-cultural similarity." Although this often results in people being "much more tolerant of superficial cultural diversity, . . . [it] obscures deep cultural differences."[20]

Everyone has gaps in their knowledge. Most everyone tends to oversimplify and conflate things they know little about or that appear similar. Consider the

---

16 A *blasé attitude* can also describe an attitude of ignorance and indifference sometimes present in the *bunker* and *barrier* responses.

17 Eboo Patel, "Building Religious Pluralism," *Religion and Foreign Policy Conference Calls* (podcast interview); also cited in Meghan A. Weiss, "Interfaith Youth Core," BA honors thesis (College of Saint Benedict and Saint John's University, Minnesota, 2016), 11.

18 E.g., the proverb "the road to hell is paved with good intentions" (origin uncertain); Ivan Illich, "To Hell with Good Intentions," Conference on InterAmerican Student Projects (CIASP), Cuernavaca, Mexico, April 20, 1968.

19 Panikkar, *Cultures and Religions in Dialogue*, 165, italics original; first appeared in *Pace e Interculturalitá*.

20 Bennett, "The Developmental Model of Intercultural Sensitivity."

common responses from an individual meeting someone's sibling or children for the first time, "you look so much like your brother" or "your children look so much alike." There is often general similarity, but those most closely related—siblings and parents—perceive stark differences because they are so well acquainted with them. Alexis de Tocqueville, in *Democracy in America*, famously observed:

Men will never establish any equality with which they will be contented. . . . When inequality of condition is the common law of society, the most marked inequalities do not strike the eye; when everything is nearly on the same level, the slightest are marked enough to hurt it. Hence the desire for equality always becomes more insatiable in proportion as equality is more complete.[21]

When different levels of material well-being, power, and wealth exist in a society as the status quo, then slight differences (marks of inequalities) are less noticeable. Likewise, when everyone is almost equal or nearly equal, then even small marks of difference (inequalities) are more noticeable. The more equal a society is (the more people are drawn to the same level), the more the slight differences stand out. Contrast two people (person A and B) observing a sporting event or activity together, for instance the World Cup alpine ski-racing women's slalom event. Person A knows little about the sport, and person B knows a great deal. Person A observes racer after racer finish the course and concludes they all looked, more or less, the same. If it weren't for the leaderboard with the posted finishing times reported by the laser-guided finishing line (to hundredths of a second), person A would have no sense of what distinguishes the fastest skiers from the slower skiers. Person B observes the same race and is able to determine the fastest racers by recognizing slight differences (e.g., errors) in the athletes' performances with much less reliance on the clock. Due to knowledge and experience with the sport, person B can detect major and minor differences that go unnoticed by person A.[22]

---

21 Alexis de Tocqueville, *Democracy in America*, trans. Henry Reeve (Penn State Electronic Classics Series Publication, 2002), chapter XIII, 607; also quoted in Alastair Greig, Frank Lewis, and Kevin White, *Inequality in Australia* (Cambridge: Cambridge University Press, 2003), 9.

22 Through my early twenties, I competed in Alpine ski racing. After every race, my parents (with cursory knowledge of ski racing) always remarked, "You looked fast!"

Religions—like siblings and sports—often share family resemblances and sometimes appear more similar to each other than they really are. Upon closer inspection, stark differences between religions unmistakably surface. Overlooking these differences can often occur when the boundaries between them are blurred or dissolved, or one takes a "blasé" attitude toward them in a manner that renders their distinctive identities all but nonexistent. This sentiment is often at the root of the common refrain, "all religions are really the same deep down; they teach the same things." Stephen Prothero recognizes such observations often come with good intentions: "One purpose of the 'all religions are one' mantra is to stop this fighting and this killing [evident in cases in which religious differences move adherents to fight and to kill]. And it is comforting to pretend that the great religions make up one big, happy family. But this sentiment, however well-intentioned, is neither accurate nor ethically responsible."[23] The blurring blasé response to diversity, although often well-intentioned, can ultimately run afoul because religions are not all the same. They do not all teach the same views nor engage in the same practices. Hence the blasé attitude that ignores difference does not really listen to what the traditions are saying. In a conversation between two people, when it becomes evident that one person is not listening then the other can easily feel disrespected, ignored, and will likely look to terminate the conversation. In a similar fashion, if a conversation partner has already defined or identified the other without their input or unique voice, they will likely not only be annoyed but also be offended. Not listening to and not recognizing the diversity between and within religions can be dangerous since it can gloss over, ignore, or disregard very disturbing movements and histories within them (e.g., Christians ignoring the roots of Nazi theology[24]). Listening to, and

---

Viewing the same performance, my coaches (with rigorous knowledge of ski racing) rarely shared my parents' view.

23 Prothero, God Is Not One, 3.

24 Stephen Prothero recounts, "When I was a professor at Georgia State University in Atlanta, I required my students to read Nazi theology. I wanted them to understand how some Christians bent the words of the Bible into weapons aimed at Jews and how these weapons found their mark at Auschwitz and Dachau. My Christian students responded to these disturbing readings with one disturbing voice: the Nazis were not real Christians, they informed me, since real Christians would never kill Jews in crematories. I found this response terrifying, and I still do, since failing to grasp how Nazism was fueled by ancient Christian hatred of Jews as 'Christ killers' allows Christians to absolve themselves of any responsibility for reckoning with how their religion contributed to these horrors. After 9/11 many Muslims absolved themselves too." God Is Not One, 10.

differentiating, traditions helps to draw lines between and within them, to the degree that such a thing is possible (given religions' dynamic, syncretic, and ever-changing nature). Panikkar advises that interreligious encounter and "interculturality demand this attitude; it seeks for harmony and agreement without reducing everything to a common denominator. . . . A common denominator does not exist. . . . The way to encounter the other is to listen to him, and the way to listen to him without misunderstanding is to love him, and the way to love him is to be free of my egoistic pride."[25]

Bridges: Effort to listen, accept, accommodate, adapt, welcome, and integrate difference into one own's purview and practice is a step toward bridgebuilding. These efforts range from bringing religiously diverse people and communities together in pursuit of a common cause or issue, to simply sharing in life's joys and sufferings in friendship, and to reflecting on one's own religious roots, upbringing, or tradition for resources to foster connection across difference. The final three ways on Bennett's DMIS continuum are *acceptance, adaptation,* and *integration.*

Acceptance of cultural difference indicates an experience in which one's own culture is experienced as just one of a number of equally complex worldviews. Acceptance does not mean agreement. . . . People at Acceptance are curious and respectful toward cultural difference.

Adaptation involves intercultural empathy, or experiencing the world to some extent "as if" one were participating in the different culture.

Integration of cultural difference indicates an experience of self that is expanded to include the movement in and out of different cultural worldviews. . . . [It] can be used to construct cultural bridges.[26]

All three can be understood as developmental degrees toward constructive bridgebuilding because they indicate a recognition of multiple ways of living, increased comfort with difference, and an ability to adapt behavior to diverse

25 Panikkar, *Cultures and Religions in Dialogue,* 143; first appeared in "Hacia una teología de la liberación," talk presented at the Fourth Parliament of World's Religions (Barcelona, Spain: 2005), in *Interculturalidad, diálogo y liberación,* ed. H. Küng, J. J. Tamayo-Acosta, and R. Fornet-Betancourt (Pamplona: Verbo Divino, 2005), 61–68.
26 Bennett, "The Developmental Model of Intercultural Sensitivity."

settings. Scholar of religion and interfaith studies Deanna Ferree Womack suggests these final three responses reflect not only an intercultural mindset but an interreligious one as well.[27] Caution and care are advised here, especially with integration. Womack recognizes that at the level of integration, in which one may see themselves as religiously hybrid and taking on practices from other traditions, "any effort to acquire an interreligious identity might look more like cultural appropriation."[28] In certain contexts, especially with important religious practices, there are ethical questions about practitioners integrating and participating in practices without being sincere and observant members of the traditions from which those practices come. Consider, for example, non-Catholics celebrating the Eucharist,[29] non-Jews hosting a Jewish Seder,[30] or non-Native Americans participating in the contemporary Lakota Sun Dance.[31] Many would deem such religious appropriation inappropriate and offensive. Hence, Womack and others are keen to point out that since full integration arises through life circumstances (e.g., interfaith marriage, multiple religious orientation) "through years of immersion, few"[32] reach this stage. Therefore, integration may not be an appropriate goal for everyone in their quests to develop an interreligious mindset. Regardless of whether one reaches the stage of full integration, it is worth recognizing the dynamic interplay and bridgebuilding potential in the relationship between (A) *religious diversity of traditions* (including internal religious diversity) and (B) *intrasubjective religious diversity* (the "diversity found within the mental cosmos of individual persons"[33]). Encounter with A can often prompt exploration of B, and, vice versa, exploration of B can motivate engagement with A.[34]

Following the confrontation stage, Panikkar's fifth and final stage of interreligious encounter maintains the spirit of bridgebuilding: *convergence and dialogue*. It entails the "discovery of a possible mutual influence" between

27 Womack, *Neighbors*, 119.

28 Womack, 24.

29 Jeffrey Vanderwilt, "Eucharistic Sharing," *Theological Studies* 63 (2002): 826–39.

30 Rich Barlow, "Are Non-Jews Who Host a Seder Sharing Jewish Culture or Hijacking It?" WBUR, April 19, 2019.

31 Ronan Hallowell, "Dancing Together," *IK: Other Ways of Knowing* 3, no. 1 (2017): 30–52.

32 Womack, *Neighbors*, 124.

33 Schmidt-Leukel, *Religious Pluralism and Interreligious Theology*, 227.

34 Hans Gustafson, "Gateways to Engagement with Religious Diversity," State of Formation, May 7, 2018.

and among cultures. "The *other* culture starts to become the other pole of our own and, perhaps its enrichment."[35] At the public civil level, convergence and dialogue, as Panikkar describes it, manifests as civic *pluralism*, a focus of the next chapter. For the present chapter it is sufficient to note an enduring characteristic of civic pluralism is that it entails not just tolerance of, but active engagement with, religious diversity in mutually enriching ways that recognize religious difference without denigrating human dignity.

THE DIGNITY OF DIFFERENCE

Tribalism (bunkers, barriers, bludgeons) and universalism (blurring, assimilation) represent two of the most common societal approaches to diversity at the macro level in the contemporary world. Tribalism refers to when societies revert to severe ingroup loyalty and tribalistic tendencies to circle the wagons, keep to their clan, stick with their own gods, "hunker down," turtle-up, and mitigate threats by staying on their own side of the river. Should they ever encounter the other, battle is waged, whether it be on the battlefield of blood or ideas. Tribalism entails a full-on fearful retreat to *bunkers* to erect *barriers* and ward off *bludgeonous* threats. Universalism refers to assimilating all peoples and cultures (all tribes) into one single way of life, whether it be a global economic or political system or a cultural worldview and way of life. Universalism embraces *blurring* the lines between difference toward common integration through assimilation. Both tribalism and universalism fall short of respecting the dignity of religious difference and advancing the common public good of respectful human flourishing.

Although religious diversity can be a liability to civilization and is often blamed for many of the societal and geopolitical chasms and conflicts that plague the world, religious diversity can also be an asset for bridging them. Rabbi Jonathan Sacks, former Chief Rabbi of the United Kingdom and Commonwealth, calls for a new religious paradigm that facilities (bridges) positive and socially cohesive ways of living with religious difference. In short, to get beyond tribalism or universalism (assimilation or "bubble")[36]—two

---

35 Panikkar, *Cultures and Religions in Dialogue*, 165, italics original; first appeared in *Pace e Interculturalità*.

36 In *From Bubble to Bridge*, Marion H. Larson and Sara L. H. Shady discuss constructive ways for college communities, especially evangelical Christian college communities

tried, tired, and inadequate responses to diversity—Sacks proposes a third option: the "dignity of difference," which argues that finding common values among faiths is not enough. Rather, religious differences must be understood, engaged, and reframed in a manner that respects and preserves them.

Since religion is an ever-present powerful shaping force in most of the world, especially in conflict zones, it ought to be included in responses that strive to bridge many of the world's conflicts.[37] Sacks's proposal responds, in part, to Samuel P. Huntington's famous theory, "the clash of civilizations," in which Huntington suggests that the source of most future conflicts in the world will be cultural,[38] which includes religion.[39] Sacks addresses two dominant theories of geopolitical conflict that arose on the heels of the Cold War: Huntington's *tribalistic* model and Francis Fukuyama's *universalist* vision. On one hand, Sacks reads Huntington's theory as a prediction for "the resurgence of older and deeper loyalties, a clash of cultures, or what [Huntington]

---

in the United States, to get beyond their monoreligious "bubbles" in an effort to "bridge" their campuses with and thoughtfully engage their religiously diverse neighbors in mutually beneficial and enriching ways. Larson and Shady, *From Bubble to Bridge* (Downers Grove, IL: IVP Academic, 2017).

37 Jonathan Sacks, "The Dignity of Difference," *The Review of Faith & International Affairs* 7, no. 2 (2009): 37.

38 Samuel P. Huntington, "The Clash of Civilizations?" *Foreign Affairs* (Summer 1993): 22.

39 TV journalist and political scientist Fareed Zakaria completed his PhD and doctoral dissertation under Huntington at Harvard University. Zakaria also served as managing editor of *Foreign Affairs* when it published Huntington's famous article on the Clash of Civilizations in 1992. Zakaria praises Huntington's core insight that in the post–Cold War world human beings and nation-states no longer identified primarily along ideological lines, but rather rediscovered their identities based on what Huntington calls "civilizations," and religion is at the heart of civilizations. According to Zakaria, Huntington correctly understood that, contrary to much of the social science at the time, religion was not going away. However, Zakaria believes Huntington went wrong when he became "too enamored with this idea [of] civilizations and the idea that they cohere . . . that part of it has never really worked." This part of the so-called "Huntington thesis" is much too oversimplified, says Zakaria. Huntington was too hyperfocused on this "clash," which depicts civilizations like billiard balls knocking into each other on a billiard table. The world is much too messy and complicated for civilizations to act monolithically and clash in this manner. After all, Zakaria claims, many of the major conflicts in the world often take place *within* particular civilizations, not *between* them. In short, a tribalistic model like Huntington's "clash," argues Sacks, is not adequate nor healthy for today's globalized world. Zakaria, interview with Sam Harris, "Episode 83: The Politics of Emergency," *Making Sense Podcast*, June 23, 2017.

called civilizations—in short, a new tribalism."[40] On the other hand, Sacks recognizes the influential proposal of Fukuyama's *End of History*, published only four years before Huntington's theory. Fukuyama speculates, "What we may be witnessing is not just the end of the Cold War, or the passing of a particular period of postwar history, but the end of history as such."[41] This is the claim that human civilization has reached its final ideological endpoint. No further evolved form of human government is possible beyond the existing version of the contemporary universal Western liberal democracy of the twentieth century. Sacks reads Fukuyama's proposal as a prediction for "an eventual, gradual spread first of global capitalism, then of liberal democracy, with the result being a new universalism, a single culture that would embrace the world."[42] In other words, a push in the direction of *blurring* the lines between difference toward common assimilation. Whereas tribalism perhaps epitomizes an ancient response to threats from outsiders and difference, universalism, Sacks explains, epitomizes the dominant response of Western Civilization for the last 2500 years (i.e., since Plato); however, like tribalism, universalism is also inadequate for the human condition. Sacks argues that universalism

is a dangerous idea, because it suggests that all differences lead to tribalism and then to war, and that the best alternative therefore is to eliminate differences and impose on the world a single, universal truth. If this is true, then when you and I disagree, if I am right, you are wrong. If I care about truth, I must convert you from your error. If I can't convert you, maybe I can conquer you. And if I can't conquer you, then maybe I have to kill you, in the name of that truth. From this flows the blood of human sacrifice through the ages.[43]

The events of September 11, 2001, argues Sacks, resulted in two civilizations with universalist worldviews clashing—"global capitalism" versus "medieval Islam"—when four large commercial airliners were hijacked by Islamist fundamentalists. Three of them were intentionally crashed into New York City's World Trade Center and the Pentagon in Washington, DC, symbolic

40 Sacks, "The Dignity of Difference," 41.
41 Francis Fukuyama, "The End of History," *The National Interest* (Summer 1989): 1.
42 Sacks, "The Dignity of Difference," 41.
43 Sacks, 38.

buildings in the United States representing global capitalism. The fourth plane, evidence suggests, was intended to be flown into the United States Capitol building but crashed in Pennsylvania.

The world is messy. Efforts to segregate (barriers, bunkers) or assimilate (blurring difference) can ultimately lead to, Sacks believes, death and violence (bludgeons). Sacks thusly asks, "Is there an alternative, not only to tribalism, which we all know is a danger, but also to universalism?"[44] Both tribalism and universalism perceive religious diversity as a problem. Sacks observes, "Societies that have lived with this difference for a long time have learned to cope with it, but for societies for whom this is new, it presents great difficulty."[45] However, religious diversity is not problematic if society has constructive and innovative ways to acknowledge, engage with, and accommodate it in respectful ways that do not dimmish, assimilate, or impose it. Hence, Sacks's proposal calls for embracing the "dignity of difference," an approach that perceives religious diversity as an asset to be leveraged.

Sacks presents his argument with a story from the Hebrew Bible about Abraham and Sarah. Their grandson Jacob (who later becomes Israel) has twelve sons, and each of their families become the twelve tribes of Israel. Despite being twelve tribes, they all belong to one family, one nation. The book of Genesis opens with two universal statements: all of humankind are created in the image of the divine (Gen 1), and God's covenant with Noah (Gen 9) instructs "all humanity to construct societies based on the rule of law, the sovereignty of justice and the non-negotiable dignity of human life."[46] There is a paradox here. Although Genesis's first eleven chapters speak of one *universal* family with one language, it quickly shifts to the *particular* in chapter 12's narrative of God's call to Abraham and Sarah to set themselves apart and to be different. Genesis 11 presents the famous Tower of Babel, the colorful narrative that depicts the introduction, and resulting confusion, of different languages to humankind. Sacks argues that in the Bible one need not "be Jewish" (chosen by God) to be a man or woman of God. Several

---

44 Sacks, 38.

45 Sacks, 37.

46 Sacks, 39. Sacks reckons these two clauses inspired Thomas Jefferson's famous line in the United States Declaration of Independence, "We hold these truths to be self-evident, that all men are created equal, that they are endowed by their Creator with certain unalienable Rights, . . ." However, Sacks argues, these truths are far from self-evident since there are clearly many groups and individuals in the history of the world who do not believe all people are equal.

biblical exemplars demonstrate divine blessing despite not being devoted to the biblical God. "The paradox is that the God of Abraham is the God of all mankind, but the faith of Abraham is not the faith of all mankind,"[47] since there are others who have different "faiths" (religions, worldviews, etc.) yet are still blessed by God. Sacks reads the story about the collapse of the Tower of Babel as God's rejection of a universal global project for humanity to be the same. Instead, Sacks interprets God to be saying "'Be different.' In fact, the word 'holy' in the Hebrew Bible, *kadosh*, actually means 'different, distinctive, set apart.' Why did God tell Abraham and Sarah to be different? To teach all of us the dignity of difference. That God is to be found in someone who is different from us."[48] Sacks's point is that his tradition, articulated in the Hebrew Bible, shifts the paradigm from tribalism and universalism toward the dignity of difference, which interprets God shouting "Be different! Being different is good, it is holy, it is dignified. People learn in the face of difference. God can be found in the face of difference, and God can be found in other people who are different from you."

For Sacks's readers who remain unconvinced by this Bible lesson, he offers two nonreligious arguments: one from natural science and one from economics. Natural science teaches about the complexity of the world, but it also discovered that the basic building blocks of life rely on the same genetic code. Out of this one basic code there are thousands of bird species (not just one Platonic idea or "form" of a bird), thousands of tree species (not just one Platonic idea or "form" of a tree), and so on. Sacks's point is that diversity comes out of unity. Basic economics relies on the diversity of skills, gifts, and resources of participants in the economy to keep the gears of commerce and trade grinding along. What one lacks in skill or resource can be made up for by others who possess it. In other words, in Sacks's view, by having a diversity of skills, gifts, and resources, everyone gains. One market produces diversity. Sacks relies on economist David Ricardo's Law of Comparative Advantage, which teaches "every one of us has something unique to contribute, and by contributing we benefit not only ourselves but other people as well."[49] A third simple example could be that a successful team (sports, business, etc.) has individuals with unique skills suited to their specific role, thus representing a great diversity and difference of overall skills. Just as a global market

---

47 Sacks, 39.
48 Sacks, 39, emphasis added.
49 Sacks, 40.

consisting of only seven billion shipbuilders is doomed to fail, so too would an American football team fail if it consisted of only eleven quarterbacks, or a soccer team fail if it consisted of only eleven goalkeepers.

Sacks's proposal for dignifying difference entails not the clashing of civilizations, which would ensure war, destruction, and destabilization for most if not all involved, especially over time. Rather, Sacks intimates, when civilizations meet, difference becomes an asset, with mutual trade, exchange, and benefit. Difference is a mutual benefit. Religious communities need not be threatened by other traditions, just as siblings need not worry about their brothers and sisters detracting from the affection their parents show them. Despite their children's differences, the parents love all of their children. Sacks concludes, "Those who are confident of their faith are not threatened but enlarged by the different faiths of others. In the midst of our multiple insecurities, we need now the confidence to recognize the irreducible, glorious dignity of difference."[50] Side-stepping tribalism and universalism (e.g., bunkers, barriers, bubbles, bombs, bludgeons, and blurring), Sacks's Dignity of Difference approach represents a bridge-building response to religious diversity. As the next chapter discusses, it embraces civic religious pluralism (energetic engagement with religious difference) and informs what Laurie Patton refers to as "pragmatic pluralism"[51] (the idea that tolerance of difference is not enough, but difference as such is a necessary good).

BEYOND THE BUBBLE AND BABEL

Religious pluralism (see chapter 11) is the reality of increased religious diversity and the increased interaction and engagement between and among individuals and groups with various religious identities. Instead of dealing with difference through inclusivism and incorporation—by absorbing newness into the fold via watering down difference and assimilation to the dominant culture—civic religious pluralism as an ideal strives for the creation of something altogether new in the process of welcoming newcomers into the fold. Sociologist of religion David Machacek reflects on two "classical approaches to understanding religious pluralism . . . the assimilation model of a cultural melting pot and the functionalist model of social

---

50 Sacks, 41–42.
51 Laurie Patton, "Plural American Needs Myths," in Patel, *Out of Many Faiths*, 156.

disorder—bubble or Babel."[52] Deeming both inadequate for understanding religious pluralism, because the reality in the United States is not necessarily one of assimilation (bubble) or disorder (Babel), Machacek claims, "The new religious immigrants are not steadily assimilating into the American way of life, but are rather actively engaged in a process of transforming it . . . [into] a culture that celebrates pluralism and a social system that is increasingly able to accommodate it."[53]

Panikkar offers three relevant principles of intercultural encounter:

1. Cultures and religions interact with each other the moment they become aware of their mutual existence. Once this moment arrives, they cannot remain mutually indifferent in *bona fide* isolation.
2. The rules of the encounter are given and found in the encounter itself. They cannot be fixed *a priori* by any of the single parties to the exclusion of the other.
3. The encounter modifies both parties. It cannot remain at the level of mere tolerance and uninfluenced coexistence. Belligerent or peaceful intercourse is their status. In both cases there is interaction.[54]

Principle (1) advocates for the impossibility of parties remaining in their bunkers or tribes, while principle (2) suggests that in order for genuine and sustainable engagement to ensue, the rules or guidelines for the encounter must be generated from within the parties themselves. Most prescient is principle (3), the encounter itself transforms all parties involved, which corresponds to Machacek's analysis of what is "new" about new religious immigrants in the United States.

Machacek marks 1965 as a crucial pivot point in American immigration history, which, with the passing of the Immigration and Nationality Act (1965), reopened the United States' doors to immigrants, prior to which immigration was significantly restricted and based on quotas. Diana Eck considers 1965 as the beginning of a "new religious America"[55] or the point

---

52 David W. Machacek, "The Problem of Pluralism," *Sociology of Religion* 64, no. 2 (2003): 151.
53 Machacek, "The Problem of Pluralism," 151.
54 Panikkar, *Cultures and Religions in Dialogue*, 96–97; first published in *Religious Syncretism in Antiquity*, ed. Pearson, 47–62.
55 Eck, *A New Religious America*, 6.

at which America's religious diversity begins to increase significantly. Machacek observes, "post-1965 immigrants, unlike earlier immigrants, stepped into a society that was rejecting a culture of communitarian consensus in favor of a culture that places a positive value on diversity and dissent—that is, a culture of pluralism."[56] With the passage of the new immigration act of 1965, Machacek argues, "instead of assimilating American social practices and cultural beliefs and values, the new immigrants, often using religion as a primary resource, appear to be actively renegotiating the terms of American social and cultural life."[57] Although the pressure to learn American English still weighs on immigrants today, there may be less stigma attached to publicly retaining one's native language and culture.

In place of the awkward and inconvenient task of assimilating one's cultural and religious practice into a dominant American framework, largely shaped by Western Protestant Christianity and American civil religion,[58] the claim—by Machacek and others—is that immigrants are more welcome to retain, maintain, and innovate their religious traditions in the context of the new religious America. Machacek concludes, "this, perhaps more than

---

56 Machacek, "The Problem of Pluralism," 148. My great grandfather was a pre-1965 immigrant who emigrated from Sweden to Minnesota in 1903. His children, which includes my grandfather, were forbidden to speak Swedish in the home or elsewhere. My family lore teaches that the decision to disallow the children to learn and speak their parents' native tongue was informed by the practical benefit of speaking the dominant language (English) of their new homeland. In all likelihood, the decision was probably more complicated. After all, "300,000 Minnesotans spoke or at least understood Swedish, which was about 15 percent of the population." This was prior to World War I in 1917, the year my grandfather was born. Eric Dregni chronicles, "Up until this point, though, Scandinavian immigrants had little incentive to learn English, since most daily business transactions happened in their native language." Then suddenly, "Scandinavian languages became traitorous, and kids were beat up for not speaking English. . . . True patriots abandoned their parents' language and Scandinavian culture to fit in and avoid suspicion. A 'hyphenated American' was not a true American." "Because Scandinavian languages are somewhat similar to German (except for Finnish), anyone caught speaking them was viewed as having 'foreign sympathies' and suspected of being a spy for Kaiser Wilhelm." Eric Dregni, *Vikings in the Attic* (Minneapolis: University of Minnesota Press, 2011), 179–80.

57 Machacek, "The Problem of Pluralism," 147.

58 The contemporary concept and theory of American Civil Religion refers to "certain common elements of religious orientation that the great majority of Americans share. These have played a crucial role in the development of American institutions and still provide a religious dimension for the whole fabric of American life, including the political sphere. This public religious dimension is expressed in a set of beliefs, symbols, and rituals." Robert N. Bellah, "Civil Religion in America," *Daedalus* 96, no. 1 (Winter 1967): 3–4.

anything else, is what is new about the 'new religious pluralism.' The new immigrants are not becoming Americans by adopting wholesale American social practices, culture, and values; they are rather becoming Americans by engaging in a process of active cultural renegotiation and institutional reform."[59] Contrary to engaging difference through assimilation and incorporation in a manner that blurs difference into one melting pot, civic religious pluralism aims at the formation of society with novel processes for welcoming newcomers. According to Eck, "pluralism is more about transformation, not incorporation."[60] Instead of incorporating newcomers into a static American civil religion informed solely by the Western Protestant Christianity of earlier immigrants from Europe, they are welcomed into the creative and innovative process of continually transforming the character and narratives of a dynamic American civil religion. Eboo Patel argues for the benefit of this model: "communities that see themselves as part of American civil religion make contributions, increase our social capital, strengthen our social cohesion, and are far less likely to develop oppositional and separatist identities."[61] By no means complete or perfect, the shift from an incorporative inclusivist vision to Eck's transformative pluralist vision as a modern ideal for civic engagement continues into the present.

Any discussion of religious diversity and pluralism in the West remains incomplete without considering the influence of secular forces (including secularity and secularization). Leaving behind the responses of bunkers, barriers, bubbles, Babel, bludgeons, and blurring, the next chapter turns to the bridgebuilding aim of civic religious pluralism, especially in secular contexts.

---

59 Machacek, "The Problem of Pluralism," 149.
60 Diana Eck, "Pluralism," *Journal of Interreligious Studies* 17, no. 17 (2015): 62.
61 Patel, *Interfaith Leadership*, 27.

11

Pluralism(s) and Secularism(s)

We don't live in a secular age; we live in a pluralist age.[1]

—Peter L. Berger

Chapter Outline

I. Secular
   a. *Secularism*
   b. *Secularization*
   c. *Secularity*
II. Pluralism(s)
   a. *Civic Pluralism*
   b. *Energetic Engagement with Diversity*
   c. *Beyond Tolerance*
   d. *Commitments*
   e. *Dialogue*

Despite Peter Berger's insight above, it may be naive to dismiss the influence, complexity, and pervasiveness of secularity (in all its manifestations) and its contribution to and impact on pluralism. The idea of a pluralist age—an era characterized by pluralism—is not entirely self-evident. "Pluralism" is a

---

1 Peter L. Berger, "The Good of Religious Pluralism," *First Things* April (2016): 40, italics original.

contested term with a few dominant definitions. Furthermore, any discussion of pluralism in the West remains incomplete without accounting for the secular.[2] Hence, this chapter heeds interreligious studies scholar Oddbjørn Leirvik's observation that "in modern pluralistic societies, debates and dialogues about religion and ethics must also include a critical conversation between religious and secular-minded citizens."[3] This chapter first addresses the enduring influence of the secular (secularism, secularization, secularity) followed by an introduction to the many modes of pluralism (especially civic pluralism with an emphasis on interfaith engagement).

SECULAR

The concept of the "secular," like pluralism, is a contested term fraught with nuance, conflation, misunderstanding, and multiple uses. The general scholarship, which includes Berger and Leirvik among others, distinguishes between three concepts: secularization (a process), secularism (a political project), and secularity (a cultural precondition or "mode of comportment to the world"[4]). The three are often conflated and used synonymously in colloquial contexts. Indeed, they share the root of "secular," which generally functions as an adjective to dissociate a noun or verb from having a "religious or spiritual basis."[5] In other words, secular is commonly used as shorthand for "nonreligious" (not "antireligious"). The term "secular" derives from the Latin *saeculum*, used by the ancient Romans to refer to the longest unit of fixed time of approximately one hundred years or a "lifetime." With the creeping influence of Christianity in late antiquity (roughly the late third to seventh centuries), *saeculum* became associated with political power to signify the present temporal era of the world (the everyday earthly here-and-now) in contrast with the Christian vision of the future eternal

---

2 Sociologist of religion José Casanova observes, "In our contemporary global secular age, what were at first divergent roads to secularization and religious pluralism are becoming ever more intertwined. More societies are becoming simultaneously more religious and more secular, though in diverse ways." Casanova, "The Karel Dobbelaere Lecture," *Social Compass* 65, no. 2 (2018): 195.

3 Leirvik, *Interreligious Studies*, 34.

4 Bradley B. Onishi, *The Sacrality of the Secular* (New York: Columbia University Press, 2018), 5.

5 *Oxford Dictionaries*, s.v. "secular," last accessed May 4, 2022.

era to come (the everlasting or heavenly hereafter).[6] The contemporary everyday use of the term "secular"—derived from *saeculum*—is associated with the nonreligious.

Secularism

Secular*ism* and secular*ity* share a close functional kinship with the root *secular*. Both can descriptively refer to a state or society distinguishing religion from nonreligion. More precisely, secularism refers to a political program or a "project to be realized"[7] that draws "a sharp distinction between religious and political powers,"[8] whereas secularity more often broadly refers to a general state or precondition of separating nonreligion from religion or remaining neutral with respect to privileging any one tradition or worldview over another. Jacques Berlinerblau teaches that political secularism "refers to legally binding actions of the secular [nonreligious] state that seek to regulate the relationship between itself and religious citizens, and between religious citizens themselves."[9] Berlinerblau alleges secularism is "the most misunderstood and mangled 'ism' in the American political lexicon. [In the American context, it refers to] a political philosophy that is predicated on a suspicion of any and all ties between government and religion."[10] It "is a guarantee of two things: freedom of religion and freedom from religion."[11] While these concepts can function descriptively, they can also function normatively and prescriptively. Secularism can refer to advancing a "societal process that makes religion less visible in public places with a corresponding decline in religious attendance."[12] One might advocate, as Leirvik does, for the benefit

---

6 Susan Bilysnkyj Dunning, "*saeculum*," in *Oxford Research Encyclopedia*, November 20, 2017.

7 Margaret Canovan, "On Being Economical with the Truth," *Political Studies* 38, no. 1 (1990): 16.

8 Leirvik, *Interreligious Studies*, 36; Oddbjørn Leirvik, "Interreligious Dialogue and Secularity," in *Secular and Sacred?* ed. Rosemaire van den Breemer, José Casanova, and Trygve Wyller (Göttingen, Germany: Vandenhoeck & Ruprecht, 2014), 263.

9 Jacques Berlinerblau, *Secularism* (London: Routledge, 2022), 5.

10 Jacques Berlinerblau, "Secularism Necessary for Religious Freedom, Professor Says," *Georgetown University News*, December 7, 2012.

11 Jacques Berlinerblau, quoted in Kimberly Winston, "Scholars Seek to Reclaim a Dirty Word," *Religion News Service*, February 22, 2013.

12 Leirvik, *Interreligious Studies*, 36.

of a secular context—with "secularity as a common language"[13]—as a precondition (constructive mediator) that opens spaces for interreligious dialogue and religious flourishing. Secularism in this sense is a political project, and secularity is its cultural precondition.

A common scholarly critique (formulated analysis) of secularism as a concept argues that it is a product of the Western religious world and more precisely of Western European Protestant Christianity.[14] Scholarship suggests secularism is best understood as "a particular iteration of Protestant Christianity... an offshoot from Christianity... something that Christianity does... another permutation of Christianity that is part of the story of Christianity"[15] (another example of Christianity's seemingly endless schismatizing or denominationalizing). This critique challenges the assumption that secularism contrasts with religion, and instead suggests that the idea of the secular grows out of a particular religious context; that religion makes secularism possible to begin with. Concurrent with this critique is the increasingly common, yet contested, view that the modern concept of religion (addressed in chapter 1) also originated with the sixteenth-century Protestant Reformation(s), "invented"[16] by Western Eurocentric Protestant sensibilities and imposed onto other cultures. Hence, the emerging debate over the (in)adequacy of the so-called World Religions paradigm, which segregates religions into neat boxes with sealed borders, and the place of secularism as a tradition within it.[17] Charles Taylor suggests that modern secularism sprouted from seeds within the Jewish and Christian traditions, which, according to Tenzan Eaghll, "implies that secularism is not some anti-religious movement in the West but is deeply *intertwined* with the rise and fall of civilization that once called itself Christendom."[18] In similar fashion, the scholarly contributors to a substantial 2014 project that examined the ambiguous relationship between the secular and the sacred in Scandinavia proposed the explanation of the situation as one of intertwinement, as seen through "a Lutheran lens, interpreting 'a hidden sacrality' in the secular,

---

13 Leirvik, 37.

14 Talal Asad, *Formations of the Secular* (Stanford, CA: Stanford University Press, 2003).

15 Donovan Schaefer, "Is Secularism a World Religion?" interviewed by Christopher R. Cotter, *The Religious Studies Project* (podcast audio), November 28, 2016.

16 E.g., Tomoko Masuzawa, *The Invention of World Religions* (Chicago: University of Chicago Press, 2007).

17 See Schaefer, "Is Secularism a World Religion?" and Tenzan Eaghll, "No, Secularism Is Not a World Religion," Religious Studies Project (website), December 16, 2016.

18 Eaghll, "No, Secularism Is Not a World Religion," italics added.

which, historically, was seen as justified, because it is through secular institutions that God's influence can be exercised."[19] Not all scholars are convinced that the secular and political secularism were born exclusively of European Protestant Christendom,[20] exported by the West throughout the world, and functioned as all-powerful hegemonic forces during the Enlightenment.[21] Others question the utility and consistency of situating secularism in simplified binaries such as "Western" and "non-Western" without considering further ethnographic investigations of the secular as a vernacular practice that more precisely describe the "ways secularisms are defined, appropriated and contested by our anthropological informants."[22]

Secularization

Secularization generally refers to a set of processes thought to be advancing in the contemporary world. Hence, the secularization thesis, as broadly articulated by José Casanova, holds three meanings: (1) the decline of religious

---

19 Rosemaire van den Breemer, José Casanova, and Trygve Wyller, "Introduction," in *Secular and Sacred?* ed. van den Breemer, Casanova, and Wyller, 10. Some visions of nonsecular secularities acknowledge the limits of human reason and human ability to fully understand and master the world. In *The Sacrality of the Secular*, Bradley Onishi asks whether it is possible to hold an "enchanted secularity" or "does secularity lead to disenchantment?" Onishi, *The Sacrality of the Secular*, 1. The term "(dis)enchantment" is used here in the spirit of Max Weber's characterization of the modern secular Western world as "disenchanted," in which the dominant modes of understanding the world through a spiritual and religious lens are replaced with an allegedly more rational and scientific approach. Onishi considers the view of William Connolly (William Connolly, *A World of Becoming* (Durham, NC: Duke University Press, 2010)), the influential twentieth-century American political scientist and theorist, to be one of an "enchanted secularity." Onishi borrows "enchanted secularity" from Jeffrey L. Kosky's *Arts of Wonder* (Chicago: University of Chicago Press, 2017) since it acknowledges the universal human need for faith ("even on the part of the nonreligious person")—faith here referring not exclusively to the transcendent—in a world that is "ultimately unmasterable by human reason." Onishi, *The Sacrality of the Secular*, 9. According to Onishi, Connolly's nonsecularist secularity, though intriguing, is not necessarily a novel proposal, for there are antecedents in nineteenth- and twentieth-century continental European philosophy of religion (Martin Heidegger, Georges Bataille, Mark Taylor, and others).

20 Charles McCrary urges, "scholars should not assume that the secular is always coterminous with Protestantism, Westernness, and whiteness." McCrary, *Sincerely Held* (Chicago: University of Chicago Press, 2022), 11.

21 Berlinerblau, *Secularism*, 16, 149–51, 182.

22 Sindre Bangstad, "Contesting Secularism/s," *Anthropological Theory* 9, no. 2 (2009): 189.

and spiritual practice and belief, (2) the privatization of religion (i.e., religion becoming increasingly a private matter instead of a public or communal affair), and (3) an amplified differentiation between religious and nonreligious institutions.[23] In short, the secularization thesis predicts not the disappearance of religion altogether, but rather the demise of religion in public life and its increased insignificance for civic life. The thesis flourished among major European sociologists (Max Weber, Émile Durkheim, Karl Marx) in the late nineteenth and early twentieth centuries and then again in the 1970s.[24] However, since the 1970s, there has been increased skepticism regarding whether and to what extent secularization is advancing. For many, it "has clearly lost validity in the historical and social sciences."[25] For instance, Nancy Ammerman makes the case for a lived-practice-based approach to the study of religion that recognizes that "it is no longer possible to imagine some inherently premodern thing called *religion* will disappear in the face of an inherently modern thing called *secularity*."[26] Ammerman captures the growing sentiment among scholars of religion that "it is increasingly evident that religion is often present in the public and private life across societies around the world."[27] Religion remains a robust feature of contemporary global life with a presence in most public and private sectors.

Peter Berger, with the publication of his well-known *The Sacred Canopy*, famously emerged in the 1960s as a major thought leader and proponent of the secularization thesis. However, in the late 1980s he changed course and concluded, "I felt reasonably sure that the empirical evidence about religion in the contemporary world did not support secularization theory."[28] In the late 1990s, he published an edited volumed titled *The Desecularization of the World*.[29] Berger's change of mind was no small matter, for one of the leading and most well-known scholars of religion abruptly changed his mind on

---

23 José Casanova, *Public Religions in the Modern World* (Chicago: University of Chicago Press, 1994), chap. 1.

24 Linda Woodhead, "The Secularization Thesis," interview with David G. Robertson, *The Religious Studies Project* (podcast audio), April 16, 2012, 00:04:30.

25 Detlef Pollack, "Secularization," in *Oxford Bibliographies*, October 29, 2013.

26 Nancy T. Ammerman, "Rethinking Religion," *American Journal of Sociology* 126, no. 1 (July 2020): 7–8, italics original.

27 Ammerman, "Rethinking Religion," 8.

28 Peter L. Berger, "Further Thoughts on Religion and Modernity," *Society* 49, no. 4 (2012): 313.

29 Peter L. Berger, ed., *The Desecularization of the World: Resurgent Religion and World Politics* (Grand Rapids, MI: Eerdmans, 1999).

an influential thesis that he helped to establish in the first place.[30] Instead of concluding that secularization was the natural evolution and normative movement of the modern world, Berger reasoned that being intensely religious remained the norm, with the geographical exception of Western and Central Europe and the sociological exception of what he deems the "international secular intelligentsia," which refers to the small group of people with high levels of formal education and cultural-political influence.[31] Berger acknowledges that "the world today is as religious as it ever was, in places more so than ever."[32] One of his central critiques of the secularization thesis, and where it went wrong, is its universalization of the European context as the global norm. It was developed in a Eurocentric context and concluded, perhaps naively, that since the modern bloc of nations known as Western Europe was trending toward nonreligion, then all up-and-coming modern societies would follow a similar path. This has not happened, at least not yet. The United States is routinely raised as an obvious counterexample: a major modern Western nation that remains predominately religious, for now. Responding to some scholars' willingness to let the United States slide by as an exception to the rule—somehow exempt from the secularization thesis—Grace Davie argues that it is Europe, not the United States, that ought to be considered the exception. Davie contends, "The religious situation in Europe is and will remain distinctive (if not exceptional)."[33] This is not to deny the existence of the secular as a profound and influential category. Rather, the observation here of Berger, Davie, Ammerman, and others is that the idea that secularization occurs as an inevitable and natural evolutionary process arising out of modernity fell flat. Hence, Berger formulates a basic proposition: "There is indeed a secular discourse resulting from modernity, but it can coexist with religious discourses that are not secular at all,"[34] and thus a secular worldview more properly belongs alongside the several religious and spiritual worldviews in a context of pluralism. Such sentiment feeds into an aspect of Berger's later "two pluralisms" proposal, which suggests a "co-existence of different religions

---

30 Johannes Quack, "Identifying (with) the Secular," in *The Oxford Handbook of Secularism*, ed. Phil Zuckerman and John R. Shook (New York: Oxford University Press, 2017), 8.

31 Berger, "Further Thoughts on Religion and Modernity," 313.

32 Berger, "The Good of Religious Pluralism," 40.

33 Grace Davie, "Is Europe an Exceptional Case?" *The Hedgehog Review* (Spring and Summer 2006): 33.

34 Berger, "Further Thoughts on Religion and Modernity," 314, italics original.

and the co-existence of religious and secular discourses."[35] Not only might it be the case that religious discourse makes secular discourse possible in the first place, and not only can secular and religious discourses coexist alongside one another in the same society, but the two discourses may very well coexist within a single person. This group of dual-belonging religio-secular citizens is very diverse with respect to the range of views (including divergent views) on the appropriate level of political entanglement with civic legislation that support, deny, or derive from particular religious traditions. One need not search too far for cases in which a group or individual advocates for quasi-theocratic legal provisions for their home tradition while crying foul of what they perceive as creeping theocracy of the religious traditions of others.[36] In short, Berger retracts his original theory of secularization to replace it with a theory of pluralization. According to Berger, "modernity does not so much change the *what* of religious faith, but the *how*."[37] In this case, the "how" includes the incorporation of "a default secular discourse [that] co-exists with a plurality of religious discourses, both in society and in consciousness."[38] Modernity does not secularize the world, it pluralizes the world.

Secularity

Secularity functions as a common language or cultural precondition that enables or advances constructive and meaningful interreligious relations. Secular conditions can paradoxically help advance nonsecular relations by providing religiously neutral spaces and language for constructive encounter. Distinct from secularism, secularity can be nonsecularist. Drawing on Charles Taylor's third form of secularity—a sociocultural condition of modernity,[39] or the way a society's culture shapes and is shaped by the beliefs and behaviors of individuals—Leirvik proposes secularity as a common space for interreligious dialogue and mutual transformation.[40] Interreligious

---

35 Peter L. Berger, *The Many Alters of Modernity* (Boston: DeGruyter, 2014), ix.
36 See Asma Uddin, *When Islam Is Not a Religion* (New York: Pegasus Books, 2019).
37 Berger, "Further Thoughts on Religion and Modernity," 316, italics original.
38 Berger, 316.
39 Charles Taylor, *A Secular Age* (Cambridge, MA: Harvard University Press, 2007), 1–2, 15; also cited in Leirvik, *Interreligious Studies*, 36.
40 Leirvik credits theorists of interreligious dialogue for their insistence on the possibility of mutual transformation in such encounters (e.g., Anne Hege Grung, "Including

dialogue not only helps shape a common language that is secular but also contributes to the transformation of the religions involved in the process. In this manner, secularity is "a way of living together in which no religion or spiritual authority has the hegemony but must share power and influence with other movements, institutions, and lines of thought."[41] Secularity refers not to spaces, discourses, and contexts free of religion, but rather to spaces, discourses, and contexts in which no one religion dominates. For instance, this occurs when two or more different religious groups or individuals come together and use a shared nonreligious (secular) language (e.g., human rights language) to uphold shared or similar values from their separate and different religious traditions. For Leirvik, when two or more religious groups arrive at a common position on a given issue, "it will often be expressed in a common language which . . . may be termed secular."[42] By emphasizing the human values that traditions often share, and by deemphasizing their unique religious interests, "interreligious declarations often lean more on human rights-inspired language than on specifically religious resources."[43] Leirvik offers the example of a Norwegian delegation consisting of Muslims and Christians that issued a joint statement opposing Pakistan's so-called "blasphemy law," the penal code that can be used to fabricate "accusations against religious minorities (Amadiyya Muslims, Shi'ites, Christians)"[44] and lead to death sentences. The 2007 statement issued by the Norwegian Coalition of Muslims and Christians employed secular (and religious) language to oppose the blasphemy law and to support instead an individual's right to religious conversion without fear of being found guilty of blasphemy or facing a death sentence, and the coalition did so by appealing to secular human-rights-based language consistent with the teachings of their respective religious traditions. Leirvik's example demonstrates how secularity can provide welcoming space for religious groups to advocate for themselves by appealing to a common, religiously neutral (secular) human-rights-based language. Furthermore, mutual transformation can occur in such instances. Not only can interreligious dialogue contribute to the shaping of "a common

---

Gender Perspective in Muslim–Christian Dialogue in Europe and Scandinavia," in *Mission to the World*, ed. T. Engelsviken, Ernst Harbakk, Rolv Olsen, and Thor Strandenæs (Oxford: Regnum, 2008), 290; cited in Leirvik, *Interreligious Studies*, 41).

41 Leirvik, *Interreligious Studies*, 38.
42 Leirvik, 42.
43 Leirvik, 42.
44 Leirvik, 47.

language that is secular—not in the sense of non-religious, but universally understandable and commonly binding"[45]—but secularity in return can provide interreligious dialogue with a religiously neutral humanistic orientation that "certainly seems to stimulate change in the religions" themselves[46] by compelling them to reflect on the humanistic values (or lack thereof) perpetrated by various individuals, communities, and sects within their traditions. For example, in Leirvik's assessment, the 2007 "joint statement on the right to conversion illustrates interreligious dialogue's 'secular' orientation towards a common, ethical language—with shared humanity as the common horizon"[47] by compelling Norwegian Muslim leaders to thoroughly discuss Islam's resources for protecting "vulnerable minorities, the right to change one's faith, and violence in close relationships."[48] Eboo Patel sketches a similar mutual dynamic that occurs in the United States concerning how "Muslims are changing America [and] present-day America is changing the Muslim Community" through the complicated negotiations that take place within and between Muslim American communities and their interactions with contemporary American political movements (e.g., social liberal progressive vs. social conservative "traditional family values").[49] Secularity not only has the potential to sustain and foster constructive interreligious relations but can also adopt a certain degree of enchantment (e.g., nonsecular secularity) of its own. It can sustain promising dominion-free (yet religiously plural) neutral zones for communication across religious difference, which may ultimately promote religious pluralism.

PLURALISM(S)

Distinguished American scholar of religion Martin E. Marty advises that pluralism ought to be referred to in the plural—pluralisms[50]—since not only

---

45 Leirvik, 46.
46 Leirvik, 51.
47 Leirvik, *Interreligious Studies*, 50; Leirvik, "Interreligious Dialogue and Secularity," 274.
48 Leirvik, "Interreligious Dialogue and Secularity," 275.
49 Patel, *Out of Many Faiths*, 88–89.
50 Marty writes, "Pluralism as spoken of during the past half century has taken on new colorations, inspired plural uses and definitions, and provoked diverse responses among those who speak of it or hear the term." Martin E. Marty, "Pluralisms," *The Annals*

do concepts of pluralism vary among scholars, but the term "pluralism" itself, like religion, is contested. Jan-Jonathon Bock and John Fahy recognize that "speaking of 'religious pluralism' fails to capture the spectrum of approaches across different contexts and circumstances, and forecloses avenues of mutual learning from other settings in which new approaches are tried and tested."[51] With Marty, Bock, Fahy, and Ole Riis, this chapter acknowledges "the very term of 'pluralism' has several meanings, depending on the respective discourse to which it refers."[52] In the study of religion, theology, and the various approaches to religious diversity and pluralism, the two most common definitions of religious pluralism are *theological* and *civic. Theological* pluralism, addressed in the next chapter,[53] refers to a theological position about the accessibility of theological truth and the access to the ultimate end (*telos*) or ends (*teloi*). This chapter addresses *civic* pluralism and, more generally, nontheological *religious* pluralism.

Pluralism is used descriptively and normatively. As a descriptive term (e.g., *religious* pluralism), it is used almost synonymously with the term "diversity" to describe the brute factual reality of the existence of multiple religious traditions and worldviews present in a given context. "Pluralism" used as a normative term (e.g., *civic* pluralism) denotes a desirable social state to be advanced—a civic project—for which the aim is to achieve social cohesion and harmony (to the degree it is possible) among individuals and communities with various religious identities. This concept of civic religious pluralism lays claim to its value as a civic good. For instance, Patel defines pluralism as "an ethic that has three main parts: respect for different identities, relationships between diverse communities, and a commitment to the common good."[54] Patel's vision exemplifies a concept of civic religious pluralism that claims to serve the common good. Scholar of law and religion John Inazu questions whether it is realistic to expect a country or neighborhood to share a commitment to *the* common good, given the diversity of views on the meaning of

of the American Academy of Political and Social Science 612, *Religious Pluralism and Civil Society* (July 2007): 15.

51 Jan-Jonathan Bock and John Fahy, "Emergent Religious Pluralisms," in *Emergent Religious Pluralisms*, ed. Jan-Jonathan Bock and John Fahy (Cham, Switzerland: Palgrave Macmillan, 2019), 7.

52 Ole Riis, "Modes of Religious Pluralism under Conditions of Globalisation," *International Journal on Multicultural Societies* 1, no. 1 (1999): 21.

53 See section "Theology of Religions" in chapter 12.

54 Patel, *Out of Many Faiths*, 20.

life, what it means to be human, definition of equality, the role of happiness, and others.[55] In other words, in communities with diverse worldviews and lifeways, challenges may arise when multiple, sometimes competing, visions of the common good exist. In this case, it may be more appropriate to speak of common *goods* in the plural. This does not mean that social cohesion within diverse communities is unrealistic. Inazu remains optimistic and hopeful that even *without a common good* "we can find common ground even when we don't agree on a common good . . . [since unity] does not require that we agree on all the reasons for our agreement."[56] With Charles Taylor, Inazu argues, "We would agree on the norms while disagreeing on why they were the right norms, and we would be content to live in this consensus."[57] It is not uncommon for religious and cultural traditions to embrace parallel ethical norms for various issues, but for different reasons and out of different worldviews.

No single definition of pluralism reigns supreme or enjoys a normative position. As with "religion" and "secular," the term "pluralism" is contested. However, this does not mean it is meaningless or useless. As with religion and secularism, pluralism is used increasingly often to convey particular ideas. Several meanings exist under a wide "banner of pluralism." Bock and Fahy demonstrate that "pluralism is far from a monolithic concept, and its contours depend on a range of social, historical and political factors that together inform approaches to managing diversity."[58] Like secularism, pluralism "does not describe a singular phenomenon, but rather a range of historically, socially and politically embedded responses to particular demographic conditions."[59] Therefore, Bock and Fahy propose a working definition of pluralism "as a particular set of evaluations of, and responses to, the accelerated diversification and amplification of religious difference, and to the concomitant ambition of the groups that constitute diversity to shape social, political and cultural processes with their values and aspirations."[60] While some use the term as shorthand for the reality of religious diversity (e.g., plurality), others take seriously the "-ism" of pluralism to denote its

---

55 John Inazu, "Hope without a Common Good," in Patel, *Out of Many Faiths*, 140.
56 Inazu, "Hope without a Common Good," 149.
57 Charles Taylor, "Conditions of an Unforced Consensus on Human Rights," in *Dilemmas and Connections* (Cambridge, MA: Belknap Press of Harvard University Press, 2011), 105; quoted in Inazu, "Hope without a Common Good," 149.
58 Bock and Fahy, "Emergent Religious Pluralisms," 4.
59 Bock and Fahy, 4.
60 Bock and Fahy, 6–7.

political and normative commitments, whether they be to some version of relativism (moral, cultural, or otherwise), or, as Diana Eck champions, an energetic engagement with religious diversity while holding firm to religious commitments (i.e., not relativism). Resonant with Inazu's point above regarding the possible lack of agreement about what constitutes the common good, David Hollenbach maintains, *"pluralism*, by definition, means that there is no agreement about the meaning of the good life,"[61] and thus, as Berger observes, it is "is often perceived as a threat to faith, associated with relativism and a loss of religious substance."[62] However, Berger argues to the contrary, "pluralism is good for faith," because it enhances the religious freedom of individuals to avoid groupthink, to critically and constructively question religious traditions (including their own), to avoid the potential oppressive and coercive authority of clergy, and to discern for themselves the core of their own religious identity and way of life.[63] For Eck and others, pluralism goes beyond mere tolerance and inclusivism; it involves an element of newness, transformation, creation, and transcendence.

Civic Pluralism

The term "pluralism," argues Berger, inherently contains an ideological position or normative vision, which sets it apart from sheer diversity. After all, plural*ism* is an *-ism*, suggesting its ideological leanings.[64] Put succinctly, although pluralism is most often used either descriptively (i.e., the fact of religious diversity) or prescriptively (i.e., something to be achieved), *civic pluralism* connotes "the coexistence, generally peaceful, of different religions, worldviews, and value systems within the same society."[65]

Despite the multidefinitional nature of pluralism, broad strokes, common characteristics, and family resemblances can be identified among its various conceptions. Although it is occasionally equated with the reality of religious diversity in the world, pluralism is more often, as Bock and Fahy recognize,

---

61 David Hollenbach, "Catholicism's Communitarian Vision," in *As Leven in the World*, ed. Thomas M. Landy (Franklin, WI: Sheed & Ward, 2001), 167, italics original.
62 Berger, "The Good of Religious Pluralism," 39.
63 Berger, 41–42.
64 Berger, 40.
65 Berger, "The Good of Religious Pluralism," 40.

"typically defined as the positive embrace of, and enthusiastic engagement with, diversity."[66] Diana Eck, who founded and directs the Pluralism Project at Harvard University, distinguishes pluralism from diversity by defining the former as "the energetic engagement with diversity."[67] Sociologist of religion David W. Machacek echoes Eck's view that pluralism is more than diversity alone and suggests that Eck's "new religious pluralism," especially in the context of the United States, refers to the phenomenon of recent immigrants to the United States who "instead of assimilating American social practices and cultural beliefs and values . . ., [and] often using religion as a primary resource, appear to be actively renegotiating the terms of American social and cultural life."[68] According to Machacek, after the 1965 Immigration and Nationality Act in the United States, immigrants "stepped into a society that was rejecting a culture of communitarian consensus in favor of a culture that placed a positive value on diversity and dissent—that is, a culture of pluralism . . . a culture in which diversity has become normative."[69] Machacek's assessment parallels Eck's distinction between the traditional model of American inclusivism and incorporation (e.g., the "melting pot" metaphor in which distinctions are absorbed and assimilated) and the new model that envisions religious pluralism characterized by transformation and newness (e.g., the "salad bowl" metaphor or Patel's "potluck" metaphor[70]). For Eck, "pluralism is more about transformation, not incorporation. The inclusivist or incorporative move is usually majoritarian,"[71] which, although enthusiastically welcoming of new and diverse members to the table, assumes that structures—the shape of the table—will not change. A pluralist model, on the other hand, assumes that structures—the shape of the table—will change as new and diverse members join.[72]

---

66 Bock and Fahy, "Emergent Religious Pluralisms," 1.
67 Diana L. Eck, "About," Pluralism Project (website).
68 Machacek, "The Problem of Pluralism," 147.
69 Machacek, 148.
70 Patel, *Out of Many Faiths*, 107–9.
71 Eck, "Pluralism," 62.
72 "The pluralist would insist that the shape of the table will change, the structures will change. The inclusivist understanding of citizenship and the polity of government is fixed, and when newcomers come, they assimilate to the way things are. The pluralists would insist that newcomers bring new perspectives. Their voices count and that the incorporative, 'melting pot,' image of America is one that is not worthy of true democracy. The incorporative move is to assume one can incorporate "others" whomever they

Traditional pluralism "concerns the fact that many religions and world-views coexist in the same society."[73] This includes the descriptive reality of religious diversity and the normative and prescriptive ideological vision of civic pluralism as an achievement. According to Berger, there is a *second pluralism*, a uniquely modern pluralism that "accentuates the first kind" by involving "the coexistence of the secular discourse with all of these religious discourses."[74] This affirms the point above from Leirvik that secularity can open a potential neutrally shared and more level space for deeper interreligious relations.[75]

Eck offers an instructive four-point[76] description of civic religious pluralism as:

1. not diversity alone, but the energetic engagement with diversity,
2. not just tolerance, but the active seeking of understanding across lines of difference,
3. not relativism, but the encounter of commitments, and
4. an ongoing process[77] (and based on dialogue[78]).

---

are into a structure of a body that is already formed. The pluralist would insist that the process of engagement, however conceived, will change everyone." Eck, "Pluralism," 62.

73 Berger, "The Good of Religious Pluralism," 40.

74 Berger, 40.

75 Interreligious studies scholar Anne Hege Grung examines how Berger's two pluralisms relate to interreligious encounter in Norway, a modern nation-state characterized as increasing in secular and religious diversity. In so doing, Grung's case study demonstrates how "interreligious encounters and particularly organized interreligious dialogues can be seen as one way for faith communities to engage actively and constructively with increased religious pluralisms." Similar to Leirvik, who suggests that secularity serves as a common space for interreligious dialogue and mutual transformation, Grung confirms Berger's thesis that the *second pluralism* (secular–religious discourse) accentuates the *first pluralism* in Norway by deepening knowledge and mutual understanding, and by providing a shared space. Aligned with Leirvik, Grung speculates that one outcome of the substantial inclusion of secular humanists in Norway's national, regional, and local dialogues is the establishment of "a shared secular language in these dialogues, marked by human-rights oriented discourse and language." Grung, "The Two Pluralisms in Norway," *Society* 54, no. 4 (2017): 434; final quotation cites Leirvik, "Interreligious Dialogue and Secularity."

76 Eck includes a fifth point specific to the United States, "pluralism in American is clearly based on the common ground rules of the First Amendment to the Constitution: "no establishment" of religion and the "free exercise" of religion. Pluralism Project, "From Diversity to Pluralism."

77 Eck, *A New Religious America*, 70–73.

78 Eck, "About."

Energetic engagement with diversity (point 1), getting beyond tolerance (point 2), the encounter of religiously committed individuals and groups (point 3), and the necessity of ongoing dialogue (point 4) form the foundation of civic religious pluralism upon which religiously diverse societies can respond to and engage religious diversity. Eck's four-point vision of civic religious pluralism, explained further in the following four subsections, is not merely academic wishful thinking but it, along with religiously neutral secular human-rights language, informs interfaith practitioners and leaders (and IRS scholars). For instance, the Minnesota Multifaith Network (MnMN), a "state-wide network that gathers the energy and passion of people of faith,"[79] cites Eck and the Pluralism Project in their expanded missional explanation:

All who associate with MnMN will uphold the principles of human rights as articulated in the UN Declaration of Human Rights which upholds the equal treatment of all people and all faiths. . . . All who associate with MnMN will support each other based on the values of religious respect, pluralism, and dialogue . . . [which] refers not to mere tolerance but to the energetic engagement of religious diversity and understanding across lines of difference.[80]

Eck's four points serve as foundational language in MnMN's missional explanation above.

Energetic Engagement with Diversity

To clearly distinguish pluralism from diversity, and to add a normative thrust, Eck enthusiastically argues that pluralism is not a given, but an achievement. Pluralism is less a noun and more a verb. It requires effort and cultivation. While diversity refers simply to the sheer reality of the existence of differing religious identities, groups, and traditions, pluralism is the integration, interaction, engagement, and encounter between, among, and within these traditions. In Eck's words, "Religious diversity is an observable fact of American life today, but without any real engagement with one another, neighboring churches, temples, and mosques might prove to be just a striking example of

---

79 Minnesota Multifaith Network, "About."
80 Minnesota Multifaith Network, "Policies Update Aug. 20, 2020."

diversity."[81] Rahuldeep Singh Gill creatively recounts the time spent in his high school cafeteria as a teenager in the Boston area. During the lunch hour, the cafeteria would teem with diversity, yet with little to no pluralism. Gill recalls the lunch tables often separated by race, ethnicity, and perhaps even gender. Looking out across the cafeteria one could immediately recognize the sheer diversity of the student body, but with very little engagement between and among the various student groups. All groups tended to sit together, tolerant of one another, but with little interaction. No, "diversity alone is not pluralism. Pluralism is not a given but must be created. . . . [It] requires participation, and attunement to the life and energies of one another."[82] Civic religious pluralism requires energetic engagement with religious diversity.

Beyond Tolerance

Tolerance refers to the human capacity to allow or endure that with which they do not necessarily agree or themselves do. It is inherently about putting up with those ideas and practices that one does not believe, do, or engage in themselves. One need not tolerate that which they already agree with, precisely because they already agree with it. To be sure, Eck endorses tolerance as a necessary good and public virtue[83] but argues that it is not sufficient to bring about sustainable constructive social cohesion and healthy engagement (pluralism) across difference. The high school cliques in the cafeteria tolerate one another—they recognize the reality of diversity without engaging it—as they sit scattered throughout the room gossiping about each other with stereotypes, clichés, and misconceptions, which, left unchecked or corrected, can lead to unhealthy fracture and conflict. For Eck, tolerance "does not require new neighbors to know anything about one another. Tolerance can create a climate of restraint but not one of understanding. Tolerance alone does little to bridge the chasms of stereotype and fear that may, in fact, dominate the mutual image of the other. . . . It is far too fragile a foundation for a society that is becoming as religiously complex as

---

81 Eck, *A New Religious America*, 70.
82 Eck, 70.
83 Raimon Panikkar speaks about tolerance as a "virtue" in "Pluralism, Tolerance, and Christianity," in *Cultures and Religions in Dialogue*, 71–84; first published as "Die Toleranz der Christenheit," in *Pluralismus, Toleranze und Christenheit* (Nürnberg: Abendändishe, 1961).

ours."[84] Though tolerance is often considered a virtue to be cultivated like any other, it proves weak in the face of learning about and engaging with the other because it does not necessarily seek to understand. Rather, it strives simply to allow for that which one may not approve. Tolerance may not push an individual to really listen to or sympathetically engage with others. It may even obstruct a promising path toward humanizing the other and possibly produce more apathy than empathy. Marshall Rosenberg, founder of the popular nonviolent (or compassionate) communication method, teaches that the "key ingredient of empathy is presence: we are wholly present with the other party and what they are experiencing."[85] If left unchecked, tolerance "leaves in place the stereotypes, the half-truths, the fears that underlie old patterns of division and violence."[86] It does little, if anything, to foster energetic encounter.

Commitments

"Pluralism is not simply relativism," but "the encounter of commitments."[87] The charge of moral, cultural, and religious relativism is often critically lobbed against pluralism. Valueless relativism, in this sense, refers to the suggestion that there exist no universal standards by which to measure morality, cultural norms, and religious worldviews, thereby rendering all equally (in)valid. This line of criticism argues that if this is what pluralism is all about, then it amounts to asking people to give up or water down their deeply held religious convictions, beliefs, and practices. Eck is quick to counter this concern, arguing that the interpretation of pluralism as relativism is "a distortion of the process of pluralism." Instead of giving up or toning down one's religious commitments in the quest for universal agreement, Eck's vision of pluralism invites citizens into "engagement with, not abdication of, differences and particularities."[88] Eck's engaged religious pluralism does not require individuals to leave their religious traditions behind. Nor does it ask them to give up their beliefs or accept all religious, spiritual, and secular worldviews and ways of life as true, equal,

---

84 Eck, *A New Religious America*, 70.
85 Marshall B. Rosenberg, *Nonviolent Communication*, 3rd ed. (Encinitas, CA: Puddle-Dancer Press, 2015), 94.
86 Eck, "About."
87 Eck, *A New Religious America*, 71.
88 Eck, 71.

and valuable. Rather, it allows them to maintain their commitments while also committing to the encounter of others who hold different commitments; hence, it is about committing to the encounter of commitments. "It means holding our deepest differences, even our religious differences, not in isolation, but in relationship to one another,"[89] and thus ongoing dialogue is the foundation upon which pluralism flourishes. The tenet of commitment embraces the spirit of Jonathan Sacks' "Dignity of Difference" addressed in the previous chapter, which Laurie Patton, as a Jew, praises since it allows for the "keeping of Jewish identity while at the same time engaging with other traditions."[90]

Dialogue

The primary means through which pluralism takes place is one of dialogue and encounter. Eck optimistically cautions that "the process of pluralism is never complete but is the ongoing work of each generation."[91] For Eck and the Pluralism Project, "dialogue means both speaking and listening, and that process reveals both common understandings and real differences."[92] By most measures of effective interreligious dialogue, the aim is not agreement or consensus. Rather, pluralism, as noted above, "involves the commitment to being at the table"—to engage, encounter, and listen to fellow citizens and neighbors—"with one's commitments."[93] Dialogue here does not refer simply to the literal act of sitting down at the table with others to engage in conversation, no matter how pleasant or disturbing that might be. Rather, dialogue here refers broadly to the diverse modes of encounter and engagement. In sum, Eck's four-point sketch of civic religious pluralism articulates a full-bodied response to religious diversity.

    ◊   ◊   ◊

The vision of civic religious pluralism sketched in this chapter, especially in the spirit of Diana Eck, aims at nurturing intimate and critical engagement

---

89 Eck, "About."
90 Patton, "Plural American Needs Myths," in Patel, *Out of Many Faiths*, 163.
91 Eck, *A New Religious America*, 72.
92 Eck, "About."
93 Eck, "About."

with religious difference. Going beyond mere tolerance, while encouraging commitment to one's own worldviews and lifeways, pluralism sidesteps the move to incorporate (dissolve) difference into a dominant narrative or assimilated culture. Rather, pluralism aims at fostering authentic civic relations by recognizing the reality of significant religious difference and diversity and advocating for ongoing change and transformation. The civic religious pluralist not only insists that diverse voices be present at the table—that the "dignity of difference" is maintained—but also insists "that the shape of the table will change"[94] in the process.

---

94 Eck, "Pluralism," 62.

12

Theological Encounters

Chapter Outline

I. "Doing Theology"
II. Theology of Religions
III. Comparative Theology
IV. Interreligious Theology
V. Transreligious Theology

One of the primary contexts in which religion is engaged is through dialogue. In the West, with its roots in Christianity, dialogue emphasizes theological discourse about the divine and its relation to humanity and the world. Historically, theological pursuits in the Western academy have been dominated by Christian theological questions, texts, and traditions. Although the Christian tradition still dominates, universities and institutions of higher education increasingly support the in-depth study of plural theological traditions by adding faculty and programs specializing in non-Christian theological traditions. A growing number of universities, including Christian-affiliated institutions, now have faculty of Islamic and Jewish theologies and offer degree programs in Islamic and Jewish theological studies.[1] These theological currents within Western academia provide spaces for interreligious

---

1 See Wolfram Weisse, Julia Ipgrave, Oddbjørn Leirvik, and Muna Tatari, eds., *Pluralisation of Theologies at European Universities* (Münster: Waxman, 2020).

encounter and nurture the blossoming of various theological methods that engage multiple religious theological traditions. This chapter introduces the most prominent theological methods of interreligious encounter in the academy today.

"DOING THEOLOGY"

Theological studies (TS) is understood in a variety of ways. In relation to the traditional academic approaches to the study of religion, or religious studies (RS),[2] covered in chapter 1, TS can be marked off as different by the confessional nature of the one "doing theology." However, some make further distinction between confessional theology and academic theology. The confessional theologian does theology—makes theological truth claims—that draws on the (re)sources available from within their religious tradition, whereas the academic theologian studies the truth claims made by confessional theologians "but employs the tools of secular disciplines as the primary methodology and guide."[3] Secular disciplines here refer to nonreligious or religiously neutral disciplines. The scholar of RS, traditionally, does not foreground her [religious] confession or faith position as a significant factor (or as a factor at all) in her scholarship. Although she may acknowledge her faith position, she's likely to minimize or bracket her religious beliefs and ideologies, to the extent possible, in her academic work. Hence, RS strives for a purely secular (nonreligious) approach to the study of religion. The RS scholar studies what *people* do and believe, today and in history, about the sacred or the divine, whereas theologians are among those doing and believing (and being studied). The academic theologian, unlike the confessional theologian, uses secular disciplines to critically engage truth claims made by theology. While academic theologians often use the secular tools, methods, and disciplines of RS for their theological inquiry, scholars of RS do not generally use TS as a tool of inquiry. However, RS scholars may study the theology espoused by various religious communities and individuals.

---

2 This chapter assumes a general synonymous relationship between the academic "study of religion" and "Religious Studies," however it acknowledges here that some scholars differentiate these from one another.

3 Paul Hedges, "Why the Theology Without Walls Program Fails Both as Scholarship and a Resource to the SBNR," *Journal of Interreligious Studies* 34 (2022): 20.

Theologian Michael J. Himes says:

Religion is the name for a way of life and action; theology is a name for reflection on the ground, meaning and goal of that way of life and action ... after you read all the best critics on Hamlet, you still need to see the play; after you are led through detailed analysis of a Mozart piano concerto, you have not replaced hearing the concerto. The work of art is richer than anything anyone can say about it. But that does not make the work of literary or musical criticism unnecessary or fruitless. The more you know about a poem or a piece of music or a painting, the more deeply, richly and fully you are able to enter into the poem or piece of music or painting. Criticism presupposes the work of art and never replaces it, but the work of art is enriched by the appreciation of the wise and perceptive critic.... Theology is not a replacement for living religiously.[4]

Those "doing" theology often commit—to varying degrees—to the truth-claims of their own tradition(s) in an effort to correlate them with truths about God (or the Gods, the divine, the transcendent), world, what it means to be human, and other questions of ultimate concern. The object of study for TS is theological truth and insight, which may include data discovered from RS. However, in the distinction between confessional and academic approaches to theology the latter utilizes secular disciplines to examine truth claims made by confessional theology.

David Ford, a theologian who writes for academic and public audiences, defines academic theology as "a subject which deals with questions of meaning, truth, beauty, and practice raised in relation to religions and pursued through a range of academic disciplines."[5] Thus, academic theologians may draw on multiple traditions and disciplines in their scholarly work. However, according to Ford, their pursuit remains distinct from RS in that their theological quest is rooted in a constructive pursuit of truth, wisdom, and beauty. RS scholarship, on the other hand, is less likely concerned (or not concerned at all) about under-standing the wisdom and beauty of God(s). Rather, RS scholarship investigates what religious *people* claim to be the wisdom and beauty of God(s). These three approaches to studying religion—confessional theology, academic theology, and religious studies—do not have tight distinct borders between them but fall

---

4 Michael J. Himes, *Doing the Truth in Love* (New York: Paulist Press, 1995), 90.
5 David Ford, *Theology* (Oxford: Oxford University Press, 1999), 29.

along a range of approaches that blur and bleed into one another.[6] The general overview offered here is far too simple to do justice to their overlap. Scholars may identify as both theologian and scholar of religion, for RS and TS are not rigid tribes to which scholars exclusively belong. Consider Paul Hedges' examples:

> religious studies about Christianity crosses over to academic theology, while a Buddhist who studies Buddhism within religious studies may also make, at times, more normative claims about their own tradition in a confessional mode. ... An atheist may teach Christian theology and identify as a theologian, while a belonging-believing Sikh may identify with religious studies and teach and research Sikhism in an entirely "secular" way.[7]

The popular undergraduate theology textbook *The Christian Theological Tradition* defines theology as "an intellectual discipline that explores *(religious) reality* from a *particular perspective, namely God* as *ultimate ground and goal of all reality*; in the words of Anselm [of Canterbury], it is '*faith seeking understanding*.'"[8] This traditional Christian and Western definition of theology is instructive on several levels.

Religious reality: Theology examines *religious* reality and not just reality as such, which is to say that theology is interested in those aspects of reality that somehow relate to, reveal, or access the divine, sacred, or God(s).

Particular perspective: Theology takes place from within the context of a particular tradition (e.g., Christian, Jewish, Islamic, etc.) and asks questions against the backdrop of this tradition.

Namely God: This definition names the *particular perspective* as *God*. Thus, theology in this sense primarily explores the reality of God. Notice that this definition posits a monotheistic understanding of God, and not Gods in the plural. Thus, it makes a specific claim about the nature of divine reality.

---

6 Hedges, "Why the Theology Without Walls Program Fails Both as Scholarship and a Resource to the SBNR," 20.

7 Hedges, 20–21.

8 Catherine A. Cory and Michael Hollerich, eds., *The Christian Theological Tradition*, 3rd ed. (Upper Saddle River, NJ: Pearson Prentice Hall, 2009), 505, italics added.

Ultimate ground and goal of all reality: This definition provides a working definition of God as the ultimate ground of all reality, thus placing all things within the purview of theological study.

In the words of Anselm: This definition privileges a classical Christian definition of theology from a well-known Christian thinker, Anselm of Canterbury, which seems appropriate given it comes from a textbook on the *Christian* theological tradition.

"Faith seeking understanding": The definition concludes with the most recognized Christian definition of theology. Notice the prerequisite of "faith," signifying that doing theology is for those already with faith who seek to understand it in relation to God and all things. Does this mean that those without faith cannot do theology? Maybe. Maybe not. It may depend on what the word "faith" means. If faith simply refers to an individual's position on God, then almost everyone can do theology including those whose position about God begins with, "I don't believe in God," which is a theological statement.

The above is but one definition of theology, albeit a traditional Christian one. Although doing theology and theological reflection are not central aims of this book, a primary context in which religion is engaged is through dialogue, which in the West, with its roots in Protestant Christianity, emphasizes theological discourse about the divine and its relation to humanity and the world. In other words, theological discourse as a mode of interreligious encounter remains prominent. Individuals who use or understand words such as God, Gods, the divine, sacred, deities, and the transcendent (among others), might be considered implicit theologians, whether they like or know it or not. For instance, theologian and philosopher Keith Ward argues that theology is not just for so-called theologians and nor is it just for those who are religious or belong to traditional religious communities. A worldview that maintains "there is no God" is still a theological worldview. For Ward, especially in the domain of comparative theology, as he conceives it, "scholars of any religious persuasion or none may engage in questions of comparative theology, the analysis of the concepts of God and of revelation."[9] Theology, by its very nature, according

---

9 Keith Ward, *Religion and Revelation* (Oxford: Clarendon Press, 1994), 45.

to Ward, is a "pluralistic discipline" in which "people of differing beliefs can co-operate, discuss, argue, and converse."[10] Theology "can be undertaken by people of many diverse beliefs,"[11] including no religious beliefs at all.

Although anyone with God-like words in their lexicon can do theology and be considered a theologian, it is useful to retain the distinction scholars make between "doing theology" and "studying religion," the former properly situated within the discipline of TS (pursued by theologians) and the latter under RS (pursued by scholars of religion). To a certain degree, individuals cannot remove themselves from the confines of the traditions or worldviews that inform their understanding of the world. Even those doing "Theology Without Walls"[12] are informed by implicit walls that confine, condition, limit, and socially construct, in part, what they see, say, and think and how they view the world.[13] Increasingly, RS scholars, not just TS scholars, recognize how the contexts and communities they belong to inform their scholarship. Within the broad field of TS—in which several subdisciplines and methods exist—methods and scholars that interreligiously engage other or multiple traditions strive to remain conscious of the contexts from which theology is done, including its limitations. Among the contemporary Western theological methods, there are formal methods that emphasize engagement with other religious traditions and their beliefs and practices. These methods include theology of religions, comparative theology, interreligious theology, and transreligious theology. It has become evident that one can no longer do theology in isolation from, or without taking seriously, the claims of the empirical and natural sciences. In similar fashion, these approaches capture the spirit of Raimon Panikkar's claim that "one can no longer practice theology in isolation or merely in one's own group"; a sentiment Panikkar expressed in the phrase "ecumenical ecumenism," which indicates "a genuine and sincere encounter between religions."[14] In other words, the doing of theology in one's own tradition can no longer be done without taking seriously the claims of other traditions.

---

10 Ward, *Religion and Revelation*, 45.

11 Ward, 46.

12 Jerry L. Martin, ed., *Theology without Walls* (London: Routledge, 2020).

13 Hedges and others contend the Theology Without Walls (TWW) project is, despite its intentions, both "confessional and walled." Paul Hedges, "Theology With and Without (W&W) Walls, Scholarship W&W Walls, and Decolonization W&W," *Journal of Interreligious Studies* 35 (2022): 97.

14 Panikkar, *Cultures and Religions in Dialogue*, 108; first published as "Vers un ecumenisme ecumènic," in *Questions de vida cristiana* no. 140 (Montserrat, 1988): 80–86, and "Ecumenisme crític," *Questions de vida cristiana* no. 144 (Montserrat, 1988): 120–23.

THEOLOGY OF RELIGIONS

Theologies of religions operate from a confessional perspective by asking whether truth can be found in traditions other than one's own and, if so, how is it related to the truth discovered in one's own tradition. Several well-known and well-worn positions emerge:

Naturalism (or atheism): truth is not found in any religion (i.e., all religious truth claims are false).

Exclusivism: truth is found exclusively in only one religious tradition.

Inclusivism: although truth may be found in more than one religious tradition, there is only "one singular maximum of that truth";[15] in other words, although many religions hold some truth, only one religion holds the most accurate optimal path to truth.

Theological Pluralism (not to be confused with civic religious pluralism): truth can be found in a plurality of religious traditions.

The above typology, in part made popular by Alan Race,[16] as described here is oversimplified and does not do justice to the rigor and seriousness with which theologians of religions engage questions of ultimate truth in the various religions. Important questions with practical outcomes emerge from this theology. For example, if a Muslim theologian concludes that non-Muslims can discover truth and know God through other religions, does it weaken any theological justifications for Muslims to preach and spread their tradition to others? If a Hindu theologian reasons that all religious traditions lead to truth and to the divine, then what, if any, special role does Hindu philosophy and teaching play in that quest? If a Christian theologian concludes truth and salvation only comes to confessional Christians, then what theological implications might Christians draw about the nature and power of God and human agency?

Related to these theological questions, posed by theologians, is the on-the-ground reality of what everyday religious people (not theologians) believe about the existence of truth and salvation or liberation in religions other than their own. The data show basic trends that describe how Americans

---

15 Schmidt-Leukel, *Religious Pluralism and Interreligious Theology*, 4.
16 Alan Race, *Christians and Religious Pluralism* (London: SCM Press, 1983).

approach these questions. A 2007 Faith Matters survey found that "Americans overwhelmingly believe that people of other religions can go to heaven" (Figure 12.1),[17] even among various Christian denominations (see Figure 12.2).[18] In his 2008 book *What Americans Really Believe*, Rodney Stark draws on a 2007 Baylor Study to conclude that "few Americans think heaven is very exclusive. Only 29 percent think that even the irreligious (non religious) are prevented from entering."[19] A reason for this, according to David Campbell and Robert Putnam, may be because "most Americans are intimately acquainted with people of other faiths."[20] Furthermore, Campbell and Putnam suggest, it is due to the Aunt Susan Principle, which is the idea that:

We all have an Aunt Susan in our lives, the sort of person who epitomizes what it means to be a saint, but whose religious background is different from our own. Maybe you are Jewish and she is a Methodist. Or perhaps you are Catholic and Aunt Susan is not religious at all. But whatever her religious background (or lack thereof), you know that Aunt Susan is destined for heaven. And if she is going to heaven, what does that say about other people who share her religion or lack of religion? Maybe they can go to heaven too. To put the Aunt Susan Principle in more technical terms: We are suggesting that having a religiously diverse social network leads to a more positive assessment of specific religious groups, particularly those with low thermometer scores.[21]

In response to the question of whether truth can be found in traditions other than one's own—a question at the center of the theology of religions— Americans also overwhelmingly believe that not only is it likely that more than one religion can be true (Figure 12.3),[22] but that there are basic truths in many religions (Figure 12.4).[23]

---

17 David E. Campbell and Robert D. Putnam, "America's Grace," *Political Science Quarterly* 126, no. 4 (Winter 2011): 627.
18 Campbell and Putnam, "America's Grace," 628.
19 Stark, *What Americans Really Believe*, 72.
20 Campbell and Putnam, "America's Grace," 620.
21 Campbell and Putnam, 620.
22 Campbell and Putnam, 637.
23 Campbell and Putnam, 634.

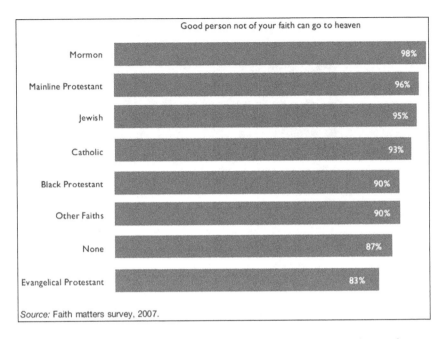

Figure 12.1. Can good people from other sects within or beyond your religious tradition go to heaven?

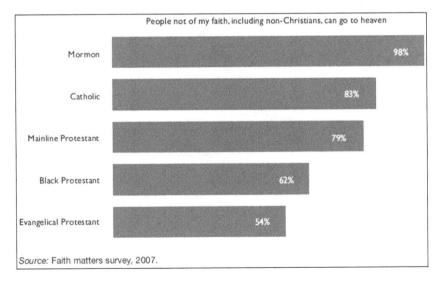

Figure 12.2. Can people from other religions go to heaven?

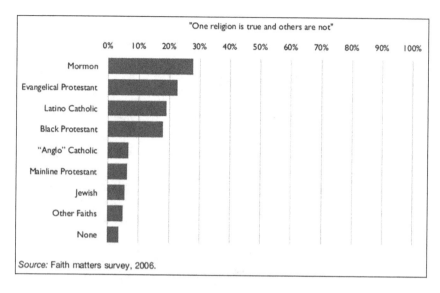

Figure 12.3. Can people from other religions go to heaven?

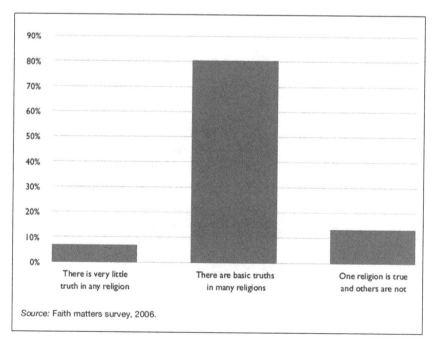

Figure 12.4. Can truth be found in many traditions?

COMPARATIVE THEOLOGY

Unlike the Theology of Religions, which begins with questions about whether truth can be found in religious traditions other than one's own, Comparative Theology (CT) commences with the basic question of what might be learned about one's home tradition by learning about and engaging with other traditions. CT focuses not first and foremost on other traditions, but on increasing one's intimacy and knowledge with their home tradition. An American Christian participant in an interfaith dialogue program captures the spirit of CT in the response, "The amazing thing is, when you learn about others, it inevitably causes you to learn about yourself."[24] Max Müller, the nineteenth-century German scholar of religion, emphasized the importance of comparison. He famously suggested about religion: "'He who knows one, knows none.'"[25] If an individual lacks knowledge of other traditions, then not only does he lack knowledge of those traditions, but he also lacks full knowledge of his own tradition. In a similar vein, Marianne Moyaert observes,

religious identity can no longer be formed and established in isolation from the "other." The permanent presence of the religious other brings about a new form of religious awareness, an awareness marked by contingency and relativity. The intimate presence of others and their vivid wisdom traditions undermine some of the certainties, non-negotiable convictions, and absolute truth claims that formed the building blocks of identity formation in the past.[26]

Drawing on this comparative spirit, CT is, as James Fredericks puts it, "the attempt to understand the meaning of . . . faith by exploring it in the light of the teachings of other religious traditions."[27] Comparative theologians argue that not only does CT achieve its primary aim of discovering deeper truths and fresh insights about one's own tradition and its secondary aim of learning about other religious traditions, but it can also transform one's own worldview in the process. For example, it is common for an individual

---

24 Pluralism Project, "America's Growing Interfaith Structure," 2020, 1.
25 Jon R. Stone, *The Essential Max Müller* (New York: Palgrave Macmillan, 2002), back cover.
26 Marianne Moyaert, *In Response to the Religious Other* (London: Lexington Books, 2014), 93–94.
27 Fredericks, *Faith among Faiths*, 169.

to gain a deeper understanding of their native first language—its structure, syntax, logic, and rules—by learning a second language. After learning how another language functions, the learner reflects on their native language with new eyes. Likewise, after learning about another religious tradition, the learner returns to their home religion with a new way of seeing. CT beckons the learner back to seek deeper knowledge of their own tradition. Seen in this light, deeper knowledge of one's own self and tradition is mutually aligned with deeper knowledge of the religious other.

This comparative principle is observed in many contexts. The experience of returning home and seeing with new eyes is common after traveling, whether one travels across the world or across the street. Consider the child who, for the first time, visits a friend's house for dinner. Accustomed to the way the evening meal proceeds at home, he discovers that his friend's family performs the ritual of dinner in different and similar ways, and it causes him to reflect on how and why his family shares the evening meal the way that they do. He left his home and immersed himself into the dinner ritual being performed in a different way with another family and then returns home and sees his family's tradition with new eyes. In the process, he gains fresh insights and generates new questions that had not yet occurred to him. Not only did he learn about the dinner tradition of his friend's family, but he gained a more intimate knowledge of his home tradition. Perhaps, at some point, he even considers adopting some of the new practices he learned at his friend's house, which then transforms his family's dinner ritual. The same spirit of comparative learning takes place in CT.

A comparative theologian, by immersing herself into the texts, teachings, and practices (if appropriate) of another tradition, begins to ask new questions about her home tradition. Hence, CT is ultimately about seeing one's home tradition in new ways with the possibility of transforming one's home tradition in light of other traditions. Comparative theologians contend that other religions provide not only interesting opportunities to learn about new traditions in their own right but also new ways to discover one's home tradition. Furthermore, other religions invite one to see their home tradition through the lens of another, to the extent possible. Judaism may look different to someone from a Hindu tradition than it does to other Jews and non-Hindus. Christianity may be understood in a variety of ways from many diverse Muslim perspectives.

The comparative method can be cyclical or iterative, returning again and again to an external tradition to gain new questions and insights each time.

In the process, the traditions themselves may change (since religious traditions are unstable, dynamic, fluid, and change over time), but the scholar is sure to change as well. For instance, a comparative theologian focused on religious texts may read back-and-forth between their home scripture (e.g., the Hebrew Bible) and texts of another tradition (e.g., the Upanishads). With each reading back-and-forth between the texts, the scholar might discover new observations each time. Even though the texts themselves do not change, the scholar is constantly changing and seeing anew with each pass. Imagine reading Plato's *Republic* at ten years old and then again at twenty years old, thirty years old, and so on. Each time, it may seem like a brand-new text. But it isn't. It is the same. It does not change. The reader changes. With each decade, the reader gains new life experiences, and it influences the way he sees the text. Hence, the reader encounters the text anew each time. A similar spirit is captured by comparative theologians in their method of moving back and forth between their home tradition and another. The aim is not to determine whether other religions are true (although a comparative theologian may concurrently pursue this question); rather, the goal of CT is to compare, learn, generate questions, and develop a deeper understanding of one's home tradition through the encounter with other traditions.

INTERRELIGIOUS THEOLOGY

Interreligious theology and transreligious theology add wrinkles to theological approaches that do theology within, between, and among multiple religious and spiritual traditions.[28] Perry Schmidt-Leukel[29] defines interreligious theology as "the form that theology assumes when it takes religious truth claims seriously, those of one's own religious tradition and those of all others. Taking them seriously means to search for possible truth in all of the religious testimonies."[30] It allows for the inclusion of both theistic and nontheistic traditions within its purview,[31] including discourse between, among, and within Abrahamic,

---

28 This section contains revised sections from Hans Gustafson, "Pansacramentalism, Interreligious Theology, and Lived Religion," *Religions* 10, no. 7: 408 (2019): 54–68.

29 Schmidt-Leukel is among contemporary thinkers doing significant work in interreligious theology; however, the method's forerunners include Keith Ward, Wilfred Cantwell Smith, and Ephraim Meir.

30 Schmidt-Leukel, *Religious Pluralism and Interreligious Theology*, 13.

31 Schmidt-Leukel, 8.

Dharmic, and nonreligious secular traditions. Schmidt-Leukel's vision of interreligious theology holds to four "principles"[32] or "starting points."[33] First, interreligious theology operates on the assumption that theological truth can be found beyond one's own tradition. Second, seeking theologically relevant truth must be "guided by the conviction that ultimately, all truth—wherever and in whatever form it might be found—must be compatible." Third, interreligious theology is done interreligiously, which is to say it seeks out encounter, engagement, and discourse with individuals and communities practicing religious traditions, worldviews, and lifeways beyond one's own. Fourth, it is an ongoing "open process"; that is, it is never finished, and "it will, therefore, be impossible for any single person to produce something like a completed interreligious theology."[34] Interreligious theology is an ongoing open process that seeks out encounter and truth with traditions other than one's own and is guided by the assumption that all truth is compatible.

The perspective of the interreligious theologian is one of integration. Although they may be confessionally committed or rooted in a particular religious tradition or ideological worldview, they remain prepared to revise, change, and transform their perspectives when necessary. Beyond the challenge of understanding multiple perspectives lays the greater challenge of imaginatively integrating insights from those perspectives within a confessional stance.[35] Interreligious theology relies on imagination. Scholars of dialogue contend that perfectly commensurable language for interreligious dialogue is impossible. No common language exists that allows for perfect one-to-one translation between religions. To overcome this, comparative theologian and scholar of religion Marianne Moyaert emphasizes imagination, which "allows people to locate differences and equivalences and question static and essentialized interpretations of religious languages. Imagination is the human capacity that makes empathy possible and enables us to cross boundaries and to enter different worlds and perspectives."[36] To empathize

---

32 Schmidt-Leukel refers to these principles respectively as (1) "a theological credit of trust," (2) "the unity of reality," (3) "tied to interreligious discourse," and (4) the "processual, essential incomplete nature" of interreligious theology. Schmidt-Leukel, *Religious Pluralism and Interreligious Theology*, 130–39.

33 Schmidt-Leukel, 130.

34 Schmidt-Leukel, 128.

35 Schmidt-Leukel, 141.

36 Marianne Moyaert, "Interreligious Dialogue and the Debate between Universalism and Particularism," *Studies in Interreligious Dialogue* 15, no. 1 (2005): 48.

with and understand the views of others—to walk a mile in their shoes—or, as Wilfred Cantwell Smith states it, in order to "understand Buddhists, we must not look at something called Buddhism but at the world so far as possible through Buddhist eyes."[37] The interreligious theologian strives to imagine the other's view in order to understand the "reasons that motivate the other in his or her belief. It means to put oneself imaginatively into the other's shoes."[38] Interreligious theology adopts the spirit of comparative theology by staying open to learning about one's own tradition in, and perhaps be transformed by, engagement with and learning about other traditions. The interreligious theologian embraces the likelihood that her self-understanding and understanding of her own religious tradition "may change if it is seen in light of the religious other."[39] Since interreligious theology is a constructive endeavor ever striving for revision and integration, interreligious theologians accept the reality of syncretism,[40] thereby embracing the likelihood that "such revisions may often take the form of reinterpretation or reconstruction."[41] Interreligious theology seeks truth through encounter with multiple religious worldviews, including nonreligious views. Guided by the assumption that all truth is compatible, it relies on imagination to grasp the diverse nature of various perspectives for the possible integration into the ongoing reinterpretation and reconstruction of their own theological vision.

TRANSRELIGIOUS THEOLOGY

The distinction between interreligious and transreligious theology is subtle and, to some extent, unclear. Preliminary observations based on various

---

37 Wilfred Cantwell Smith, *Towards a World Theology* (Maryknoll, NY: Orbis, 1989), 82, first published 1981. Also quoted in Schmidt-Leukel, *Religious Pluralism and Interreligious*, 143.

38 Schmidt-Leukel, 142.

39 Schmidt-Leukel, 143.

40 Schmidt-Leukel writes, "I do not see any problems with syncretism as such. All great religions are, after all, the produce of syncretistic processes. . . . Currently one of the biggest obstacles to the idea of conscious interreligious borrowing seems to be the widespread fear of syncretism. Yet this fear ignores the syncretistic nature of all major religious traditions: They originated from and further developed under the influence of various other religions." Schmidt-Leukel, *Religious Pluralism and Interreligious Theology*, 138, 144–45; Schmidt-Leukel, *Transformation by Integration*, 67–89.

41 Schmidt-Leukel, *Religious Pluralism and Interreligious Theology*, 144.

scholars' work provide some insight. The prefix *trans-* generally connotes a degree of transcendence, while *inter-* does not. Inter- generally assumes interaction between and among two or more relatively stable religious entities, while transreligious interaction, according to some advocates, more rigorously recognizes the fluidity of religious entities. The prefix trans- can signal the generation of something novel beyond (transcendent of) sum total of that which is being integrated or synthesized. Thus, transreligious theology, perhaps unlike interreligious theology, generates something new that did not previously exist in the same way. It may be that the transreligious theologian is distinct from the interreligious theologian in that the former *trans*cends the traditions, practices, and disciplines from which they draw and, in so doing, generate a novel perspective, while the interreligious theologian, although integrating multiple diverse religious theological perspectives, may not necessarily claim to be generating a novel theological perspective beyond the traditions being integrated. On the question of novel generation, there is not a clear consensus yet among scholars about precisely where the line can be drawn, if one is to be drawn at all, between interreligious theology and transreligious theology. Maybe transreligious processes (transcendence and the creation of novel perspectives) are assumed within interreligious theology, which makes transreligious concerns inherent to interreligious theology.

Beyond the context of theology, in advocating for transreligious over interreligious, Anne Hege Grung argues that

> to replace "inter" with the term "trans" requires the acknowledgement of a larger fluidity in the encounter between people of different religious affiliation, and opens it up for addressing thematizing *intra-religious* differences. It may also make the relevant contextual power relations influencing the dialogue more visible. On the other hand, the term "trans" instead of "inter" may be understood as a challenge or a threat to religious boundaries the participants in the dialogue wish to keep stable in order to feel secured in their own religious identity.[42]

Furthermore, advocates claim, transreligious more adequately accounts for the internal diversity of religious traditions, the porous borders between

---

42 Anne Henge Grung, "Inter-Religious or Trans-Religious," *Journal of Interreligious Studies* 13 (2014): 11, italics original.

traditions, and the fluidity of religious identities.[43] In other words, transreligious more rigorously foregrounds the reality that religions are not stable entities with fixed boundaries, but rather are dynamic internally diverse and ever-fluid movements with shifting and porous boundaries.[44] Furthermore, Grung argues that the domain of the transreligious more properly recognizes the intrapersonal dynamics of multiple religious belonging and representation. Hence, the benefit of transreligious over interreligious is its emphasis on the religiosity of the individual over institutions, of religious practitioners over religious traditions. The claim is that the term "transreligious" more accurately and dynamically captures the reality of lived religious experience than the term "interreligious." Hence, Oddbjørn Leirvik's speculation about the future of academic theology: "university theology will be done in the third space between established faith traditions—that is, interreligiously . . . [and] beyond that, in response to the complex reality of fluid identities and multiple belongings, theology must also increasing be done *trans*religiously."[45] The conversation about the distinction between interreligious and transreligious theology, and the move from the former to the latter, is in its infancy. To be sure, the two are related and may offer useful differences on their own, with interreligious theology emphasizing integration and transreligious theology emphasizing the creation of something new beyond that which becomes integrated. It seems reasonable to employ both methods concurrently while privileging one over the other, depending on one's context and aims.

❧　❧　❧

Given the prominence and historical legacy of theological approaches in the practice and construction of religion in the West, any discussion about interreligious studies and interfaith engagement (with a focus on the West) is incomplete without acknowledging the major theological approaches that

---

43 See Leirvik, "Interreligious Studies: A New Academic Discipline?" 34–35; and Gustafson, "Is Transreligious Theology Unavoidable in Interreligious Theology and Dialogue?" 248–60.

44 Grung, "Inter-Religious or Trans-Religious," 11–14; Anne Hege Grung, "Inter-religious or Transreligious?" in *Interreligious Studies*, ed. Gustafson, 58–65.

45 Oddbjørn Leirvik, "Pluralisation of Theologies at Universities," in *Pluralisation of Theologies at European Universities*, ed. Weisse et al., 33.

involve engaging multiple religious traditions. Theology is but one mode of engagement across religious difference. Despite having beliefs about God or the Gods, ranging from belief to agnosticism to indifference to disbelief, most people do not fancy themselves as theologians or engage in regular theological discourse across religious difference. Far more common are relationships, friendships, and personal encounters of everyday life with others from various religious orientations. These relationships hold significant potential to be sustained over time and produce lifelong impact (and create the conditions for meaningful theological discourse if so desired). It is to the topic of friendship across difference and its potential for transformation that the next chapter turns.

13

Friendship across Difference

Chapter Outline

I.   Interreligious Friendship and Living Religion
II. My Friend Al and the Spillover Effect
III. Forging Solidarities
IV. Friendship and Interfaith Dialogue
V.   Inter/Intrapersonal Changemaking

Relationships are vital to the human experience, and they are invaluable for interreligious encounter. At their best, all dialogues and encounters across difference humanize those involved. With time, some may foster meaningful relationships, perhaps friendships. This chapter explores interreligious relationships and friendships as promising, long-lasting, and sustainable means to bridge differences. This includes exploring (1) the concept of interreligious friendship in the context of lived religious encounter, (2) social science on friendship across religious difference, (3) how interfaith solidarity develops in the face of the logic of identity, (4) the prominence of friendship in interfaith dialogue, and (5) the value of friendship for inter- and intrapersonal changemaking.

Raimon Panikkar recounts a story about "a European lady science teacher" in sub-Saharan Africa teaching young African children about the cycle of malaria, an awful disease that takes many victims in that region. After explaining it, she sensed the children did not really understand it. A child protested,

"But you didn't explain to us why my grandad died of malaria. That's what I want to know!" Panikkar distinguishes between appealing to the concept and appealing to the heart. To truly understand something, beyond the mere concept or scientific explanation, Panikkar argues for an appeal to the heart. To understand a concept at the deepest intimate levels, "it is necessary to use the heart rather than the mind"; it is necessary to "abandon the concept and be 'caught' by the 'thing' that we expect to understand." Appealing to the heart, to the person, to the lived experience, often goes further and deeper to concretize—to drive home—a concept, than relying solely on a theoretical appeal to the concept. Panikkar suggests there is a kind of knowledge "based on participation and experience, a knowledge that is not just rational living but the total intuition of the person who is *con-vinta* by who knows. To know (*co-naître* in French) is to be reborn together with the known thing." Knowledge about religious difference—being religiously literate—is one thing. Encountering dynamic living embodiments of religious difference in others is quite another thing.[1] Not only does interreligious friendship offer an intimate, interactive, and dynamic window into religious difference, it also functions to sharpen one's interreligious phronesis.

Building relationships and establishing friendships is an intuitive way to bridge divides, shatter stereotypes, break down walls, and establish deep connections. No question, people are different from one another. They are complicated. However, this premise does not rule out the reality of people connecting at fundamental levels of common humanity. Consider Daryl Davis, a Black American race reconciliation activist who befriends white supremacist Ku Klux Klan members with the aim to convince them to leave their hateful ideology behind. Through the power and influence of complicated friendships, Davis successfully shatters through the hate to their humanity. Also consider The Parents Circle—Families Forum (PCFF), a joint Israeli–Palestinian organization that brings together families on both sides of the conflict who have lost an immediate family member. In facing each other, sharing in each other's loss, and connecting on a common human level, the families support initiatives that "prevent bereavement, [and] promote dialogue, tolerance,

---

1 This paragraph is adapted from a section in Gustafson, "Vitality of Lived Religion Approaches," in *Interreligious Studies*, ed. Gustafson, 91. All quotations in this paragraph are from Raimon Panikkar, *Cultures and Religions in Dialogue*, 125, italics original; originally published as "Tres grandes interpretaciones de la interculturalidad," in *Interculturality, Gender, and Education*, 27–44.

reconciliation and peace."[2] Davis and the Parents Circle are but two among countless stories that speak to what many find deeply intuitive: when it comes to tearing down walls of hate, building bridges of trust, establishing friendships, and softening the hearts of others, real human relationships outperform arguments reliant on hard data, facts, or theo-philosophical models.

INTERRELIGIOUS FRIENDSHIP AND LIVING RELIGION

The Elijah Interfaith Institute, an international interfaith organization in Jerusalem, explicitly calls out friendship in their mission, which is to "foster unity in diversity, creating a harmonious world" in the spirit of "wisdom, inspiration, friendship and hope across religious traditions."[3] The institute distinguishes between neighbor and friend, the former being a person with whom one may share a common life in proximity, while the latter is a "person with whom we cultivate a deeper, more intentional, more focused, more intimate and ultimately more spiritual relationship."[4] The Elijah Institute grounds its understanding of interreligious friendship in the recognition of the "fundamental similarities that serve as its foundations," its function as a "means of attaining and propagating these higher goods, commonly recognized by our different religions," and its characteristics of mutual reciprocity.[5] The institute is among the global leaders in promoting relationships and friendships across religious difference; hence, its convictions about the nature of human relationships serve as a powerful foundation for thinking about interreligious friendship.

Chapters 5 and 6 sketched a Lived Religion (LR) approach to the study of religion and interreligious encounter. The spirit of the approach, which is hyperdevoted to the lived nuances and details of religion as lived in messy, complicated ways by particular people in particular places at particular times, can be harnessed in relationships to bridge religious differences. Within the broad multi- and interdisciplinary study of religion, LR approaches commence by examining, first and foremost, the ways individuals and communities practice their religious, spiritual, and secular traditions in the day-to-day rhythms of life. Energized by scholars such as Nancy Ammerman, Robert

---

2 The Parents Circle, "About PCFF."
3 Elijah Institute, "About."
4 Elijah Institute, "Friendship across Religions."
5 Elijah Institute, "Friendship across Religions."

Orsi, Meredith McGuire, and others, LR avoids looking past the messiness of concrete human religious practice and social life. Recall that for Ammerman, LR examines the "material, embodied aspects of religion as they occur in everyday life, in addition to listening for how people explain themselves. . . . Finding religion in everyday life means looking wherever and however we find people invoking a sacred presence."[6] Recall that Orsi observes, "'religion' cannot be neatly separated from the other practices of everyday life, from the ways that human beings work on the landscape, for example, or dispose of corpses, or arrange for the security of their offspring."[7] Likewise, recall McGuire's reminder that although "studies of religious organizations and movements are still relevant, they cannot capture the quality of people's everyday religious lives. As messy as these lives may be in practice, individuals' lived religions are what really matters to them."[8] Complicated relationships and friendships are central to the disordered messiness of human life. The LR approach, focusing less on textbook knowledge or preached teachings and more on lived practice, offers a window into the ordinariness of everyday friendship in the context of religion and interreligious friendship.

The term "interreligious" refers to the interaction, encounter, and relations between, among, and within individuals and communities with various religious, spiritual, and secular identities, traditions, worldviews, and ways of living. It is used in a broad and expansive manner to also account for the vast internal differences that are always present (but often overlooked) within particular traditions, communities, and individuals themselves. Hence, interreligious friendship can occur between two or more individuals who differ across these lines. As authentic friendship across religious, spiritual, and secular difference, the term intimately exposes the complicated messiness of human relations in a striking way. Therefore, in addition to providing the rich fruits of human relationship, interreligious friendship can also increase the lived (inter)religious literacy for those involved in the relationship.

Furthermore, human encounters, especially intimate friendships, often challenge individuals to reevaluate their convictions and practices (worldviews

---

6 Ammerman, "2013 Paul Hanly Furfey Lecture," 190–91; also cited in Gustafson, "Vitality of Lived Religion Approaches," 93.

7 Orsi, "Everyday Miracles," 6–7; also cited in Gustafson, "Vitality of Lived Religion Approaches," 93.

8 McGuire, Lived Religion, 213; also cited in Gustafson, "Vitality of Lived Religion Approaches," 94.

and lifeways) about the world, others, and themselves. The working definition of friendship is a bilateral mutual partnership that seeks the good of the
other without seeking (or expecting) anything in return. Seeking the good
of the other for their sake requires resilient honesty, trust, integrity, and
acceptance of the mutual reciprocation (i.e., a mutual assent to the social
contract of friendship). Friends with significant difference in lifeway or lifestance may be more likely to explicitly and implicitly challenge one another's
core beliefs and practices. Lifeways and lifestances of ultimate purpose or
concern (including religious, spiritual, and secular practices and beliefs of
ultimacy) are powerful contexts and catalysts for embodying and articulating
one's foundational beliefs and practices. Interreligious relationships, especially friendships, understood broadly, functionally epitomize lived religion
(religion as it is authentically lived in the world) insofar as they expose the
messy imperfection of the human condition in the fragile intimate vulner-
ability of human relationships. Dialogue and modes of encounter, especially
dialogue that humanizes, are primary ways for individuals, especially friends,
to interact. Stated more simply, friends readily serve as ultimate partners in
dialogue by constructively sparring[9] with each other. Friends incessantly (re)
craft one another's beliefs and practices in a hyperpersonal "cosmic dance"[10] of
mutual upbuilding dialogue as they advance one another toward greater self-
knowledge and mutual change.[11] Such dynamic mutual sharpening reflects a
foundational principle of dialogue articulated by the first principle of Leonard
Swidler's famous *Dialogue Decalogue*: "The essential purpose of dialogue is
to learn, which entails change. At the very least, to learn that one's dialogue
partner views the world differently is to effect a change in oneself. Recipro-
cally, change happens for one's partner as s/he learns about her/himself."[12]
Friendships with individuals with varying worldviews and lifeways provide promising opportunities for challenging dialogue, vulnerable learning,
mutual growth, and self-discovery for all parties involved.

---

9 See chapter 8 for more on the concept of friendly sparring.
10 Leonard Swidler, "The Cosmic Dance of Dialogue," in *Dialogue for Interreligious
Understanding* (New York: Palgrave Macmillan, 2014), 15–18.
11 Referencing John Cobb Jr., Anne Hege Grung, Emmanuel Levinas, and Simone de
Beauvoir, Oddbjørn Leirvik observes that "in many definitions of dialogue, the notion of
mutual change appears a pivotal one." Leirvik, "Philosophies of Interreligious Dialogue,"
Approaching Religion 1, no. 1 (2011): 21–22.
12 Swidler, "Dialogue Principles."

MY FRIEND AL AND THE SPILLOVER EFFECT

Political scientists David E. Campbell and Robert D. Putnam, in their popular study about Americans' engagement with religious diversity, propose the My Friend Al Principle and the related spillover effect. The My Friend Al Principle, which they deem a corollary of the Aunt Susan Principle introduced in the previous chapter, states that interreligious friendships often result not from intentionally seeking out relationships with others who differ religiously, rather they result coincidentally in the wake of friendships developed over a nonreligious circumstance, such as being coworkers, classmates, or neighbors, sharing devotion to the same professional sports team, or a love of similar music,[13] to name a few.[14] For example, Campbell and Putnam explain, the My Friend Al Principle occurs as follows:

You become friends with Al for, say, your shared affinity for beekeeping. As you get to know Al, you learn that in addition to his regard for apiculture, he is also an evangelical Christian. Prior to learning that, you may have been suspicious of evangelicals. But if your pal Al is an avid beekeeper—just like you—and is also an evangelical, then perhaps evangelicals are not so bad after all . . . upon realizing that you can become friends with Al, a member of a religious group you once viewed with suspicion, you come to reevaluate your perception of other religious groups too.[15]

The My Friend Al Principle suggests that becoming friends with someone from a religious group one once viewed with suspicion often leads to a reevaluation of one's perceptions of other religious groups as well. This is the spillover effect. The newfound empathy *spills over* and extends to groups other than

---

13 E.g., Daryl Davis recounts his first encounter with a white Supremacist Ku Klux Klan member with whom he struck up conversation over their shared love of boogie-woogie blues piano music.

14 Campbell and Putnam cite sociologist Robert Wuthnow, who argues that inter-religious encounter "occurs because a friend happened to belong to another religion, not because the person was actively engaged on a quest for new spiritual experiences. Often this exposure is involuntary . . . or focuses less on religion and more on sports, music, and other interests." Wuthnow, *America and the Challenges of Religious Diversity* (Princeton, NJ: Princeton University Press, 2005), 139; also cited in Campbell and Putnam, "America's Grace," 624.

15 Campbell and Putnam, "America's Grace," 624.

the initial group reevaluated, which shows the potential for relationships across religious difference to promote self-growth and awareness of one's attitudes and feelings toward groups and individuals who hold worldviews different than one's own.

FORGING SOLIDARITIES

Building relationships across difference—forging solidarities with those outside one's group—does not happen without intentional effort or action.[16] Diversity can be an asset, but without engagement it can easily become divisive, lead to conflict, and result in deeper division. Forging solidarities across difference entails the recognition that personal and group identities are dynamic and embedded in multiple contexts, which provides multiple opportunities for connections between and among several different groups. Social psychologist Henri Tajfel famously carried out experiments in the early 1970s to investigate intergroup relations by dividing groups along arbitrary and irrelevant lines. For instance, one experiment separated people into two groups at random. One group was told they overestimated the number of dots on a page while the other group was told they underestimated. Demonstrating the power of in-group bias and tribalism, members of each group showed favoritism toward those in their own group, despite not knowing or ever speaking to them.[17] Consider the (in)famous 1954 Robbers Cave State Park experiment in Oklahoma (USA) led by the American social psychologist Muzafer Sherif. The experiment divided twenty-two eleven-year-old boys attending a summer camp into two groups, the Eagles and the Rattlers, and pitted them against one another. All the boys shared a white, Protestant, middle-class background and did not know each other prior to the experience. The boys developed an attachment to one another in their respective groups. During four days of competitions between the groups, conflict and prejudice emerged. Verbal conflict and bragging led to the Eagles burning the Rattler's flag, which led to the Rattlers vandalizing the Eagles' cabin in revenge. At one point, camp

---

16 This section adapted from Hans Gustafson, "Is Transreligious Theology Unavoidable in Interreligious Theology and Dialogue?" 248–60, and Hans Gustafson, "'They're Not Really Christians.'"

17 Henri Tajfel, "Social Identity and Intergroup Behavior," *Social Science Information* 13, no. 65 (1974): 65–93.

staff had to physically separate the boys because they became too aggressive with one another. Each group showed a tendency to describe their group in favorable terms and the other group as unfavorable. When effort was made to reduce the conflict between the groups, increased contact only led to more conflict. However, camp staff eased tensions by artificially creating situations in which the groups needed to work together to reach common goals. For instance, the water to the camp was shut off and the two groups had to work together to get it fixed. Likewise, the food truck became stuck in the ditch and required the strength of both groups to pull it out with a rope. Both scenarios were artificially devised by the researchers to test whether cooperative action toward a common and mutually beneficial goal might soften edges, break down walls, and ease tension between the groups. Toward the end of the experiment, the researchers found the relations between the groups improved, name calling subsided, and some of the campers wanted to ride home from camp on the same bus as the other group.[18]

It is not self-evident that diversity is an asset, rather it is by nature divisive.[19] Without intentional action or effort (e.g., civic pluralism), diversity is likely to fester and leave misconceptions and ill-formed prejudices in place. In other words, diversity on its own without constructive engaged pluralism (action between groups and individuals) likely leads to conflict. Chapter 2 introduced the claim by the Religions in Schools Task Force that religions are, among other things, (1) "not internally homogeneous but diverse," (2) "dynamic and changing as opposed to static and fixed," and (3) "collections of ideas, practices, values, and stories that are all embedded in cultures and not isolated from them."[20] These claims hold true not just for religious traditions but for individuals' religious identities as well. Chapter 2 also introduced Jeannine Hill Fletcher's observation that "identities are not constructed on a singular feature (e.g., gender or religion) but that persons are located in multiple spaces and that these aspects of identity are mutually informing."[21]

---

18 Muzafer Sherif, O. J. Harvey, B. Jack White, William R. Hood, and Carolyn W. Sherif, *Intergroup Conflict and Cooperation* (Norman, OK: The University Book Exchange, 1954/61); also cited in Patel, *Interfaith Leadership*, 54–55.

19 Jonathan Haidt, "True Diversity Requires Generosity of Spirit," Heterodox Academy, November 2015; also noted by Patel that "diversity isn't always or necessarily positive," in *Interfaith Leadership*, 53.

20 AAR Religions in Schools Task Force and Moore, "Guidelines for Teaching about Religion in K–12 Public Schools in the United States," 12–14.

21 Fletcher, "Shifting Identity," 14–15.

Given the common human experience of multiple modes of identity—that is, hybridity of identity—people often implicitly accept the diverse and fragmented nature of their groups' identities as well as their own personal identity. Fletcher recognizes the benefit of this: "The hybridity of my identity means that although I do not identify completely with any one given category or community, I partially identify with many. The idea of hybrid identities and incomplete identification *within* a category can be embraced as the potential for Christians to forge solidarities[22] *outside* the Christian community."[23] A variation of the spillover effect: if someone recognizes that they can feel at home with groups they identify with in some but not all ways (e.g., a group that shares their religious worldview but is different in countless other ways), then they likely conclude there may be other groups with which they can also find common ground (or "forge solidarity with") despite not sharing their religious view or other major identity orientations.

Fletcher draws on feminist thought to confront the "logic of identity," which was introduced in chapter 2. The theory assumes distinctions between things by appealing to some (often ill-defined) firmly set boundaries and criteria between the 'things' and on the assumption that other things are the same as or identical to one another. For instance, a religious essentialist, implicitly operating on the logic of identity, might assume that "all Christians practice X and believe Y." The logic of identity provides a handy method to distinguish between things in a given class: e.g., in this case, to determine who is and is not a Christian based on whether they practice X and believe Y. Applied to religious identities, the logic of identity refers to the "grouping of persons into the various categories of 'the religions' and the assumptions made on the basis of those groupings."[24] Fletcher recognizes the inherent exclusion operative in this mode of classification insofar as it excludes certain members of groups. It also "too easily erase[s] the diversity and difference within any one community,"[25] which also too easily dilutes the rich internal diversity of a religious tradition by lumping together all Muslims (regardless of whether they identify as Sunni, Shia, etc.), lumping together all Christians (regardless of denominational affiliation or creedal confession), and so on. By erasing or

---

22 Fletcher, 5–24.
23 Fletcher, 19.
24 Fletcher, 14; Fletcher draws on Iris Marion Young to apply the logic of identity to personal identities.
25 Fletcher, 14.

minimizing "the diversity and difference"[26] within the traditions, the logic of identity reinforces the problematic nature of essentialism. However, the logic of identity can be useful insofar as it provides some parameters and meaning to "things." Although all religions are internally diverse, scholars and practitioners still need to make useful distinctions, such as a Jew who states unequivocally, "I am Jewish, not Christian. I do not believe Jesus of Nazareth was the Messiah as most Christians do." Fletcher recognizes that people still identify with certain groups and do not identify with others, but contends these group identifications are not in perfect lockstep with the others in any rigidly defined group. Consider the Christian who states "I am a Christian, but not a Christian in the same way as those Christians down the street. We share some beliefs and practices, but certainly not all. Yet, we are all still Christians." According to Fletcher, the logic of identity allows individuals to forge solidarities with various groups, stemming from their hybrid identities. This can bring together individuals with different identities not only within a broad intrareligious group (e.g., Protestants with Roman Catholics with Eastern Orthodox) but also across interreligious groups (Jews with Hindus with Jains, and so on). For instance, if a Christian is comfortable with other Christians with whom she only partially identifies, then there are likely other groups with whom she will feel comfortable despite not wholly identifying with them, including non-Christian groups.

A single individual can identify themselves in countless ways throughout the course of a day or week: father, son, coworker, mentor, teacher, student, brother, husband, friend, humanist, American, European, fan of a particular sport or sports team, beekeeper, male, English speaker, and on and on and on. These are all legitimate aspects of an individual's identity that places them within or outside particular groups, which are all internally diverse themselves. Fletcher's argument for the benefit of hybrid identities' potential to forge solidarities suggests that since one's community—for example, Christian community—is internally diverse, then it may potentially serve as a model to forge relationships with non-Christians, who also belong to multiple internally diverse groups. Most people can recall instances in which they identified more closely with—forged solidarities with—people in groups other than their own, such as having more in common with people from another religion, family, community, race, language, culture, country, town, team, etc., than in their own. Often these forged solidarities are founded

26 Fletcher, 14.

on other—perhaps more prevalent—identities beyond religious or spiritual affiliation, worldview, or practice.

FRIENDSHIP AND INTERFAITH DIALOGUE

There is increasing evidence from recent studies that demonstrate the benefit of interreligious friendships and their impact on personal self-discovery and the understanding of others. The IDEALS research survey (Interfaith Diversity Experiences & Attitudes Longitudinal Survey), conducted from 2015 to 2019, assessed "undergraduate [student] encounters with religious and worldview diversity" in the United States.[27] It found evidence for the spillover effect among its central findings. "Evidence suggests that the benefits of friendships across difference can extend beyond the friends themselves building appreciation for and reducing prejudice toward members of other cultural groups."[28] In other words, "the positive effects of gaining a close friend in one group also appear to generalize to other outgroups."[29] Although it is not clear whether the IDEALS project used a hard-and-fast definition of "friend" (as distinct from neighbor or acquaintance), it is clear that "evidence from IDEALS shows that friendship matters over and above conditions and experiences such as a welcoming campus climate, support to freely express one's worldview, and meaningful yet challenging encounters with diverse peers."[30] IDEALS demonstrates the influence of interreligious friendship to elicit inter- and intrapersonal change: "friendships that students develop in their first year on campus seem to do more than shape intergroup dynamics; they appear to have the power to influence students' inner development and core features of their self-understanding and personal identity."[31] Unsurprisingly, IDEALS lends evidence to suggest that friendships have significant impact on learning across worldview and lifeway difference among American university students.

Chapter 6 introduced the 2014 case study on interfaith dialogue in which ethnographer Martin Stringer observed a six-month, small-group interfaith dialogue program in the religiously diverse city of Birmingham (UK).

---

27 Interfaith Youth Core, "Interfaith Diversity Experiences & Attitudes Longitudinal Survey: 2015–2019."
28 Rockenbach et al., "Friendships Matter," 1.
29 Rockenbach et al., 13.
30 Rockenbach et al., 11.
31 Rockenbach et al., 16.

In the study, the group's focus on everyday friendship stood out. The dialogue sessions emphasized everyday lived (religious) experience. Stringer reports that among his several findings, "One of the things that particularly struck me, given that these were interreligious conversations, was just how little specifically religious language or discourse was being used within the conversations. . . . By focusing on 'lived religion' and people's everyday experiences, the language used to express feelings and interrelations tended not to be that of religion."[32] When the group's dialogue participants were asked about what gives them hope in challenging times, although responses such as God, scripture, prayer were common, "the one that was generally picked up and shared most widely, however, was that of reaching out to others, of 'friendship.' . . . Relationships, friendship, sharing, hospitality, companionship, all of these were expressed both as important resources available from within the religious traditions, but also seen as being necessary for future dialogue."[33] These responses imply a clear recognition of the vital need for and value of deep interpersonal relationships for a long-term hope-filled future within diverse communities. The dialogue group, a sponsored program of the Birmingham Conversations project, was organized by a collaboration called Faiths, Neighbors, Changemakers (FNC). Appropriately, FNC recognizes the powerful tether between friendship and *changemaking*, especially in the context of strengthening the local neighborly fabric across the Birmingham area. The final section of this chapter reflects on the role of relationships and friendships in inter- and intrapersonal changemaking. Encounters that center relationship-building can help develop one's interreligious phronesis by increasing one's self-awareness and openness to intrapersonal change.

INTER/INTRAPERSONAL CHANGEMAKING

The concept of changemaking (and changemaker) is slowly gaining traction.[34] On the frontlines of this trend is Ashoka, a forty-year-old American organization with a global presence founded by social entrepreneur Bill Drayton,

---

32 Stringer, "Lived Religion and Difficult Conversations," 10–11.
33 Stringer, "Lived Religion and Difficult Conversations," 11.
34 This section is adapted from a section in the forthcoming Hans Gustafson, "Friends in Foxholes," in *Friends in This World*, ed. Anne-Marie Ellithorpe, Hussam S. Timani, and Laura Duhan Kaplan (Minneapolis: Fortress Press, forthcoming).

which "identifies and supports the world's leading social entrepreneurs, learns from the patterns in their innovations, and mobilizes a global community that embraces these new frameworks to build an 'everyone a changemaker world.'"[35] The Ashoka organization defines a changemaker as "anyone who is taking creative action to solve a social problem."[36] Changemaking can occur in several contexts (personal, local, national, global) and at various levels of impact (direct service, scaled direct service, systems change, and framework change).[37] Strategies to incite social change vary widely. For instance, Campus Compact, an American organization that "advances the public purposes of colleges and universities by deepening their ability to improve community life and to educate students for civic and social responsibility," identifies up to twenty major strategies for social change: advocacy and raising awareness, volunteering and direct service, community building, economic development, deliberative and reflective dialogue, mutual aid, social innovation and enterprise, socially responsible daily behavior, protests and demonstrations, voting and formal political activities, and others.[38] Changemaking occurs in local, national, and global contexts, but also concurrently at *intra-* and *inter*personal levels.

In relation to these changemaking contexts, levels, and strategies, relationships—in particular, friendship across worldview and lifeway difference—are especially beneficial for *intra*personal and *inter*personal changemaking. Personal changemaking emphasizes the various ways, modes, and strategies that happen between and among individuals and communities as well as the intrapersonal change that takes place within an individual. Intrapersonal changemaking occurs in coordination with the various levels of impact and major strategies denoted above. The focus here remains on how intrapersonal changemaking is catalyzed by friendship across religious worldview and lifeway difference in "deliberative and reflective dialogue" as an instrument for leadership cultivation. Campus Compact articulates deliberative and reflective dialogue as "exchanging and evaluating different ideas and approaches around particular issues in a public setting, [and] learning about the experiences and stories of others by listening fully and actively."[39] Dialogue—and

---

35 Ashoka United States, "About Ashoka."
36 Ashoka United States, "Frequently Asked Questions."
37 Marina Kim, "Rethinking the Impact Spectrum," AshokaU, April 30, 2015.
38 Minnesota Campus Compact, "Social Change Wheel 2.0 Toolkit," June 16, 2020.
39 Iowa and Minnesota Campus Compact, "Social Change Wheel 2.0 Toolkit," 2.

often the dialogue that surfaces naturally but not always effortlessly among friends—can stimulate interpersonal change, which refers to the dynamic nature of the relationship between two or more individuals.

Dialogue need not refer exclusively to literal conversation, but broadly includes activities and phenomena pertaining to any meaningful encounters between people. For many people, interreligious learning, friendship, and engagement often occur, and are easily understood and recognized, in the sharing and empathizing with the seemingly ordinary, mundane, everyday tasks common to all humanity: from the challenge and joys of raising children, to the struggle to earn a living, to contributing to one's neighborhood and community, and to the suffering and sorrows of burying dead loved ones. In short, dialogue is not just conversation about ideas and worldviews but includes the dialogue of life: lived encounter with bodies and souls operating and struggling in the world.

Part and parcel of interpersonal change that occurs between individuals—especially between friends devoted to willing the good of the other—is intrapersonal change, which refers to the self-reflexive interior change of an individual. Intrapersonal change can manifest in myriad ways ranging from change in belief, ethics, and ideology to the altering of one's attitudes and actions toward specific issues and contexts. It can include the self-discovery of personal traits not previously known, such as discerning one's natural tendency toward self-destructive habits or seeking grudge-bearing conflict or an inclination toward taking on the burden of others. Encounters between individuals invite them to develop their self-awareness (foundational to leadership and intercultural competencies) through the (re)evaluation of their core beliefs and ideas about the world, others, and self-identity. Dialogue, in the context of trust, mutuality, and goodwill for the other, can serve as a primary mode of encounter that enables the surfacing of significant difference. The face of difference, especially when difference is unveiled through trustworthy and respectful friendship, can constructively burden individuals to see themselves in new light and through the eyes of the other. This newfound self-knowledge is not only vital for intrapersonal change, but foundational for cultivating practical interfaith wisdom for everyday living and leadership, the central foci of the remaining two chapters.

14

Practical Interfaith Wisdom

Chapter Outline

I. Interfaith Wisdom as *Phronesis*
    a. *Phronesis* as Wherewithal
    b. *Phronesis* as Virtue
    c. Interreligious *Phronesis* as Guiding Virtue

II. Four Dimensions of Interreligious *Phronesis*
    a. Know What (*episteme*)
    b. Know Who (*empatheia*)
    c. Know Why (*sophia*)
    d. Know How (*techne*)

III. For the Right *Reasons*

"The dominant American attitude toward other faith traditions is indifference,"[1] claims David Roozen, director of the Hartford Institute for Religion Research. Indifference runs parallel to the common response to religious diversity (from chapter 10) of blurring, minimizing, ignoring, dismissing, or a blasé attitude. Developing Interreligious Phronesis (IP), the central focus of this chapter, entails getting beyond a state of indifference toward practical engagement with religious diversity by becoming aware of potential tensions or opportunities in (inter)religiously complex situations and having

---

1 Michelle Boorstein, "Interfaith Movement Struggles to Adapt to Changing Religious Landscape," *Washington Post*, August 16, 2013.

the wherewithal (ability and resources) to responsibly act in a constructive manner through thoughtful action, leadership, and motivation of others in ways that benefit individuals and groups in pursuit of common public goods. This chapter sketches interfaith wisdom as interreligious *phronesis*, a guiding virtue with four dimensions (know what, know who, know why, and know how), and concludes with an examination of the vital ethical component of IP.

INTERFAITH WISDOM AS *PHRONESIS*

Developing the wherewithal to act in concrete situations in accordance with virtue requires time, education, and experience. According to Aristotle, virtues are characteristics of good behavior guided by *phrónēsis* (φρόνησῐς), often translated as "practical wisdom,"[2] which enable one to do the right thing in the right place at the right time with the right people for the right reasons. *Phronesis* is not just wisdom for wisdom's sake but emphasizes a particular practical and agency-based dimension. *Phronesis* is "concerned with action,"[3] entails "the ability to deliberate"[4] and act in a manner that is prudent,[5] is "neither a pure science nor an art,"[6] and allows individuals to see what is good not only for themselves but for the common public good as well.[7] *Phronesis* entails wisdom, which, strikingly similar to Aristotle's description, is commonly defined by contemporary psychology as

meta-cognitive processes and strategies grounded in moral aspirations... [that] entail considering multiple perspectives, balancing different view-points, integrating opposing views, reflection, and adapting problem solutions to their specific contexts. Moral aspirations relevant to wisdom include the willingness to balance one's interests with those of others, the pursuit of truth, and an orientation towards shared humanity without defaulting to in-group favoritism and out-group negativity.[8]

---

2 Aristotle, *Nichomachean Ethics*, trans. Martin Ostwald (Englewood Cliffs: Prentice Hall, 1962), 1144b25.

3 Aristotle, *Nichomachean Ethics*, 1141b22.

4 Aristotle, 1140a32.

5 Aristotle, 1143a8.

6 Aristotle, 1140b.

7 Aristotle, 1140b7, 20.

8 Mengxi Dong and Marc A. Fournier, "What Are the Necessary Conditions for Wisdom?" *Collabra: Psychology* 8, no. 1 (2022): 1; citing Igor Grossman et al.,

As a virtue, *phronesis* is cultivated over a lifetime of practice, experience, education, and exposure. It is a practice, a craft, a skillset, an orientation, and more. A chief aim among many scholar-practitioners of interreligious studies is to facilitate the development of interreligious *phronesis*, or practical wisdom to be utilized in religiously complex contexts. This aim resonates with what is referred to elsewhere as interreligious wherewithal, "that virtue of being aware of a potential tension or opportunity in (inter)religiously complex situations and having the skill to do something constructive about it through thoughtful action, leadership, and motivation of others."[9] Interfaith wisdom as *phronesis* provides guidance for navigating religiously complex situations with constructive action and leadership, which requires wherewithal.

Phronesis as Wherewithal

Interfaith wisdom as *phronesis* requires not just the knowledge and awareness to act, but also the ability, skill, and resources to act.[10] Imbibing a steady diet of American sports television broadcasts, especially American professional football, one is likely to eventually hear the commentor remark about the "wherewithal" of a player to make an exceptional play. In an article for ESPN, the multinational sports media network owned by Disney and self-described "Worldwide Leader in Sports," sportswriter Greg Garber, in an attempt to make the case that Miami Dolphins quarterback Dan Marino was the best pure passer in the history of American football, writes, "quarterback is the most difficult position to play in professional sports. The athlete must have the vision to see the defense, the brain to assimilate the information, the *wherewithal* to quickly choose a course of action and the physical skill to deliver the ball where it will do the most damage."[11] Wherewithal is used often enough in this context that it has adopted a broader more colloquial definition beyond its traditional usage as a noun to refer "the means or resources one has at one's disposal,"[12] referring to financial capital and resources. In

---

"The Science of Wisdom in a Polarized World," *Psychological Inquiry* 31, no. 2 (2020): 103–33.

9 Hans Gustafson, "Interreligious Wherewithal," State of Formation, November 16, 2017.

10 This section draws on and revises Gustafson, "Interreligious Wherewithal."

11 Greg Garber, "Call Dan the Greatest . . . Passer," ESPN.com, November 19, 2003.

12 *Merriam-Webster*, s.v. "wherewithal," accessed October 26, 2017, https://tinyurl.com/5fb7zd9x.

the context of athletic performance, the term takes on an expanded usage without losing sight of its root.

"Wherewithal" is a curious word. Part of the English lexicon since the sixteenth century, it functions as a pronoun, noun, conjunction, and was probably originally used exclusively as a conjunction bringing together "where" and "withal," the latter an outdated term that can simply mean "with." The conjunction "wherewith" can also mean "that with" or "by which," which is similar to the usage of the pronoun function of wherewithal. For instance, the King James Bible preaches "So shall I have wherewith to answer him that reproacheth me: for I trust in thy word."[13]

"Wherewithal" in the context of IP and interreligious encounter captures the essential feature of having the ability and resources coupled with a certain posture, approach, attitude, orientation, awareness, or disposition in (inter) religiously complex situations. Retaining the essence of "wherewithal," which alludes to "possessing what one needs to make something happen," the word can also connote the state of being present in a particular place and time (one's specific context) with others, that is, where-with-all. This is a departure from its historic and intended usage, but no less instructive. Having wherewithal in this sense means to be aware of and sensitive to the needs, concerns, and desires of others—particularly those not regularly or adequately seen or heard—in a given context, but also having the ability to make something happen. Truly being with-all is to remain conscious of individual and community needs while having the foresight to surmise how particular actions might produce particular consequences down the road.

However, simply being aware or having such a posture is not enough to qualify as the virtue of wherewithal. Wherewithal goes beyond mere awareness. It includes having the ability and resources to engage and act in a deliberate manner. An individual may have the utmost awareness about how the position of quarterback ought to be performed and where to "deliver the ball where it will do the most damage," but without the ability, skill, and resources at his disposal to actually do it, the awareness is rendered less useful (perhaps useless). Likewise, wherewithal is not just about being conscious of the concerns and circumstances of others, but requires the ability to do something about it, to take responsibility and make something happen. Wherewithal includes skill, ability, resources, and competency in addition to knowledge and awareness.

---

13 Psalm 119:42.

Phronesis as Virtue

The classic Western Aristotelian approach to virtue (*aretê*) refers to a virtue as "an excellent trait of character."[14] More precisely, an individual possessing a particular virtue is one for whom the virtue is an all-encompassing attitude, orientation, or disposition that permeates the whole of one's persona "to notice, expect, value, feel, desire, choose, act, and react in certain characteristic ways."[15] Hence, the ethical theory of virtue ethics does not focus on particular ethical issues or questions, but on the person as a moral agent, since the virtuous person strives for the good and to act in accordance with virtue in all situations. The term "virtuoso" is often used to describe a musician that has achieved peak excellence in her craft; she plays the piano seemingly without even thinking about it. The music seamlessly flows from her through the instrument as she plays every note precisely and perfectly and on time: not too slow, not too fast, not too loud, not too soft; but just right, achieving the pinnacle of perfection. Hitting the mark just right—not too much or too little—according to Aristotle, lies "between excess and deficiency." He preaches that "an expert in any field avoids excess and deficiency, but seeks the median and chooses it—not the median of the object but the median relative to us."[16] The right amount of a particular action varies relative to the context in which the person operates. Some situations call for a tremendous amount of courage, an amount which in other situations may be reckless. Other situations call for less courage, which in other situations might be cowardly fear. Virtuous action lies in hitting the mark "at the right time, toward the right objects, toward the right people, for the right reason, and in the right manner."[17] The pianist, not playing out of habit but virtue, strikes the right note at the right time with the right force and in the right manner. She is a virtuous pianist.

Virtue is rooted deeper than habit. It is a holistic disposition of one's persona. Disposition refers to a deliberately chosen attitude and not an instinctual, natural inclination, or propensity to a particular mode of behavior. An individual possessing the virtue of honesty will not only be habitually honest, but honesty will permeate all facets of his life: he will be concerned

---

14 Rosalind Hursthouse and Glen Pettigrove, "Virtue Ethics," in *The Stanford Encyclopedia of Philosophy*, Winter 2018 ed., ed. Edward N. Zalta.

15 Hursthouse and Pettigrove, "Virtue Ethics."

16 Aristotle, *Nichomachean Ethics*, 1106b5–6.

17 Aristotle, 1106b20.

with honesty in all matters of life and relations, he will surround himself with honest friends, and will harbor disdain for dishonesty (perhaps even disliking fictional stories of dishonesty and cheating). Honesty is part of his inner and outer everyday persona that orients the way he lives in the world. Like the pianist who seemingly plays the piano effortlessly and perfectly, the individual with virtuous honesty will not struggle to be honest, rather it flows naturally.

An individual that possesses a virtue (whether it be courage, justice, temperance, honesty, pride, moderation, etc.) has "a certain complex mindset . . . [which includes] the wholehearted acceptance of a distinctive range of considerations as reasons for action."[18] Developing IP as a virtue refers not only to developing a general awareness or habit of knowing the complex ways in which "religion is always in the room"[19] and impacts particular situations but also to fostering a moral excellence deeply entrenched in one's character that summons a complex mindset to consider and implement a range of constructive and collaborative responses that draw on available resources and assets.

Interreligious Phronesis as Guiding Virtue

As a guiding virtue, IP strives for the good. It seeks the good life, the morally good life, not only for the possessor but for the common public goods as well. Cultivating the moral character of virtues for IP involves *consistency, develops over time*, and requires ongoing *education* and *practice*.

Consistency: As personal characteristics, moral virtues remain relatively consistent. A virtuously honest person is not honest one day and dishonest the next. Integrated into one's character, honesty remains consistent, steady, and present day-in-day-out. Over time, individuals develop virtues in a way that enables them to act with consistency in multiple situations. An individual with a high degree of IP remains steady in their attunement to how religion may play pivotal roles in various contexts, and they act consistently and accordingly over time in responding to, and leading in the face of, opportunities and challenges.

---

18 Hursthouse and Pettigrove, "Virtue Ethics."
19 Liz Kineke, www.lizkineke.com, accessed July 30, 2021.

Longitudinal Development: Virtues develop over time through experience and practice. Though people may be born with natural tendencies, no one is born with perfectly formed virtues aligned for the world into which they are thrust. Natural tendencies can still be developed, grown, curbed, and shaped over a lifetime through experience, practice, and encounters with friends, parents, siblings, teachers, role models, and others. The next chapter details aspects of personal and leadership development through the cultivation of self-awareness. It sketches how an individual, in becoming more aware of their problematic and promising habitual tendencies, can develop their virtuous capacities and integrate them into their full persona. No individual is born with a perfectly developed capacity of IP. As with all virtues, IP develops through practice, mistakes, experience, and role models. Over time, an individual may identify strengths and shortcomings within their capacity for IP and focus their development accordingly. As the *Tao of Leadership* instructs, "consciousness or awareness . . . is the source of your ability. Learn to become increasingly conscious."[20]

Education and Practice: Developing virtues involves education and practice. Teachers, mentors, parents, role models, and experience are all important. Aristotle famously taught that virtues are acquired through practice:

we acquire by first having put them into action, and the same is also true of the arts (technical skills). For things which we have to learn before we can do them we learn by doing: men become builders by building houses, and harpists by playing the harp. Similarly, we become just by the practice of just actions, self-controlled by exercising self-control, and courageous by performing acts of courage.[21]

Learning to swim is difficult, if not impossible, without getting wet. Likewise, *being* virtuous without *acting* virtuously is impossible. Learning to swim properly, efficiently, and in a timely manner requires knowledgeable instructors and mentors who not only provide appropriate education, but also serve as role models. Furthermore, simply being knowledgeable about a particular skill or virtue is not the same as acquiring it. It must be practiced. It is not enough to have deep conceptual knowledge of compassion in order

---

20 John Haider, *The Tao of Leadership* (Palm Beach, FL: Green Dragon Books, 2015), 117.

21 Aristotle, *Nichomachean Ethics*, 1103a30–35, parenthetical added.

to be compassionate. One must also perform acts of compassion, which may be difficult at first, nor come naturally. Over time, being compassionate may become less difficult and eventually habitual. It may become part of one's persona as one becomes a virtuously compassionate person. Consider the following analogy: Many people have an adequate conceptual understanding of mindfulness mediation, its theory, method, and utility. However, they find it difficult, unnatural, and rarely practice it. Meditation is not a habitual or virtuous part of their overall persona. If they slowly devote more time to practicing it on a regular basis (e.g., begin with one minute a day and then keep adding a minute), not only is it likely to become easier but they may also develop a deep-seated yearning and need to practice it on a regular basis as it becomes part of who they are. Virtues are not habits, but they can become habituated through conscious, intentional, and deliberate choices to learn about and practice them. One chooses to be virtuous by practicing a virtue and habituating oneself to it through practice and knowledge. IP requires education and opportunities to put it into practice. Over time, one may develop the virtue of IP by engaging opportunities and challenges in which religious diversity or interreligious encounter is present. The virtue of IP can develop over time for those who learn to act consistently in various situations. Consistent with theoretical virtue ethics, focus is not on determining universal answers to particular questions or issues. Rather, focus is on the person practicing IP and striving for the good in all situations. No one universal action or answer is sufficient to apply across all situations. Prudent actions differ depending on the multivariable contexts and are determined accordingly by the individual operating with the virtue of IP. In other words, as the virtue of IP strives for the good (moral goods and the common public goods), the virtuous practitioner of IP maintains the ability to consistently determine appropriate courses of action in various contexts.

FOUR DIMENSIONS OF INTERRELIGIOUS PHRONESIS[22]

For the development of everyday leadership for (inter)religiously complex contexts that require thoughtful agency for the common good, the guiding

---

22 This section is adapted from Hans Gustafson, "An Emerging *Phronetic* Framework in Interfaith and Interreligious Studies Courses in the United States," *Journal of Interreligious Studies* 36 (2022): 64–74.

virtue of *phronesis* provides an integrative synthesis of knowledge (know what), empathy (know who), wisdom (know why), and technical skill-craft (know how).[23] The introduction and chapter 1 offer various definitions of interreligious studies (IRS).[24] The civic-oriented and practitioner approach to IRS described by Eboo Patel and complemented by Kate McCarthy are the most relevant for this chapter's focus. Patel's vision for the field emphasizes the implications of interreligious encounter "for communities, civil society, and global politics,"[25] with a "research agenda for a civic approach to interfaith studies [that] focuses on how interactions among diverse orientations around religion—both in the lives of individuals and in the practices of institutions—impact civic space."[26] McCarthy stresses the need for IRS to serve "the public good by bringing its analysis to bear on practical approaches to issues in religiously diverse societies,"[27] and therefore "must frame its values and goals in terms appropriate to the secular academy, aimed at the cultivation of civic rather than religious dispositions."[28] Marianne Moyaert acknowledges that this approach is not unique to the United States but also informs contemporary trends in Europe, where, "Universities increasingly agree that for students to become successful, responsible citizens of pluralized societies they need to acquire interfaith skills, to sensitively and effectively relate to people who believe and practice differently."[29] IP provides a holistic framework for interreligious studies, especially for its emerging scholar-practitioner dimensions.

Increasingly, IRS as a pedagogy, especially at the Bachelor and Professional levels, involves developing or building practical capacities to face complex

---

23 Elsewhere I address how the popular "cultural competence" model shares a kinship to the phronetic model proposed here. "The cultural competence framework develops individuals' ability to navigate culturally diverse contexts while critically examining their own attitudes, awareness, knowledge, and skills, all four of which loosely map on to the fourfold *phronetic* framework proposed here. Interreligious *phronesis* goes beyond the cultural framework to include—and emphasize—the role and context of religiosity. *Phronesis* lends itself to cultivating leadership competencies." Gustafson, "An Emerging *Phronetic* Framework in Interfaith and Interreligious Studies Courses in the United States," 64–74.

24 See the introduction to this volume, note 3.

25 Patel, "Toward a Field of Interfaith Studies."

26 Patel, "A Civic Approach to Interfaith Studies," 30.

27 McCarthy, "(Inter)Religious Studies," 12.

28 McCarthy, "Secular Imperatives," 172.

29 Moyaert, "Interfaith Learning in Academic Spaces," 35.

problems in everyday life, especially what psychologist Robert Sternberg refers to as the "weighty matters" of resolving disputes with neighbors, partners, coworkers, and clients.[30] A trend among IRS and other academic pedagogies in the humanities is the integration of applied practical dimensions in academic environments increasingly characterized by "decreasing enrollments and increased pressure to justify themselves on market grounds."[31] McCarthy observes that students today, perhaps more than ever, are under "the triple threat of educational debt, stagnant job markets, and a wider culture that increasingly defines the value of education in terms of its immediate economic payoff."[32] IRS scholars Wakoh Shannon Hickey and Margarita M. W. Suárez contend that "liberal arts education has come under attack in recent years by those who argue that colleges should provide practical training in skills that will net graduates high-paying jobs."[33] Some religious studies, theology, and IRS programs have responded by adding applied dimensions to their programs' missions, "framed in terms of civic and professional (rather than religious) values and skills."[34] Deanna Womack reports that some IRS programs are embedded within the curriculum of other programs in an effort to serve as a "bridge linking the question of religion to STEM fields and pre-professional degree programs that no longer require students to show any knowledge of religious and theological studies."[35] For instance, an IRS degree or certificate might be embedded within a bachelor's degree program in business leadership, nursing, or education not only to provide relevant basic religious literacy training for the preprofessional students (which may no longer be part of the general liberal arts course sequence) but also to introduce them to increasingly necessary interpersonal skills for effectively navigating diverse religious identities among colleagues, consumers, clients, vendors, and various publics.

Despite the trendy nature of integrating applied learning experiences and cultivating transferrable skills and competencies into the curriculum, Jenn Lindsay argues that knowledge acquisition remains a primary or "front-line task," even prior to the basic building blocks of developing attitudes and skills, for the capacity-building project of developing

---

30 Sternberg, "Where Have All the Flowers of Wisdom Gone?" 17.
31 McCarthy, "(Inter)Religious Studies," 4.
32 McCarthy, "(Inter)Religious Studies," 4.
33 Hickey and Suárez, "Meeting Others, Seeing Myself," 120.
34 McCarthy, "(Inter)Religious Studies," 14.
35 Womack, "From History of Religions to Interfaith Studies," 24.

students' interreligious competence.[36] Hence, there is increasing momentum and focus on primary, postprimary, and undergraduate curricula that build students' basic religious literacy in addition to their practical knowledge and wisdom (phronesis) of other religious traditions. This curricular framework is comprised of four dimensions of interreligious phronesis for everyday leadership: *know what* (e.g., basic religious literacy), *know who* (empathetic lived engagement), *know why* (self-knowledge and awareness), and *know how* (technical knowledge of dialogue and leadership).

Know What (*episteme*)

Know What aims at conveying or producing *epistemic* knowledge about various topics in various ways.[37] Trina Janiec Jones' and Cassie Meyer's study of faculty teaching IRS in the United States corroborates Lindsay's argument above about knowledge acquisition serving as the primary frontline task for developing interreligious understanding. Jones and Meyer report, "among the courses we observed, one thing is constant: the 'facts' about religious traditions are considered important—vital even—but not as ends in themselves."[38] Acquiring basic vital facts, not as ends in themselves but as practical knowledge, comes through the development of basic religious and interreligious literacy (see chapter 7). Congruent with current trends in leadership studies, knowledge (literacy) ought not be confused with an accumulation of information, but rather understood to reflect the understanding of key underlying principles, facts, and concepts characteristic to the domain of action (in this case, religiously diverse contexts).[39] Acquiring epistemic knowledge and

---

36 Jenn Lindsay, "Growing Interreligious and Intercultural Competence in the Classroom," *Teaching Theology and Religion* 23 (2020): 17–33. Lindsay argues, "Rather than emphasizing a change in *attitude* first, we argue a different strategy for improving intercultural and in interreligious competence: *knowledge* of other cultures must come prior to the development of skills to interact with them, thereby paving the way, finally, for the area of competence most deep-seated in cognition and the most resistant to change: the attitude," 22, italics original.

37 *Know What* corresponds to Jones's and Meyers's fourth dominant theme of contemporary interreligious and interfaith studies pedagogy: "Interfaith Literacy and Religious Literacy." Jones and Meyer, "Interfaith and Interreligious Pedagogies," 23–25.

38 Jones and Meyer, "Interfaith and Interreligious Pedagogies," 23.

39 Michael D. Mumford, Stephen J. Zaccaro, Francis D. Harding, T. Owen Jacobs, and Edwin A. Fleishman, "Leadership Skills for a Changing World," *Leadership Quarterly* 11, no. 1 (2000): 20.

basic vital facts (i.e., becoming religiously literate) includes reflecting on with whom authority lies with regards to measuring and determining the epistemologically correct or "right" ways of knowing about religion. This question becomes especially important in cases that involve actors with competing interests or divergent ultimate aims (ranging from respect, tolerance, and pluralism that strive to serve the common good to disrespect, exclusion, and fear that foment hate and division). Although chapter 7 detailed (inter)religious literacy, a few points are worth stressing here in chapter 14. Religious literacy is often understood as an "operative knowledge"[40] that contributes to the civic welfare of the individual and common good. Beyond acquiring textbook knowledge or collecting facts, dates, definitions, and names, the religiously literate person is equipped to navigate the complicated, nuanced, and messy realities of contemporary religiously diverse societies. In fact, as Barbara McGraw argues, "Religious literacy is not about knowing every religion—which is impossible—but being well-informed enough generally to know what one needs to find out to be effectively literate for the situation at hand."[41] Similarly, Eboo Patel references this ability to recognize what one does *not* know and the ability to find out as part of what it means to build

---

40 Kevin Minister, quoted in Jones and Meyer, "Interfaith and Interreligious Pedagogies," 26.
41 McGraw, "Toward a Framework for Interfaith Leadership," 6.

"a radar screen for religious diversity."[42] Interreligious or interfaith literacy, some argue, goes beyond knowledge—beyond basic religious literacy—to the practice of breaking down barriers and addressing conflicts and misunderstandings that result from the reality of religious diversity.[43] According to Moyaert, interreligious learning is "not focused on textbook knowledge about different religious traditions, but rather on promoting interreligious literacy. The goal is to equip students with the necessary competencies to address religious diversity."[44] The trend to foster interreligious/interfaith literacy beyond religious literacy may stem from the concern over the (in)efficacy of the latter[45] to be of value in professional settings, to "bring social benefits or cure societal ills,"[46] or to prove successful in motivating citizens to serve the common public good. A powerful means to advance Moyaert's vision of interreligious literacy—to get beyond the textbook and put a human face on religion—is through direct empathetic engagement with real people as articulated by the second dimension of interreligious *phronesis*: know who.

Know Who (*empatheia*)

Know Who aims to foster *empathetic* engagement with real people across religious difference or with religious diversity, often through lived or experiential learning.[47] The intuition that both parties have the potential for change and transformation through direct encounter is evident in several comparative and contact theories. As this book advocates, Lived Religion approaches to the study of religion (see chapter 5) and their potential to optimize IRS (see

---

42 Patel, *Interfaith Leadership*, 135.

43 In *Teaching Religious Literacy to Combat Religious Bullying*, W. Y. Alice Chan argues that teaching religious literacy in secondary schools promotes understanding and tolerance while influencing religious bullying, positively and negatively.

44 Moyaert, "On the Role of Ritual in Interfaith Education," 59.

45 Tenzan Eaghll challenges the "cliché" (or false platitude) that "learning about religion leads to tolerance" in "Learning about Religion Leads to Tolerance," in *Stereotyping Religion*. See also Wolfart, "'Religious Literacy,'" 1–28.

46 Wolfart, "'Religious Literacy,'" abstract.

47 *Know Who* corresponds to Jones's and Meyers's first dominant theme of contemporary interreligious and interfaith studies pedagogy—"Experiencing Religious Diversity"—as well as the third and seventh themes of "Dialogue" and "Personal Reflection and Self-Disclosure." Jones and Meyer, "Interfaith and Interreligious Pedagogies," 15–17, 19–22, 30–32.

chapter 6) rests on the premise that IRS primarily investigates people and their relations between and among each other.[48] Hence, direct engagement advances knowledge of other and self. Fostering empathy, a dimension of *phronesis*, Catherine Cornille suggests, "may be located somewhere on the border between knowledge and skill. It involves experiential knowledge of the other that may be more innate as a personal skill in some, while requiring more effort in others."[49] Empathy is the "ability to resonate with the beliefs and practices of the other[, which] helps to break down barriers, while the inability to do so tends to cast the religious other as strange and threatening."[50] Empathetic knowledge of others (*know who*) facilitates, in part, the process of knowing one's self, which is a major aim not only of leadership development (chapter 15) but also of the third dimension of interreligious *phronesis*: know why.

Know Why (*sophia*)

Know Why aims to impart transcendent wisdom (*sophia*) for a deeper understanding of self, world, and life.[51] Phronesis concerns doing the right thing in the right place at the right time to the right person(s) for the right reasons. The *know why* dimension of IP involves the agent's reflection on their own personal worldview, values, practices, and ways of living insofar as they are able to articulate and justify proper courses of action. In large part, it requires self-knowledge, self-awareness, and the ability to articulate one's self through narrative and action. Psychologists Carolyn Aldwin and Michael Levenson argue that practical wisdom is based on self-knowledge and self-transcendence. "Without reflection on how and from where our values and beliefs have risen, we cannot see through the illusions fostered by those who seek to influence us or those reflecting the consequences of

---

48 Gustafson, "Vitality of Lived Religion Approaches," 92.

49 Cornille, "Interreligious Empathy," 223.

50 Cornille, 223.

51 *Know Why* corresponds to Jones's and Meyers's sixth dominant theme of contemporary interreligious and interfaith studies pedagogy: "Students' Personal Religious Journeys" as well as the second, third and seventh themes of "Case Study Snapshots," "Dialogue" and "Personal Reflection and Self-Disclosure." Jones and Meyer, "Interfaith and Interreligious Pedagogies," 19–22, 30–32.

poorly chosen actions for our own health and well-being."[52] Self-transcendence refers to building one's capacity "to stand outside of their immediate sense of time and place to view life from a larger, more objective perspective."[53] Foundational for several models and theories of leadership development is the sentiment that "becoming a leader begins when you come to understand who you are, what you care about, and why you do what you do. Developing yourself as a leader begins with knowing you own key convictions; it begins with your value system."[54] Cultivating self-exploration, self-knowledge,[55] and self-discovery are foundational for effective leadership development[56] in community, civic, and professional environments. Hence, commonly utilized leadership development techniques and pedagogical practices include storytelling, spiritual autobiography,[57] vocational discernment reflection exercises,[58] and journaling. The greater degree to which a leader is self-aware, the more equipped they will be to leverage and improve their strengths, acknowledge their shortcomings, and lead others. To "know thyself"—about which Aristotle alleged serves as the beginning of wisdom (*sophia*)—is facilitated not only through self-reflective autobiographical

---

52 Carolyn M. Aldwin and Michael R. Levenson, "The Practical Applications of Self-Transcendent Wisdom," in *Applying Wisdom to Contemporary World Problems*, ed. Sternberg et al., 297.

53 R. L. Piedmont, "Does Spirituality Represent the Sixth Factor of Personality?" *Journal of Personality* 67 (1999): 988; cited in Aldwin and Levenson, "The Practical Applications of Self-Transcendent Wisdom," 298.

54 James M. Kouzes and Barry Z. Posner, "Leadership Begins with an Inner Journey," in *Contemporary Issues in Leadership*, 2nd ed., ed. Rosenbach et al., 119.

55 Lindsay argues that "cultivation of self-awareness also falls into the 'knowledge' pursuit of intercultural and interreligious competence, as increased self-awareness is also knowledge-building process, focus inwardly." Lindsay, "Growing Interreligious and Intercultural Competence in the Classroom," 27.

56 E.g., "Authentic Leadership" is among the several emerging leadership models and theories of the past two decades that "draws from both positive psychological capacities and a highly developed organizational context, which results in both greater self-awareness and self regulated positive behaviors on the part of leaders and associates, fostering positive self development." Fred Luthans and Bruce J. Avolio, "Authentic Leadership," in *Positive Organizational Scholarship*, ed. K. S. Cameron, J. E. Dutton, and R. E. Quinn (San Francisco: Barrett-Koehler, 2003), 243.

57 E.g., Matthew Maruggi and Martha E. Stortz, "Teaching the 'Most Beautiful Stories,'" in *Interreligious/Interfaith Studies*, ed. Patel et al., 85–97.

58 E.g., Hans Gustafson, "Interreligious Studies and Personal Changemaking Pedagogy for Leadership and the Common Good," *Teaching Theology and Religion* 24 (2021): 42–48.

personal inventorying[59] and storytelling exercises, but also—and perhaps more vitally—through lived encounter and dialogue with others who constructively illuminate and reflect one's selfhood back to one.[60]

Know How (techne)

Know How aims to cultivate the craft or technical (techne) skillset and competencies necessary for navigating and flourishing in complicated and religiously diverse contexts.[61] Moyaert argues, "Whether one becomes a doctor, a teacher, a lawyer, or a businesswoman working for a multinational, the added value of knowing how to navigate culturally and religiously diverse worlds is clear and employers are looking for people who have experience of solving 'problems with people whose views differ from their own.'"[62] Patel, in an interview about his vocation and interfaith vision, suggests that the organization he founded and directs, Interfaith America (formerly Interfaith Youth Core), is "not about opening your diary to the world . . . [rather it is,] like learning how to play jazz or do surgery, is about becoming very very very good at a particular craft, which takes a great deal of study."[63] Developing one's craft requires time, study, practice, experience, and exposure. It involves developing

---

59 Similarly, Lindsay reports on the utility of learning experiences in religious studies classes to "help students live a 'life examined' as they determine their own personality types, rate their own empathy tendencies and levels of personal resiliency, assess their moral foundation and attachment styles, and understand their personal approach to conflict. Knowledge of self and these theoretical tools lays a foundation for the broadening of Skills and Attitudes." Lindsay, "Growing Interreligious and Intercultural Competence in the Classroom," 29.

60 Such is the spirit of Hickey and Suárez's chapter on interfaith learning titled "Meeting Others, Seeing Myself." Related, Jones and Meyer discovered that students in the interreligious courses they examined "articulated the purpose or value of site visits primarily in terms of an opportunity for their *own* self-discovery." Jones and Meyer, "Interfaith and Interreligious Pedagogies," 15, italics added.

61 *Know How* corresponds to Jones's and Meyers's fifth dominant theme of contemporary interreligious and interfaith studies pedagogy—"Connecting to Professional Skills"—and is most significantly developed by the second and third themes, "Case Study Snapshots" and "Dialogue." Jones and Meyer, "Interfaith and Interreligious Pedagogies," 25–28, 18–22.

62 Moyaert, "Interfaith Learning in Academic Spaces," 38; citing Hart Research Associates, "Falling Short?" Association of American Colleges and Universities (2015), 4.

63 Eboo Patel, interviewed by Erin VanLaningham and Hannah Schell, "Charisma and Craft," *Callings* (podcast audio), January 28, 2021, 00:45:00.

technical skills and building interreligious competencies. Patel suggests that craft is among "those seemingly intangible qualities that separate excellent interfaith leaders from good ones."[64] It "is not just about commitment to a particular endeavor; it's about knowing the things—big and little—you need to focus on to achieve excellence."[65]

Since developing craft and excellence requires experience and knowledge in real-world situations, it should be no surprise that the case-study method is among the signature pedagogies of IRS.[66] Several IRS instructors use the well-crafted interreligious case studies prepared by the Pluralism Project[67] as teaching aids to approximate real-world simulation, promote agency, and develop practical skills and decision making. According to the Harvard Business School, the case-study method rests on the premise that "the best way to learn a skill is to practice in a simulation-type process."[68] Similar case-method pedagogical approaches are common in the study of law with an eye to forming moral judgment and practical wisdom.[69] Case studies require action in situations for which being neutral or doing nothing is not a viable option. They invite personal reflection on (1) responding to real-world, complex situations in which there are sometimes few, if any, good solutions (often only bad and worse options), and (2) determining what assets, strengths, and skills one brings to a situation in working toward an outcome. Case-study exercises promote agency to respond to messy problems in which having the relevant facts and figures alone remains insufficient. Unlike multiple-choice or short-answer problems in which formulae exist to calculate the proper outcome or "where the correct answer is obtained by a well-structured path to solution and is unique among all of the possible answers," case studies more accurately reflect the complicated nature of reality by presenting

---

64 Patel, *Interfaith Leadership*, 156.

65 Patel, 162.

66 Jones and Meyer, drawing Elinor Pierce and the Pluralism Project, assert, "If interfaith and interreligious studies has something like a 'signature' pedagogy, the case study method is arguably it." Jones and Meyer, "Interfaith and Interreligious Pedagogies," 18.

67 Ellie Pierce, "Using the Case Studies Method in Interfaith Studies Classrooms," in *Interreligious/Interfaith Studies*, ed. Patel et al., 84.

68 Pierce, "Using the Case Studies Method in Interfaith Studies Classrooms," 77.

69 E.g., "Putting the Judgement Back into Judging" and "The Ethical Lawyer," in Barry Schwartz and Kenneth E. Sharpe, *Practical Wisdom* (New York: Riverhead Books, 2010), 235–51.

ill-structured problems that (1) involve arbitrating among competing interests and stakeholders, (2) have no clear path to solution, and (3) can only be resolved through the application of practical wisdom (*phronesis*).[70] Case studies promote the development not only of practical skills but also of a civic orientation toward serving common public goods.[71] Case-study analysis directly aids the development of *phronesis*, which, according to Timothy Furlan, "is primarily about performing a particular social practice well, such as being a good friend, parent, doctor, teacher, or citizen and that means figuring out the right way to do the right thing in a concrete set of circumstances, with a particular person, at a particular time, and so on."[72] Developing *phronesis* through case-study reflection and simulation is "not musing about how someone else in a hypothetical situation ought to act. It is about 'what am I to do?' right here and now, with this person. A practically wise person doesn't merely speculate or theorize about what is proper, crucially, he or she actually does it."[73] The case-study method is likely to remain a premier way to invite individuals to continually develop their knowledge, skills, and craft for responding with IP in real-world situations.

Unsurprisingly, *phronesis* continues to receive "attention in management studies as a basis for rethinking leadership and management education and more recently managing change."[74] Furthermore, phronesis becomes particularly crucial in situations for which policies and codes of conduct either fall short or fail to anticipate proper application. Marthe Hurteau and Caroline Gagnon argue for the utility of phronesis in situations that require ethical decision making in professional contexts: "To solve problems, one should always refer first to codes of conduct (standards) and codes of ethics. However, such codes do not effectively resolve problems in all circumstances, and in such cases, practical wisdom is a framework that supports finding an

---

70 Sternberg, "Where Have All the Flowers of Wisdom Gone?" 3–4.
71 This attitude is documented by Jones and Meyer among instructors who use case studies, for whom case studies are "not 'just' about skills and action, but also about the kinds of analysis, critical thinking, and development of a civic orientation that are arguably central to the project of liberal education." Jones and Meyer, "Interfaith and Interreligious Pedagogies," 19.
72 Timothy J. Furlan, "Cultivating Practical Wisdom," *Harvard Medical School Bioethics Journal*, January 1, 2020.
73 Furlan, "Cultivating Practical Wisdom."
74 Elena P. Antonacopoulou, "The Capacity of *Phronesis*," in *Academic–Practitioner Relationships*, ed. Jean M. Bartunek and Jane McKenzie (London: Routledge, 2017), 1.

ethical solution."[75] This leads to the ethical component of phronesis: acting virtuously for the right reasons.

FOR THE RIGHT *REASONS*

Phronesis entails performing not only the right action in the right context but for the right *reasons* as well, which is to say it is not only an intellectual and practical virtue, but a moral virtue: it assumes an ethical foundation. It is not sufficient for an individual to merely perform the right virtues, since virtues and intentions can be performed for wrong or short-sighted reasons and, more devastatingly, lead to undesired outcomes.[76] Phronesis guides one's intentions in deploying the proper balance of virtue toward the ethically desired outcomes. For interfaith engagement and leadership, and for IRS scholarship, phronetically adopting the appropriate balance of virtuous intention toward desired outcomes is crucial. To illustrate, consider the two following examples, one relating to *interreligious studies* and one relating to *interfaith engagement.*

Interreligious Studies (a critical academic discipline) and its relationship to interfaith engagement (a normative, community-based civic project) is raised by scholar of religion Brian K. Pennington, who expresses concern with the neoliberal agenda of the twenty-first-century university and argues for keeping central the impetus for scholarly critique, especially for any movements that promote social change and oppose anything that may prompt the need for interfaith engagement.[77] Well-intentioned and virtuous urgent calls for interfaith cooperation can potentially be blindly corrupted or malformed by neoliberal forces or produce unintended outcomes. Pennington calls attention to the seemingly "impossible grip"[78] of the (neo)liberal realities that stealthily subjugate interreligious studies (and

---

75 Marthe Hurteau and Caroline Gagnon, "Contribution of Practical Wisdom to Resolving Ethical Issues," *Evaluation* 28, no. 2 (2022): 189.

76 E.g., the proverb "the road to hell is paved with good intentions" (origin uncertain); Ivan Illich, "To Hell with Good Intentions," address to American students at the Conference on InterAmerican Student Projects (CIASP), Cuernavaca, Mexico, April 20, 1968.

77 Brian K. Pennington, "(Neo)Liberal Challenges," in *Interreligious Studies*, ed. Gustafson, 179–80.

78 Lucia Hulsether, "The Grammar of Racism," *Journal of the American Academy of Religion* 86, no. 1 (2018): 32; cited in Pennington, "(Neo)Liberal Challenges," 181.

the interfaith movement) to "global capitalism and the nation-state that facilitates and sanctifies that economic order[,] . . . the subjection of higher education to the logic of the market[,] . . . [and] the inextricability of the state from global markets and the corporatized university."[79] Pressure from these (neo)liberal forces, argues Pennington, could influence the ways in which the field of IRS develops, is carried out, and serves its students. For instance, the increasing corporatization of the university as an employment training center to equip students with the competencies most sought after by employers may pressure IRS scholars and instructors to focus their research questions and teaching emphases on how the field best serves the needs of their job-seeking students, as well as the global business communities. These concerns extend beyond scholars of IRS to practitioners in the interfaith movement, both of whom likely proceed with virtuous intentions. In their nearly universally shared interest to reduce conflict, promote understanding, and emphasize "cooperation across lines of religious difference," Pennington points out, IRS scholars (and IFE practitioners) locate "the sources of inter-religious conflict among people and groups rather than in the imperialism of global markets or highly militarized nation-states."[80] In doing so, they are more likely to miss, ignore, or avoid complicated aspects of interreligious conflict stemming from (neo)liberal legacies and forces beyond the conflicting people and groups. Mindful of this possibility, Pennington invites a more serious "interrogation of the (neo)liberal imaginaire that has so thoroughly infiltrated our understanding of social relations and social change, just as it has colonized our academic institutions."[81] Pennington's critique exposes an instance in which the function of the guiding virtue of phronesis may aid IRS scholars and IFE practitioners in balancing their virtuous intentions to achieve their intended outcomes with more accurate knowledge and realistic outcomes.

Interfaith Engagement focuses on community- and civic-oriented approaches to fostering tolerance, respect, and social cohesion in religiously diverse societies. It is carried out most often at local community levels but can include state level geopolitical relations. In the wake of the infamous 2013 Boston Marathon bomb attack, in which two terrorists planted two homemade pressure cooker bombs near the finish line that killed three

---

79 Pennington, "(Neo)Liberal Challenges," 181.
80 Pennington, 180.
81 Pennington, 181.

people and injured hundreds of others, Patel asked whether the view that interfaith efforts matter more than ever holds "up to analysis, or is it just a surface salve for a really deep wound?"[82] Patel answers affirmatively—interfaith efforts do matter—for three reasons: (1) they help to "harmonize people's various identities," (2) they "help us to separate the worst elements of communities from the rest," and (3) they "remind us [that] America is about welcoming the contributions of all communities and nurturing cooperation between them."[83] Lucia Hulsether thoughtfully responds to Patel and asks whether "interfaith dialogue [can] cure religious violence?" Among Hulsether's several points, two stand out:

1. Appeals to interfaith dialogue often trade in binaries, just like the discourses that they seek to resist. Instead of "Christians" versus "everyone else," or "Americans" versus "Muslims," we have a new formulation that pits "extremists" against "pluralists."
2. In their attempts to reach a larger base, mainstream interfaith projects sometimes gloss over material conflicts and replace them with driving oppositional formulations between "interfaith" participants and those who refuse to participate out of their own intolerance.[84]

Hulsether's critique invites interfaith practitioners to reflect on potential harmful and unintended outcomes of their well-intentioned efforts. Interfaith efforts risk replacing one binary with another and, like Pennington's concern above, sometimes (often) look past the more divisive systemic forms of material and social inequality laden in the contexts of the conflicts. While acknowledging common ground with Hulsether, Patel responds with an attempt to further nuance and complicate the messiness of navigating the terrain of conflicts that involve interfaith relations. More to the point, Patel focuses on what he considers to be the "central problem interfaith work seeks to solve: how are all of us, with our deep differences, to share a nation and a world together? I believe that is primarily a question of civic space, not

82 Eboo Patel, "3 Reasons Interfaith Efforts Matter More Than Ever," *Huff Post*, April 23, 2013.
83 Patel, "3 Reasons Interfaith Efforts Matter More Than Ever."
84 Lucia Hulsether, "Can Interfaith Dialogue Cure Religious Violence?" Religion Dispatches, April 26, 2013.

political ideology."[85] In this friendly sparring match (see chapter 8), Huls-ether and Patel sharpen one another's scope of the various real-world ideas and consequences involved. They share similar needs and views. In fact, Patel acknowledges that his "views on most political issues are probably in the same general universe as Hulsether's."[86] Both share well-founded and virtuous intentions to produce outcomes that serve the common good for the flourishing of all persons and groups; however, the difference in their approaches may not have been initially apparent to one another, and to their readers, prior to their eloquent sparring match. Their exchange showcases the value of reflecting on and striving for virtuous interfaith action for the right and ethical reasons. Furthermore, it offers an instance of the vital role friendly sparring partners can play in developing IP.

$$\diamond \quad \diamond \quad \diamond$$

Phronesis helps individuals "sum up a situation, weigh up various factors, and work out what to do to promote or achieve [their] objectives. Often enough, because of [their] experience and wisdom, [these individuals] can see straight off the best thing to do, without having to go through a process of deliberation."[87] Individuals with IP draw on lived experience, basic religious literacy (*know what*), and awareness of self and others to efficiently assess an (inter)religiously complex situation, empathetically account for the various and often competing needs of the stakeholders involved (*know who*), and proficiently discern and act with skill, craft, art, and technique (*know how*) in the moment toward the right outcomes for the right reasons (*know why*), in service of the common goods for all parties involved. Developing practi-cal interfaith wisdom as IP for everyday leadership (and scholarship) does not happen overnight. It develops over a lifetime of experience, chock-full of personal and social failures and successes. Questions about developing *phronesis* and other leadership qualities is of growing interest for scholars, especially for educators interested in developing leaders. Leadership scholars

85 Eboo Patel, "What Is Interfaith Cooperation For?" Religion Dispatches, May 6, 2013.

86 Patel, "What Is Interfaith Cooperation For?"

87 John Lloyd Ackrill, *Aristotle's Ethics* (London: Faber & Faber, 1973), 28; cited in Gaberial J. Costello, *The Teaching of Design and Innovation* (Cham, Switzerland: Springer, 2020), 20.

Teresa Rothausen and Sara Christensen show that although "most leadership development occurs in experiences of leading, . . . not everyone learns from experience alone, and for most people more is learned when integrated with"[88] the activities of goal setting, reflection, assessment, relationships, and education. Many scholars of IRS, especially in the United States, have a particular interest in the applied role of the field for developing not only citizens and professionals but "leaders."[89] The final chapter explores the nature and development of IP that are markedly relevant for everyday leadership in professional, personal, and civic contexts.

88 Teresa J. Rothausen and Sara M. Christenson, "Leadership," in *Wiley Encyclopedia of Management*, vol. 2: *Business Ethics*, 3rd ed., ed. Cary L. Cooper (Chichester: Wiley, 2014), 272.

89 Brian K. Pennington, "The Interreligious Studies Agenda," in *The Georgetown Companion to Interreligious Studies*, ed. Lucinda Mosher (Washington, DC: Georgetown University Press, 2022), 20.

15

Everyday Leadership

Chapter Outline

I. Everyday Leadership
    a. *Everyday*
    b. *Leadership*
    c. *Professional Application*
II. IP for Leadership
    a. *Awareness*
    b. *Self-Discovery*
    c. *Yogas*
III. Concluding Unscientific Postscript: A Reflexive Account

The claim that "leaders are born, not made" is likely to elicit stern pushback amidst leadership scholars, coaches, and professionals.[1] Alternatively, consider the overused quotes from Leadership Studies pioneer Warren Bennis and legendary American football coach Vince Lombardi:

---

1 While the question of whether leaders are "born or made" may be asked, "the budgets dedicated to leadership development by organizations (estimates range from $15 billion annually worldwide), the numbers of books aimed at improving leadership, and the thriving specialty of executive coaching suggest that many experienced organizational managers and consultants believe leaders can be made. Research supports them to a large degree." Rothausen and Christenson, "Leadership," 272.

The most dangerous leadership myth is that leaders are born—that there is a genetic factor to leadership. That's nonsense; in fact, the opposite is true. Leaders are made rather than born.

—Warren Bennis

Leaders aren't born, they are made. And they are made just like anything else, through hard work. And that's the price we'll have to pay to achieve that goal, or any goal.

—Vince Lombardi

This final chapter sketches approaches to leadership development for the everyday person[2] in everyday religiously diverse contexts. Furthermore, in the ever-changing complexity of the world, most everyone is eventually thrown into situations that demand leadership regardless of whether or not they chose to be there or are trained for it. Henry Kimsey-House's Co-Active Leadership model embraces this reality: "Sooner or later we all have leadership thrust upon us. It may be an employee, a team, a family, or an organization in your community. Eventually, everyone gets called upon to stand up and say, 'Follow me.'"[3] According to Vinita Bali, an Indian business leader with experience leading and serving several multinational food corporations, "what distinguishes effective leaders from others is not just their technical or functional expertise, but their ability to handle adaptive challenges, that is, those situations or circumstances that cannot be predicted but can occur at any time."[4] Hence, for Bali, "leadership is a capability that each of us has within us."[5] Leadership nor leadership development need not fit into perfect one-size-fits-all boxes confined to rigid definition, creeds, protocols, or prescribed methods. People are not all the same, nor do they share similar learning styles. Therefore, leadership models and theories vary in efficacy from person to person. Furthermore, leadership need not be confined to pure science or pure art; rather, it strikes several points along the spectrum of

---

2 "Leadership skills and subsequent performance are not viewed as the province of a few gifted individuals. Instead, leadership is held to be a potential in many individuals—a potential that emerges through experience and the capability to learn and benefit from experience." Mumford et al., "Leadership Skills for a Changing World," 21.

3 Henry Kimsey-House and David Skibbins, *The Stake* (San Rafael, CA: Co-Active Press, 2013), 1.

4 Vinita Bali, "Leadership Lessons from Everyday Life," in *Contemporary Issues in Leadership*, 2nd ed., ed. Rosenbach et al., 231.

5 Bali, "Leadership Lessons from Everyday Life," 229.

this artificial binary. With an eye to the fluid dancing spirit of phronesis and the diversity of leadership development methods, this chapter attends to the personal and professional utility of cultivating Interreligious Phronesis (IP) for leadership in everyday contexts. The chapter concludes with a personal reflexive account of an instance of utilizing a particular method to promote self-actualization and to foster greater knowledge and awareness of self and others for IP.

EVERYDAY LEADERSHIP

IP, sketched in the previous chapter, refers to the ability to draw on lived experience, basic religious literacy (*know what*), and awareness of self and others to efficiently assess (inter)religiously complex situations, empathetically account for the various and often competing needs of the stakeholders involved (*know who*), and proficiently discern and act with skill, craft, art, and technique (*know how*) in the moment toward the right outcomes for the right reasons (*know why*) for the common goods of all parties involved. Leadership is not only for top-level managers or charismatic sages on stages. Leaders are found everywhere every day, and everyone can be a leader in various professional and nonprofessional contexts.

Everyday

In the context of everydayness, IP has a certain utility that makes it readily accessible in one's quiver to be deployed at a moment's notice. Like an elite archer who draws arrow from quiver or the sharpshooter who draws pistol from holster, the individual with IP skillfully and seamlessly deploys it with no noticeable action or effort. To illustrate, consider the three following sketches detailed below: (1) ancient Chinese religion (Daoism), (2) a musical virtuoso (Miles Davis), and (3) a twentieth-century Hungarian British philosopher with Jewish heritage and Christian commitments (Michael Polanyi).

In Daoism, the Dao is generally translated as "the way"; that is, the way of reality or the way the world works, which is often mysterious. It can refer to the chaotic but somehow harmonious way nature expresses itself, observed in its Yin and Yang of patterns and processes. Dao is the way of nature—or the natural way—which the human is invited to tap into, unite with, go with, and live resonantly with. Hence, "to live in the way of the Dao is to attune to the force of nature, go with it, and refrain from struggling against it; like a skier or surfer gracefully going with gravity down the mountain or the wave like a dance, not a fight."[6] In other words, the leader who utilizes IP and embraces the "Dao of Phronesis" for leadership exemplifies the principle of *wu wei* (無爲), which translates literally as "nonaction," but in an active way. *Wu wei* is the ideal of effortlessness or acting-without-acting. It is not passivity, but the effortless action displayed by, for example, world-class athletes or musicians who perform their craft so well it appears effortless (e.g., the surfer or skier dancing down the wave or mountain, the golfer flawlessly swinging her club). Leadership blogs and articles frequently cite a passage attributed to the *Daodejing*, the central text that informs the Daoist way of life and allegedly authored by Laozi. The quote reads, "The best of all rulers is but a shadowy presence to his subjects."[7] In this noncoercive or nonassertive action, there is no wasted or extra movement, and nothing is missing.[8] Leaders who utilize the "Dao of Phronesis" effortlessly and noncoercively lead others in the moment in such a humble manner that those involved—various stakeholders—may not readily notice. Such is the epitome of this humble approach to leadership relevant for the everyday utility of IP.

Miles Davis, iconic American musician and trumpet virtuoso, is praised by fellow musician Herbie Hancock in the latter's recollection of Davis' improvisation during a public musical performance in which Hancock played the wrong chord mid-performance: "Miles took a breath and then played some notes, and the notes made my chord right. . . . Somehow, what he chose to play fit my chords to the structure of the music. . . . What I learned from that is that Miles didn't hear the chord as being wrong. He just heard it as something new that happened."[9] As a musical virtuoso, Miles Davis had the musical phronetic ability at-hand to seamlessly act in the moment to what the context presented him. He effortlessly played the right note at the right time with the right person and for the right reason and, as the Daoist principle of *wu wei* embraces, played in a manner undetectable to those in the room (except for Hancock). Davis actively led in the moment through nonactive

---

6 Gustafson, "Suppressing the Mosquitoes' Coughs," 9.

7 Lao Tzu, *Tao Te Ching*, trans. D. C. Lau (New York: Penguin, 1963), chap. 17.

8 Gustafson, "Suppressing the Mosquitoes' Coughs," 10.

9 Herbie Hancock, interview by Jim Lehrer, *PBS News Hour*, September 16, 2010 (video); cited in Diane Millis, *Deepening Engagement* (Woodstock, VT: Skylight Paths, 2015), 127.

humble action in a manner that served the context and those around him. He didn't just know how to play; he knew how to play in the moment for the right reasons and in the right manner. Such is the way of practical *know how*, or phronetic leadership and "wisdom as moral jazz."[10]

Michael Polanyi investigated *know how* under the designation "tacit knowledge," which he distinguished from explicit knowledge (knowledge transferred through explanation). His well-known example of tacit knowledge is the implicit knowledge of riding a bike.[11] "We can know how to ride a bicycle without being able to tell anyone the rules for riding, and we seem to learn to ride without being given any of the rules in an explicit way—our knowledge of the ability to ride a bike is tacit."[12] Polanyi suggests "the fact that we can know more than we can tell . . . seems obvious enough. . . . Take an example. We know a person's face, and can recognize it among a thousand, indeed a million. Yet we usually cannot tell how we recognize a face we know. So most of this knowledge cannot be put into words."[13] Hence, "tacit knowledge is knowledge that is not explicated."[14] Developing IP involves discovering any implicit or tacit knowledge one already has.

Although many agree that people are not born leaders, it may be that people are born *to learn to become* leaders. More specifically, people are "born to be wise."[15] Relying on modern psychological research, psychologist Barry Schwartz and political scientist Kenneth Sharpe argue that developing the moral skills related to phronesis (perceptiveness, nuanced thinking, appreciation of context, integration of intellect and emotion, empathy) is not

---

10 Schwartz and Sharpe, *Practical Wisdom*, 41.

11 For case studies that illustrate the various visions of tacit knowledge from philosophy (Wittgenstein's "rules of action," and the somatic tacit knowledge the human body elicits in its relations to the world), developmental psychology (children's learning through bodily relation to their environment), sociology (collective tacit knowledge of laboratory scientists to repeat functioning consistent and accurate laboratory manipulations), and management (relational knowledge of kneading dough for breadmaking to design of breadmaking machine), see Harry Collins, *Tacit and Explicit Knowledge* (Chicago: University of Chicago Press, 2010), 2–4.

12 Collins, *Tacit and Explicit Knowledge*, 2. Author Karl Ove Knausgaard observes, "I have met many grown-ups who don't know how to drive a car or who can't swim, but I have never met an adult who didn't know how to ride a bicycle." Karl Ove Knausgaard, *Summer* (New York: Penguin, 2018), 355.

13 Michael Polanyi, *The Tacit Dimension* (Chicago: University of Chicago Press, 1966), 4.

14 Collins, *Tacit and Explicit Knowledge*, 1.

15 Schwartz and Sharpe, *Practical Wisdom*, 51–68.

"hardwired" in people, but is within the grasp of everyone. People are "born to be wise in the way that is similar to the way we are born to master language. We don't come into the world equipped with 'English,' but we *do* come into the world equipped to *learn* English, or Japanese, or any other language, with relative ease."[16] Likewise, people are born with the tacit knowledge to become wise and to become leaders by discovering and cultivating those implicit abilities inherent to their personhood. Tacit knowledge, though not the same as practical wisdom, is a "core feature of wisdom" in that the application of tacit knowledge allows leaders to "maximize a balance of various self-interests (intrapersonal) with other people's interests (interpersonal) and aspects of the context in which they live (extrapersonal)."[17] In other words, practical wisdom (phronesis), unlike tacit knowledge, is morally oriented toward "the maximization of a common good, rather than individual well-being."[18] Such is the case with the nature and development of IP for everyday leadership.

The complicated everydayness of life, whether it be in the workplace, in the community, or at home, teems with *aporias*, those unresolvable dilemmas and uncertainties in which simply having brute, fact-based epistemic knowledge is insufficient for discerning the proper action (even when all the relevant facts are known). This can be especially true in interpersonal relationships and in professional workplaces. "Professional practitioners draw on relevant epistemological knowledge, but the application of that knowledge calls for a quite different form of knowledge from that episteme alone, one that embraces the messiness of practice."[19] All the knowledge of jazz and trumpet playing in the world is likely insufficient for one to play virtuously in the moment like Miles Davis. Contexts that involve religious, spiritual, and secular identities can be complicated. Having all the facts or an exhaustive religious literacy, which is not only impossible but impractical and unhelpful (see chapter 7), cannot alone solve complicated *aporetic* dilemmas. Knowledge of the physics

---

16 Schwartz and Sharpe, 52, italics original.

17 Hannes Zacher and Ute Kunzemann, "Wisdom in the Workplace," in *Applying Wisdom to Contemporary World Problems*, ed. Sternberg et al., 260–61; citing Robert J. Sternberg, "A Balance Theory of Wisdom," *Review of General Psychology* 2, no. 4 (1998): 347–65.

18 Zacher and Kunzemann, "Wisdom in the Workplace," 260–61; citing Sternberg, "A Balance Theory of Wisdom," 347–65.

19 Elizabeth Anne Kinsella and Allan Pittman, "Engaging Phronesis in Professional Practice and Education," in *Phronesis as Professional Knowledge*, ed. Elizabeth Anne Kinsella and Allan Pittman (Rotterdam, The Netherlands: Sense Publishers, 2012), 6.

and mechanics of surfing or skiing do not readily translate into being able to surf or ski. That comes with the tacit knowledge cultivated over time. Rather, IP can assist individuals in navigating and leading others in the everyday messiness of life, with the seemingly effortlessness of the Dao and with an eye to serving the common goods for those involved.

Leadership

Leadership scholars Teresa Rothausen's and Sara Christensen's proposed "meta-theory" of leadership is that of a function of the leader, followers, the connection between them, and their context. Additionally, "there are a number of traits, behaviors, sources of power, and influence tactics that can be leveraged in leadership and different combinations of these may be effective with different followers and in different situations."[20] Within the scope of leadership, IP carries a social dimension focused on assessing the needs, goals, and interests of individual and group stakeholders, and on guiding the outcomes toward serving the common goods. Although no particular model of leadership is the ultimate one-and-only model for IP, the Leadership-as-Practice (LAP) model is an accessible one to begin with since it resonates soundly with IP's stress on everydayness. Unlike the worn-out and tiresome "heroic, command-and-control leadership style" that has "a dampening effect on the creativity and energy of people in our organizations and communities," LAP emphasizes "leadership in everyday practices, those regularized and sometime emergent activities performed by various actors within an organization or community."[21] Emphasizing traditionally recognized areas of study for leadership research—traits, behaviors, skills, competencies, influence tactics, and contexts—the models of leadership proposed by Barbara A. McGraw and Eboo Patel are appropriate for religiously diverse contexts because they take into consideration the degrees to which religious identities impact leadership, followership, and personal and social agency in collaborative contexts.

The value of interfaith understanding for "new-genre leadership" models includes shared, servant, collaborative, relational, authentic, and spiritual

---

20 Rothausen and Christenson, "Leadership," 275.
21 Joe Raelin, "In Leadership, Look to the Practices Not the Individual," *Academia Letters*, article 34 (2020): 1.

leadership.[22] These models emphasize "charismatic leader behavior, vision-ary, inspiring, ideological and moral values, as well as transformational leadership approaches"[23] such as that of James MacGregor Burns.[24] Trans-formational leadership focuses not primarily on a leader's competencies and characteristics, but on the creative interaction between leader and follower, by developing the leader to appeal to the intrinsic needs and values of their team of followers.[25] McGraw argues that Burns's transformational leadership model is effective for motivating individuals and teams, and "is particularly relevant for innovative business leaders who employ creative collaboration and/or adopt corporate social responsibility strategies, especially for moral reasons."[26] However, in order to fully utilize a transformational approach while remaining grounded in a value-based foundation, the leader ought to be sufficiently equipped not only with "a much more nuanced understanding of the particularities of constituents' cultural perspectives," but with sympathies for the ways, discussed below, "deep religious roots shape their perspec-tives, values, and customs, and the social assumptions and orientations that inform them."[27] The new-genre transformational leader, in appealing to the intrinsic value-based needs of their constituents, not only considers cross-cultural dimensions of individuals and teams, but is also (inter)religiously literate "about the religious roots of those cultures"[28] and about how those roots influence intrapersonal and intergroup dynamics. A transformational leader exhibits IP by actively applying knowledge to action for the common goods of the team or groups. New-genre transformational leaders recognize the ways in which religious roots influence cultural norms and exhibit IP accordingly by remaining aware of potential tensions and opportunities in complex situations and demonstrating the skill to drive toward constructive solutions with thoughtful action and motivation of others.

---

22 Barbara McGraw, "Cross-Cultural Leadership as Interfaith Leadership," in *Inter-religious Studies*, ed. Gustafson, 217.

23 Bruce J. Avolio, Fred O. Walumbwa, and Todd J. Weber, "Leadership," *Annual Review of Psychology* 60 (2009): 428.

24 James MacGregor Burns, *Transforming Leadership* (New York: Grove, 2003); cited by McGraw, "Cross-Cultural Leadership as Interfaith Leadership," 217.

25 McGraw, 217.

26 McGraw, 217.

27 McGraw, 218.

28 McGraw, 218.

Patel's book *Interfaith Leadership* examines the various public spaces of significant interaction (what Patel refers to as the "civic interfaith landscape"), which include "schools, parks, college campuses, companies, organizations, libraries, sports leagues, [and] hospitals," where people with various religious and nonreligious orientations "interact with one another with varying degrees of ignorance and understanding, tension and connection, division and cooperation, *when their faith identities are implicated by that interaction*."[29] Eschewing the common image of interfaith leaders as high-level state officials or ordained religious clergy, Patel articulates the identity of interfaith leaders as common people of all ages, gender, backgrounds, professions, and social locations. For Patel, "Interfaith leaders are people who cause other people to change their attitudes and actions with respect to religious diversity."[30] In other words, Patel's "Interfaith Leaders" practice IP in moving others, including themselves, from a state of indifference or opposition (from Barriers, Blasé, and Bombs) to one of practical engagement (to Bridges) with religious diversity by becoming aware of potential tensions or opportunities in (inter) religiously complex situations and having the skill and resources to drive toward constructive solutions through thoughtful action, leadership, and motivation of others in ways that benefit individuals and groups in pursuit of common goods.

Many leadership curricula offer techniques designed to assist individuals to know themselves better and to identify ways they relate to others. Many IRS courses require experiential learning experiences (e.g., community engagement, service-learning, direct encounter beyond the classroom, and interfaith leadership capacity building) because they help "students to understand the dynamics of interreligious dialogue in a more existential way that has practical implications for their own lives."[31] Patel argues that IRS (or "Interfaith Studies") in the classroom ought to center on the reflexive question of "How would you lead in any given interreligiously complex situation?" For Patel, a priority of IRS is to "recognize the importance of training people who have the knowledge base and skill set needed to engage religious diversity in a way that promotes peace, stability,

---

29 Patel, *Interfaith Leadership*, 6, italics original.
30 Patel, 13.
31 Dunbar, "The Place of Interreligious Dialogue in the Academic Study of Religion," 462; cited in Oddbjørn Leirvik, "Interreligious Studies," *Journal of Interreligious Studies* 13 (February 2014): 16.

and cooperation—and to begin offering academic programs that certify such leaders."[32] Utilizing the case-study method (see chapter 14), Patel suggests IRS curricula develop leaders by igniting student discussions about messy interreligious encounters for which leadership is called. For instance, Patel imagines a classroom discussion about whether and how YMCA directors and school principals in Minneapolis should educate themselves and respond to the "faith practices of the Somali Muslims, Hmong Shamanists, and Native Americans of the area."[33] Among the myriad stories Patel weaves throughout his ongoing work to cultivate interfaith leaders and to articulate the concreteness of interfaith leadership is his unshakably clear vision of a democracy in need of interfaith leaders, who, as Russ Arnold contends, "are necessary in every office, every classroom, every workplace, and every neighborhood."[34] With the Western world increasing in religious diversity, especially in professional and civic spaces, the likelihood of being thrust into a position or situation that calls for thoughtful interfaith leadership is also increasing. As Kimsey-House and Skibbins preach (above), "everyone gets called upon to stand up and say, 'Follow me.'"[35] It is impossible to be perfectly prepared for these moments or for all possible scenarios involving interreligious conflicts or opportunities in the civic interfaith landscape of a religiously diverse democracy. However, cultivating IP through transformational leadership development can help individuals anticipate these moments and be equipped to meet them more fully. With respect to every office and workplace—and without losing sight of the equally important contexts of the neighborhood and classroom—the next section turns to the application of IP for leadership in professional contexts.

Professional Application

According to a 2019 survey, 70 percent of Americans indicate their workplace is the top location for the most frequent interaction with people who do not

32 Patel, "Toward a Field of Interfaith Studies."
33 Patel, "Toward a Field of Interfaith Studies."
34 Russell C. D. Arnold, "Making Interfaith Conversations Central to our Jesuit Mission," *Conversations on Jesuit Higher Education*, April 19, 2017.
35 Kimsey-House and Skibbins, *The Stake*, 1.

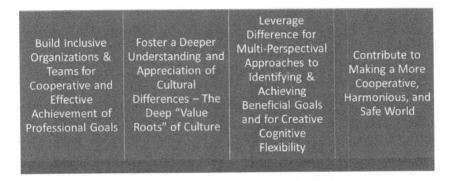

Figure 15.1. "Four Purposes of Interfaith Leadership in Business," Barbara McGraw, 2021.

share their religion.[36] Furthermore, global religious populations are projected to grow at a rate twenty-three times higher than religiously unaffiliated populations.[37] Religion is not going anywhere, yet, and religious diversity is only likely to grow in the American workplace. McGraw's vision of "interfaith leadership" is, at its core, the ability to investigate "the deep roots of culture in a region's traditional religion for an in-depth understanding of underlying values that shape people's vision of the good society and the good life within it."[38]

Needless to say, IP includes this core competency (Figure 15.1).[39] Since all professionals need to work effectively in organizations and teams, and with diverse communities, clients, and collaborators, McGraw's four purposes of business leadership transfer broadly across professional and vocational sectors regardless of context (public, private, for-profit, nonprofit).[40]

---

36 Robert P. Jones and Maxine Najle, "American Democracy in Crisis," PRRI, February 22, 2019.

37 Brian J. Grim and Phillip Connor, "Changing Religion, Changing Economies," Religious Freedom and Business Foundation, October 21, 2015.

38 McGraw, "Cross-Cultural Leadership as Interfaith Leadership," 213.

39 All content in this section on McGraw's "Four Purposes of Business Leadership" is from the following source unless cited otherwise: Barbara McGraw, "Why Interfaith Leadership Matters to Business and the Professions," Center for Engaged Religious Pluralism at Saint Mary's College of California, February 19, 2021 (educational video).

40 Including professional fields of education, law, health, social work, small business, entrepreneurship, entertainment, public relations, financial services, marketing, journalism, construction, engineering, real estate, research, public service, etc.

The first three purposes[41] are particularly instructive for understanding the value of IP in religiously diverse professional contexts, which are ripe for opportunities and challenges, since the model articulates benefits for the leader, their team, and other stakeholders.

To *build inclusive organizations and teams for cooperative and effective achievement of professional goals,* leaders need to work toward understanding how the deep "value roots" of their colleagues, coworkers, managers, supervisees, and clients inform the many cultural assumptions about leadership, followership, collegiality, and professionalism that exist in the workplace. Consider the case of the Muslim junior sales manager at a software corporation in Paris who uncomfortably refrained from the traditional *faire la bise* cheek-kiss greeting with members of the opposite sex,[42] or the case of the Muslim woman who was deemed by a Swedish Labor Court to have been "discriminated against in a job interview for refusing to shake hands on religious grounds."[43] Such cases—sometimes costly[44]—might be avoided. With IP or interfaith leadership, conflicts can be prevented that needn't arise in the first place. Furthermore, opportunities for collaboration and innovation can be foreseen. McGraw rhetorically asks about a diverse organization with constant clashes and frustration stifling progress and innovation, "What if there had been better understanding of those expectations and an effort to bridge them through appreciation of differences?"[45]

Fostering a deeper understanding and appreciation of cultural differences embedded in the deep "value roots" of culture can build more individual and

---

41 The fourth purpose—*contributing to making a more cooperative harmonious, and safer world*—echoes the moral dimension of IP for the workplace in serving common goods beyond the workplace. McGraw envisions, "business, law, health care, education, government, nonprofit, and public sector professionals have an opportunity to employ collaborative leadership . . . galvanizing everyone in mutual respect and equal dignity to achieve professional goals. [They also have the opportunity] to contribute to making the world a better place as those kinds of attitudes and understandings and cooperation spread throughout all the professions and the world." McGraw, "Why Interfaith Leadership Matters to Business and the Professions," 11:37–12:25.

42 Università della Svizzera italiana, "Fasting the Month of Ramadan at the Workplace," Master of Advanced Studies in Intercultural Communication (MIC).

43 Christina Anderson, "Muslim Job Applicant Who Refused Handshake Wins Discrimination Case in Sweden," *New York Times*, August 16, 2018.

44 The Muslim job applicant in the previous sentence was awarded 40,000 SEK (approximately $4,350 USD), paid out by the company that discriminated against her.

45 McGraw, "Why Interfaith Leadership Matters to Business and the Professions," 08:27–08:58.

collective capacity to leverage all team members as assets. Omar Ishrak, chairman of the board at Intel Corporation and former chairman of the board for Medtronic, two of the largest multinational companies in the world, preaches the common intuition that "diversity breeds differences, and differences of opinion breeds a better and more innovative business culture."[46] McGraw argues that it is a mistake to embrace the common Western tendency to "set religion aside and think of it as a private separate matter," because "religion is everywhere a main motivator of many people," including the religiously unaffiliated who often unknowingly inherit values from their cultural heritage, which "almost always" have deep religious roots.[47] For example, McGraw points to the deep religious "value roots" of the United States in the Calvinist Puritan "Protestant Work Ethic" that began in New England and was based and expressed, in part, on the belief that "idle hands are the devil's playground." Such an attitude (alongside other strong Calvinist theological underpinnings), so goes the general argument, cultivated the value and necessity of labor and hard work for the greater glory of God, and hence the United States and its citizens continue to reckon with their seemingly workaholic psyches. McGraw argues that the professions today need leaders who understand how these deep value roots influence individual performance and motivation and team chemistry and cooperation.

Leveraging difference for multiperspectival approaches to identifying and achieving beneficial goals and for creative, cognitive flexibility entails finding innovative ways to put people in positions to think outside the box. Encouraging everyone to bring their differences to the table, far from being time-consuming and burdensome, assists individuals and groups to "overcome monoculture and group think." In so doing, McGraw contends, leaders create the "opportunity for a shift in perspective" that surfaces both commonalities and differences while strengthening trust, respect, and empathy in the process.

---

46 Omar Ishrak, in "Diversity Leadership," DiversityInc.com, May 16, 2013. Such sentiment is backed by countless others. E.g., Orlando Richard, "Racial Diversity, Business Strategy, and Firm Performance," *Academy of Management Journal* 43, no. 2 (2000): 164–77; Society for Human Resource Management. "Impact of Diversity Initiatives on the Bottom Line" (Alexandria, VA: 2001); Sylvia Ann Hewlett, Melinda Marshall, and Laura Sherbin, "How Diversity Can Drive Innovation," *Harvard Business Review*, December 1, 2013.

47 McGraw, "Why Interfaith Leadership Matters to Business and the Professions," 03:54–04:40.

Bringing differences to the table can generate innovative opportunities for team members to learn from others in ways that create shifts in perspectives and helps everyone to see a wider picture for themselves, their organizations, and teams.[48]

McGraw's fourfold scheme sketching the purpose of interfaith leadership in business can be implemented at the individual and team levels by providing training and teambuilding opportunities for sharing and learning about each other's value roots, religious and cultural heritages, and multiperspectival approaches to organizational mission, convictions, and vision. It can also be worthwhile to explore the value roots of external organizational groups such as consumers, clients, and vendors to better understand and serve their needs and behaviors. The fourfold scheme is applicable not only across the professions and in civic roles but also for everyday interaction in religiously diverse societies.

IP FOR LEADERSHIP

In the parlance of the times, the term "cultivate," from the Latin *colere*, is most often used in the context of either agriculture or personal development. The former refers to the preparation and utilization of the land or soil to grow valuable crops. The latter refers to the preparation, development, and utilization of the person to grow in valuable skills, competencies, and virtues. In either case, cultivation requires time, resources, tact, and assistance. This final section—the culmination of this book—explores the cultivation of IP under three headings: awareness, self-discovery, and yogas (or paths).

Awareness

Cultivating IP, at the most basic level, is about developing ears to hear and eyes to see; it is about being sensitive, mindful, attentive, and aware. In fact, Deanna Ferree Womack proposes a "Model of Interfaith *Awareness*,"[49]

48 McGraw, 10:57–11:29.
49 Womack, *Neighbors*, 107–26, italics added.

based on Milton Bennett's model of intercultural "sensitivity,"[50] for building constructive Christian–Muslim relations. Similarly, among Patel's five
key skills for interfaith leadership is "Building a radar screen for religious
diversity,"[51] which refers to having a general awareness of, and actionable
language for, religious diversity issues when they arise. Unsurprisingly,
awareness sits atop most shortlists of essential components of leadership.
Daniel Goleman identifies self-awareness—"the ability to recognize and
understand your moods, emotions and drives, as well as their effect on
others"[52]—among the top five components of emotional intelligence, which
is an ability he argues that most effective leaders have. Reinforcing the
importance for a leader with IP to empathetically account for the various
and often competing needs of the stakeholders involved (know who), Brad
Jackson and Ken Parry observe, "frequently, when you look at leadership
failure, it comes down to emotional issues and not cognitive ones."[53] Likewise, the Co-Active Leadership Model identifies awareness as one among
five primary skills of leadership, for it enables leaders to empathetically
balance the needs of various stakeholders by reading "the emotional energies in a room and to sense what's going on in the space between everyone,
rather than what's going on with just one or two people individually."[54]
Developing attentiveness, awareness, and mindfulness for IP are necessary
for effective leadership in religiously diverse contexts. Hence, a major path
(yoga) for cultivating IP focuses on growing in mindfulness and the ability to pay attention. Individuals can grow in their ability to pay attention
to themselves and to others through life experience and various exercises
and methods (explored more below). Although IP is ultimately about being
aware of and sensitive to how religious diversity impacts others in everyday
contexts for the common good, an individual's cultivation of IP is often
grounded in developing greater awareness of one's self. In short, the journey

---

50 Milton Bennett, *Basic Concepts of Intercultural Communication*, 2nd ed. (Boston: Intercultural Press, 2013), 88; see chapter 10 for more on applying Bennet's Developmental Model of Intercultural Sensitivity (DMIS) to interfaith engagement and responding to religious diversity.
51 Patel, *Interfaith Leadership*, 135–39.
52 Daniel Goleman, "What Makes a Leader?" in *Contemporary Issues in Leadership*, 2nd ed., ed. William E. Rosenbach et al. (London: Taylor & Francis, 2014), 23.
53 Brad Jackson and Ken Parry, *A Very Short, Fairly Interesting and Reasonably Cheap Book about Studying Leadership*, 3rd ed. (London: Sage, 2018), 126.
54 Kimsey-House and Skibbins, *The Stake*, 53–4.

of self-discovery, the development of self-awareness and awareness of others are mutually beneficial and interdependent.

Self-Discovery

The personal growth and self-improvement industry (i.e., "self-help" products and programs) is a massive market, estimated to be worth 56.6 billion USD by 2027.[55] It capitalizes on the common intuition that attending to and healing the destructive self-centered aspects of the self is "a lifelong path that every leader must travel."[56] Understandably, consumers develop a healthy level of skepticism for any product that emerges from such a robust and lucrative industry. Psychologist Svend Brinkmann sardonically argues that one of the most important twenty-first-century skills is to "turn on your bullshit-detector,"[57] especially when confronted with trendy lists of skills and competencies littered with buzzwords. Although this book—and especially this section on self-discovery—does not aspire to be listed among these self-help products, it does not shy away from embracing evidence-based methods for leadership development. This book aspires to fall closer to the spirit Brinkmann embraces in *Stand Firm*, a book he describes not as a self-help book but one that offers alternative approaches to self-awareness and "self-actualization." Everyday wisdom, especially for leadership in a pluralistic world, entails a journey of self-discovery. This journey includes the ability to sort through what works and what does not work. Instead, aspiring leaders may consider embracing the spirit of Mahayana Buddhism's teaching of *upāya* (उपाय), or skillful means, which recognizes that people learn differently, have different skills, and are at different stages of their spiritual journey. It encourages the use of practical methods given the situation to achieve the goal. If a method falls flat, then it ought to be set aside. Likewise, once a method has served its purpose then it is to be discarded so as not to be confused with the goal. The method is left behind, "like a raft lying on the bank by a man who has crossed a stream and

---

55 Grand View Research, "Personal Development Market Size, Share & Trends Analysis Report by Instrument (Books, e-Platforms, Personal Coaching/Training, Workshops), by Focus Area, by Region, and Segment Forecasts, 2020—2027," Grandviewresearch.com, July 2020.

56 Kimsey-House and Skibbins, *The Stake*, 18.

57 Svend Brinkmann (@svendbrinkmann), "Tænd for din bullshit-detektor," Twitter, October 6, 2019, 5:24 a.m.

needs it no more."[58] Sometimes an individual can become too attached to and dependent on a particular self-help or leadership development method or tool, to the point where their training and development become more important than implementing the lessons and tools in real-life contexts. If the method itself usurps the aim of the method, then the individual can miss the forest for the trees. In such cases it may be more helpful to leave the forest, dropping the method altogether until such time as they can reenter with a renewed perspective on the relationship between the training (the trees) and its goals (the forest). Likewise, becoming too fixated on the methods and practices that cultivate the self, without keeping an eye on the larger forest or the distant shore, can sometimes lead to an unhealthy obsession of the self that risks being counterproductive to more authentically seeing oneself and engaging others. The point here is for individuals to consider evidence-based methods for leadership development for IP while granting themselves permission to use their bullshit detector to root out lousy methods or leave them behind once they have served their purpose, become distractions, or proven futile.

Leadership begins with the self. According to leadership scholars James M. Kouzes and Barry Z. Posner, leadership "is first an inner quest to discover who you are and what you care about, and it's through this process of self-examination that you find the awareness needed to lead.... The mastery of the art of leadership comes with the mastery of the self, and so developing leadership is a process of developing the self."[59] Scholar of business organizational behavior Richard Daft echoes this: "the first job of leadership is often getting the best out of yourself."[60] Importantly, a primary aim of cultivating deeper self-awareness and self-knowledge for IP is for the purpose of being sensitive to *others* and serving the common public goods. Hence, Brinkmann argues not only that too much self-reflection can become unhealthy, unproductive, overly obsessive, and result in disappointment and meaninglessness[61] (especially if it feeds one's self-destructive tendencies to judge, betray the self, justify, excuse, and revisit the old stories we tell ourselves time and again[62])

58 Michael Pye, *Skilful Means* (London: Routledge, 2003), 1.
59 Kouzes and Posner, "Leadership Begins with an Inner Journey," 117.
60 Richard L. Daft, "First, Lead Yourself," in *Contemporary Issues in Leadership*, 2nd ed., ed. Rosenbach et al., 126.
61 Brinkman suggests that "once a year is enough when it comes to self-analysis." Svend Brinkman, *Stand Firm*, trans. Tam McTurk (Cambridge: Polity Press, 2014), 15.
62 E.g., "The Destructive Self" of "Level One Awareness" in the Co-Active Leadership Model. Kimsey-House and Skibbins, *The Stake*, 17.

but also that self-actualization often comes through and requires others.[63] Although it may be true that "Leadership begins as an inside job"[64] in the sense that an individual must first discern their purpose to lead from personal values, convictions, and experiences that come from deep within, it is also true that this process often requires others to help one realize one's deepest values, convictions, and experiences. Almost every leadership development program or theory preaches that for one to be an effective authentic leader, they must first absolutely know who they are, to the extent that it is possible. Hence, significant focus on self-knowledge and self-awareness generally finds a home on most shortlist compilations of effective leadership traits, characteristics, and competencies. Co-Active Leadership teaches, "Finding out who you are and what you stand for is the genesis of leadership. The leader's connection with his or her fundamental strengths, foundational beliefs, and core principles is central to effective leadership."[65] McGraw extends the necessity of this leadership trait to knowing one's own inherited religious heritage, of which many may be initially unaware: "leaders who do not recognize their own particular religio-cultural influences, which inform leaders' habits and practices, can undermine their efforts at effective leadership."[66] This involves a leader understanding not only how they perceive themselves, but how others perceive them as well. These insights cannot be gained without others going alongside the leader in trusting fashion to help illuminate and reflect back to them their particular strengths, some of which the leader may be unaware. Although the cultivation of the self receives the lion's share of attention in leadership development, its inherent interdependency on *others* ought not be deprioritized or lost.

Unsurprisingly, some scholars identify spiritual dimensions to the journey of self-cultivation for fostering leadership development and IP. In the Upanishadic tradition of Sanātana Dharma (Hinduism), the enduring insight of *tat tvam asi*, or "thou art that," prevails. That is, through deep examination of self and detachment from impermanent superficial affiliations (age, occupation, body, desires, memories, etc.), an individual can discover who they already are, or more precisely that they are already that. They are already their

---

63 Brinkman suggests learning "to look outwards, not inwards; to be open to other people, cultures, and natures. Brinkmann, *Stand Firm*, 16.
64 Kimsey-House and Skibbins, *The Stake*, 26.
65 Kimsey-House and Skibbins, 27.
66 McGraw, "Cross-Cultural Leadership as Interfaith Leadership," 216.

underlying true self, which is divine and veiled by their superficial affiliations. The Co-Active Leadership model, which is not affiliated with any religious or spiritual traditions, utilizes language and concepts resonant of religious language. In particular, it strikes a similar tone to theologian Paul Tillich's concept of religion as the name for an individual's ultimate concern. Chapter 1 introduced Tillich's proposal of religion as the "state of being grasped by an ultimate concern."[67] Co-Active Leadership invites leaders to identify their "Life Purpose Statement," which is "the meaning, purpose, and reason why you were born on this planet at this time, and it defines the work you were meant to do."[68] Furthermore, with language laden with unmistakable spiritual resonance, the Co-Active model preaches that "your Life Purpose is the current pulling you along and moving you onward through your life . . . [and] influences any Stake you choose to set, and any Stake you set is wrapped around the unshakable core of your Life Purpose."[69] Discovery and awareness of self are essential for identifying one's life purpose and their various Stakes within it. *Yogas* are methods for yoking one's self to their "Life Purpose," "Ultimate Concern," and deepest knowledge of self, passions, values, and convictions.

Yogas

One of the most ancient instances of any Indo-European language is found in the *Rigveda*. The word "yoga" appears in its original Indo-European usage to denote a "yoke," which is used to tether a bull or horse to a plow or chariot. Over time, yoga became less associated with the yoke as such (the mechanism that binds horse to chariot) and came to denote the chariot itself, and the war chariot in particular. By heroically falling on the battlefield, "one could become metaphorically 'yoked' to a heavenly war chariot"[70] that whisks one away to the heavenly realm of gods and heroes (akin to Valhalla in Norse traditions). In the *Mahabharata*, the Vedic sense of "yoga" lives on, "where

---

67 Tillich, *The Future of Religions*, 3.
68 Kimsey-House and Skibbins, *The Stake*, 24.
69 Kimsey-House and Skibbins, *The Stake*, 24.
70 Bjarne Wernicke-Olesen, "Hinduism and Meditation," in *The Oxford Handbook of Meditation*, ed. Miguel Farias, David Brazier, and Mansur Lalljee (Oxford: Oxford University Press, 2020), 5.

dying heroes travel in their 'yoga' or divine chariot" to the heavens.[71] Later texts, such as the *Katha Upanishad*, use yoga soteriologically to denote a method of ultimate liberation.[72] Yoga denotes a path, a way, or a method to ultimate meaning or liberation. Yogas are methods that bind an individual to the task of reaching an ultimate goal. To accommodate the plurality of personality types and diverse range of learning styles and means by which people learn and grow, the Hindu traditions are well known for endorsing a rich tapestry of various yogas (or paths) to achieve liberation. Whether one is a student, instructor, scholar, practitioner, leader, or all of these and more, in the spirit of the Hindu traditions, aspiring leaders seeking IP should consider exploring the several rich time-tested and emerging yogas or methods to yoke one's self to the goal of growing in practical everyday wisdom for interreligious encounter. If IP is a leadership virtue, and virtues can be cultivated, then the quest(ion) becomes a matter of determining the best methods or yogic paths (or skillful means for that matter) through which each individual can foster IP.

Just as swimming cannot be learned without getting wet, IP cannot be learned without experience. Practical wisdom is not attained primarily through texts, lectures, and writing. It must be learned through encounters in the world. It must be applied.[73] Rather, like the implicit tacit *know how* described above, IP must be learned by doing and found in the practices of one's experience. For instance, "Practical wisdom is embedded in the actual practices of being a lawyer or a teacher or a doctor or a banker or a military officer or a violence counselor or a custodian . . . wisdom is associated with experience. But it's not just any experience. Experience must be structured in ways that 'cause wisdom to be learned.'"[74] Although researchers generally agree that "leadership is something that is largely and primarily learned through experience,"[75] and there exists no replacement for the actual lived experience and practices that foster IP—just as there are no replacements for

---

71 Wernicke-Olesen, "Hinduism and Meditation," 5.

72 Wernicke-Olesen, 5.

73 "Practical wisdom is not something that can be taught, at least in the narrow sense of listening to classroom lectures, reading books, and doing exams or papers. And it can't be learned as an isolated subject' or even as a general skill that we can go around 'applying.'" Schwartz and Sharpe, *Practical Wisdom*, 271.

74 Schwartz and Sharpe, 271–72.

75 Jackson and Parry, *A Very Short, Fairly Interesting and Reasonably Cheap Book about Studying Leadership*, 3rd ed. (London: Sage, 2018), 123.

learning to ride a bike other than just simply getting on the bike—there are paths and methods to more efficiently assist an individual with developing greater IP. Depending on each learner's character, learning style, and context, several practical and theoretical methods exist to increase one's leadership and IP. These include ancient practices such as mindfulness training[76] (akin to *rāja* yoga) and Ignatian spirituality,[77] immersive practice-oriented and selfless-service oriented experience (akin to *karma* yoga), ultimate loving devotion to others and work (akin to *bhakti* yoga),[78] friendship and deep relationships,[79] inspiration from role models and moral exemplars,[80] Confucian-inspired humble leadership development and apprenticeship,[81] self-interrogation and self-authoring development models[82] through reading literature or writing exercises, and the ever-growing catalogue of leadership development models and styles (such as Appreciative, Authentic, Charismatic, Co-Active, Cross-Cultural, Genuine, Global, Nordic, Positive, Servant, Spiritual, Transactional, Transformational, and all the other old and New-Genre leadership theories). Several offer constructive commencement points in the quest for greater awareness of self and of others, and are foundational to cultivating practical interfaith leadership as IP for everyday living. Students may choose a method and try it, instructors may select a method to adapt to their teaching in service of their student learning goals, and scholars and practitioners may exercise a method for greater awareness of self and of others in their professional and community leadership. For individuals discerning a method, "look for a programme that has stood the test of time. Avoid programmes that emphasize the latest and greatest techniques. Leadership is an ancient art—in

76 There is an almost endless growing list of works on mindfulness meditation for awareness and leadership, e.g., Amishi P. Jha, *Peak Mind* (New York: HarperOne, 2021).

77 Teresa J. Rothausen, "Integrating Leadership Development with Ignatian Spirituality," *Journal of Business Ethics* 145 no. 4 (2017): 811–29.

78 Satinder Dhiman, *Bhagavad Gītā and Leadership* (Cham, Switzerland: Palgrave MacMillan, 2019), 157–77.

79 Gustafson, "Friends in Foxholes."

80 Megan Mischinski and Eranda Jaywickreme, "Can Moral Exemplars Promote Wisdom?" in *Applying Wisdom to Contemporary World Problems*, ed. Sternberg et al., 173–200.

81 Gary K. Y. Chan, "Confucianism, Virtue, and Leadership," in *Handbook of Virtue Ethics in Business and Management*, ed. Alejo José G. Sison, Gregory R. Beabout, and Ignacio Ferrero (Dordrecht: Springer, 2017), 445–55.

82 Hans Gustafson, "Interreligious Studies and Personal Changemaking Pedagogy for Leadership and the Common Good," 42–48.

truth, not much has changed"[83]—therefore, and since "a completely secular understanding of wisdom may be incomplete,"[84] this book has throughout drawn on the depths of various ancient wisdom traditions of, to name a few, Daoism, Hinduism, Buddhism, and Aristotle. Neuropsychologist Amishi Jha discovered this when her lab at the University of Miami researched how to train the brain to be more attentive and found the answer in the ancient wisdom of mindfulness mediation.[85] In the same way that learning to play an instrument requires the buildup of tacit knowledge through using the language, cultivating IP requires putting oneself or others in positions to experience in real time those contexts and situations that call for IP.

Although leadership development programs cannot train leaders, they can make leadership more likely to occur.[86] Programs can help individuals develop behaviors and skills by engaging in dialogue and encounter in a variety of (inter)religiously civic, professional, and public contexts accompanied by self-reflexive tools and resources from the above-mentioned leadership development theories and methods[87] for reflecting on, and growing in, one's everyday IP for interreligious encounter and leadership. Vinita Bali offers wisdom about everyday leadership: "More than anything else, leadership is about character and authenticity. It is about taking ownership for changing something and making it better than you found it. . . . Leadership is exercised every day—in schools, homes, and other institutions."[88] Inspired by Bali's spirit of everyday leadership set within contexts and spaces of interreligious

---

83 Jackson and Parry, *A Very Short, Fairly Interesting and Reasonably Cheap Book about Studying Leadership*, 126.

84 Juensung J. Kim, Stephanie Morris, Phillip Rajewicz, Michael Ferrari, and John Vervaeke, "Walk in Wisdom's Path," *Journal of Religion, Spirituality, and Aging* (2022): 17.

85 Jha, *Peak Mind*, 13, 70.

86 Jonathan Gosling and Ian Sutherland, "Diverse Approaches to Leadership Development," in *The Routledge Companion to Leadership*, ed. John Store, Jean Hartley, Jean-Louis Denis, Paul 't Hart, and David Ulrich (New York: Routledge, 2017), 550; cited in Jackson and Parry, *A Very Short, Fairly Interesting and Reasonably Cheap Book about Studying Leadership*, 124–25.

87 E.g., meditation, self-authoring, narrative pedagogy, selfless service, direct encounter and engagement, simulations and role playing, group dynamics training, action learning, case study analysis, coaching, outdoor adventure team building, roundtables, art-based approaches, gamification methods, deep relationships, great literature. Gosling and Sutherland, "Diverse Approaches to Leadership Development," 550; citing Jackson and Parry, *A Very Short, Fairly Interesting and Reasonably Cheap Book about Studying Leadership*, 124–25.

88 Bali, "Leadership Lessons from Everyday Life," 230.

encounter, this book invites readers to reflect on their "Stake" in relation to developing interreligious practical wisdom for leadership in the everyday world. Additionally, this book, which aspires to good scholarship, invites readers to critically investigate every claim made by the book and to reflect on where they stand in their own responses to those claims (and then critically interrogate their own claims as well). Such reflection will undoubtedly prove to be, in part, what drives any relevance for this book but more importantly for the readers' benefit.

〽 〽 〽

CONCLUDING UNSCIENTIFIC POSTSCRIPT: A REFLEXIVE ACCOUNT

Incorporating theories and methods of self-discovery and leadership development for IP into one's life—whether it be through academic course-work, pedagogy, scholarship, leadership training, self-improvement, or otherwise—can stimulate greater discovery of one's subjective inward truth (self-awareness) and increased mindfulness of others for everyday wisdom and leadership in an interreligiously complex world. They can also promote self-actualization, that is, the journey of becoming more fully human. They can facilitate the process of knowing more intimately who you already are, an inner journey all leaders must take. Leadership Studies pioneer Warren Bennis famously preached, "To become a leader, you must become yourself; become the maker of your own life,"[89] and hence, as Vinita Bali suggests, "leadership is less about what we do and more about what we become—and in the process how we influence and learn from those around us."[90] Cultivating everyday practical wisdom and leadership in the contemporary world does not need to be complicated. It can be as simple as choosing a method or point of entry and trying it out. Find a path that speaks to you and move forward with it. At worst, you will fail and need to adopt another method. Failing in this way can be a welcome invitation for growth.

---

89 Warren G. Bennis and Patricia Ward Biederman, *The Essential Bennis* (Hoboken, NJ: Wiley, 2015), 214; cited in Kouzes and Posner, "Leadership Begins with an Inner Journey," 119.

90 Bali, "Leadership Lessons from Everyday Life," 235.

It was a watershed moment for me when I learned that "there is no leadership without risk, and there is no risk without failure."[91] The image of "failing forward, . . . the only way a baby learns to walk or a leader learns to lead,"[92] granted me the license and motivation to accept risks and failures as necessary for growth, not only in interfaith leadership or leadership in general, but in the greater scope of flourishing in life.[93]

After both my parents died, only four months apart, I attempted a method that spoke to my sensibilities. I stumbled upon psychologist Svend Brinkmann's book *Stand Firm*, which he describes as an "anti-self-help book," that is, "a seven-step guide on how to ignore seven-step guides. Because there is no key, there is no solution—there is just life, with all its problems."[94] At that time in my life, Brinkmann's stoic-ridden sentiment of treading through life in a chaotic imperfect messy world struck a deep chord. Such an outlook may fall flat on the ears of many, as it probably would have for me had I considered it a year earlier. Not all paths speak to all persons at all times. However, Brinkmann's anti-self-help self-help orientation, during a time in which I grasped for a foothold in the reality of death and mortality, challenged me to follow his "Step 6: Read a novel—not a self-help book or biography." Brinkmann argues that literature ought to "be considered as qualitative research in itself" and, moreover, "it enables readers to understand the world and themselves better than they did before and may even animate them to act differently, both of which are legitimate aims of research."[95] Brinkmann reminded me that great works of literature and fictional novels "enable you to understand human life as complex and unmanageable,"[96] and can function as a type of Foucauldian "technology of the self."[97] They depict life as "complex, random, chaotic and multifaceted,"[98] and invite the reader to share in that reality.

---

91 Kimsey-House and Skibbins, *The Stake*, 35.

92 Kimsey-House and Skibbins, 35.

93 For a personal example of failing forward in an interreligious context, see Hans Gustafson, "Deflecting Myself: A Failure of Leadership," in *With the Best of Intentions: Interrogating Interfaith Mistakes*, ed. Lucinda Mosher, Ellie Pierce, and Or Rose (Maryknoll, NY: Orbis Books, 2023).

94 Independent.ie, "There Is No Key, There Is Just Life," March 7, 2017.

95 Svend Brinkmann, "Literature as Qualitative Inquiry," *Qualitative Inquiry* 15, no. 8 (2009): 1392.

96 Brinkmann, *Stand Firm*, 86.

97 Michael Foucault, *Technologies of the Self*, ed. Luther H. Martin, Huck Gutman, and Patrick H. Hutton (London: Tavistock, 1988); cited in Brinkmann, *Stand Firm*, 93.

98 Brinkmann, *Stand Firm*, 88.

Upon Brinkmann's recommendation, I tackled the nearly four-thousand-page autofictional novel *My Struggle* by Karl Ove Knausgaard. I quickly discovered Brinkmann's assessment was accurate in that *My Struggle*, lacking illusions and focusing on mundane and negative aspects of life, offered deep and striking insight into my own life.[99] Although I did not realize it at first, I slowly came to understand what one book reviewer meant by the line, "Karl Ove makes me see better. I have not wanted his books to end because I have not wanted to unmerge with him."[100] It is difficult to imagine any therapist, life coach, rigorous self-help book, or fancy leadership development program could at that time have reflected my life and past back to me in the way Knausgaard did in his writing. Reading a novel helped me to see myself better, become more human, relate more intimately to others, and grow as a leader with a greater sense of how others identify and view the world, religiously and otherwise. It helped me further to cultivate IP to a degree previously unknown to me.

Seven years after the death of my parents, the Office for Spirituality at my university invited me to write a brief Advent reflection to publish on their website, to which I reluctantly agreed. I didn't consider myself to be very religious, and I dreaded writing reflections of this kind. They require the writer to reflect on preselected Scripture passages from the New Testament and Hebrew Bible, and then write a brief public reflection. Such short and potentially personally charged reflections often take more of my time and emotional energy than a standard twenty-page academic article. I knew the assignment, if it were to be of any substance, demanded significant time and soul-searching, two requests for which I lacked bandwidth at that point amidst my end-of-semester duties. I received the two Scripture selections and never made it past reading the first one from the Hebrew Bible: Isaiah 40:1–11. It described a wasteland, a rugged land, and a rough country with withering grass and wilting flowers. A world in which all flesh is grass and all people are grass. It transported me back to the death of my parents, the chaos in which I flailed trying to make sense of it. It also simultaneously transported me back to Knausgaard's stunningly direct and ordinary prose about his own father's death in *My Struggle*. The two memories came together in me like a sedate bolt of lightning emanating up from the ground to its origin in the

---

99 Brinkmann, 97.

100 Nina MacLaughlin, "Recapturing the World with Karl Ove Knausgaard," *Los Angeles Review of Books*, May 23, 2013.

atmosphere. Knausgaard's blunt depiction of the brutal mundane ordinary details of the lived experience of a parent's death coupled with the memory of my dead parents, set within the context of Brinkmann's stoic reminder about the healthy passing of life, helped me see myself, others, and the world better—and it helped me to appreciate the often-significant differences among the ways people, communities, and traditions experience and understand such weighty matters of life. The Advent reflection flowed seamlessly henceforth from my pen and was subsequently published.[101]

Had it not been for the subtle nudge to self-interrogate by simply reading a novel, I may not have come to terms—my own terms—with my parents' deaths. Such was an appropriate path for me at that particular point in my life. Not only did it help me see what was already there but, perhaps more importantly, it revealed aspects of myself and history that had always been there. Nor would I have developed a greater awareness of and appreciation for the diverse ways individuals, groups, and traditions approach death and endure the grieving process. My experience of becoming more self-aware simultaneously included becoming more aware of others. For leadership development and ultimately for cultivating IP, the lesson here for me was to remain opportunistic and open to the diverse voices, methods, processes, people, and yogas that may speak to me at different times and in different places. It taught me to utilize diverse experiences and methods to self-reflect and to always begin with the question, "What does this reveal about me and my relations to the world and to others?" After considering such a necessary preliminary question like this, I often discover that I am in a healthier and more effective place to inquire about how I leverage my assets, resources, and experiences to serve, recognize, and balance the needs and concerns—(inter) religious or otherwise—of all stakeholders involved, hopefully with an eye to serving the common public good(s) in ways that enable persons and communities to flourish.[102]

---

101 Hans Gustafson, "Tuesday of the Second Week of Advent," University of St. Thomas, December 10, 2019.

102 Bernard V. Brady, "Persons and the Common Good," in *Essential Catholic Social Thought*, 2nd ed. (Maryknoll, NY: Orbis Books, 2017), 34–50.

Acknowledgments

The number of individuals and groups needing thanks is too great to list here. If your name appears in this book, or if you've crossed paths with me in professional, civic, or community settings, whether it be at an AAR conference, an interfaith gathering, in a classroom, in Minnesota, online Zoom, or elsewhere, chances are very high that you have influenced my evolution of thought. This group includes Amy Allocco, Russ Arnold, Patrice Brodeur, Catherine Cornille, Diana Eck, Jeannine Hill Fletcher, Anne Hege Grung, Paul Hedges, Amir Hussain, J. R. Hustwit, Andrew Johnson, Mike Klein, Dave Krueger, Oddbjørn Leirvik, Dominic Longo, Matt Maruggi, Kate McCarthy, Barbara McGraw, John Merkle, Rachel Mikva, Kevin Minister, Younus Mirza, Lucinda Mosher, Marianne Moyaert, Eboo Patel, Jenny Peace, Brian Pennington, Ellie Pierce, Carolyn Roncolato, Perry Schmidt-Leukel, Noah Silverman, Marty Stortz, Kim Vrudny, Wolfram Weisse, and many others. From the heart, thank you for your friendship. Above all, it is the relationships I've developed with all of you that I cherish the most. A special thanks to Will Bergkamp and the team at Fortress Press for believing in this book and supporting its publication. A very special thanks to Bethany Dickerson for her keen eye and substantive editorial review of the manuscript. Her significant contributions to the book make it not only infinitely more readable but more intelligent, engaging, and relevant.

Acknowledgment and appreciation are due to all the publishers and editors that granted permission to adapt and revise my previously published thought. The section "Interreligious Studies" in chapter 1 is adapted from "Defining the Academic Field of Interreligious Studies," *Interreligious Studies and Intercultural Theology* 4, no. 2 (2020): 131–54, © Equinox Publishing Ltd 2020; and "Interreligious and Interfaith Studies in Relation to Religious Studies and Theological Studies," State of Formation, January 6, 2015. Four paragraphs in the section "Personal and Social Identities" in chapter 2 are adapted and revised from "'They're Not Really Christians,'" State of Formation, May 27,

2018. Portions of chapter 6 on lived interreligious encounter are inspired by and adapted from "Vitality of Lived Religion Approaches" by Hans Gustafson (Copyright © 2020 by Baylor University Press. Used with permission. All rights reserved). Chapter 7 on (inter)religious literacy expands significantly on "What Does It Mean to Be (Inter)Religiously Literate," State of Formation, April 27, 2018. Chapter 8 on the relationship of interreligious studies to interfaith engagement is adapted, revised, and extended from "Sparring with Spider Silk," in Copyright 2022 by Georgetown University Press. Hans Gustafson, "Chapter 4 Sparring with Spider Silk". From The Georgetown Companion to Interreligious Studies, Lucinda Mosher, Editor, pp. 32–40. Reprinted with permission. www.press.georgetown.edu. The section "Interfaith or Interreligious?" in chapter 9 is adapted and extended from Hans Gustafson, "'Interfaith' Is 1970s!" State of Formation, April 12, 2018. The section "Interreligious Theology" in chapter 12 contains revised sections from "Pansacramentalism, Interreligious Theology, and Lived Religion," *Religions* 10, no. 7: 408 (2019): 54–68. A paragraph in the introduction to chapter 13 is adapted and revised from a section in "Vitality of Lived Religion Approaches" by Hans Gustafson (Copyright © 2020 by Baylor University Press. Used with permission. All rights reserved). The section "Forging Solidarities" in chapter 13 is adapted and revised from "Is Transreligious Theology Unavoidable in Interreligious Theology and Dialogue?" *Open Theology* 2, no. 1 (2016): 248–60, and "'They're Not Really Christians': Acknowledging Oppression and Violence in Our Traditions for the Sake of Interreligious Understanding," State of Formation, May 27, 2018. The section "Phronesis as Wherewithal" in chapter 14 draws on "Interreligious Wherewithal," State of Formation, November 16, 2017. The section "Four Dimensions of Interreligious Phronesis" in chapter 14 is adapted and revised from "An Emerging Phronetic Framework in Interfaith and Interreligious Studies Courses in the United States," *Journal of Interreligious Studies* 36 (2022): 64–74. It is used with permission of the publishers.

Bibliography

AAR Religions in Schools Task Force, and Diane L. Moore. "Guidelines for Teaching about Religion in K–12 Public Schools in the United States." American Academy of Religion, 2010. https://tinyurl.com/2p8ewu3v.

Abdi, Cawo. "Where Is My Islam? The Identity Crisis of 21st Century Muslims." CNN.com, August 24, 2015. https://tinyurl.com/msve96fn.

Ackrill, John Lloyd. *Aristotle's Ethics*. London: Faber & Faber, 1973.

Ahmad, Aisha-Nusrat, Maik Fielitz, Johanna Leinius, and Gianna Magdalena Schlichte. "Introduction: Critical Interventions in Knowledge Production from within and without Academia." In *Knowledge, Normativity and Power in Academia: Critical Interventions*, edited by Aisha-Nusrat Ahmad, Maik Fielitz, Johanna Leinius, and Gianna Magdalena Schlichte, 7–26. Frankfurt: Campus Verlag, 2018.

Aldwin, Carolyn M., and Michael R. Levenson. "The Practical Applications of Self-Transcendent Wisdom." In *Applying Wisdom to Contemporary World Problems*, edited by Robert J. Sternberg, Howard C. Nusbaum, and Judith Glück, 293–307. Cham, Switzerland: Palgrave Macmillan, 2019.

Allocco, Amy L., Geoffrey D. Clausen, and Brian K. Pennington. "Constructing Interreligious Studies: Thinking Critically about Interfaith Studies and the Interfaith Movement." In *Interreligious/Interfaith Studies: Defining a New Field*, edited by Eboo Patel, Jennifer Howe Peace, and Noah Silverman, 36–48. Boston: Beacon Press, 2018.

Amarasingam, Amarnath, Hicham Tiflati, and Nathan C. Walker. "Religious Literacy in Law: Anti-Muslim Initiatives in Quebec, the United States, and India." *Religion & Education* 48, no. 1 (2021): 121–40. https://doi.org/10.1080/1550739 4.2021.1881028.

American Academy of Religion. "AAR Guidelines: What US College Graduates Should Understand about Religion." Draft 3.1 authors: Eugene V. Gallagher, Diane L. Moore, Amir Hussain, Cherie Hughes, Eugene Lowe, Margaret Lowe, Brian Pennington, and Martha Reineke. Hardcopy distributed at the American Academy of Religion annual conference, Boston, MA, November 18, 2017.

——. "Religious Literacy Guidelines for College Students." American Academy of Religion (website). Last accessed December 5, 2018. https://www.aarweb.org/about/religious-literacy-guidelines-for-college-students.

Ammerman, Nancy Tatom. "Rethinking Religion: Toward a Practice Approach." *American Journal of Sociology* 126, no. 1 (July 2020): 6–51.

———. *Studying Lived Religion: Contexts and Practices.* New York: New York University Press, 2021.

———. "2013 Paul Hanly Furfey Lecture: Finding Religion in Everyday Life." *Sociology of Religion* 75, no. 2 (2014): 189–207.

Anderson, Christina. "Muslim Job Applicant Who Refused Handshake Wins Discrimination Case in Sweden." *New York Times*, August 16, 2018. https://tinyurl.com/2p89v3db.

Andreassen, Bengt-Ove. "'Knowledge about Religions' and Analytical Skills in Religious Education: Reflections from a Norwegian Context." *Religion, Education, and the Challenges of Contemporary Societies* 9, no. 4 (2019): 73–90.

Antonacopoulou, Elena P. "The Capacity of *Phronesis.*" In *Academic–Practitioner Relationships: Developments, Complexities and Opportunities*, edited by Jean M. Bartunek and Jane McKenzie, 178–93. London: Routledge, 2017.

Aristotle. *Nichomachean Ethics.* Translated by Martin Ostwald. Englewood Cliffs: Prentice Hall, 1962.

Arnold, Russell C. D. "Complicating Religious Identity." In *Interreligious Studies: Dispatches from a Field*, edited by Hans Gustafson, 185–90. Waco: Baylor University Press, 2020.

———. "Making Interfaith Conversations Central to Our Jesuit Mission: Why and How to Get Started." *Conversations on Jesuit Higher Education* 51, no. 24 (2017). https://tinyurl.com/2fxputmx.

The Art of Dr. Seuss Collection (website). "Dr. Seuss' Use of Racist Images." Accessed May 4, 2020. https://tinyurl.com/j2nyksf3.

Asad, Talal. *Formations of the Secular: Christianity, Islam, Modernity.* Stanford, CA: Stanford University Press, 2003.

Ashoka United States. "About Ashoka." Accessed September 6, 2020. https://tinyurl.com/mp4wpnv6.

———. "Frequently Asked Questions." Accessed September 6, 2020. https://tinyurl.com/2p83rt4r.

Avolio, Bruce J., Fred O. Walumbwa, and Todd J. Weber. "Leadership: Current Theories, Research, and Future Directions." *Annual Review of Psychology* 60 (2009): 421–49. https://doi.org/10.1146/annurev.psych.60.110707.163621.

Baatz, Ursula. "Territory, Relationship or Path: A Brief Survey of Metaphors of 'Double Religious Belonging.'" *Open Theology* 3 (2017): 144–55.

Baird, Robert D. *Category Formation and the History of Religion.* The Hague and Paris: Mouton, 1971.

Bali, Vinita. "Leadership Lessons from Everyday Life." In *Contemporary Issues in Leadership*, 2nd ed., edited by William E. Rosenbach, Robert L. Taylor, and Mark A. Youndt, 229–35. London: Taylor & Francis, 2014.

Bangstad, Sindre. "Contesting Secularism/s: Secularism and Islam in the Work of Talal Asad." *Anthropological Theory* 9, no. 2 (2009): 188–208.

Barlow, Rich. "Are Non-Jews Who Host a Seder Sharing Jewish Culture or Hijacking It?" WBUR, April 19, 2019. https://tinyurl.com/52hffmey.

Barnes, Michael, and Jonathan D. Smith. "Religious Literacy as *Lokahi*: Social Harmony through Diversity." In *Religious Literacy in Policy and Practice*, edited by Adam Dinham and Matthew Francis, 77–97. Bristol: Policy Press, 2016.

Beck, Ulrich. *A God of One's Own: Religion's Capacity for Peace and Potential for Violence*. Cambridge: Polity Press, 2010.

Bell, David M. "Religious Identity." In *Encyclopedia of Psychology and Religion*, edited by David A. Leeming, Kathryn Madden, and Stanton Marlon, 778. New York: Springer, 2009.

Bellah, Robert N. "Civil Religion in America." *Daedalus* 96, no. 1 (Winter 1967): 1–21.

Bennett, Milton. *Basic Concepts of Intercultural Communication: Paradigms, Principles, and Practices*, 2nd ed. Boston: Intercultural Press, 2013.

———. "The Developmental Model of Intercultural Sensitivity." IDRInstitute, 2014. Accessed April 28, 2022. https://tinyurl.com/949pfu8k.

Bennis, Warren G., and Patricia Ward Biederman. *The Essential Bennis*. Hoboken, NJ: Wiley, 2015.

Berger, Peter L., ed. *The Desecularization of the World: Resurgent Religion and World Politics*. Grand Rapids, MI: Eerdmans, 1999.

———. "Further Thoughts on Religion and Modernity." *Society* 49, no. 4 (2012): 313–16.

———. "The Good of Religious Pluralism." *First Things* April (2016): 39–42.

———. *The Many Alters of Modernity: Toward a Paradigm for Religion in a Pluralist Age*. Boston: DeGruyter, 2014.

Berghuijs, Joantine. "Multiple Religious Belonging in the Netherlands: An Empirical Approach to Hybrid Religiosity." *Open Theology* 3 (2017): 19–37.

Berghuijs, Joantine, Hans Schilderman, André van der Braak, and Manuela Kalsky. "Exploring Single and Multiple Religious Belonging." *Journal of Empirical Theology* 31 (2018): 18–48.

Berkley Center for Religion, Peace, and World Affairs. "A Discussion with Anna Halafoff." Georgetown University, September 22, 2016. https://tinyurl.com/35mtryf9.

Berlinerblau, Jacques. *Secularism: The Basics*. London: Routledge, 2022.

———. "Secularism Necessary for Religious Freedom, Professor Says." *Georgetown University News*, December 7, 2012. https://tinyurl.com/2p8eyjma.

Berthong, John. *The Divine Deli: Religious Identity in the North American Cultural Mosaic*. Maryknoll, NY: Orbis, 1999.

Blumenthal, David R. "Where Does 'Jewish Studies' Belong?" *Journal of the American Academy of Religion* 44, no. 3 (1976): 535–46.

Bobrowicz, Ryszard. "Keeping Religion in the Closet: How Legible Religion Shapes Multi-Faith Spaces." Doctoral diss., Lund University, Sweden, 2022.

Bock, Jan-Jonathan, and John Fahy. "Emergent Religious Pluralisms: Ideals and Realities in a Changing World." In *Emergent Religious Pluralisms*, edited by Jan-Jonathan Bock and John Fahy, 1–19. Cham, Switzerland: Palgrave Macmillan, 2019.

Boorstein, Michelle. "Interfaith Movement Struggles to Adapt to Changing Religious Landscape." *Washington Post*, August 16, 2013. https://tinyurl.com/2p8fct8r.

Borneman, John, and Abdellah Hammoudi, eds. *Being There: The Fieldwork Encounter and the Making of Truth*. Berkeley: University of California Press, 2009.

Bowker, John, ed. *The Concise Oxford Dictionary of World Religions*. Oxford: Oxford University Press, 2000.

Brady, Bernard V. *Essential Catholic Social Thought*, 2nd ed. Maryknoll, NY: Orbis Books, 2017.

——. "Persons and the Common Good." In *Essential Catholic Social Thought*, 2nd ed. Maryknoll, NY: Orbis Books, 2017.

Brinkmann, Svend. "Literature as Qualitative Inquiry: The Novelist as Researcher." *Qualitative Inquiry* 15, no. 8 (2009): 1376–94.

——. *Stand Firm: Resisting the Self-Improvement Craze*. Translated by Tam McTurk. Cambridge: Polity Press, 2014.

——. "Tænd for din bullshit-detektor." @svendbrinkmann, Twitter, October 6, 2019, 5:24 a.m. https://tinyurl.com/yjxar395.

Brodd, Jeffrey, Layne Little, Bradley Nystrom, Robert Platzner, Richard Shek, and Erin Stiles, ed. *Invitation to World Religions*. Oxford: Oxford University Press, 2012.

Brodeur, Patrice, and Eboo Patel. "Introduction." In *Building the Interfaith Youth Movement: Beyond Dialogue to Action*, edited by Eboo Patel and Patrice Brodeur, 1–13. Lanham, MD: Rowman & Littlefield, 2006.

Bruce, Steve. "Multiple Religious Belonging: Conceptual Advance or Secularization Denial?" *Open Theology* 3 (2017): 611–12.

Bullivant, Stephen, Miguel Farias, Jonathan Lanman, and Lois Lee. "Understanding Unbelief: Atheists and Agnostics around the World." Interim findings from 2019 research in Brazil, China, Denmark, Japan, the United Kingdom, and the United States. Understanding Unbelief, 2019. https://tinyurl.com/3tykercy.

Burke, Peter J., and Jan E. Stets. *Identity Theory*. New York: Oxford University Press, 2009.

Burns, James MacGregor. *Transforming Leadership*. New York: Grove, 2003.

Byock, Jesse L. *Viking Age Iceland*. London: Penguin, 2001.

Cabrera, Danie. "Mayo Clinic Includes Social Media Scholarship Activities in Academic Advancement." Mayo Clinic Social Media Network, May 25, 2016.

Caldwell, Tommy. "How Becoming a Hostage and Losing a Finger Made Him a Better Climber." *National Geographic*, June 25, 2017. https://tinyurl.com/kmjvw3z7.

Campbell, David E., and Robert D. Putnam. "America's Grace: How a Tolerant Nation Bridges Its Religious Divides." *Political Science Quarterly* 126, no. 4 (Winter 2011): 611–40.

Cannella, Gaille S., and Yvonna S. Lincoln. "Predatory vs. Dialogic Ethics: Constructing an Illusion or Ethical Practice as the Core of Research Methods." *Qualitative Inquiry* 13, no. 3 (2007): 315–35.

Canovan, Margaret. "On Being Economical with the Truth: Some Liberal Reflections." *Political Studies* 38, no. 1 (1990): 5–19.

Casanova, José. "The Karel Dobbelaere Lecture: Divergent Global Roads to Secularization and Religious Pluralism." *Social Compass* 65, no. 2 (2018): 187–98.

——. *Public Religions in the Modern World*. Chicago: University of Chicago Press, 1994.

Chan, Gary K. Y. "Confucianism, Virtue, and Leadership: The Focus on Humble Leadership." In *Handbook of Virtue Ethics in Business and Management*, edited by Alejo José G. Sison, Gregory R. Beabout, and Ignacio Ferrero, 445–55. Dordrecht: Springer, 2017.

Chan, W. Y. Alice. *Teaching Religious Literacy to Combat Religious Bullying: Insights from North American Secondary Schools*. New York: Routledge, 2021.

Chan, W. Y. Alice, and Jessica Sitek. "Religious Literacy in Healthcare." *Religion & Education* 48, no. 1 (2021): 102–20. https://doi.org/10.1080/15507394.2021.1889 453.

Cheetham, David. "The University and Interfaith Education." *Studies in Interreligious Dialogue* 15, no. 1 (2005): 16–35.

Chryssides, George D., and Stephen E. Gregg. *The Insider/Outside Debate: New Perspectives in the Study of Religion.* Sheffield, UK: Equinox, 2020.

Coleman, Monica A. "The Womb Circle: A Womanist Practice of Multi-Religious Belonging." *Practical Matters* 4 (Spring 2011): 1–12.

Collier, Stephen J., and Aihwa Ong. "Global Assemblages, Anthropological Problems." In *Global Assemblages: Technology, Politics, and Ethics as Anthropological Problems,* edited by Aihwa Ong and Stephen J. Collier, 3–21. Malden, MA: Blackwell, 2005.

Collins, Harry. *Tacit and Explicit Knowledge.* Chicago: University of Chicago Press, 2010.

Connolly, William. *A World of Becoming.* Durham, NC: Duke University Press, 2010.

Conroy, James C. "Religious Illiteracy in School Religious Education." In *Religious Literacy in Policy and Practice,* edited by Adam Dinham and Matthew Francis, 167–85. Bristol: Policy Press, 2016.

Convergence on Campus. "Mission Statement." Last accessed October 24, 2019. www.convergenceoncampus.org/our-plan. Now at https://www.convergencestrategies.org/.

Cooper, Travis Warren. "Taxonomy Construction and the Normative Turn in Religious Studies." *Religions* 8, no. 12: 270 (2017): 1–25.

Cornille, Catherine. "Conditions for Interreligious Dialogue." In *The Wiley-Blackwell Companion to Inter-Religious Dialogue,* edited by Catherine Cornille, 26–28. Hoboken, NJ: Wiley, 2013.

——. "The Dynamics of Multiple Belonging." In *Many Mansions? Multiple Religious Belonging and Christian Identity,* edited by Catherine Cornille, 1–6. Maryknoll, NY: Orbis Books, 2002.

——. "Empathy and Inter-Religious Imagination." *Religion and the Arts* 12, no. 1–3 (2008): 102–18. Also published in *Traversing the Heart: Journeys of Interreligious Imagination,* edited by Richard Kearney and Eileen Rizo-Patron, 107–21. Leiden: Brill, 2009.

——. "Empathy and Otherness in Interreligious Dialogue." In *Dynamics of Difference: Christianity and Alterity,* edited by Ulrich Schmiedel and James Matarazzo, 221–30. New York: Continuum/T&T Clark, 2014.

——. *The Im-Possibility of Interreligious Dialogue.* New York: Crossroad Publishing, 2008.

——. "Interreligious Empathy." In *Interreligious Studies: Dispatches from the Field,* edited by Hans Gustafson, 223–27. Waco: Baylor University Press, 2019.

——. "Multiple Religious Belonging and Christian Identity." The Santa Clara Lecture (2011). https://tinyurl.com/2p92bfnw.

Cory, Catherine A., and Michael Hollerich, eds. *The Christian Theological Tradition,* 3rd ed. Upper Saddle River, NJ: Pearson Prentice Hall, 2009.

Costello, Gaberial J. *The Teaching of Design and Innovation*. Cham, Switzerland: Springer, 2020.

Cracknell, Kenneth. "'We Talking about Us': Wilfred Cantwell Smith's Relevance to Theology without Walls." *Journal of Ecumenical Studies* 51, no. 4 (2016): 517–23.

Daft, Richard L. "First, Lead Yourself." In *Contemporary Issues in Leadership*, 2nd ed., edited by William E. Rosenbach, Robert L. Taylor, and Mark A. Youndt, 125–33. London: Taylor & Francis, 2014.

Davie, Grace. "Is Europe an Exceptional Case?" *The Hedgehog Review* (Spring and Summer 2006): 23–34.

Del Vecchio, Kristi, and Noah J. Silverman. "Learning from the Field: Six Themes from the Interfaith/Interreligious Studies Curriculum." In *Interreligious/Interfaith Studies: Defining a New Field*, edited by Eboo Patel, Jennifer Howe Peace, and Noah Silverman, 49–57. Boston: Beacon Press, 2018.

Department for Communities and Local Government. "Face to Face and Side by Side: A Framework for Partnership in Our Multi Faith Community." London, 2008. https://tinyurl.com/yfzzm7pe.

Dhiman, Satinder. Bhagavad Gītā *and Leadership: A Catalyst for Organizational Transformation*. Cham, Switzerland: Palgrave MacMillan, 2019.

Diller, Jeanine. "Toward a Field of Interfaith Studies: Emerging Questions and Considerations." In roundtable with Jeanine Diller, Eboo Patel, Jennifer Peace, and Colleen Windham-Hughes. *Journal of Interreligious Studies* 16 (2015): 5–13.

Dinham, Adam, and Matthew Francis, eds. *Religious Literacy in Policy and Practice*. Bristol: Policy Press, 2016.

Dinham, Adam, and Matthew Francis. "Religious Literacies: The Future." In *Religious Literacy in Policy and Practice*, edited by Adam Dinham and Matthew Francis, 257–70. Bristol: Policy Press, 2016.

——. "Religious Literacy: Contesting an Idea and Practice." In *Religious Literacy in Policy and Practice*, edited by Adam Dinham and Matthew Francis, 3–25. Bristol: Policy Press, 2016.

Dinham, Adam, and Stephen H. Jones. "Religious Literacy Leadership in Higher Education: An Analysis of Challenges of Religious Faith, and Resources for Meeting Them, for University Leaders." A Report from the Religious Literacy Leadership in Higher Education Programme. York, UK: 2010. Accessed October 30, 2018. https://tinyurl.com/57726ajw.

Dong, Mengxi, and Marc A. Fournier. "What Are the Necessary Conditions for Wisdom? Examining Intelligence, Creativity, Meaning-Making, and the Big-Five Traits." *Collabra: Psychology* 8, no. 1 (2022): 33145. https://doi.org/10.1525/collabra.33145.

Dregni, Eric. *Vikings in the Attic: In Search of Nordic America*. Minneapolis: University of Minnesota Press, 2011.

Drescher, Elizabeth. *Choosing Our Religion: The Spiritual Lives of America's Nones*. New York: Oxford University Press, 2016.

Drew, Rose. "Christian and Hindu, Jewish and Buddhist: Can You Have a Multiple Religious Identity?" In *Controversies in Contemporary Religion: Education, Law, Politics, Society, and Spirituality*, edited by Paul Hedges, 248–51. Santa Barbara: Praeger, 2014.

Droogers, André. "The Future of New Worldview Studies." In *Methods for the Study of Religious Change: From Religious Studies to Worldview Studies*, edited by André Droogers and Anton van Harskamp, 165–79. Sheffield, UK: Equinox, 2014.

——. "Syncretism: The Problem of Definition, the Definition of the Problem." In *Dialogue and Syncretism: An Interdisciplinary Approach*, edited by Jerald Gort, Hendrik Vroom, Rein Fernhout, and Anton Wessels, 7–25. Grand Rapids, MI: Eerdmans, 1989.

——. "The World of Worldviews." In *Methods for the Study of Religious Change: From Religious Studies to Worldview Studies*, edited by André Droogers and Anton van Harskamp, 25–42. Sheffield, UK: Equinox, 2014.

Droogers, André, and Anton van Harskamp, eds. *Methods for the Study of Religious Change: From Religious Studies to Worldview Studies*. Sheffield, UK: Equinox, 2014.

Dunbar, Scott Daniel. "The Place of Interreligious Dialogue in the Academic Study of Religion." *Journal of Ecumenical Studies* 35, no. 3–4 (1998): 455–69.

Dunning, Susan Bilysnkyj. "Saeculum." In *Oxford Research Encyclopedia*, November 20, 2017. https://doi.org/10.1093/acrefore/9780199381135.013.8233.

Durkheim, Emil. *The Elementary Forms of Religious Life*. Translated by Carol Cosman. Oxford: Oxford University Press, 2001.

Eaghll, Tenzan. "Learning about Religion Leads to Tolerance." In *Stereotyping Religion: Critiquing Clichés*, edited by Bard Stoddard and Craig Martin, 113–30. London: Bloomsbury, 2017.

——. "No, Secularism Is Not a World Religion." The Religious Studies Project (website). December 16, 2016. https://tinyurl.com/48z73a5w.

Eck, Diana L. "About." Pluralism Project (website). Accessed May 30, 2020. https://tinyurl.com/3bxnmvn9.

——. *A New Religious America: How a "Christian Country" Has Become the World's Most Religiously Diverse Nation*. San Francisco: HarperCollins, 2001.

——. "Pluralism: Problems and Promise." *Journal of Interreligious Studies* 17, no. 17 (2015): 54–62.

——. "Preface." In *Building the Interfaith Youth Movement: Beyond Dialogue to Action*, edited by Eboo Patel and Patrice Brodeur, ix. Lanham, MD: Rowman & Littlefield, 2006.

Eck, Diana, Diane Moore, Eboo Patel, and Mara Willard. "Religious Literacy: How Knowing Your Neighbor Can Save the World." Harvard Divinity School YouTube Channel, November 13, 2013. Accessed March 7, 2002. https://tinyurl.com/34s5mrfs.

Edwards, John. *Language and Identity*. Cambridge: Cambridge University Press, 2009.

Eliade, Mircea. *No Souvenirs: Journal, 1957–1969*. New York: Harper & Row, 1977.

Elijah Institute. "About." Last accessed September 11, 2020. https://elijah-interfaith.org/about-elijah.

——. "Friendship across Religions: An Interreligious Manifesto." Last accessed September 11, 2020. https://elijah-interfaith.org/addressing-the-world/friendship-across-religions.

Elon University. "Interreligious Studies Minor." Accessed September 3, 2019. https://tinyurl.com/ntue9s74.

Enstedt, Daniel. "Religious Literacy in Non-Confessional Religious Education and Religious Studies in Sweden." *Journal of Humanities and Social Science Education* 1 (2022): 26–48.

Fahy, John, and Jan-Jonathan Bock. "Introduction: Interfaith and Social Movement Theory." In *The Interfaith Movement: Mobilising Religious Diversity in the 21st Century*, edited by John Fahy and Jan-Jonathan Bock, 1–27. London: Routledge, 2019.

Fletcher, Jeannine Hill. "The Promising Practice of Antiracist Approaches to Interfaith Studies." In *Interreligious/Interfaith Studies: Defining a New Field*, edited by Eboo Patel, Jennifer Howe Peace, and Noah Silverman, 137–46. Boston: Beacon Press, 2018.

——. "Scholarship as Activism." In *Interreligious Studies: Dispatches from the Field*, edited by Hans Gustafson, 249–53. Waco: Baylor University Press, 2020.

——. "Shifting Identity: The Contribution of Feminist Thought to Theologies of Religious Pluralism." *Journal of Feminist Studies in Religion* 19, no. 2 (2003): 5–24.

Flood, Gavin. *Beyond Phenomenology: Rethinking the Study of Religion*. London: Cassell, 1999.

Ford, David. *Theology: A Very Short Introduction*. Oxford: Oxford University Press, 1999.

Foucault, Michael. *Technologies of the Self*. Edited by Luther H. Martin, Huck Gutman, and Patrick H. Hutton. London: Tavistock, 1988.

Fredericks, James L. *Faith among Faiths*. New York: Paulist, 1999.

The Free Dictionary. "Idioms and Phrases." https://tinyurl.com/43tkzfa7.

Freud, Sigmund. *The Future of an Illusion*. Translated by Gregory C. Richter. Peterborough, ON: Broadview Press, 2012.

——. "Lecture 35: The Question of a *Weltanschauung*." In *New Introductory Lectures on Psycho-Analysis*, translated by James Strachey, 195–226. New York: W. W. Norton, 1965.

Fukuyama, Francis. "The End of History." *The National Interest* (Summer 1989): 3–18.

Furlan, Timothy J. "Cultivating Practical Wisdom." *Harvard Medical School Bioethics Journal* January 1 (2020). https://tinyurl.com/2ywzmufd.

Furseth, Inger. "The Return of Religion in the Public Sphere? The Public Role of Nordic Faith Communities." In *Institutional Change in the Public Sphere: Views on the Nordic Model*, edited by Fredrik Engelstad, Hakon Larsen, Jon Rogstad, and Kari Steen-Johnsen, 221–40. Warsaw: De Gruyter Open, 2017.

Gallie, Walter B. "Essentially Contested Concepts." *Proceedings of the Aristotelian Society* S6, no. 1 (1956): 167–98.

Garber, Greg. "Call Dan the Greatest . . . Passer." ESPN.com, November 19, 2003. https://tinyurl.com/r9erdvja.

Gardner, John W. "The Antileadership Vaccine." In *Contemporary Issues in Leadership*, 2nd ed., edited by William E. Rosenbach, Robert L. Taylor, and Mark A. Youndt, 287–95. London: Taylor & Francis, 2014.

Gates, Henry Louis, Jr., and Manning Marable. "A Debate on Activism in Black Studies." In *Companion to African-American Studies*, edited by Jane Anna Gordon and Lewis Gordon, 96–101. Oxford: Wiley Blackwell, 2006.

Geertz, Clifford. "Religion as a Cultural System." In *The Interpretation of Cultures: Selected Essays*, 90. London: Fontana Press, 1993.

Georgetown University. "Interfaith Programs and Services." Campus Ministry (website). Accessed July 16, 2019. https://tinyurl.com/my7pbdcp.

Gill, Rahuldeep Singh. "From Safe Spaces to Resilient Places: A Role for Interfaith Cooperation in Contentious Times." *Journal of College and Character* 18, no. 3 (2017): 202–7.

Giorda, Maria Chiara. "Different Illiteracies for Different Countries: Are There No Data for Religious Literacy?" In *Religious Literacy, Law and History: Perspectives on European Pluralist Societies*, edited by Alberto Melloni and Francesca Cadeddu, 29–45. Oxford: Routledge, 2019.

Glatzer, Nahum A. "The Beginnings of Modern Jewish Studies." In *Studies in Nineteenth-Century Jewish Intellectual History*, edited by Alexander Altmann, 27–46. Cambridge, MA: Harvard University Press, 1964.

Goleman, Daniel. "What Makes a Leader?" In *Contemporary Issues in Leadership*, 2nd ed., edited by William E. Rosenbach, Robert L. Taylor, and Mark A. Youndt, 21–35. London: Taylor & Francis, 2014.

Goodman, Kathleen, Mary Ellen Giess, and Eboo Patel. "Introduction." In *Educating about Religious Diversity and Interfaith Engagement: A Handbook for Student Affairs*, edited by Kathleen Goodman, Mary Ellen Giess, and Eboo Patel, 1–4. Sterling, VA: Stylus Publishing, 2019.

Gordon, Jane Anna. "Some Reflections on Challenges Posed to Social Scientific Method by the Study of Race." In *Companion to African-American Studies*, edited by Jane Anna Gordon and Lewis Gordon, 279–304. Oxford: Wiley Blackwell, 2006.

Gosling, Jonathan, and Ian Sutherland. "Diverse Approaches to Leadership Development." In *The Routledge Companion to Leadership*, edited by John Storey, Jean Hartley, Jean-Louis Denis, Paul 't Hart, and David Ulrich, 545–65. New York: Routledge, 2017.

Graff, Harvey J. *The Literacy Myth: Literacy and Social Structure in the Nineteenth-Century City*. New York: Academic Press, 1979.

Grand View Research. "Personal Development Market Size, Share & Trends Analysis Report by Instrument (Books, e-Platforms, Personal Coaching/Training, Workshops), by Focus Area, by Region, and Segment Forecasts, 2020—2027." Grand View Research (website), July 2020. https://tinyurl.com/hpcptdt5.

Green, Todd. *Presumed Guilty: Why We Shouldn't Ask Muslims to Condemn Terrorism*. Minneapolis: Fortress Press, 2018.

Gregg, Heather. "Three Theories of Religious Activism and Violence: Social Movements, Fundamentalists, and Apocalyptic Warriors." *Terrorism and Political Violence* 28, no. 2 (2016): 338–60.

Gregg, Stephen. "The British Association for the Study of Religions (BASR) and the Impact of Religious Studies." Panel with Steve Sutcliffe, Stephen Gregg, Christopher Cotter, Suzanne Owen, and David Robertson. *The Religious Studies Project* (podcast audio), March 12, 2018. https://tinyurl.com/34rcj55v.

Greig, Alastair, Frank Lewis, and Kevin White. *Inequality in Australia*. Cambridge: Cambridge University Press, 2003.

Griffiths, Morwenna. *Feminisms and the Self: The Web of Identity*. London: Routledge, 1995.

Grim, Brian J. "Religious Literacy and Diversity for Business." In *Reimagining Faith and Management*, edited by Edwina Pio, Robert Kilpatrick, and Timothy Pratt, 236–50. New York: Routledge, 2021.

Grim, Brian J., and Phillip Connor. "Changing Religion, Changing Economies: Future Global Religious and Economic Growth." Religious Freedom and Business Foundation, October 21, 2015. https://tinyurl.com/yckv7nr6.

Grossman, Igor, Nic M. Weststrate, Monica Ardelt, Justin Brienza, Mengxi Dong, Michael Ferrari, Marc A. Fournier, Chao. S. Hu, Howard Nussbaum, and John Vervaeke. "The Science of Wisdom in a Polarized World: Knowns and Unknowns." *Psychological Inquiry* 31, no. 2 (2020): 103–33. https://doi.org/10.1080/1047840X.2020.1750917.

Grung, Anne Hege. "Including Gender Perspective in Muslim–Christian Dialogue in Europe and Scandinavia—a Disturbance of Bridge-Building or a Contextual Necessity?" In *Mission to the World: Communicating the Gospel in the 21st Century, Essays in Honour of Knud Jørgensen*, edited by Tormod Engelsviken, Ernst Harbakk, Rolv Olsen, and Thor Strandenæs, 289–397. Oxford: Regnum, 2008.

———. "Interreligious or Transreligious?" In *Interreligious Studies: Dispatches from an Emerging Field*, edited by Hans Gustafson, 58–65. Waco: Baylor University Press, 2020.

———. "Inter-Religious or Trans-Religious: Exploring the Term 'Inter-Religious' in a Feminist Postcolonial Perspective." *Journal of Interreligious Studies* 13 (2014): 11–14.

———. "The Two Pluralisms in Norway." *Society* 54, no. 5 (2017): 432–38.

Gustafson, Hans. "Defining the Academic Field of Interreligious Studies." *Interreligious Studies and Intercultural Theology* 4, no. 2 (2020): 131–54.

———. "Deflecting Myself: A Failure of Leadership." In *With the Best of Intentions: Interrogating Interfaith Mistakes*, edited by Lucinda Mosher, Ellie Pierce, and Or Rose. Maryknoll, NY: Orbis Books, 2023.

———. "Descandalizing Multiple Religious Identity with Help from Nicholas Black Elk and His Spirituality: An Exercise in Interreligious Learning." *Journal of Ecumenical Studies* 51, no. 1 (Winter 2016): 80–113.

———. "An Emerging Phronetic Framework in Interfaith and Interreligious Studies Courses in the United States: A Response to Jones and Meyer." *Journal of Interreligious Studies* 36 (2022): 64–74.

———. *Finding All Things in God: Pansacramentalism and Doing Theology Interreligiously*. Eugene, OR: Pickwick, 2016.

———. "Friends in Foxholes: Interreligious Friendship, Changemaking, and Leadership." In *Friends in This World: Multi-Religious Reflections on Friendship*, edited by Anne-Marie Ellithorpe, Hussam S. Timani, Laura Duhan Kaplan. Minneapolis: Fortress Press, forthcoming.

———. "Gateways to Engagement with Religious Diversity." State of Formation, May 7, 2018. https://tinyurl.com/4xk3wpsf.

———. "'Interfaith' Is So 1970s!" State of Formation, April 12, 2018. https://tinyurl.com/4k78xuz6.

———. "Interreligious and Interfaith Studies in Relation to Religious Studies and Theological Studies." State of Formation, January 6, 2015. https://tinyurl.com/dc7k2h85.

———. ed. *Interreligious Studies: Dispatches from an Emerging Field.* Waco: Baylor University Press, 2020.

———. "Interreligious Studies and Personal Changemaking Pedagogy for Leadership and the Common Good: The My Story Assignment." *Teaching Theology & Religion* 24 (2021): 42–48. https://doi.org/10.1111/teth.12572.

———. "Interreligious Wherewithal: Cultivating a Leadership Virtue." State of Formation, November 16, 2017. https://tinyurl.com/vp38h36p.

———. "Introduction." In *Interreligious Studies: Dispatches from an Emerging Field,* edited by Hans Gustafson, 1–14. Waco: Baylor University Press, 2020.

———. "Is Transreligious Theology Unavoidable in Interreligious Theology and Dialogue?" *Open Theology* 2 (2016): 248–60.

———. "Pansacramentalism, Interreligious Theology, and Lived Religion." *Religions* 10, no. 7: 408 (2019): 1–15. Special issue, *Sacramental Theology: Theory and Practice from Multiple Perspectives,* edited by Bruce Morrill. https://doi.org/10.3390/rel10070408.

———. "Sparring with Spider Silk: Models for the Relationship between Interreligious Studies and the Interfaith Movement." In *The Georgetown Companion to Interreligious Studies,* edited by Lucinda Mosher, 32–40. Washington, DC: Georgetown University Press, 2022.

———. "Suppressing the Mosquitoes' Coughs: An Introduction to Holy Envy." In *Learning from Other Religious Traditions: Leaving Room for Holy Envy,* edited by Hans Gustafson, 1–12. Cham, Switzerland: Palgrave Macmillan, 2018.

———. "'They're Not Really Christians': Acknowledging Oppression and Violence in Our Traditions for the Sake of Interreligious Understanding." State of Formation, May 27, 2018. https://tinyurl.com/4y67sbbm.

———. "Tuesday of the Second Week of Advent." University of St. Thomas (website), December 10, 2019. https://tinyurl.com/4vsdwkkp.

———. "Vitality of Lived Religion Approaches." In *Interreligious Studies: Dispatches from an Emerging Field,* edited by Hans Gustafson, 91–97. Waco: Baylor University Press, 2020.

———. "What Does It Mean to Be (Inter)Religiously Literate." State of Formation, April 27, 2018. https://tinyurl.com/2y8rcetr.

Haider, John. *The Tao of Leadership: Lao Tzu's* Tao Te Ching *Adapted for a New Age.* Palm Beach, FL: Green Dragon Books, 2015.

Haidt, Jonathan. "True Diversity Requires Generosity of Spirit." *Heterodox Academy: The Blog,* November 18, 2015. https://tinyurl.com/5xmaxbk8.

Halafoff, Anna. *The Multifaith Movement: Global Risks and Cosmopolitan Solutions.* Dordrecht: Springer, 2013.

Hall, David D. "Lived Religion." In *Encyclopedia of Religion in America,* edited by Charles H. Lippy and Peter W. Williams, 1282–89. Washington, DC: CQ Press, 2010.

Hall, Stuart. "Introduction: Who Needs Identity?" In *Questions of Cultural Identity,* edited by Stuart Hall and Paul Du Gay, 1–17. London: Sage, 1996.

Hallowell, Ronan. "Dancing Together: The Lakota Sun Dance and Ethical Intercultural Exchange." *IK: Other Ways of Knowing* 3, no. 1 (2017): 30–52.

Hampton, K. "Transforming School and Society." *Scholar-Practitioner Quarterly* 4, no. 2 (2009): 185–92.

Hancock, Herbie. Interview by Jim Lehrer (video). *PBS News Hour*, September 16, 2010. https://tinyurl.com/275rjv2x.

Hanshaw, Mark E., and Usra Ghazi. "Interfaith Studies and the Professions: Could Heightened Religious Understanding Seed Success within Secular Careers?" In *Interreligious/Interfaith Studies: Defining a New Field*, edited by Eboo Patel, Jennifer Howe Peace, and Noah Silverman, 196–208. Boston: Beacon Press, 2018.

Harris, Grove. "Pagan Involvement in the Interfaith Movement: Exclusions, Dualities, and Contributions." *CrossCurrents* 55, no. 1, "Current Issues in Interfaith Work" (Spring 2005): 66–76.

Hart Research Associates. "Falling Short? College Learning and Career Success." Association of American Colleges and Universities, 2015. https://tinyurl.com/577awppd.

Harvard Business School. "The HBS Case Method." Accessed May 18, 2018. https://tinyurl.com/4rk34ec8.

Heath, Rachel A. "Multiple Religious Belonging and Theologies of Multiplicity: Confluences of Oneness and Porosity." *Journal of Interreligious Studies* 21 (October 2017): 23–36.

Heckman, Donald "Bud." "Appendix A: A Taxonomy of Interfaith." In *InterActive Faith: The Essential Interreligious Community-Building Handbook*, edited by Donald Heckman with Rori Picker Neiss, 223–30. Woodstock, VT: SkyLight Paths Publishing, 2008.

———. "Why the 'Interfaith Movement' Must Rebrand." *Huffington Post*, March 11, 2013. https://tinyurl.com/ync2y5nr.

Hedges, Paul. *Controversies in Interreligious Dialogue and the Theology of Religions.* London: SCM, 2010.

———. "Decolonising the Study of Religion (in Relation to the Social and Human Sciences)." *Paul Hedges Weblog*, March 12, 2018. https://tinyurl.com/yckwnyh8.

———. "Editorial Introduction: Interreligious Studies." *Journal for the Academic Study of Religion* 27, no. 2 (2014): 127–31.

———. "Encounters with Ultimacy? Autobiographical and Critical Perspectives in the Academic Study of Religion." *Open Theology* 4 (2018): 355–72.

———. "Interreligious Studies." In *Encyclopedia of Sciences and Religion*, edited by Anne Runehov and Lluis Oviedo, 1176–80. New York: Springer, 2012.

———. "Interreligious Studies: A New Direction in the Study of Religion?" *Bulletin of the British Association for the Study of Religions* (November 2014): 13–14.

———. "Multiple Religious Belonging after Religion: Theorising Strategic Religious Participation in a Shared Religious Landscape as a Chinese Model." *Open Theology* 3 (2017): 48–72.

———. "Theology With and Without (W&W) Walls, Scholarship W&W Walls, and Decolonization W&W: A Rejoinder to Rory D. McEntee." *Journal of Interreligious Studies* 35 (2022): 80–99.

———. *Understanding Religion: Theories and Methods for Studying Religiously Diverse Societies.* Oakland: University of California Press, 2021.

———. "Why the Theology Without Walls Program Fails Both as Scholarship and a Resource to the SBNR: A Friendly Condemnation." *Journal of Interreligious Studies* 34 (2022): 18–33.

Hedges, Paul, and Angela Coco. "Belonging, Behaving, Believing, Becoming: Religion and Identity." In *Controversies in Contemporary Religion: Education, Law, Politics, Society, and Spirituality,* edited by Paul Hedges, 163–90. Santa Barbara: Praeger, 2014.

Hegel, G. W. F. *Philosophy of History.* Translated by J. Sibree. Mineola, NY: Dover Publications, 1956.

Hemingway, Ernest. *A Farewell to Arms.* New York: Scribner, 1929, 2014.

Henderson, Gabe. "I Guess There's One Thing Both #Vikings & #Bears Fans Can Agree On 😊." @GabeAHenderson, Twitter, January 8, 2023, 2:24 p.m. https://tinyurl.com/3ussur2d.

Henriksen, Jan-Olav. "Normative Dimensions in Empirical Research on Religion, Values, and Society." In *Difficult Normativity: Normative Dimensions in Research on Religion and Theology,* edited by Jan-Olav Henriksen, 17–36. Frankfurt am Main: Peter Lang, 2011.

Henry, Andrew M. "Religious Literacy in Social Media: A Need for Strategic Amplification." *Religion & Education* 48, no. 1 (2021): 89–101. https://doi.org/10.1080/15507394.2021.1876507.

———. "What Is Religion?" Religion for Breakfast (YouTube channel), January 12, 2016. 01:15–01:18. https://tinyurl.com/mrsw9awu.

Hervieu-Léger, Danièle. "'What Scripture Tells Me': Spontaneity and Regulation within the Catholic Charismatic Renewal." In *Lived Religion in America: Toward a History of Practice,* edited by David D. Hall, 22–40. Princeton, NJ: Princeton University Press, 1997.

Hewitt, John P. *Dilemmas of the American Self.* Philadelphia: Temple University Press, 1989.

Hewlett, Sylvia Ann, Melinda Marshall, and Laura Sherbin. "How Diversity Can Drive Innovation." *Harvard Business Review,* December 1, 2013. https://tinyurl.com/3fcr8xxr.

Hickey, Wakoh Shannon, and Margarita M. W. Suárez. "Meeting Others, Seeing Myself: Experiential Pedagogies in Interfaith Studies." In *Interreligious/Interfaith Studies: Defining a New Field,* edited by Eboo Patel, Jennifer Howe Peace, and Noah Silverman, 108–21. Boston: Beacon Press, 2018.

Hijmans, Ellen, and Adri Smaling. "Over de relatie tussen kwalitatief onderzoek en levensbeshouwing: Een inleading." In *Kwalitatief onderzoek en levensbeshouwing,* edited by Adrei Smaling and Ellen Hijmans, 15–20. Amsterdam: Boom, 1997.

Himes, Michael J. *Doing the Truth in Love: Conversations about God, Relationships, and Service.* New York: Paulist Press, 1995.

———. "Living Conversation: Higher Education in a Catholic Context." *Conversations on Jesuit Higher Education* 8, no. 1, art. 5 (October 1995): 2–8.

Hirsch, E. D. *Cultural Literacy: What Every American Needs to Know.* New York: Vintage Books, 1988.

Hirst, Jacqueline Suthren, and John Zavos. "Riding a Tiger? South Asia and the Problem of 'Religion.'" *Contemporary South Asia* 14, no. 1 (2005): 3–20.

Hitlin, Steven. "Values as the Core of Personal Identity: Drawing Links between Two Theories of Self." In "Social Identity: Sociological and Social Psychological Perspectives," edited by Michael A. Hogg and Cecilia L. Ridgeway. Special issue, *Social Psychology Quarterly* 66, no. 2 (2003): 118–37.

Hoffman, Andrew J. *The Engaged Scholar: Expanding the Impact of Academic Research in Today's World.* Stanford, CA: Stanford University Press, 2021.

Hollenbach, David. "Catholicism's Communitarian Vision: The Church in the Modern World." In *As Leven in the World: Catholic Perspectives on Faith, Vocation, and the Intellectual Life,* edited by Thomas M. Landy, 167–76. Franklin, WI: Sheed & Ward, 2001.

Horkheimer, Max. "Traditional and Critical Theory (1937)." In *Critical Theory: Selected Essays,* edited by M. O'Connell, 188–243. New York: Continuum Press, 1999.

Hulsether, Lucia. "Can Interfaith Dialogue Cure Religious Violence?" Religion Dispatches, April 26, 2013. https://tinyurl.com/3w3v8pnn.

———. "The Grammar of Racism: Religious Pluralism and the Birth of the Interdisciplines." *Journal of the American Academy of Religion* 86, no. 1 (2018): 1–41. https://doi.org/10.1093/jaarel/lfx049.

Huntington, Samuel P. "The Clash of Civilizations?" *Foreign Affairs* 72, no. 3 (Summer 1993): 22–49.

Hursthouse, Rosalind, and Glen Pettigrove. "Virtue Ethics." In *The Stanford Encyclopedia of Philosophy,* Winter 2018 ed., edited by Edward N. Zalta. https://tinyurl.com/24tbbee3.

Hurteau, Marthe, and Caroline Gagnon. "Contribution of Practical Wisdom to Resolving Ethical Issues." *Evaluation* 28, no. 2 (2022): 182–91.

Hustwit, J. R. "Empty Selves and Multiple Belonging: Gadamer and Nāgārjuna on Religious Identity's Hidden Plurality." *Open Theology* 3 (2017): 107–16.

Hutchinson, Elizabeth. "Spirituality, Religion, and Progressive Social Movements: Resources and Motivation for Social Change." *Journal of Religion and Spirituality in Social Work: Social Thought* 31, no. 1–2 (2012): 105–27.

Illich, Ivan. "To Hell with Good Intentions." Address to American students at the Conference on InterAmerican Student Projects (CIASP). Cuernavaca, Mexico, April 20, 1968.

Inazu, John. "Hope without a Common Good." In *Out of Many Faiths: Religious Diversity and the American Promise,* by Eboo Patel, 133–50. Princeton, NJ: Princeton University Press, 2018.

Independent.ie. "There Is No Key, There Is Just Life." *Independent.ie,* March 7, 2017. https://tinyurl.com/47m72jue.

Ingesman, Per. "Introduction." In "The 'Long Reformation' in Nordic Historical Research." Report edited by Per Ingesman on behalf of Head of the Nordic Reformation History Working Group and prepared for discussion at the 28th Congress of Nordic Historians in Joensuu, Finland, 4–44. August 14–17, 2014. Accessed July 24, 2018. https://tinyurl.com/ysxpvvck.

Interfaith Youth Core. "Interfaith Cooperation." Last accessed October 24, 2019. www.ifyc.org/interfaith.

———. "Interfaith Diversity Experiences & Attitudes Longitudinal Survey: 2015–2019." Last accessed September 12, 2020. https://ifyc.org/ideals.

———. "Mission and Programs." Last accessed May 11, 2018. https://www.ifyc.org/mission.

———. "Module 2.2: Models of Religious Diversity" (video). Last accessed December 31, 2019. https://www.ifyc.org/interfaithleadership/lesson2.

Iowa and Minnesota Campus Compact. "Social Change Wheel 2.0 Toolkit." Accessed September 7, 2020. https://tinyurl.com/yckz5seb.

Ipgrave, Julia, Thorsten Knauth, Anna Körs, Dörthe Vieregge, and Marie von der Lippe, eds. *Religion and Dialogue in the City: Case Studies on Interreligious Encounter in Urban Community and Education*. Münster: Waxmann, 2018.

Ishrak, Omar. "Diversity Leadership." DiversityInc.com, May 16, 2013. https://tinyurl.com/48yhznb6

Jackson, Brad, and Ken Parry. *A Very Short, Fairly Interesting and Reasonably Cheap Book about Studying Leadership*, 3rd ed. London: Sage, 2018.

Jackson, Michael. *Paths toward a Clearing: Radical Empiricism and Ethnographic Inquiry*. Bloomington: Indiana University Press, 1989.

Jacobsen, Douglas, and Rhonda Hustedt Jacobsen. *No Longer Invisible: Religion in University Education*. New York: Oxford University Press, 2012.

Janson, Marloes. "Unity through Diversity: A Case Study of Chrislam in Lagos." *Africa* 86, no. 4 (2016): 646–72.

Jenkins, Richard. *Social Identity*, 3rd ed. London: Routledge, 2008.

Jetzkowitz, Jens. *Co-Evolution of Nature and Society: Foundations for Interdisciplinary Sustainability Studies*. Cham, Switzerland: Palgrave Macmillan, 2019.

Jha, Amishi P. *Peak Mind: Find Your Focus, Own Your Attention, Invest 12 Minutes a Day*. New York: HarperOne, 2021.

Johnson, Andrew. *If I Give My Soul: Faith behind Bars in Rio de Janeiro*. New York: Oxford University Press, 2017.

Johnson, Todd M., and Brian J. Grim, with Gina A. Bellofatto. *The World's Religions in Figures: An Introduction to International Religious Demography*. Chichester: Wiley Blackwell, 2013.

Jones, Robert P., and Maxine Najle. "American Democracy in Crisis: The Fate of Pluralism in a Divided Nation." PRRI, February 22, 2019. https://tinyurl.com/m9e88s9r.

Jones, Trina Janiec, and Cassie Meyer. "Interfaith and Interreligious Pedagogies: An Assessment." *Journal of Interreligious Studies* 36 (2022): 9–34.

Jörg, Ton. *New Thinking in Complexity for the Social Sciences and Humanities: A Generative, Transdisciplinary Approach*. Dordrecht: Springer, 2011.

Kamstra, Jacques H. *Synkretisme: Op de Grens tussen Theologie en Godsdienstfenomenologie*. Leiden: Brill, 1970.

Kasimow, Harold. "Leonard Swidler: Dialogue Pioneer and Peacemaker." *Journal of Ecumenical Studies* 50, no. 1 (Winter 2015): 37–41.

Kaufman, Tone Stangeland. "Normativity as Pitfall or Ally?" *Ecclesial Practices* 2 (2015): 9–34.

Keenan, John P. *The Meaning of Christ: A Mahāyāna Theology*. Maryknoll, NY: Orbis Press, 1989.

Kerby, Lauren. "Teaching for Tolerance: The Case for Religious Studies in American Public Schools." *Colgate Academic Review* 6 (2012): art. 7.

Kerry, John. "John Kerry: 'We Ignore the Global Impact of Religion at Our Peril.'" *America Magazine*, September 2, 2015. https://tinyurl.com/m9knawhc.

——. "Speech—To Announce the Launch of the State Department's Office of Faith-Based Community Initiatives." C.SPAN, August 7, 2013. https://tinyurl.com/m46rfcuz.

Kim, Marina. "Rethinking the Impact Spectrum." AshokaU, April 30, 2015. https:// tinyurl.com/yvapuajp.

Kim, Juensung J., Stephanie Morris, Phillip Rajewicz, Michael Ferrari, and John Vervaeke. "Walk in Wisdom's Path: Contributions of Faith, Age, and Personal Wisdom to Ideas of Cultivating Wisdom." *Journal of Religion, Spirituality, and Aging* (2022): 1–20. https://doi.org/10.1080/15528030.2022.2041532.

Kimsey-House, Henry, and David Skibbins. *The Stake: The Making of Leaders*. San Rafael, CA: Co-Active Press, 2013.

King, Anna S., and Paul Hedges. "What Is Religion? Or, What Is It We Are Talking About?" In *Controversies in Contemporary Religion: Education, Law, Politics, Society, and Spirituality*, edited by Paul Hedges, 1–30. Santa Barbara: Praeger, 2014.

Kineke, Liz. www.lizkineke.com. Accessed July 30, 2021.

Kinsella, Elizabeth Anne, and Allan Pittman. "Engaging Phronesis in Professional Practice and Education." In *Phronesis as Professional Knowledge: Practical Wisdom in the Professions*, edited by Elizabeth Anne Kinsella and Allan Pittman, 1–11. Rotterdam, The Netherlands: Sense Publishers, 2012.

Klein, Mike, Amy Finnegan, and Jack Nelson-Pallmeyer. "Circle of Praxis Pedagogy for Peace Studies." *Peace Review: A Journal of Social Justice* 30, no. 3 (2018): 270–78.

Knausgaard, Karl Ove. *Summer*. New York: Penguin, 2018.

Kosky, Jeffrey L. *Arts of Wonder: Enchanting Secularity*. Chicago: University of Chicago Press, 2017.

Kouzes, James M., and Barry Z. Posner. "Leadership Begins with an Inner Journey." In *Contemporary Issues in Leadership*, 2nd ed., edited by William E. Rosenbach, Robert L. Taylor, and Mark A. Youndt, 117–23. London: Taylor & Francis, 2014.

Kraemer, Hendrik. *De Wortelen van het Syncretisme*. The Hague, The Netherlands: Boekencentrum, 1937.

Kubeck, Elizabeth. "Common Ground: Imagining Interfaith Studies as an Inclusive, Interdisciplinary Field." In *Interreligious/Interfaith Studies: Defining a New Field*, edited by Eboo Patel, Jennifer Howe Peace, and Noah Silverman, 26–35. Boston: Beacon Press, 2018.

Kyung, Chung Hyun. *Struggle to Be the Sun Again: Introducing Asian Women's Theology*. Maryknoll, NY: Orbis, 1990.

Lambert, Paul. "An Interview with Paul Lambert: Understanding the Importance of Religious Literacy." The Fletcher Forum of World Affairs, November 17, 2017. https://tinyurl.com/2p8t9u8w.

Lander, Shira. "The Role of the Religious Voice in the Twenty-First Century—A Jewish Perspective." In *Religious Identity and Renewal in the Twenty-First Century: Jewish, Christian, and Muslim Explorations*, edited by Simone Sinn and Michael Reid Trice, 77–91. Leipzig: Evangelische Verlagsanstalt, 2015.

Landnámabók (The Book of Settlements). Translated by Herman Pálsson and Paul Edwards. Winnipeg: University of Winnipeg Press, 1972, reprinted 2006.

Lane, Belden. "Writing in Spirituality as a Self-Implicating Act: Reflections on Authorial Disclosure and the Hiddenness of the Self." In *Exploring Christian Spirituality: Essays in Honor of Sandra M. Schneiders*, edited by Bruce H. Lescher and Elizabeth Liebert, 53–69. New York: Paulist Press, 2006.

BIBLIOGRAPHY

Lao Tzu. *Tao Te Ching*. Translated by D. C. Lau. New York: Penguin, 1963.

Larson, Marion H., and Sara L. H. Shady. *From Bubble to Bridge: Educating Christians for a Multifaith World*. Downers Grove, IL: IVP Academic, 2017.

Leatham, Miguel. "Practical Religion and Peasant Recruitment to Non-Catholic Groups in Latin America." *Religion and the Social Order* 6 (1996): 175–90.

Leirvik, Oddbjørn. "Area, Field, Discipline." In *Interreligious Studies: Dispatches from an Emerging Field*, edited by Hans Gustafson, 17–28. Waco: Baylor University Press, 2020.

———. "Interreligious Dialogue and Secularity: The Secular as Non-Hegemonic Condition." In *Secular and Sacred? The Scandinavian Case of Religion in Human Rights, Law and Public Space*, edited by Rosemarie van den Breemer, José Casanova, and Trygve Wyller, 261–77. Göttingen, Germany: Vandenhoeck & Ruprecht, 2014.

———. "Interreligious Studies: A New Academic Discipline?" In *Contested Spaces, Common Ground: Spaces and Power Structures in Multireligious Societies*, edited by Ulrich Winkler, Lidia Rodriguez, and Oddbjørn Leirvik, 33–42. Leiden: Brill Rodopi, 2016.

———. *Interreligious Studies: A Relational Approach to Religious Activism and the Study of Religion*. New York: Bloomsbury, 2014.

———. "Interreligious Studies: A Relational Approach to the Study of Religion." *Journal of Interreligious Studies* 13 (February 2014): 15–19.

———. "Philosophies of Interreligious Dialogue: Practice in Search of Theory." *Approaching Religion* 1, no. 1 (2011): 16–24. https://doi.org/10.30664/ar.67466.

———. "Pluralisation of Theologies at Universities: Approaches and Concepts." In *Pluralisation of Theologies at European Universities*, edited by Wolfram Weisse, Julia Ipgrave, Oddbjørn Leirvik, and Muna Tatari, 25–34. Münster: Waxman Verlag, 2020.

Leopold, Anita Maria, and Jeppe S. Jensen. *Syncretism in Religion: A Reader*. New York: Routledge, 2004.

Lester, Emile, and Patrick. S. Roberts. "Learning about World Religions in Modesto, California: The Promise of Teaching Tolerance in Public Schools." *Politics and Religion* 4, no. 2 (2011): 264–88.

———. *Learning about World Religions in Public Schools: The Impact on Student Attitudes and Community Acceptance in Modesto, California*. Nashville: First Amendment Center, 2006.

Lévi-Strauss, Claude. *The Savage Mind*. Chicago: University of Chicago Press, 1966.

Levine, Amy-Jill. *The Misunderstood Jew: The Church and the Scandal of the Jewish Jesus*. San Francisco: HarperCollins, 2006.

Levine, Deborah J. "The Why and How of Religious Diversity Training." *Huffington Post*, December 29, 2015. https://tinyurl.com/5355bpsa.

Lewis, Thomas A. "The Inevitability of Normativity in the Study of Religion: Theology in Religious Studies." In *Theology and Religious Studies in Higher Education: Global Perspectives*, edited by Darlene L. Bird and Simon G. Smith, 87–98. London: Continuum, 2009.

Li, Vivienne. "Spider Silk: Properties, Uses, and Production." The Molecule of the Month (website), University of Bristol. Accessed June 28, 2019. https://tinyurl.com/32dfwehu.

Lindheim, Tone. "Developing Religious Literacy through Conversational Spaces for Religion in the Workplace." *Nordic Journal of Religion and Society* 33, no. 1 (2020): 16–29.

Lindsay, Jenn. "Growing Interreligious and Intercultural Competence in the Classroom." *Teaching Theology and Religion* 23 (2020): 17–33.

Lowery, Charles. "The Scholar-Practitioner Ideal: Toward a Socially Just Educational Administration for the 21st Century." *Journal of School Leadership* 26 (February 2016): 34–60.

Luthans, Fred, and Bruce J. Avolio. "Authentic Leadership: A Positive Developmental Approach." In *Positive Organizational Scholarship*, edited by Kim S. Cameron, Jane E. Dutton, and Robert E. Quinn, 241–61. San Francisco: Barrett-Koehler, 2003.

Machacek, David W. "The Problem of Pluralism." *Sociology of Religion* 64, no. 2 (2003): 145–61.

MacLaughlin, Nina. "Recapturing the World with Karl Ove Knausgaard." *Los Angeles Review of Books*, May 23, 2013. https://tinyurl.com/bp4wmx3r.

Maduro, Otto. "Directions for a Reassessment of Latina/o Religion." In *Enigmatic Powers: Syncretism with African and Indigenous Peoples' Religions among Latinos*, edited by Anthony M. Stevens-Arroyo and Andrés I. Pérez y Mena, 47–68. New York: Bildner Center for Western Hemisphere Studies, 1995.

Marcus, Benjamin P. "Religious Identity Formation: The 3B Framework: Beliefs, Behavior, Belonging." Religious Freedom Center. Last accessed June 20, 2018. www.religiousfreedomcenter.org/grounding/identity.

——. "Religious Literacy in American Education." In *The Oxford Handbook of Religion and American Education*, edited by Michael D. Waggoner and Nathan C. Walker. New York: Oxford University Press, 2018. https://doi.org/10.1093/oxfordhb/9780199386819.013.38.

Martí, Gerardo. "Found Theologies versus Imposed Theologies: Remarks on Theology and Ethnography from a Sociological Perspective." *Ecclesial Practices* 3 (2016): 157–72.

——. "Religious Reflexivity: The Effect of Continual Novelty and Diversity on Individual Religiosity." *Sociology of Religion* 76, no. 1 (2015): 1–13.

Martin, Jerry L., ed. *Theology without Walls: The Transreligious Imperative*. London: Routledge, 2020.

Marty, Martin E. "Pluralisms." *The Annals of the American Academy of Political and Social Science* 612, *Religious Pluralism and Civil Society* (July 2007): 14–25.

Maruggi, Matthew, and Martha E. Stortz. "Teaching the 'Most Beautiful Stories': Narrative Reflection as a Signature Pedagogy for Interfaith Studies." In *Interreligious/Interfaith Studies: Defining a New Field*, edited by Eboo Patel, Jennifer Howe Peace, and Noah Silverman, 85–97. Boston: Beacon Press, 2018.

Marx, Karl. *Critique of Hegel's Philosophy of Right*. Translated by Annette Jolin and Joseph O'Malley. Cambridge: Cambridge University Press, 1970.

Masao, Abe. "Faith and Self-Awakening: A Search for the Fundamental Category Covering All Religious Life." *The Eastern Buddhist* 31, no. 1 (1998): 12–24.

Masuzawa, Tomoko. *The Invention of World Religions: Or, How European Universalism Was Preserved in the Language of Pluralism*. Chicago: University of Chicago Press, 2007.

——. "The Production of 'Religion' and the Task of the Scholar: Russell McCutcheon among the Smiths, Culture and Religion." *Culture and Religion* 1, no. 1 (2000): 123–30. https://doi.org/10.1080/01438300008567146.

Maxwell, Nicholas. "How Wisdom Can Help Solve Global Problems." In *Applying Wisdom to Contemporary World Problems*, edited by Robert J. Sternberg, Howard C. Nusbaum, and Judith Glück, 337–80. Cham, Switzerland: Palgrave Macmillan, 2019.

McCarthy, Kate. "(Inter)Religious Studies: Making a Home in the Secular Academy." In *Interreligious/Interfaith Studies: Defining a New Field*, edited by Eboo Patel, Jennifer Howe Peace, and Noah Silverman, 2–15. Boston: Beacon Press, 2018.

——. "Secular Imperatives." In *Interreligious Studies: Dispatches from an Emerging Field*, edited by Hans Gustafson, 171–77. Waco: Baylor University Press, 2020.

McCloud, Sean. "Everything Blended: Engaging Combinations, Appropriations, Bricolage, and Syncretisms in Our Teaching and Research." *Implicit Religion* 21, no. 2 (2018): 362–82.

McConeghy, David. "Where Does the Word Religion Come From?" In *Religion in 5 Minutes*, edited by Aaron W. Hughes and Russel T. McCutcheon, 8–10. Sheffield, UK, and Bristol, CT: Equinox, 2017.

McCrary, Charles. *Sincerely Held: American Secularism and Its Believers*. Chicago: University of Chicago Press, 2022.

McCutcheon, Russell T. *Critics Not Caretakers: Redescribing the Public Study of Religion*. Albany: SUNY Press, 2001.

——, ed. *The Insider/Outsider Problem in the Study of Religion*. London: Continuum, 2014.

——. "Religion, Ire, and Dangerous Things." *Journal of the American Academy of Religion* 72, no. 1 (2004): 173–93.

——. *Studying Religion: An Introduction*. New York: Routledge, 2014.

——. "What Is the Future of 'Religion'?" In *Religion in 5 Minutes*, edited by Aaron W. Hughes and Russell T. McCutcheon, 299–306. Sheffield, UK, and Bristol, CT: Equinox, 2017.

McGraw, Barbara. "Cross-Cultural Leadership as Interfaith Leadership." In *Interreligious Studies: Dispatches from an Emerging Field*, edited by Hans Gustafson, 213–22. Waco: Baylor University Press, 2020.

——. "From Prison Religion to Interfaith Leadership for Institutional Change." In *Interreligious/Interfaith Studies: Defining a New Field*, edited by Eboo Patel, Jennifer Howe Peace, and Noah Silverman, 183–95. Boston: Beacon Press, 2018.

——. "Toward a Framework for Interfaith Leadership." *Engaging Pedagogies in Catholic Higher Education (EPiCHE)* 3, no. 1, *Interfaith Opportunities for Catholic Higher Education* (2017): 1–9.

——. "Why Interfaith Leadership Matters to Business and the Professions." Center for Engaged Religious Pluralism at Saint Mary's College of California, February 19, 2021 (educational video). https://tinyurl.com/yc3m9hf7.

McGuire, Meredith B. "Embodied Practices: Negotiation and Resistance." In *Everyday Religion: Observing Modern Religious Lives*, edited by Nancy Ammerman, 187–200. New York: Oxford University Press, 2008.

———. *Lived Religion: Faith and Practice in Everyday Life*. New York: Oxford University Press, 2008.

Menocal, Rosa. *The Ornament of the World: How Muslims, Jews, and Christians Created a Culture of Tolerance in Medieval Spain*. New York: Back Bay Books, 2012.

Meyer, Brigit, and David Morgan, Crispin Paine, and S. Brent Plate. "The Origin and Mission of Material Religion." *Religion* 40 (2010): 207–11.

Miedema, Siebren. "A Plea for Inclusive Worldview Education in All Schools: Original Research." *Vir Christelike Wetenskap* 77, no. 1 (2012): 1–7.

Mikva, Rachel S. *Dangerous Religious Ideas: The Deep Roots of Self-Critical Faith in Judaism, Christianity, and Islam*. Boston: Beacon Press, 2020.

———. "Reflections in the Waves: What Interreligious Studies Can Learn from the Evolution of Women's Movements in the US." *Journal of Ecumenical Studies* 53, no. 4 (2018): 461–82.

———. "Six Issues That Complicate Interreligious Studies and Engagement." In *Interreligious/Interfaith Studies: Defining a New Field*, edited by Eboo Patel, Jennifer Howe Peace, and Noah Silverman, 124–46. Boston: Beacon Press, 2018.

Millis, Diane. *Deepening Engagement: Essential Wisdom for Listening and Leading with Purpose, Meaning Joy*. Woodstock, VT: Skylight Paths, 2015.

Minnesota Campus Compact. "Social Change Wheel 2.0 Toolkit." June 16, 2020. https://tinyurl.com/yckz5seb.

Minnesota Multifaith Network. "About." Accessed May 10, 2022. https://tinyurl.com/4ftsh47y.

———. "Policies Update Aug. 20, 2020." Accessed May 10, 2022. https://tinyurl.com/53e5p48s.

Mischinski, Megan, and Eranda Jaywickreme. "Can Moral Exemplars Promote Wisdom?" In *Applying Wisdom to Contemporary World Problems*, edited by Robert J. Sternberg, Howard C. Nusbaum, and Judith Glück, 173–200. Cham, Switzerland: Palgrave Macmillan, 2019.

Moberly, R. W. L. "Knowing God and Knowing about God: Martin Buber's *Two Types of Faith* Revisited." *Scottish Journal of Theology* 64, no. 4 (2012): 402–20.

Mogel, Wendy. *The Blessing of a Skinned Knee: Using Jewish Teachings to Raise Self-Reliant Children*. New York: Scribner, 2001.

Molloy, Michael. *Experiencing the World's Religions: Traditions, Challenge, and Change*, 4th ed. New York: McGraw Hill, 2008.

Moore, Diane L. "Core Principles." Religion and Public Life, Harvard Divinity School. Accessed January 17, 2022. https://tinyurl.com/bddymb22.

———. "What Is Religious Literacy?" Harvard Divinity School Religious Literacy Project. Accessed October 30, 2018. https://tinyurl.com/2fmbhdzc.

Moyaert, Marianne. *In Response to the Religious Other: Ricoeur and the Fragility of Interreligious Encounters*. London: Lexington Books, 2014.

———. "Interfaith Learning in Academic Spaces." In *Pluralisation of Theologies at European Universities*, edited by Wolframm Weisse, Julia Ipgrave, Oddbjørn Leirvik, and Muna Tatari, 35–46. Münster: Waxman, 2020.

———. "Interreligious Dialogue and the Debate between Universalism and Particularism: Searching for a Way out of the Deadlock." *Studies in Interreligious Dialogue* 15, no. 1 (2005): 36–51.

——. "On the Role of Ritual in Interfaith Education." *Religious Education* 113, no. 1 (2018): 49–60.

——. "The Scholar, the Theologian, and the Activist." In *Interreligious Studies: Dispatches from an Emerging Field*, edited by Hans Gustafson, 34–42. Waco: Baylor University Press, 2020.

Mumford, Michael D., Stephen J. Zaccaro, Francis D. Harding, T. Owen Jacobs, and Edwin A. Fleishman. "Leadership Skills for a Changing World: Solving Complex Social Problems." *Leadership Quarterly* 11, no. 1 (2000): 11–35.

Myth Busters Jr. "Episode 8: Bug Special." Science Channel, February 6, 2018.

National Center for Educational Statistics. "Environmental Studies." CIP 03.0103 (CIP 2000). Classification of Instructional Programs. Accessed August 21, 2019. https://tinyurl.com/yc8kr3u5.

——. "Peace Studies and Conflict Studies." CIP 30.0501 (CIP 2020). Classification of Instructional Programs. Accessed March 22, 2022. https://tinyurl.com/29ws7t5w.

——. "Sustainability Studies." CIP 30.3301 (CIP 2000). Classification of Instructional Programs. Accessed August 21, 2019. https://tinyurl.com/2wp86768.

Nealon, Kevin. "Kevin Nealon: Now Hear Me Out!" (stand-up comedy). Vivendi Entertainment, 2009.

Njal's Saga. Translated by Robert Cook. London: Penguin, 2001.

Norris, Pippa, and Ronald Inglehart. *Sacred and Secular: Religion and Politics Worldwide.* Cambridge: Cambridge University Press, 2004.

Numrich, Paul D. "Epilogue: Understanding a Decentralised Social Movement." In *The Interfaith Movement: Mobilising Religious Diversity in the 21st Century*, edited by John Fahy and Jan-Jonathan Bock, 219–28. London: Routledge, 2019.

O'Leary, Joseph S. "Toward a Buddhist Interpretation of Christian Truth." In *Many Mansions? Multiple Religious Belonging and Christian Identity*, edited by Catherine Cornille, 29–43. Maryknoll, NY: Orbis Books, 2002.

Omer, Atalia. "Can a Critic Be a Caretaker Too? Religion, Conflict, and Conflict Transformation." *Journal for the American Academy of Religion* 79, no. 2 (2011): 469–96.

Onishi, Bradley B. *The Sacrality of the Secular: Postmodern Philosophy of Religion.* New York: Columbia University Press, 2018.

Orsi, Robert A. "Everyday Miracles: The Study of Lived Religion." In *Lived Religion in America: Toward a History of Practice*, edited by David D. Hall, 3–21. Princeton, NJ: Princeton University Press, 1997.

——. "Is the Study of Lived Religion Irrelevant to the World We Live In? Special Presidential Plenary Address, Society for the Scientific Study of Religion, Salt Lake City, November 2, 2002." *Journal for the Scientific Study of Religion* 42, no. 2 (2003): 169–74.

Otto, Rudolf. *The Idea of the Holy.* Translated by John W. Harvey. New York: Oxford University Press, 1958.

Owen, Suzanne. "The World Religions Paradigm: Time for a Change." *Arts & Humanities in Higher Education* 10, no. 3 (2011): 253–68.

Panikkar, Raimon. *Cultures and Religions in Dialogue: Part One, Pluralism and Interculturality.* Edited by Milena Carra Pavan. Maryknoll, NY: Orbis Press, 2018.

——. "Die Toleranz der Christenheit." In *Pluralismus, Toleranze und Christenheit*, 117–42. Nürnberg: Abendändishe, 1961.

——. "Ecumenisme critic." *Questions de vida cristiana* no. 144 (Montserrat, 1988): 120–23.

——. "Hacia una teologia de la liberación." Talk presented at the Fourth Parliament of the World's Religions. Barcelona, Spain, 2005. In *Interculturalidad, dialogo y liberació*, edited by H. Kung, J. J. Tamayo-Acosta, and R. Fornet-Betancourt, 61–68. Pamplona: Verbo Divino, 2005.

——. "The Myth of Pluralism: The Tower of Babel—A Meditation on Nonviolence." *CrossCurrents* 29 (Summer 1979): 197–230.

——. *Pace e Interculturalitá: Una riflessione filosofica.* Edited by Milena Carrara Pavan. Milan: Jaca Book, 2002, reprinted 2006.

——. "Religious Identity and Pluralism." In *A Dome of Many Colors: Studies in Religious Pluralism and Unity*, edited by A. Sharma and K. M. Dugan, 23–47. Harrisburg, PA: Trinity International Press, 1999.

——. *Religious Syncretism in Antiquity: Essays in Conversation with Geo Widengren.* Edited by B. A. Pearson. Missoula, MT: Scholars Press, 1975.

——. "Some Notes on Syncretism and Eclecticism: Related to the Growth of Human Consciousness." In *Religious Syncretism in Antiquity: Essays in Conversation with Geo Widengren*, edited by B. A. Pearson, 47–62. Missoula, MT: Scholars Press, 1975.

——. "Tres grandes interpretaciones de la interculturalidad." In *Interculturality, Gender, and Education*, edited by Raul Fornet-Betancourt, 27–44. Frankfurt am Main and London: Iko, 2004. Inaugural talk given by Panikkar at Congress of Intercultural Philosophy, Olavide Cultural Center in Carmona in 2004.

——. "Vers un ecumenisme ecumenic." *Questions de vida Cristiana* no. 140 (Montserrat, 1988): 80–86.

The Parents Circle. "About PCFF." Accessed June 30, 2021. https://tinyurl.com/3r7hu4ad.

Patel, Eboo. "Building Religious Pluralism." *Religion and Foreign Policy Conference Calls* (podcast interview). Accessed December 31, 2019. https://tinyurl.com/mdd4efd4.

——. "A Civic Approach to Interfaith Studies." In *Interreligious Studies: Dispatches from an Emerging Field*, edited by Hans Gustafson, 29–33. Waco: Baylor University Press, 2020.

——. "Dynamic Tensions." Panel presentation at Symposium on Religion and the Liberal Aims of Higher Education. Boisi Center for Religion and American Public Life. Boston College, November 9, 2012. https://tinyurl.com/3dh39e25.

——. *Interfaith Leadership: A Primer.* Boston: Beacon Press, 2016.

——. *Out of Many Faiths: Religious Diversity and the American Promise.* Princeton, NJ: Princeton University Press, 2018.

——. "3 Reasons Interfaith Efforts Matter More Than Ever." *Huff Post*, April 23, 2013. https://tinyurl.com/4akf45yf.

——. "Toward a Field of Interfaith Studies." *Liberal Education* 99, no. 4 (2013): 38–43.

——. "What Is Interfaith Cooperation For?" Religion Dispatches, May 6, 2013. https://tinyurl.com/2njzdywh.

Patel, Eboo, and Cassie Meyer. "Teaching Interfaith Leadership." In *Teaching Interfaith Encounters*, edited by Marc A. Pugliese and Alexander Y. Hwang, 297–310. New York: Oxford University Press, 2017.

Patton, Laurie. "Plural American Needs Myths: An Essay in Foundational Narratives in Response to Eboo Patel." In *Out of Many Faiths: Religious Diversity and the American Promise* by Eboo Patel, 151–79. Princeton, NJ: Princeton University Press, 2018.

Peace, Jennifer. "Toward a Field of Interfaith Studies: Emerging Questions and Considerations." In roundtable with Jeanine Diller, Eboo Patel, Jennifer Peace, and Colleen Windham-Hughes. *Journal of Interreligious Studies* 16 (2015): 5–13.

Peace, Jennifer Howe, and Or N. Rose. "The Value of Interreligious Education for Religious Leaders." In *Interreligious/Interfaith Studies: Defining a New Field*, edited by Eboo Patel, Jennifer Howe Peace, and Noah Silverman, 172–82. Boston: Beacon Press, 2018.

Pedersen, Kusumita P. "The Interfaith Movement: An Incomplete Assessment." *Journal of Ecumenical Studies* 41, no. 1 (2004): 74–94.

Pennington, Brian K. "The Interreligious Studies Agenda." In *The Georgetown Companion to Interreligious Studies*, edited by Lucinda Mosher, 15–23. Washington, DC: Georgetown University Press, 2022.

——. "(Neo)Liberal Challenges." In *Interreligious Studies: Dispatches from an Emerging Field*, edited by Hans Gustafson, 178–84. Waco: Baylor University Press, 2020.

Pew Research Center. "America's Changing Religious Landscape." May 12, 2015. https://tinyurl.com/yc76ehtt.

——. "Being Christian in Western Europe." May 29, 2018, 47. https://tinyurl.com/yt6syybw.

——. "The Changing Global Religious Landscape." April 5, 2017. https://tinyurl.com/489nc96j.

——. "Eastern, New Age Beliefs Widespread: Many Americans Mix Multiple Faiths." December 2009. https://tinyurl.com/uzr2xs88.

——. "Europe's Growing Muslim Population." November 29, 2017. https://tinyurl.com/2p93uh48.

——. "The Future of World Religions: Population Growth Projections, 2010–2050." April 2, 2015. https://tinyurl.com/46pptvkc.

——. "A Portrait of Jewish Americans." October 1, 2013. https://tinyurl.com/59c9b7py.

——. "Religion in Everyday Life." April 12, 2016. https://tinyurl.com/2w5cnvp2.

——. "When Americans Say They Believe in God, What Do They Mean?" April 25, 2018. https://tinyurl.com/mr7dvtp3.

Piedmont, R. L. "Does Spirituality Represent the Sixth Factor of Personality? Spiritual Transcendence and the Five-Factor Model." *Journal of Personality* 67, no. 6 (1999): 985–1013.

Pierce, Ellie. "Using the Case Studies Method in Interfaith Studies Classrooms." In *Interreligious/Interfaith Studies: Defining a New Field*, edited by Eboo Patel, Jennifer Howe Peace, and Noah Silverman, 72–84. Boston: Beacon Press, 2018.

Pluralism Project. "America's Growing Interfaith Structure." Accessed May 11, 2022. https://tinyurl.com/yz6vxfap.

——. "From Diversity to Pluralism." Accessed November 22, 2020. https://tinyurl.com/4uwcm5mm.

Polanyi, Michael. *The Tacit Dimension*. Chicago: University of Chicago Press, 1966.

Pollack, Detlef. "Secularization." In *Oxford Bibliographies*. Last modified October 29, 2013. https://tinyurl.com/37ukrhph.

Pope Francis. "Audience with a Delegation of the Emouna Fraternité Alumni Association." Oral address, Sala dei Papi of the Apostolic Palace, June 23, 2018. https:// tinyurl.com/yv23zn9a.

Primiano, Leonard Norman. "Vernacular Religion and the Search for Method in Religious Folklife." *Western Folklore* 54, no. 1 (1995): 42.

Prothero, Stephen. *God Is Not One: The Eight Rival Religions That Run the World*. New York: HarperOne, 2011.

——. *Religious Literacy: What Every American Needs to Know—and Doesn't*. New York: HarperOne, 2007.

——. "World Religions 101: Buddhism." *Interfaith Voices* (podcast audio), August 27, 2014. Hosted by Maureen Fiedler. https://tinyurl.com/bdfpebzk.

Putnam, Robert. "*E Pluribus Unum*: Diversity and Community in the 21st Century: The 2006 Johan Skytte Prize Lecture." *Scandinavian Political Studies* 30, no. 2 (June 2007): 137–74.

Pye, Michael. *Skilful Means: A Concept in Mahayana Buddhism*. London: Routledge, 2003.

——. "Syncretism and Ambiguity." *Numen* 18 (1971): 83–93.

Quack, Johannes. "Identifying (with) the Secular: Description and Genealogy." In *The Oxford Handbook of Secularism*, edited by Phil Zuckerman and John R. Shook. New York: Oxford University Press, 2017. https://doi.org/10.1093/ oxfordhb/9780199988457.013.2.

Race, Alan. *Christians and Religious Pluralism*. London: SCM Press, 1983.

Raelin, Joe. "In Leadership, Look to the Practices Not the Individual." *Academia Letters* art. 34 (2020): 1–6. https://doi.org/10.20935/AL34.

Repko, Allen F., and Rick Szostak. *Interdisciplinary Research: Process and Theory*, 3rd ed. Los Angeles: Sage, 2017.

Richard, Orlando. "Racial Diversity, Business Strategy, and Firm Performance: A Resource-Based View." *Academy of Management Journal* 43, no. 2 (2000): 164–77.

Riis, Ole. "Modes of Religious Pluralism under Conditions of Globalisation." *International Journal on Multicultural Societies* (IJMS) 1, no. 1 (1999): 20–34.

Ringgren, Helmer. "The Problems of Syncretism." In *Syncretism: Based on Papers Read at the Symposium on Cultural Contact, Meeting of Religions, Syncretism Held at Abo on the 18th–10th of September 1966*, edited by Sven S. Hartman, 7–14. Stockholm: Almqvist and Wiksell, 1969.

Roberts, Michelle Voss. "Religious Belonging and the Multiple." *Journal of Feminist Studies in Religion* 26, no. 1 (Spring 2010): 43–62.

Rockenbach, Alyssa N., Tara D. Hudson, Matthew J. Mayhew, Benjamin P. Correia-Harker, Shauna Morin, and Associates. "Friendships Matter: The Role of Peer Relationships in Interfaith Learning and Development." Chicago: Interfaith Youth Core, 2019. https://tinyurl.com/ymu6e6dm.

Rosenberg, Marshall B. *Nonviolent Communication: A Language of Life*, 3rd ed. Encinitas, CA: PuddleDancer Press, 2015.

Rothausen, Teresa J. "Integrating Leadership Development with Ignatian Spirituality." *Journal of Business Ethics* 145, no. 4 (2017): 811–29. https://doi.org/10.1007/ s10551-016-3241-4.

Rothausen, Teresa J., and Sara M. Christenson. "Leadership." In *Wiley Encyclopedia of Management*, vol. 2: *Business Ethics*, 3rd ed., edited by Cary L. Cooper, 271–77. Chichester: Wiley, 2014.

Rubens, Heather Miller, Homayra Ziad, and Benjamin E. Sax. "Towards an Inter-religious City: A Case Study." In *Interreligious/Interfaith Studies: Defining a New Field*, edited by Eboo Patel, Jennifer Howe Peace, and Noah Silverman, 209–19. Boston: Beacon Press, 2018.

Rudolph, Kurt. "Synkretismus vom Theologischen Scheltwort zum religionswissenshaftlichen Begriff." In *Humanitas Religiosa: Festschrift für Harlds Biezais zu seinem 70 Geburtstag*, 193–212. Stockholm: Almqvist and Wiksell, 1979.

Sacks, Jonathan. "The Dignity of Difference: Avoiding the Clash of Civilizations." *The Review of Faith & International Affairs* 7, no. 2 (2009): 37–42.

Sahgal, Neha. "10 Key Findings about Religion in Western Europe." Pew Research Center, May 29, 2018. https://tinyurl.com/2ztad483.

Schaefer, Donovan. "Is Secularism a World Religion?" Interview with Christopher R. Cotter. *The Religious Studies Project* (podcast audio), November 28, 2016. https://tinyurl.com/yu7dpc4a.

Schmidt-Leukel, Perry. "A Fractal Interpretation of Religious Diversity." In *New Paths for Interreligious Theology: Perry Schmidt-Leukel's Fractal Interpretation of Religious Diversity*, edited by Alan Race and Paul Knitter, 3–22. Maryknoll, NY: Orbis Books, 2019.

——. *Religious Pluralism and Interreligious Theology: The Gifford Lectures.* Maryknoll, NY: Orbis, 2017.

——. *Transformation by Integration: How Inter-Faith Encounter Changes Christianity.* London: SCM Press, 2009.

Schulson, Michael. "When Religious Disagreement Seems the Least of Our Problems: The Future of 'Interfaith' in a Divided Society." Religion Dispatches, December 6, 2016. https://tinyurl.com/22ruue66.

Schwartz, Barry, and Kenneth Sharpe. *Practical Wisdom: The Way to Do the Right Thing.* New York: Riverhead Books, 2010.

Shaw, Martha. "Towards a Religiously Literate Curriculum—Religion and World-view Literacy as an Educational Model." *Journal of Beliefs and Values* 41, no. 2 (2020): 150–61.

Shaw, Rosalind, and Charles Stewart. "Introduction: Problematizing Syncretism." In *Syncretism/Anti-Syncretism: The Politics of Religious Synthesis*, edited by Charles Stewart and Rosalind Shaw. London: Routledge, 1994.

Sheldrake, Philip. "Spirituality and Its Critical Methodology." In *Exploring Christian Spirituality: Essays in Honor of Sandra M. Schneiders*, edited by Bruce H. Lescher and Elizabeth Liebert, 15–34. New York: Paulist Press, 2006.

Sherif, Muzafer, O. J. Harvey, B. Jack White, William R. Hood, and Carolyn W. Sherif. *Intergroup Conflict and Cooperation: The Robbers Cave Experiment.* Norman, OK: The University Book Exchange, 1954/61.

Smart, Ninian. *Worldviews: Crosscultural Explorations of Human Beliefs*, 3rd ed. Upper Saddle River, NJ: Prentice Hall, 2000.

Smith, Jonathan Z. *Imagining Religion: From Babylon to Jonestown*. Chicago: University of Chicago Press, 1982.

Smith, L. Shakiyla, and Natalie Wilkins. "Mind the Gap." *Journal of Public Health Management and Practice* 24, no. 1 (2018): S6–S11.

Smith, Wilfred Cantwell. *Faith and Belief: The Difference between Them*. Oxford: Oneworld, 1998.

——. *Towards a World Theology: Faith and the Comparative Study of Religion*. Philadelphia: Westminster Press, 1981. 2nd ed. 1989, Maryknoll, NY: Orbis.

Snook, Jennifer. *American Heathens: The Politics of Identity in a Pagan Religious Movement*. Philadelphia: Temple University Press, 2015.

Society for Human Resource Management. "Impact of Diversity Initiatives on the Bottom Line." Alexandria, VA: 2001.

Soules, Kate E., and Sabrina Jafralie. "Religious Literacy in Teacher Education." *Religion & Education* 48, no. 1 (2021): 37–56. https://doi.org/10.1080/15507394.2021.1876497.

Stark, Rodney. *What Americans Really Believe*. Waco: Baylor University Press, 2008.

Stendahl, Krister. "From God's Perspective We Are All Minorities." *Journal of Religious Pluralism* 2 (1993). https://tinyurl.com/4fx9ed5u.

Sternberg, Robert J. "A Balance Theory of Wisdom." *Review of General Psychology* 2, no. 4 (1998): 347–65. https://doi.org10.1037/1089-2680.2.4.347.

——. "Where Have All the Flowers of Wisdom Gone? An Analysis of Teaching for Wisdom over the Years." In *Applying Wisdom to Contemporary World Problems*, edited by Robert J. Sternberg, 255–92. Cham, Switzerland: Palgrave MacMillan, 2019.

Stewart, Charles. "Relocating Syncretism in Social Science Discourse." In *Syncretism in Religion: A Reader*, edited by A. M. Leopold and J. S. Jensen, 264–85. New York: Routledge, 2004.

Stone, Jon R. *The Essential Max Müller: On Language, Mythology, and Religion*. New York: Palgrave Macmillan, 2002.

Stringer, Martin D. "Lived Religion and Difficult Conversations." Birmingham Conversations of the Faith, Neighbors, Changemakers Collaboration, 2015. Last accessed October 10, 2019. http://www.fncbham.org.uk/wp-content/uploads/2015/05/Lived-Religion-and-Difficult-Conversations.pdf.

——. "Professor Martin Stringer: Religion and Religious Diversity." University of Birmingham: Institute for Research into Superdiversity (IRiS) (interview). Last accessed July 25, 2018. https://www.birmingham.ac.uk/research/activity/super-diversity-institute/research/martin-stringer.aspx.

Stryker, Sheldon. *Symbolic Interactionism: A Social Structural Version*. Menlo Park, CA: Benjamin/Cummings, 1980.

Stryker, Sheldon, and Peter J. Burke. "The Past, Present, and Future of an Identity Theory." *Social Psychology Quarterly* 63 (2000): 284–97.

Sweetman, Will. "Against Invention: A Richer History for 'Hinduism.'" Interview with Thomas White. *The Religious Studies Project* (podcast audio), February 19, 2018. https://tinyurl.com/5r4uwhht.

Swidler, Leonard. *The Age of Global Dialogue*. Eugene, OR: Wipf & Stock, 2016.

——. *Dialogue for Interreligious Understanding: Strategies for the Transformation of Culture-Shaping Institutions*. New York: Palgrave Macmillan, 2014.

——. "Dialogue Principles." Dialogue Institute. Accessed September 20, 2016. https://tinyurl.com/55r8w33n.

——. "The History of Inter-Religious Dialogue." In *The Wiley-Blackwell Companion to Inter-Religious Dialogue*, edited by Catherine Cornille, 3–19. Oxford: Wiley Blackwell, 2013.

——. "Nobody Knows Everything about Anything!" *Journal of Ecumenical Studies* 45 (Spring 2010): 175–77.

Tajfel, Henri. "Social Identity and Intergroup Behavior." *Social Science Information* 13, no. 65 (1974): 65–93. https://doi.org/10.1177/053901847401300204.

Taleb, Nassim Nicholas. *Antifragile: Things That Gain from Disorder*. New York: Random House, 2012.

——. *Skin in the Game: Hidden Asymmetries in Daily Life*. New York: Random House, 2018.

Taves, Ann. "Finding and Articulating Meaning in Secular Experience." In *Religious Experience*, edited by Dan Fleming, Eva Leven, and Ulrich Riegel, 11–22. Munich: Waxman Verlag, 2018.

——. "Studying Religions as Worldviews and Ways of Life." Gunning Lectures, University of Edinburgh, Scotland, March 19, 2018. https://tinyurl.com/44dz7pdm.

——. "What Is Nonreligion? On the Virtues of a Meaning Systems Framework for Studying Nonreligious and Religious Worldviews in the Context of Everyday Life." *Secularism and Nonreligion* 7, no. 9 (2018): 1–6. https://doi.org/10.5334/snr.104.

——. "Worldviews and Ways of Life." Interview by David G. Robertson. *The Religious Studies Project* (podcast), May 21, 2018. Podcast transcript by Helen Bradstock, version 1.1, May 16, 2018. https://tinyurl.com/23bcamk7.

Taves, Ann, Egil Asprem, and Elliot Ihm. "Psychology, Meaning Making and the Study of Worldviews: Beyond Religion and Non-Religion." *Psychology of Religion and Spirituality* 10, no. 3 (2018): 207–17.

Taves, Ann, and Graham Ward. "Normativity in the Study of Religion: A Dialogue about Theology and Religious Studies." Religious Studies News, March 22, 2016. https://tinyurl.com/4hysuhuv.

Taylor, Charles. "Conditions of an Unforced Consensus on Human Rights." In *Dilemmas and Connections*. Cambridge, MA: Belknap Press of Harvard University Press, 2011.

——. *A Secular Age*. Cambridge, MA: Harvard University Press, 2007.

Taylor, William B. *Magistrates of the Sacred: Priests and Parishioners in Eighteenth-Century Mexico*. Stanford, CA: Stanford University Press, 1996.

Thatamanil, John. "We Are All Multiple: Identity and Conversion after 'Religion.'" Paper presented to the American Academy of Religion, Baltimore, MD, November 25, 2013.

Tillich, Paul. *The Future of Religions*. New York: Harper & Row, 1966.

Tocqueville, Alexis de. *Democracy in America*. Translated by Henry Reeve. Penn State Electronic Classics Series Publication, 2002. https://tinyurl.com/2tezjbbc.

TOI Staff. "At 70, Israel's Population Is 8.842 Million, 43% of World Jewry." *Times of Israel*, April 16, 2018. https://tinyurl.com/3s5ztn46.

Tylor, Edward Burnett. *Primitive Culture: Researches into the Development of Mythology, Philosophy, Religion, Language, Art, and Custom*, vol. 1. New York: G. P. Putnam's Sons, 1920.

Uddin, Asma. *When Islam Is Not a Religion: Inside America's Fight for Religious Freedom*. New York: Pegasus Books, 2019.

United Nations Educational, Scientific and Cultural Organization. "International Day of Tolerance." UNESCO. Accessed April 9, 2022. https://tinyurl.com/2p9bvhx7.

United States Air Force. "Cadet Chapel." Accessed April 9, 2022. https://tinyurl.com/yzn4e4tc.

Università della Svizzera italiana. "Fasting the Month of Ramadan at the Workplace." Master of Advanced Studies in Intercultural Communication (MIC). Accessed November 28, 2021. https://tinyurl.com/5n978r5r.

University of Oslo. "Horizon Document for a Planned Program in Interreligious Studies." Version 16.10.00. University of Oslo, Norway, Faculty of Theology, 2000. https://tinyurl.com/3443a5hs.

University of St. Thomas. "Justice and Peace Studies Homepage." Accessed August 16, 2019. https://tinyurl.com/mrr4czcx.

van den Breemer, Rosemaire, José Casanova, and Trygve Wyller. "Introduction." In *Secular and Sacred? The Scandinavian Case of Religion in Human Rights, Law and Public Space*, edited by Rosemaire van den Breemer, José Casanova, and Trygve Wyller, 9–20. Göttingen, Germany: Vandenhoeck & Ruprecht, 2014.

van der Leeuw, Gerardus. *Phänomenologie der Religion*. Tübingen, Germany: Mohr, 1965.

van der Veer, Peter. "Syncretism, Multiculturalism, and the Discourse of Tolerance." In *Syncretism/Anti-Syncretism: The Politics of Religious Synthesis*, edited by Charles Stewart and Rosalind Shaw, 185–200. London: Routledge, 1994.

Vanderwilt, Jeffrey. "Eucharistic Sharing: Revising the Question." *Theological Studies* 63 (2002): 826–39.

VanLaningham, Erin, and Hannah Schell. "Charisma and Craft: A Conversation with Eboo Patel." *Callings* (podcast audio), January 28, 2021. https://tinyurl.com/2trkcbth.

Varnon-Hughes, Stephanie L. *Interfaith Grit: How Uncertainty Will Save Us*. Eugene, OR: Wipf & Stock, 2018.

Vernacular Architecture Forum (website). Last accessed July 13, 2018. www.vernaculararchitectureforum.org.

Vikings name plaque (photograph). Wikimedia Commons, February 8, 2018. https://tinyurl.com/bdhtwh7w.

von der Lippe, Marie, and S. Undheim. "Why Common Compulsory RE in School?" In *Religion i skolen: Didaktiske perspektiver på religions- og livssynsfaget*, edited by Marie von der Lippe and S. Undheim, 35–53. Oslo: Universitetsforlaget, 2017.

Wakelin, Michael, and Nick Spencer. "Religious Literacy and the Media: The Case of the BBC." In *Religious Literacy in Policy and Practice*, edited by Adam Dinham and Matthew Francis, 227–36. Bristol: Policy Press, 2016.

Wald, Kenneth, Adam Silverman, and Kevin Fridy. "Making Sense of Religion in Political Life." *Annual Review of Political Science* 8 (2005): 121–34.

Walker, Nathan C., W. Y. Alice Chan, and H. Bruce McEver. "Religious Literacy: Civic Education for a Common Good." *Religion & Education* 48, no. 1 (2021): 1–16. https://doi.org/10.1080/15507394.2021.1876508.

Ward, Keith. *Religion and Revelation: A Theology of Revelation in the World's Religions*. Oxford: Clarendon Press, 1994.

Washington Post. "Nigeria's Boko Haram Kills 49 in Suicide Bombings." November 18, 2015. https://tinyurl.com/awzrn29z.

Weiss, Meghan A. "Interfaith Youth Core: Theology and Religious Commitment in One of America's Most Prominent Youth Interfaith Organizations." BA honors thesis. College of Saint Benedict and Saint John's University, Minnesota, 2016. https://tinyurl.com/4t3cd2ce.

Weisse, Wolfram, Julia Ipgrave, Oddbjørn Leirvik, and Muna Tatari, eds. *Pluralisation of Theologies at European Universities*. Münster: Waxman, 2020.

Wernicke-Olesen, Bjarne. "Hinduism and Meditation: Yoga." In *The Oxford Handbook of Meditation*, edited by Miguel Farias, David Brazier, and Mansur Lalljee. Oxford: Oxford University Press, 2020. https://doi.org/10.1093/oxfordhb/9780198808640.013.5.

Wertheimer, Linda K. *Faith Ed: Teaching about Religion in an Era of Intolerance*. Boston: Beacon Press, 2015.

Wexler, Jay. *Our Non-Christian Nation: How Wiccans, Satanists, Atheists, and Other Non-Christians Are Demanding Their Rightful Place in American Public Life*. Stanford, CA: Redwood Press, 2020.

Winston, Kimberly. "Scholars Seek to Reclaim a Dirty Word: Secularism." Religion News Service, February 22, 2013. https://tinyurl.com/2p87uw7d.

Wittgenstein, Ludwig. *Philosophical Investigations*. Translated by G. E. M. Anscombe. Oxford: Blackwell, 1958.

Wolfhart, Johannes C. "'Religious Literacy': Some Considerations and Reservations." *Method and Theory in the Study of Religion* (published online ahead of print, 2022): 1–28.

Womack, Deanna Ferree. "From History of Religions to Interfaith Studies: A Theological Educator's Exercise in Adaptation." In *Interreligious/Interfaith Studies: Defining a New Field*, edited by Eboo Patel, Jennifer Howe Peace, and Noah Silverman, 16–25. Boston: Beacon Press, 2018.

——. *Neighbors: Christians and Muslims Building Community*. Louisville, KY: Westminster John Knox Press, 2020.

Woodhead, Linda. "The Secularization Thesis." Interview with David G. Robertson. *The Religious Studies Project* (podcast audio), April 16, 2012. https://tinyurl.com/29pmpr4s.

Wuthnow, Robert. *America and the Challenges of Religious Diversity*. Princeton, NJ: Princeton University Press, 2005.

Yeager, David Scott, and Carol S. Dweck. "Mindsets That Promote Resilience: When Students Believe That Personal Characteristics Can Be Developed." *Educational Psychologist* 47, no. 4 (2012): 302–14.

Zacher, Hannes, and Ute Kunzemann. "Wisdom in the Workplace." In *Applying Wisdom to Contemporary World Problems*, edited by Robert J. Sternberg, Howard C. Nusbaum, and Judith Glück, 255–92. Cham, Switzerland: Palgrave Macmillan, 2019.

Zakaria, Fareed. "Episode 83: The Politics of Emergency." Conversation with Sam Harris. *Making Sense* (podcast audio), June 23, 2017. https://tinyurl.com/2p8pzvsy.

Index of Names

A

Abdi, Cawo, 122–23, 123n12, 124
Abraham, 228, 229
Ackrill, John Lloyd, 308n87
Ahmad, Aisha-Nusrat, 188n97
Alcoholics Anonymous (AA), 11, 11n9
Aldwin, Carolyn, 300, 301n52, 301n53
Allocco, Amy L., 24n53, 26n66, 26n67,
    26n68, 26n69, 26n70, 29n80,
    29n81, 128n31, 128n32, 175n39,
    176n42, 189n98, 189n99,
    189n100
Alston, William, 17n28
Altmann, Alexander, 178n49
Amarasingam, Amarnath, 152n63
American Academy of Religion (AAR),
    36n124, 60, 146–47
American Historical Association
    (AHA), 36n124
American Political Science Association
    (APSA), 36n124
Ammerman, Nancy, 59, 59n65, 95–96,
    96n3, 96n4, 97n10, 98n12, 102,
    103n35, 121n5, 188n93, 240,
    240n26, 240n27, 241, 275, 276n6
Anacombe, G. E. M., 16n25
Anderson, Christina, 322n43
Andreassen, Bengt-Ove, 158, 158n91
Ansari, Aziz, 214n1
Anselm, 106n53, 259
Antonacopoulou, Elena P., 304n74
Aquinas, Thomas, 69, 70, 106n53
Aristotle, 69, 70, 106n53, 288n2, 288n3,
    288n4, 288n5, 288n6, 288n7, 291,
    291n16, 291n17, 293, 293n21

Arjuna, 192
Arnold, Russell C. D., 210, 210n45,
    210n46, 210n47, 320, 320n34
Asad, Talal, 238n14
Asprem, Egil, 206n31
Association for the Sociology of
    Religion (ASR), 36n124
Association of Interreligious/Interfaith
    Studies (AIIS), 36n124
Augustine, 106n53
Averroes, 106n53
Avolio, Bruce J., 301n56, 318n23

B

Baatz, Ursula, 56n57, 86, 86n27
Baird, Robert D., 71
Balboa, Rocky, 161, 166, 168, 170, 190,
    193
Bali, Vinita, 312, 312n4, 312n5, 332,
    332n88, 333, 333n90
Bangstad, Sindre, 239n22
Barlow, Rich, 224n30
Barnes, Michael, 146, 146n30, 146n31,
    154, 154n77, 155n78
Bartunek, Jean M., 304n74
Bataille, Georges, 239n19
Beabout, Gregory R., 331n81
Beauvoir, Simone de, 277n11
Beck, Ulrich, 136n80
Bell, David, 65, 65n3
Bellah, Robert N., 232n58
Bellofatto, Gina A., 39n3
Bennett, Milton J., 217, 217n7, 218, 218n9,
    220n20, 223, 223n26, 325, 325n50
Bennis, Warren, 311, 312, 333, 333n89

Berger, Peter L., 235, 235n1, 236, 240, 240n28, 240n29, 241, 241n31, 241n32, 241n34, 242, 242n35, 242n37, 242n38, 247, 247n62, 247n63, 247n64, 247n65, 249, 249n73, 249n74, 249n75
Berghuijs, Joantine, 65, 65n5, 84n15, 85, 85n22, 114, 115n94, 116n98, 116n99
Berlinerblau, Jacques, 237, 237n9, 237n10, 237n11, 239n21
Berthong, John, 82n10
Biederman, Patricia Ward, 333n89
Bird, Darlene L., 185n84
Blumenthal, David R., 177–78, 177n45, 177n46, 177n47, 178n48, 178n49, 178n50, 178n51
Bobrowicz, Ryszard, 202n20
Bock, Jan-Jonathan, 172n20, 173, 173n28, 174, 174n29, 174n31, 174n32, 174n33, 174n34, 175n37, 245, 245n51, 246, 246n58, 246n59, 246n60, 247, 248n66
Boorstein, Michelle, 1n2, 287n1
Borneman, John, 182n72
Bowker, John, 99n20
Bradstock, Helen, 11n9
Brady, Bernard V., 336n102
Brazier, David, 329n70
Brinkmann, Svend, 326, 326n57, 327, 327n61, 328n63, 334–35, 334n95, 334n96, 334n97, 334n98, 335n99, 336
Brodd, Jeffrey, 18n31, 20
Brodeur, Patrice, 172, 172n22, 190, 190n103
Bruce, Steve, 82n11, 83, 83n14, 115, 115n95, 115n96, 115n97, 135, 135n71, 135n72, 136, 136n73, 136n74, 136n75, 136n76, 136n77, 136n78, 136n79, 136n80
Buber, Martin, 155
Bullivant, Stephen, 106n51
Burke, Peter J., 49n32, 50, 50n35, 50n36, 80n1
Burns, James MacGregor, 318, 318n24

Bush, George W., 141
Byock, Jesse, 90, 90n44, 90n45

C

Cabrara, Daniel, 4n12
Cadeddu, F., 148n41
Caldwell, Tommy, 168, 169, 169n12, 169n13, 170, 171n18, 181
Cameron, K. S., 301n56
Campbell, David, 262, 262n17, 262n18, 262n20, 262n21, 262n22, 262n23, 278, 278n14, 278n15
Cannella, Gaille, 188, 188n97
Canovan, Margaret, 237n7
Carrara Pavan, Milena, 54n53
Casanova, José, 20, 20n40, 20n41, 236n2, 237n8, 239n19, 240n23
Chan, Gary K. Y., 331n81
Chan, W. Y. Alice, 151n57, 152n62, 158n92, 299n43
Christensen, Sara, 309, 309n88, 311n1, 317, 317n20
Chryssides, George D., 25n58
Clausen, Geoffrey D., 24n53, 128n31
Cobb, John, Jr., 277n11
Coco, Angela, 49n30, 49n33, 49n34, 52, 52n44, 53n49, 57, 57n62, 61n72, 66, 66n7, 66n8
Coleman, Monica, 72, 72n37
Collier, Stephen J., 92, 93n51, 93n56
Collins, Harry, 315n11, 315n12, 315n14
Connolly, William, 239n19
Connor, Phillip, 321n37
Conroy, James, 145–46, 146n29
Cook, Robert, 91n46
Cooper, Cary L., 309n88
Cooper, Travis Warren, 186n86
Cornille, Catherine, 81n6, 89n37, 156n83, 300, 300n49, 300n50
Correia-Harker, Benjamin P., 211
Cory, Catherine A., 258n8
Costello, Gaberial J., 308n87
Cotter, Christopher, 123n13, 238n15
Cracknell, Kenneth, 201n18
Creed, Apollo, 166

D

Daft, Richard, 327, 327n60
Damocles, 168
Davie, Grace, 241, 241n33
Davis, Daryl, 274, 275, 278n13
Davis, Miles, 314–15, 316
Denis, Jean-Louis, 332n86
Dhiman, Satinder, 331n78
Diller, Jeanine, 22n50, 31n98, 35, 35n116,
    36, 36n125, 80n5, 82n11, 83n12
Dinham, Adam, 141, 143, 143n17, 145,
    145n27, 145n28, 146, 146n29,
    146n32, 149n44, 149n45, 149n46,
    150, 150n47, 150n48, 150n49,
    150n50, 150n51, 150n52, 150n53,
    151n54, 152n60
Dong, Mengxi, 288n8
Dostoevsky, Fyodor, 192
Drayton, Bill, 284
Dregni, Eric, 232n56
Drescher, Elizabeth, 48, 48n27
Drew, Rose, 82n11, 87, 87n30, 89n36,
    89n38, 135, 135n69
Droogers, André, 67n10, 68n15, 68n20,
    69n21, 71n27, 71n28, 71n29,
    71n30, 71n31, 73, 73n42, 75,
    75n51, 76n53, 80n2, 130, 130n40,
    130n41, 137, 205, 205n25,
    205n26, 205n27, 205n29
Du Guy, Paul, 52n45
Dugan, K. M., 73n43
Dunbar, Scott Daniel, 24, 24n54, 24n55,
    28–29, 28n78, 29n79, 31–32,
    32n101, 32n102, 319n31
Dunning, Susan Bilysnkyj, 237n6
Durkheim, Émile, 13, 14, 14n17, 240
Dutton, J. E., 301n56
Dweck, Carol S., 167n7

E

Eaghll, Tenzan, 158n90, 159, 159n94,
    159n95, 160, 238, 238n17,
    238n18, 299n45
Eck, Diana, 134n60, 148, 148n42,
    157n87, 173, 173n23, 231–32,

231n55, 233, 233n60, 247, 248,
    248n67, 248n71, 249, 249n72,
    249n76, 249n77, 249n78, 250–52,
    251n81, 251n82, 252–53, 252n84,
    252n86, 252n87, 252n88, 253,
    253n89, 253n91, 253n92, 253n93
Edwards, John, 66n7
Edwards, Paul, 91n47
Eliade, Mircea, 209, 209n44
Elijah Interfaith Institute, 275
Ellithorpe, Anne-Marie, 284n34
Elon University, 23–24, 26
Engelstad, Fredrik, 198n3
Engelsviken, T., 243n40
Enstedt, Daniel, 159, 159n96, 159n97,
    160
European Society of Intercultural
    Theology and Interreligious
    Studies (ESITIS), 36n124
Eyvindarason, Helgi "Magri (the Lean),"
    91

F

Fahy, John, 172n20, 173, 173n28, 174,
    174n29, 174n31, 174n32, 174n33,
    174n34, 175n37, 245, 245n51,
    246, 246n58, 246n59, 246n60,
    247, 248n66
Faiths, Neighbors, Changemakers
    (FNC), 284
Farias, Miguel, 106n51, 329n70
Fernhout, Rein, 67n10
Ferrari, Michael, 332n84
Ferrero, Ignacio, 331n81
Fielitz, Maik, 188n97
Finnegan, Amy, 181n65
Fleishman, Edwin A., 297n39
Fletcher, Jeannine Hill, 28, 28n76,
    28n77, 52n46, 53, 53n50, 57,
    57n61, 57n63, 57n64, 59, 59n66,
    60, 60n67, 60n68, 60n70, 61,
    61n71, 67n12, 89n40, 175,
    175n40, 180n59, 192n110, 280,
    280n21, 281–82, 281n22, 281n23,
    281n24, 281n25, 282n26

Flood, Gavin, 32n103
Ford, David, 257, 257n5
Fornet-Betancourt, R., 54n53, 223n25
Foucault, Michael, 334n97
Fournier, Marc A., 288n8
Francis (Pope), 68, 68n16
Francis, Matthew, 145, 145n27, 145n28, 146, 146n29, 146n32, 150, 150n49, 150n50, 150n51, 150n52, 150n53, 151n54, 152n60
Fredericks, James L., 200n7, 265, 265n27
Freud, Sigmund, 14, 14n14, 14n15, 14n16
Fridy, Kevin, 173n28
Fukuyama, Francis, 226, 227, 227n41
Furlan, Timothy, 304, 304n72, 304n73

G

Gagnon, Caroline, 304, 305n75
Gallagher, Eugene V., 146, 146n35
Gallie, Walter B., 11n4
Garber, Greg, 289, 289n11
Gardner, John W., 4, 4n14, 5n15
Gates, Henry Louis, Jr., 178, 178n53, 179–80, 179n54, 179n55, 179n56, 179n57, 180n58
Geertz, Clifford, 13, 15, 15n19
Geisel, Theodor Seuss (Dr. Seuss), 214–16, 214n1, 218
Georgetown University, 173n25
Ghazi, Usra, 30n89
Giess, Mary Ellen, 173n26
Gill, Rahuldeep Singh, 167, 167n7, 251
Giorda, Maria Chiara, 148, 148n41
Glatzer, Nahum A., 178n49
Glück, Judith, 3n10
God, 228, 229
Goldmill, Mickey, 165, 165n2, 166, 170, 190
Goleman, Daniel, 325, 325n52
Goodman, Kathleen, 173n26
Gordon, Jane Anna, 178n53, 180, 180n60, 180n61, 180n62
Gordon, Lewis, 178n53

Gort, Jerald, 67n10
Gosling, Jonathan, 332n86, 332n87
Graff, Harvey J., 160n104
Green, Todd, 125n24
Gregg, Heather, 174n30
Gregg, Stephen E., 25n58, 123–24, 123n13, 123n14, 123n15, 124n16, 124n17
Greig, Alastair, 221n21
Griffiths, Morwanna, 67n12, 89n40
Grim, Brian J., 39, 39n3, 152n59, 321n37
Grossman, Igor, 288n8
Grung, Anne Hege, 204, 242n40, 249n75, 270, 270n42, 271, 271n44, 277n11
Gustafson, Hans, 2n3, 21n44, 23n52, 34n112, 51n42, 82n10, 101n26, 121n4, 140n5, 153n73, 165n1, 175n40, 176n41, 198n2, 224n34, 267n28, 271n43, 274n1, 276n6, 276n7, 276n8, 279n16, 284n34, 289n9, 289n10, 294n22, 295n23, 300n48, 301n58, 314n6, 314n8, 331n79, 331n82, 334n93, 336n101
Gutman, Huck, 334n97

H

Haider, John, 1n1, 293n20
Haidt, Jonathan, 280n19
Halafoff, Anna, 175, 175n37, 192n110
Hall, David D., 96n2, 97n7, 98n11, 101n27
Hall, Stuart, 52, 52n45
Hallowell, Ronan, 224n31
Hammoudi, Abdellah, 182n72
Hampton, K., 191n108
Hancock, Herbie, 314, 314n9
Harbakk, Ernst, 243n40
Harding, Francis D., 297n39
Harris, Grove, 189n101
Harris, Sam, 226n39
Hart, Paul't, 332n86
Hartley, Jean, 332n86

Hartman, Sven S., 68n20
Harvey, O. J., 280n18
Heath, Rachel A., 72n37
Heckman, Donald "Bud," 172, 172n21, 197
Hedges, Paul, 1n3, 10n3, 15n20, 15n21, 15n22, 15n23, 16n26, 20, 20n38, 20n39, 21–22, 21n43, 22n45, 24n57, 28, 28n74, 28n75, 30, 30n94, 31n99, 35, 35n118, 35n119, 37n132, 37n133, 37n134, 49n30, 49n33, 49n34, 52, 52n44, 53n49, 57, 57n62, 61n72, 66, 66n7, 66n8, 71, 72n32, 84, 84n18, 84n19, 85, 85n20, 85n21, 86n24, 86n25, 86n26, 125n21, 187, 187n91, 187n92, 203n21, 256n3, 258, 258n6, 258n7, 260n13
Hege Grung, Anne, 70, 71n26
Hegel, G. W. F., 14n13
Heidegger, Martin, 239n19
Hemingway, Ernest, 168, 168n11
Henderson, Gabe, 52n47
Henriksen, Jan-Olav, 186n87, 186n88
Henry, Andrew M., 10n1, 152n61
Henshaw, Mark E., 30n89
Hervieu-Léger, Danièle, 102, 102n32
Hewitt, John P., 50n38
Hickey, Wakoh Shannon, 29, 29n85, 296, 296n33, 302n60
Hijmans, Ellen, 205n28
Himes, Michael, 103, 103n37, 257, 257n4
Hirsch, E. D., 139n2, 140
Hitlin, Steven, 50n37, 50n38, 80, 80n4
Hoffman, Andrew J., 4n12
Hogg, Michael A., 50n37
Hollenbach, David, 247, 247n61
Hollerich, Michael, 258n8
Hood, William R., 280n18
Horkheimer, Max, 175, 175n40
Hudson, Tara D., 211
Hughes, Aaron W., 10n2
Hughes, Cherie, 146n35
Hulsether, Lucia, 305n78, 307, 307n84, 308

Huntington, Samuel P., 56n58, 56n59, 226, 226n38, 226n39, 227
Hursthouse, Rosalind, 291n14, 291n15, 292n18
Hurteau, Marthe, 304, 305n75
Hussain, Amir, 146n35
Hustedt Jacobsen, Rhonda, 141, 142n13, 143n14, 143n15, 143n16
Hustwit, J. R., 67n13, 72n35, 81, 81n7, 81n8, 205, 206n30
Hutchinson, Elizabeth, 174n29
Hutton, Patrick H., 334n97
Hwang, Alexander Y., 22n50
Hwelett, Sylvia Ann, 323n46
Hydra, 168

I
Ihm, Elliot, 206n31
Inazu, John, 246n55, 246n56
Inter-Belief Conversation Café, 203
Interfaith America (Interfaith Youth Core), 29, 200, 302
Ipgrave, Julia, 3n9, 22n48, 28n72, 30n91
Ishrak, Omar, 323, 323n46

J
Jackson, Brad, 325, 325n53, 330n75, 332N83, 332n86, 332n87
Jacob, 192, 228
Jacobs, T. Owen, 297n39
Jacobsen, Douglas, 141, 142, 142n13, 143, 143n14, 143n15, 143n16
Jacobsen, Rhonda Hustedt, 141, 142n13, 143n14, 143n15, 143n16
Jafralie, Sabrina, 151n58
James, William, 50
Janson, Marloes, 92–93, 92n50, 92n51, 92n52, 92n53, 92n54, 92n55, 92n57, 92n58, 103n36
Jaywickreme, Eranda, 331n80
Jefferson, Thomas, 228n46
Jenkins, Richard, 61n72
Jensen, Jeppe S., 67n14, 68n18
Jetzkowitz, Jens, 184, 184n81, 184n82, 184n83

Jha, Amishi P., 331n76, 332n85
Johnson, Andrew, 16n24
Johnson, Lyndon, 4
Johnson, Todd M., 39, 39n3
Jones, Robert P., 321n36
Jones, Stephen H., 143, 143n17, 149n44,
    149n45, 149n46, 150n47, 150n48
Jones, Trina Janiec, 178n52, 297,
    297n37, 297n38, 299n47, 300n51,
    302n60, 302n61, 303n66, 304n71
Jörg, Ton, 34n111
Jorgenson, Kevin, 171n18
Juergensmeyer, Mark, 207n39

K

Kalsky, Manuela, 84n15
Kaplan, Laura Duhan, 284n34
Kasimow, Harold, 86n28
Kaufman, Tone Stangeland, 186n87,
    186n88, 188, 188n94, 188n96
Kearney, Richard, 156n83
Keenan, John, 70, 70n24
Kerby, Lauren, 158n92
Kerry, John, 142, 142n11
Ketilsdottir, "Hyrna," 91
Kilpatrick, Robert, 152n59
Kim, Juensung J., 332n84
Kim, Marina, 285
Kimsey-House, Henry, 312, 312n3, 320,
    320n35, 325n54, 326n56, 327n62,
    328n64, 328n65, 329n68, 329n69,
    334n91, 334n92
Kineke, Liz, 292n19
King, Anna S., 15n20, 15n21, 15n22,
    15n23, 16n26, 20, 20n39, 21,
    21n43, 203n21
King, H., 54n53
Kinsella, Elizabeth Anne, 316n19
Klein, Mike, 181n65, 182n70, 182n71,
    182n73, 183, 183n74, 183n75,
    183n76, 183n77, 183n78, 183n79,
    190n102, 192n109
Knausgaard, Karl Ove, 315n12, 335–36,
    335n100
Knitter, Paul, 88n33

Kosky, Jeffrey L., 239n19
Kouzes, James M., 301n54, 327, 327n59,
    333n89
Kraemer, Hendrik, 71
Krishna, 192
Kubek, Elizabeth, 33, 34n110, 34n113
Küng, H., 223n25
Kunzemann, Ute, 316n17, 316n18
Kyung, Chung Hyun, 59

L

Lalljee, Mansur, 329n70
Lambert, Paul, 144n20
Lander, Shira, 125–26, 126n25,
    126n26
Landy, Thomas M., 247n61
Lane, Belden, 33, 33n107, 33n108,
    33n109
Lanman, Jonathan, 106n51
Lao Tzu, 314n7
Larsen, Hakon, 198n3
Larson, Marion H., 225n36, 226n36
Lau, D. C., 314n7
Lee, Lois, 106n51
Leeming, David A., 65n3
Lehrer, Jim, 314n9
Leinius, Johanna, 188n97
Leirvik, Oddbjørn, 1–2n3, 3n9, 22,
    22n47, 22n49, 25, 25n60, 30,
    30n92, 30n93, 31, 31n95, 31n100,
    32, 35n115, 35n121, 36–37,
    36n122, 37n131, 37n136, 236,
    236n3, 237n8, 237n12, 238n13,
    242, 242n40, 243, 243n41,
    243n42, 243n43, 243n44, 244,
    244n45, 244n46, 244n47, 244n48,
    249n75, 271, 271n43, 271n45,
    277n11, 319n31
Leopold, Anita Maria, 67n14, 68n18
Lester, Emile, 158n92
Levenson, Michael, 300, 301n52,
    301n53
Lévi-Strauss, Claude, 89n35
Levinas, Emmanuel, 277n11
Levine, Amy-Jill, 51n43

Levine, Deborah, 145, 145n23, 145n24, 145n25, 145n26
Lewis, Frank, 221n21
Lewis, Thomas A., 185, 186n85, 188n95
Li, Vivienne, 167n4
Lincoln, Bruce, 17n28
Lincoln, Yvonna, 188, 188n97
Lindbeck, George, 57
Lindheim, Tone, 156n85, 156n86, 157
Lindsay, Jenn, 3n11, 160n100, 296, 297n36, 301n55, 302n59
Lippy, Charles H., 96n2
Little, Layne, 18n31
Lombardi, Vince, 311–12
Lowe, Eugene, 146n35
Lowe, Margaret, 146–47n35
Lowery, Charles, 191n108
Luthans, Fred, 301n56

M

Machacek, David, 230, 231, 231n52, 231n53, 232–33, 232n56, 232n57, 233n59, 248, 248n68, 248n69
MacLaughlin, Nina, 335n100
Madden, Kathryn, 65n3
Maimonides, 106n53
Marable, Manning, 178, 178n53, 179–80, 179n54, 179n55, 179n56, 179n57, 180n58
Marcus, Benjamin P., 49n31, 141, 147, 147n37, 147n38, 147n39
Marino, Dan, 289
Marlon, Stanton, 65n3
Marshall, Melinda, 323n46
Martí, Gerardo, 133, 133n58, 133n59, 134, 134n60, 134n61, 134n62, 134n63, 134n64, 134n65, 134n66, 135n67, 135n68, 136n80, 187, 187n89, 187n90
Martin, Craig, 158n90
Martin, Jerry L., 260n12
Martin, Luther H., 334n97
Marty, Martin E., 244, 244n50, 245
Maruggi, Matthew, 301n57

Marx, Karl, 13, 14, 14n13, 240
Masao, Abe, 201, 201n15, 201n16, 201n17, 202
Masuzawa, Tomoko, 200, 200n10, 238n16
Matarazzo, James, 156n83
Maxwell, Nicholas, 4, 4n13
Mayhew, Matthew J., 211
Mcbean, Sylvester McMonkey, 214
McCarthy, Kate, 2, 2n7, 2n8, 22, 22n51, 25–26, 25n61, 26n63, 26n64, 26n65, 31, 31n96, 35, 35n117, 36, 36n126, 36n127, 36n128, 36n129, 36n130, 128n30, 175, 175n38, 295, 295n27, 295n28, 296, 296n31, 296n32, 296n34
McCloud, Sean, 67n14, 72, 72n36, 112–13, 113n81
McConeghy, David, 10n2
McCrary, Charles, 239n20
McCutcheon, Russel T., 10n2, 13, 13n12, 15n18, 17, 17n29, 19, 19n35, 21, 21n42, 24, 24n56, 25, 25n58, 135n70, 200n10
McEver, H. Bruce, 151n57
McGraw, Barbara A., 30n88, 143, 143n18, 148–49, 149n43, 154, 154n75, 154n76, 298, 317, 318, 318n22, 318n24, 318n25, 318n26, 318n27, 318n28, 321, 321n38, 321n39, 322, 322n41, 322n45, 323, 324, 324n48, 328, 328n66
McGuire, Meredith, 51, 51n39, 51n40, 51n41, 63, 63n1, 65, 65n4, 66, 66n9, 68n18, 68n19, 72, 73, 73n38, 73n40, 75, 75n52, 76, 76n56, 76n57, 81n6, 81n9, 87, 88n32, 89n35, 89n39, 90n42, 90n43, 91, 92n48, 97, 97n8, 98n12, 102, 102n34, 103, 103n38, 104n39, 104n40, 104n41, 104n42, 120, 121n3, 129, 129n35, 129n36, 129n37, 130, 130n38, 130n39, 276, 276n8
McKenzie, Jane, 304n74

McTurk, Tam, 327n61
Meir, Ephraim, 267n29
Melloni, A., 148n41
Meyer, Brigit, 98n13, 99n14, 99n15,
    99n16, 99n17, 99n18, 99n19
Meyer, Cassie, 22n50, 178n52, 297,
    297n37, 297n38, 299n47, 300n51,
    302n60, 302n61, 303n66, 304n71
Michael, George, 200
Miedema, Siebren, 158n92
Mikva, Rachel, 27, 27n71, 32, 32n104,
    32n105, 55, 55n56, 124n19, 125,
    125n20, 125n22, 125n23, 177n44,
    199n4, 200n9
Millis, Diane, 314n9
Mills, C. Wright, 135
Mischinski, Megan, 331n80
Moberly, R. W. L., 201n12, 201n13
Mogel, Wendy, 181, 181n64
Molloy, Michael, 18, 18n32, 18n33
Moore, Diane L., 60n69, 65, 65n6,
    141, 144, 144n21, 144n22, 146,
    146n35, 148, 157n87
Morgan, David, 98n13
Morin, Shauna, 211
Morris, Stephanie, 332n84
Mosher, Lucinda, 165n1, 309n89,
    334n93
Moyaert, Marianne, 3n9, 28, 28n73,
    126, 126n27, 155–56, 155n79,
    155n80, 155n81, 156n82, 156n84,
    157, 161, 175, 176, 176n41,
    265, 265n26, 268, 268n36, 295,
    295n29, 299n44, 302, 302n62
Müller, Max, 265
Mumford, Michael D., 297n39,
    312n2

N

Najle, Maxine, 321n36
Nealon, Kevin, 199n5
Neiss, Rori Picker, 172n21
Nelson-Pallmeyer, Jack, 181n65
Nisbet, Robert, 178
Noah, 228

Numrich, Paul D., 172n20, 173, 173n27
Nusbaum, Howard C., 3n10
Nystron, Bradley, 18n31

O

O'Connell, M., 175n40
O'Leary, Joseph S., 87n31
Olsen, Rolv, 243n40
Omer, Atalia, 25, 25n59
Ong, Aihwa, 92, 92n56, 93n51
Onishi, Bradley B., 236n4, 239n19
Orsi, Robert, 97, 97n9, 101n27, 101n28,
    101n29, 101n30, 101n31, 102,
    102n33, 121–22, 121n6, 122n7,
    122n8, 122n9, 127n28, 127n29,
    128n33, 275–76, 276n7
Ostwald, Martin, 288n2
Otto, Rudolf, 12, 12n11
Owen, Suzanne, 11n5, 123n13, 159,
    159n98, 160

P

Paine, Crispin, 98n13
Pálsson, Herman, 91n47
Panikkar, Raimon, 54, 54n53, 54n54,
    68, 68n17, 72n34, 73, 73n43,
    74n44, 77, 77n59, 77n60, 78,
    78n62, 78n63, 80n3, 213, 217n5,
    218, 218n10, 219n13, 220n19,
    223, 225, 225n35, 231, 231n54,
    251n83, 260, 260n14, 273–74,
    274n1
Parents Circle-Families Forum (PCFF),
    58, 274–75
Parry, Ken, 325, 325n53, 330n75,
    332n83, 332n86, 332n87
Patel, Eboo, 2, 2n5, 2n6, 22, 22n50, 29,
    29n82, 29n84, 31n98, 35, 35n114,
    35n120, 56, 56n59, 57n60, 143,
    143n19, 153, 153n71, 153n72,
    154n74, 156n83, 157n87, 160,
    160n101, 172, 172n22, 173n26,
    174n35, 190, 190n103, 191,
    191n104, 191n105, 191n106,

200, 213, 214n1, 216, 216n2,
217n4, 218, 218n8, 218n11,
219, 219n12, 219n14, 220n17,
233, 233n61, 244, 244n49, 245,
245n54, 248n70, 280n19, 295,
295n25, 295n26, 298, 299n42,
302, 302n63, 303, 303n64,
303n65, 307, 307n82, 307n83,
308, 308n85, 308n86, 317, 319,
319n29, 319n30, 320, 320n32,
320n33, 325, 325n51
Patton, Laurie, 230n51, 253,
253n90
Pavan, Milena Carrara, 217n6
Peace, Jennifer, 22n50, 30n87,
31n98
Pearson, B. A., 68n17
Pedersen, Kusumita P., 172n20, 174,
175n36
Pennington, Brian K., 24n53, 128n31,
147n35, 305, 305n77, 305n78,
306, 306n79, 306n80, 306n81,
307, 309n89
Pettigrove, Glen, 291n14, 291n15,
292n18
Phoenix, 168
Piedmont, R. L., 301n53
Pierce, Elinor, 303n66, 303n67, 303n68,
334n93
Pio, Edwina, 152n59
Pittman, Allan, 316n19
Plate, S. Brent, 98n13
Plato, 106n53, 267
Platzner, Robert, 18n31
Plotinus, 106n53
Pluralism Project, 250, 253
Polanyi, Michael, 313, 315, 315n13
Pollack, Detlef, 240n25
Posner, Barry Z., 301n54, 327, 327n59,
333n89
Pratt, Timothy, 152n59
Primiano, Leonard Norman, 100n21,
100n25
Prothero, Stephen, 18, 18n34, 124n18,
140, 140n6, 140n7, 141, 141n9,
142, 142n10, 142n12, 143, 148,
151, 151n56, 153n70, 160n99,
222, 222n23, 222n24
Pugliese, Marc A., 22n50
Putnam, Robert, 217n3, 262, 262n17,
262n18, 262n20, 262n21, 262n22,
262n23, 278, 278n14, 278n15
Pye, Michael, 67n11, 68, 69n21, 327n58

Q
Quack, Johannes, 241n30
Quinn, R. E., 301n56

R
Race, Alan, 88n33, 134n60, 261, 261n16
Raelin, Joe, 317n21
Rahner, Karl, 57
Rajewicz, Phillip, 332n84
Reeve, Henry, 221n21
Reineke, Martha, 147n35
Religious Literacy Project (RLP)
(Religion and Public Life (RPL))
(Harvard University), 144
Ricardo, David, 229
Richard, Orlando, 323n46
Ridgeway, Cecilia L., 50n37
Riis, Ole, 245, 245n52
Ringgren, Helmer, 68n20
Rizo-Patron, Eileen, 156n83
Roberts, Michelle Voss, 75, 75n50,
82n11, 83, 83n13, 84, 84n16,
84n17, 85, 85n23, 87, 87n31,
90n41
Roberts, Patrick S., 158n92
Robertson, David G., 11n9, 123n13
Rockenbach, Alyssa N., 211, 283n28,
283n29, 283n30, 283n31
Rodriguez, Lidia, 2n3
Rogstad, Jon, 198n3
Roozen, David, 1, 287
Rose, Or N., 30n87, 334n93
Rosenbach, William E., 4n14, 312n4,
325n52
Rosenberg, Marshall, 252, 252n85

Rothausen, Teresa, 309, 309n88, 311n1, 317, 317n20, 331n77
Rubens, Heather Miller, 30n90
Rudolph, Kurt, 71

S

Sacks, Jonathan, 213, 225, 226, 226n37, 226n39, 227, 227n40, 227n42, 227n43, 228, 228n44, 228n45, 228n46, 229, 229n47, 229n48, 229n49, 230, 230n50, 253
Sahgal, Neha, 109n67
Sarah, 228, 229
Sax, Benjamin E., 30n90
Schaefer, Donovan, 238n15, 238n17
Schell, Hannah, 302n63
Schilderman, Hans, 84n15
Schlichte, Gianna Magdalena, 188n97
Schmidt-Leukel, Perry, 67n11, 69n22, 70, 70n25, 72n33, 73n41, 74, 74n45, 74n46, 74n47, 74n48, 74n49, 76, 77, 77n58, 88, 88n33, 224n33, 261n15, 267, 267n29, 267n30, 267n31, 268, 268n32, 268n33, 268n34, 268n35, 269n37, 269n38, 269n39, 269n40, 269n41
Schmiedel, Ulrich, 156n83
Schulson, Michael, 56n60
Schwartz, Barry, 303n69, 315, 315n10, 315n15, 316n16, 330n73, 330n74
Seuss, Theodor Seuss, 213
Shady, Sara L. H., 225n36, 226n36
Sharma, A., 73n43
Sharpe, Kenneth E., 303n69, 315, 315n10, 315n15, 316n16, 330n73, 330n74
Shaw, Martha, 139n3
Shaw, Rosalind, 72n33, 73, 73n39
Shek, Richard, 18n31
Sheldrake, Philip, 101, 101n26
Sherbin, Laura, 323n46
Sherif, Carolyn W., 280n18
Sherif, Muzafer, 279, 280n18
Shook, John R., 241n30

Silverman, Noah, 36, 36n123, 173n28
Sinn, Simone, 126n25
Sison, Alejo José G., 331n81
Skibbins, David, 312n3, 320, 320n35, 325n54, 327n62, 328n64, 328n65, 329n68, 329n69, 334n91, 334n92
Smaling, Adri, 205n28
Smart, Ninian, 17, 17n27, 159, 207n39
Smith, J. Shakiyla, 191n107, 192n111
Smith, Jonathan D., 146, 146n30, 146n31, 154, 154n77, 155n78
Smith, Jonathan Z., 19, 19n36
Smith, Simon G., 185n84
Smith, Wilfred Cantwell, 200, 200n7, 200n8, 201, 201n11, 201n14, 201n18, 202, 267n29, 269, 269n37
Snook, Jennifer, 54n51
Soules, Kate E., 151n58
Spencer, Nick, 152n60
Stark, Rodney, 47n26, 107, 108n63, 113n86, 262, 262n19
Steen-Johnsen, Kari, 198n3
Stendahl, Krister, 153, 153n73, 160
Sternberg, Robert J., 3n10, 296, 296n30, 304n70, 316n18
Stets, Jan E., 49n32, 50, 50n35, 50n36, 80n1
Stewart, Charles, 68, 68n18, 72n33, 73, 73n39
Stiek, Jessica, 152n62
Stiles, Erin, 18n31
Stoddard, Bard, 158n90
Stone, Jon R., 265n25
Store, John, 332n86
Stortz, Martha E., 301n57
Strandenæs, Thor, 243n40
Stringer, Martin D., 97n6, 130–33, 130n42, 130n43, 130n44, 130n45, 130n46, 130n47, 132, 132n48, 132n49, 132n50, 132n51, 132n53, 133n54, 133n55, 133n57, 283, 284n32, 284n33
Stryker, Sheldon, 80n4
Suárez, Margarita, 29, 29n85, 296, 296n33, 302n60

Sutcliffe, Steve, 123n13
Sutherland, Ian, 332n86, 332n87
Suthren Hirst, Jacqueline, 11n5
Sweetman, Will, 19n37
Swidler, Leonard, 11, 11n8, 54, 54n52,
    86, 86n29, 141n8, 172n20,
    203n22, 277, 277n10, 277n12

T

Tajfel, Henri, 279n17
Taleb, Nassim Nicholas, 167, 168,
    168n8, 168n9, 168n10, 169–70,
    180–81, 181n63
Tamayo-Acosta, J. J., 54n53, 223n25
Tatari, Muna, 3n9
Taves, Ann, 11n7, 11n9, 18n30, 205,
    206n31, 206n32, 206n33, 207,
    207n34, 207n35, 207n36, 207n37,
    207n38, 207n39, 208, 208n40,
    208n41, 209, 209n42, 209n43, 210
Taylor, Charles, 238, 242, 242n39, 246,
    246n57
Taylor, Mark, 239n19
Taylor, Robert L., 4n14
Thatamanil, John, 82n10
Thorkelson, Thorgeir, 90
Tiflati, Hicham, 152n63
Tillich, Paul, 11, 11n6, 329, 329n67
Timani, Hussam S., 284n34
Tocqueville, Alexis de, 221, 221n21
Trice, Michael Reid, 126n25
Tylor, Edward Burnett, 12, 12n10

U

Uddin, Asma, 242n36
Ulrich, David, 332n86
Undheim, S., 158n91
US Air Force, 202

V

van den Breemer, Rosemaire, 237n8,
    239n19
van der Leeuw, Gerard, 71

van der Veer, Peter, 72, 72n33
Van Harshkamp, Anton, 75n51, 205n25,
    205n26
Vanderwilt, Jeffrey, 224n29
VanLaningham, Erin, 302n63
Varnon-Hughes, Stephanie L., 156n83
Vecchio, Kristi Del, 36, 36n123
Vervaeke, John, 332n84
von der Braak, André, 84n15
von der Lippe, Marie, 158n91
Voss Roberts, Michelle, 75, 75n50,
    82n11, 83, 83n13, 84, 84n16,
    84n17, 85, 85n23, 87, 87n31,
    90n41
Vroom, Hendrik, 67n10

W

Waggoner, Michael D., 147n37
Wakelin, Michael, 152n60
Wald, Kenneth, 173n28
Walker, Nathan C., 147n37, 151n57,
    152n63, 152n64, 158n93
Walumbwa, Fred O., 318n23
Ward, Keith, 259, 259n9, 260n10,
    260n11, 267n29
Weber, Max, 240
Weber, Todd J., 318n23
Weigel, George, 56
Weisse, Wolframm, 3n9, 220n17
Wernicke-Olesen, Bjarne, 329n70,
    330n71, 330n72
Wertheimer, Linda K., 158n92
Wessels, Anton, 67n10
Wexler, Jay, 152, 152n65, 152n67
White, B. Jack, 280n18
White, Kevin, 221n21
Wieseltier, Leon, 214n1
Wilhelm, Kaiser, 232n56
Wilkins, Natalie, 191n107, 192n111
Williams, Peter W., 96n2
Williard, Mara, 157n87
Windham-Hughes, Colleen, 22n50,
    31n98
Winkler, Ulrich, 2n3

Winston, Kimberly, 237n11
Wittgenstein, Ludwig, 16, 16n25, 315n11
Wolfhart, Johannes C., 139n3, 140n4, 148, 148n40, 152n68, 153n69, 157n88, 158n89, 160, 160n103, 299n46
Womack, Deanna Ferree, 29, 30n86, 31n97, 32, 32n106, 37n135, 217n7, 224, 224n27, 224n28, 224n32, 296, 296n35, 324, 324n49
Woodhead, Linda, 240n24
Wuthnow, Robert, 278n14
Wyller, Trygve, 237n8, 239n19

Y

Yeager, David Scott, 167n7
Youndt, Mark A., 4n14
Young, Iris Marion, 53n50, 281n24

Z

Zaccaro, Stephen J., 297n39
Zacher, Hannes, 316n17, 316n18
Zakaria, Fareed, 226n39
Zalta, Edward N., 291n14
Zavos, John, 11n5
Ziad, Homayra, 30n90
Zuckerman, Phil, 241n30

Index of Subjects

A

academic theology, 257
acceptance, 223
action planning, 183
activism, 28
adaption, 223
adversity, 170
agnosticism, 106. *See also* unaffiliated religious identity
American Civil Religion, 232n58
antifragility, 167–69, 170
antireductionism, 16
anti-self-help, 334
Antisemitism, 29. *See also* Jews/Judaism
antisyncretism, 76
appealing to the heart, 274
applied dimension, of interreligious studies (IRS), 29, 296
appreciative knowledge, of religions, 153–54
architecture, vernacular, 100
articulated worldview, 207
Ashoka, 284–85
assemblage, 92–94
assimilation, 227, 231, 233
astrology, 113
atheism, 46, 47, 106. *See also* unaffiliated religious identity
Aunt Susan Principle, 262, 278
Australia, 47
authentic identity, 53–54
authentic leadership model, 301
awareness, 324–26

B

Babel concept, 230–33
barriers, 217–19, 225, 228
"Being there," 182n72
belief, 200–1
belonging, 84, 86
bereavement, 274–75, 335–36
Birmingham Conversations, 131
Black Protestants, 106
Black studies, 178–81
blasé attitude, 220, 220n16, 222
blasphemy law (Pakistan), 243
The Blessing of the Skinned Knee (Mogel), 181
bludgeons, 219, 225
blurring, 219–23, 225, 227, 228
Boko Haram, 122–23
Boston Marathon bomb attack, 306–7
both religious and spiritual (BRS), 110
Boundless Openness, 201–2
boxing, 166, 170
bricolage, 89
bridges, 223–25
broken nose analogy (Rocky Balboa), 166, 170
bubble concept, 230–33
Buddhism, 12, 17, 41, 43–44, 269
bunkers, 216–17, 225, 228
business, 144n20, 148, 152, 321–24, 322n41

C

Cadet Chapel (US Air Force), 202
Campus Compact, 285

Canada, 47
case-study method, 302–4, 320
casting curses (evil eye), 113
Catholicism, 66, 103, 107, 108, 113
changemaking, 284–86
China, 43, 44
Chrislam, 93, 103, 121–22
Christianity
  assemblage and, 93
  assumptions regarding, 121–22
  communal conversion within,
    90–91
  cultural understandings within, 90
  dangerous religious ideas regarding,
    125
  differences within, 58
  diversity within, 282
  domination of, 141
  family resemblance approach and, 17
  identity of, 54, 282
  Japanese, 70n23
  Korean, 59–60
  literacy within, 141
  Native American, 70n23
  natural increase and, 45
  North American, 59
  in politics, 141–42
  public opinion regarding, 110
  religious identity of, 57–58, 59–60
  secularism and, 238
  single religious belonging (SRB)
    and, 83
  solidarity outside of, 281
  statistics regarding, 40, 41–42, 57,
    106–7
  yoga and, 113
The Circle of Praxis, 182–83, 191
civic competency, 148
civic interfaith landscape, 319
civic interfaith leadership, 191
civic pluralism, 225, 245, 247–50,
  253–54
civilizations, 226n39, 230
clash of civilizations theory/thesis, 56,
  56n59, 226, 226n39

Co-Active Leadership model, 312, 325,
  328–29
code, within religion, 18
codes of conduct and ethics, 304–5
coexistence, 220
Cold War, 226, 226n39
collective hybridity, 90
commitment, pluralism, 252–53
communication, intercultural encounter
  and, 220. See also conversation;
  dialogue
community, within religion, 18
Comparative Theology (CT), 260,
  265–67, 269
compassion, 294
condemnation, 219
conquest, 219
contempt, 218
convergence, bridgebuilding and,
  224–25
conversation. See also dialogue
  changemaking and, 285–86
  interspiritual, 203
  personal and social identity within,
    51
  religious, 150, 156–57
  research as, 32n103
  secularity and, 242–44
conversion, communal, 90–91
COVID-19 pandemic, 186
craft, development of, 302–3
creed, 18
cross-cultural similarity, 220
cultivation, 324
cultural competence model, 295n23
cultural differences, 322–23
culture, research of religion within,
  32n103
cultus, 18

D
dancing, 209
dangerous religious ideas, 125–27
Daodejing, 314
Daoism, 313–14

"Dao of Phronesis," 314
The Dawn Wall, 168–69
Declaration of Independence, 228n46
defense, 218
denial, 217
descriptive analysis, 182–83
descriptive usage, of interreligious
    studies (IRS), 23–27
Developmental Model of Intercultural
    Sensitivity (DMIS), 217
developmental psychology, 315n11
dialogue. *See also* conversation
    bridgebuilding and, 224–25
    changemaking and, 285–86
    function of, 255, 277, 286
    interfaith, 283–84, 307
    interfaith, friendship and, 283–84
    pluralism and, 253
    study of, 31–32
Dialogue Decalogue, 203n22
difference
    barriers response to, 217–19, 225,
        228
    blasé attitude toward, 220, 220n16
    bludgeons response to, 219, 225
    blurring response to, 219–23, 225,
        227, 228
    bridges response to, 223–25
    bunker response to, 216–17, 225, 228
    cultural, 322–23
    dignity of, 225–30, 254
    leveraging, 323–24
    as mutual benefit, 230
    status quo and, 221
disenchantment, 239n19
disposition, 291
diversity
    as asset, 280
    barriers response to, 217–19, 225,
        228
    bludgeons response to, 219, 225
    blurring response to, 219–23, 225,
        227, 228
    bridges response to, 223–25
    bunker response to, 216–17, 225, 228

divisiveness within, 280
    energetic engagement with, 250–51
    misconceptions regarding, 280
    pluralism *versus,* 248
    tribalism and, 225
    unity and, 229
    universalism and, 225
dreams, 113
dual-belonging religio-secular citizens,
    242
Dutch/The Netherlands, 110, 115,
    115n94, 116
duties, within religion, 10

E
Easter, 92n49
economics, 229
ecumenical, 198
education
    Christian tradition within, 255
    interfaith movement within, 173n26
    interreligious studies (IRS) within,
        319–20
    multiculturalism within, 173n26
    religious literacy and, 151, 157–58
    theological currents within, 255–56
emotion, religious experience and, 132
empathy, 252, 300
enacted worldview, 207
enchanted secularity, 239n19
encounter
    challenges from, 276–77
    interreligious, 278
    religious literacy and, 161
    self-awareness from, 286
    through relationship, 272, 273
End of History (Fukuyama), 227
enlightenment, 210
Environmental Studies, 183–84
essentialism, 120–24
essentialist approach, 12–13
ethnic studies, 178
Eurocentric context, 241
Europe, 40–41, 42, 45, 241
Evangelicals, 106

evil eye (casting curses), 113
excellence, development of, 302–3
exclusivism, 261
experience, 208–9, 330–31
Experiencing the World's Religions
(Molloy), 18
extraterrestrials, 113

F

faith, 200–1, 259
faith communities, 26
family resemblance approach, 16–18,
222
favoritism, 279
feminist thought, 60, 281
Folk Religions, 40, 41, 44, 99n20
forged solidarity, 52–53
fractal theory of religious diversity, 88
fragility, 168
France, 47
freedom from religion, 136n80, 237
freedom of religion, 13, 136n80, 237
friendship
changemaking and, 284
cosmic dance of, 277
defined, 277
encounters through, 272
importance of, 273
interfaith dialogue and, 283–84
inter/intrapersonal changemaking
and, 284–86
interreligious, 274, 275–77
mutual sharpening within, 277
religious difference and, 133
solidarities through, 279–83
spillover effect and, 278–79
team work and, 280
functionalist approach, 13–16

G

geopolitical relations, religious literacy
within, 148
Germany, 47
ghosts, 113

global capitalism, 227–28
God
attributes of, 106
belief statistics regarding, 105–10,
111, 112
classical theistic account of, 106n53
difference and, 229
influence of, 239
personal response to, statistics
regarding, 109
God Is Not One (Prothero), 18
good intentions, 220
Great Britain, 47
The Great Pioneers, 82n11
grief, 274–75, 335–36

H

healthcare, religious literacy within,
144, 152
heart, appealing to, 274
heaven, 262–64
Hinduism, 40, 41, 43
history, interreligious studies (IRS)
within, 35
Holy Envy, 153–54, 153n73, 160
Homeland, 77
honesty, 291–92
horoscopes, 113
hunkering down, 216–17
Huntington thesis, 226n39
The Hybrid, 82n11
hybrid identities, 281, 282
hybridity, religious, 89–92

I

Iceland, 90–92
identity
authentic, 53–54
categories of, 55, 58
defined, 48–49
hybridity of, 281, 282
logic of, 53, 281–82
personal, 50–51
as pluralistic, 79–80

relationships and, 55–61
social, 50–51
theory of, 79–80
types of, 282
identity, religious. *See* religious identity
identity wheel, 210
ignorance, 217
imagination, interreligious theology
    and, 268
immersion, Comparative Theology
    (CT) and, 266
immigration, 231–33, 232n56
Immigration and Nationality Act,
    231–32
inclusivism, 248, 261
incorporation, 248
India, 43, 54
indifference, 3, 218, 287
Indonesia, 42–43
in-group bias, 279
insertion, 182, 183
integration, 223, 224, 268
interbelief, 203
intercultural encounter, 231
interdisciplinary usage, of interreligious
    studies (IRS), 34–38
interfaith, concept of, 197, 198–204
interfaith dialogue, 283–84, 307. *See
    also* conversation; dialogue
Interfaith Diversity Experiences &
    Attitudes Longitudinal Survey
    (IDEALS) research survey, 283
Interfaith Engagement (IFE)
    categorizing within, 121
    civic religious pluralism, 26
    critiques of, 189n100
    defined, 25–26, 172, 184
    interreligious studies (IRS) as
        mutually beneficial to, 176–85,
        192–93
    interreligious studies (IRS) *versus,*
        170–71, 189–90
    Lived Religion (LR) approach and,
        128
    normative commitments of, 185

overview of, 306–7
purpose of, 307
interfaith leadership, 143–44, 321–24,
    322n41, 325
interfaith literacy, 299
interfaith movement
    characteristics of, 173–74
    defined, 172
    goals of, 175
    interreligious studies (IRS) *versus,*
        25–26, 175
    motives for, 174–75
    term use by, 199–200
interfaith studies, 29–30
interfaith wisdom, 288–94
inter/intrapersonal changemaking,
    284–86
interlifeway, 204–11
international secular intelligentsia,
    241
interreligious awareness, 32–33
interreligious conflict, 306
interreligious conversations, 130–33
interreligious dialogue, 242–44
interreligious encounter, 157
interreligious friendship, 274, 275–77
interreligiousity, 198–204, 276
interreligious learning, 137–38, 299
interreligious literacy
    benefits of, 299
    experiential encounters and, 156
    interreligious sensibility and, 156
    lokahi (harmony through diversity)
        and, 154–55
    overview of, 153–57
    religious literacy *versus,* 155
    sufficiency of, 157–61
interreligious phronesis (IP). *See also*
    phronesis
    consistency of, 292
    defined, 4, 157
    development of, 4, 287–88
    dimensions of, 294–305
    education and practice of, 293–94
    everyday leadership and, 313–24

experience importance within, 330–31
as guiding virtue, 292–94
interfaith wisdom within, 308
Know How (techne) of, 302–5, 313, 315
Know What (episteme) of, 297–99, 313
Know Who (empatheia) of, 299–300, 313
Know Why (sophia) of, 300–2, 313
for leadership, 324–33
longitudinal development of, 293
right reasons and, 305–8
scholar-practitioner model and, 192
social dimension of, 317
wherewithal and, 289–90
interreligious studies (IRS)
as academic field, 25–26
applied dimension of, 29, 296
benefits of, 2
case-study method within, 302–4
categorizing within, 121
civic approach to, 191
contextual aids to, 175–76
critiques of, 189n100
defined, 1–2, 1–2n3, 21–22, 171
descriptive characteristic of, 23–27
field role of, 309
function of, 189
indifference regarding, 3
interactions and, 23
Interfaith Engagement (IFE) as mutually beneficial to, 176–85, 192–93, 305
Interfaith Engagement (IFE) versus, 170–71, 189
interfaith movement versus, 25–26, 175
interfaith solidarity and, 28
interreligious phronesis (IP) and, 295
Lived Religion (LR) benefits to, 118–28
multi-, inter-, and transdisciplinary characteristic of, 34–38

normative characteristic of, 27–30
overview of, 21–23, 38
practical capabilities from, 295–96
prescriptive characteristic of, 27–30
purpose of, 295
relations and, 23
research agenda for, 2
scholar-activism within, 175
self-implicating characteristic of, 30–34
transparency of, 185
interreligious theology, 260, 267–69, 271
Interreligious Understanding core value (Georgetown University), 173n25
intersectionality, 55, 60
interspirituality, 203
interworldview, 204–11
intragroup diversity, 61
intragroup friendship, 61
intrasubjective religious diversity, 224
Invitation to World Religions textbook, 18
Ireland, 110
ISIS, 122–23
Islam
assemblage and, 93
assumptions regarding, 121–22
dangerous religious ideas regarding, 125n24
growth of, 123
misinformation and, 149
natural increase and, 45
reclaiming, 122–23
September 11, 2001 and, 122, 227–28
statistics regarding, 40, 41, 42–43
value roots within, 322
isolation, 217
Italy, 110

J

Japan, 43
Japanese Christianity, 70n23
Jesus, 107

Jewish studies, 177–78
Jews/Judaism
  dangerous religious ideas regarding,
    125
  misinformation and, 149
  multiple religious belonging (MRB)
    of, 114–15
  religious practices of, 114
  statistics regarding, 40, 41, 44–45,
    106–7, 108, 109
"jumping into the fray," 180, 192
Justice and Peace Studies, 181–82,
    181n65

K

Know How (techne), of interreligious
  phronesis (IP), 302–5, 313, 315
knowledge
  academic dogma and, 178
  acquisition, as front-line task,
    296–99
  application of, 316
  construction of new knowledge
    from, 191
  direct engagement and, 300
  gaps in, 220–21
  participation and, 274
  personal experience and, 274
  practice *versus*, 293–94
  production, 3–4
  tacit, 315, 315n11
Know What (episteme), of interreligious
  phronesis (IP), 297–99, 313
Know Who (empatheia), of
  interreligious phronesis (IP),
  299–300, 313
Know Why (sophia), of interreligious
  phronesis (IP), 300–2, 313

L

language, 66, 266, 316
Law of Comparative Advantage, 229
leadership
  authentic leadership model of, 301

awareness within, 324–26
as born or made, 311–12, 311n1
capability of, 312
characteristics of, 137, 317
civic interfaith, 191
Co-Active Leadership model for,
  312, 325, 328–29
in context, 314–15
creative interactions of, 318
curricula for, 319
Daoism and, 313–14
defined, 327
development factors of, 301, 308–9
development programs of, 332
difference leveraging by, 323–24
everyday, 313–24
experience importance within,
  330–31
interfaith, 143–44, 319, 321–24,
  322n41, 325
interreligious phronesis (IP) for,
  324–33
knowledge application within, 316
Leadership-as-Practice (LAP) model
  of, 317
learning for, 315
meta-theory of, 317
new-genre, 317–18
overview of, 4–5, 332, 333–36
perspective shift of, 323–24
potential of, 312n2
professional application of, 320–24
purposes of, in business, 321–24,
  322n41
religious literacy and, 143–44
risk and failure within, 333–34
self-awareness of, 301
self-discovery and, 326–29
significant interaction of, 319
transformational, 318
types of, 312
value roots and, 322
Leadership-as-Practice (LAP) model,
  317
Life Purpose Statement, 329

lifestance, 277
lifeway, 204–11, 277
literacy, 139, 140. *See also* interreligious literacy; religious literacy
lived experience, 208
lived-practice-based approach, to religion, 240
Lived Religion (LR) approach
  benefit of, 101–4
  dangerous religious ideas and, 125–27
  friendship and, 133
  for interfaith dialogue, 130–33
  Interfaith Engagement (IFE) and, 128
  interreligious encounter and, 128–29
  interreligious friendship and, 275–77
  interreligious studies (IRS) benefits of, 118–28
  kindred approaches to, 98–101
  multiple religious orientation and, 133–36
  overview of, 95–104, 125–26, 299–300
  political discourse and, 123
  porous borders and, 127–28
  practices and blending within, 112–17
  putting human face on, 137–38
  reflexivity and, 133–36
  relevance of, 121–22
  religious difference and, 128–29
  religious orientation and, 126
  secularization and, 133–36
  self-critical faith and, 125–27
  self-implication and, 127–28
  storytelling within, 132–33
  in the United States, 105–10
living religion, 275–77
logic of identity, 53, 281–82
lokahi (harmony through diversity), 146, 154–55
Long Reformation, 129n34, 130

M

malaria, 273–74
management studies, 304, 315n11
material religion, 98–99
media, 151, 152
meditation, 113, 294
melting pot metaphor, 248
memorized worldview, 207
migration, 45
minimization, 220
Minnesota Multifaith Network (MnMN), 250
Model of Interfaith Awareness, 324–25
movement, 172, 172n20
multiculturalism, 173n26
multidisciplinary usage, of interreligious studies (IRS), 34–38
multifaith, 201–2
multiple religious belonging (MRB)
  defined, 80, 114n94
  dimensions of, 116
  lived religious reality of, 114–15
  reconsideration of, 135
  secularization and, 136
  single religious belonging (SRB) and, 83
  study of, 84
multiple religious identity (MRI), 80, 82–83, 134
multiple religious orientation (MRO), 80–88, 115n94, 133–36
multiple religious participation (MRP), 80, 83–84, 85, 89, 114, 116
music, 291, 292, 314–15
My Friend Al Principle, 278–79
mysterium tremendum, 12
My Struggle (Ove Knausgaard), 335–36

N

Native American Christianity, 70n23
natural increase, 45
naturalism, 261
natural science, 229
Nazis, 124, 222n24

neither religious nor spiritual (NRNS), 110
neoliberalism, 305–6
Nepal, 43
The Netherlands/Dutch, 110, 115, 115n94, 116
New Zealand, 47
nones, 46, 48, 105–7, 109, 110–11. *See also* unaffiliated religious identity
nonhumans, worldview of, 206n33
nonreligious, defined, 236. *See also* secular; unaffiliated religious identity
nonreligious worldview, 207
normative analysis, 183
normative turn, 185–89
normative usage, of interreligious studies (IRS), 27–30
normativity, 186n88

O

objectivity, 188
organisms, 206n33
Other Religions, 44

P

Pakistan, 43, 243
peace studies, 181–83, 190
personal identity, 50–51
philosophy, 315n11
phronesis. *See also* interreligious phronesis (IP)
  Dao of, 314
  defined, 192, 288
  intentions and, 305
  interfaith wisdom as, 288–94
  in management studies, 304
  overview of, 308–9
  right reasons and, 305–8
  as a virtue, 289, 291–92
  as wherewithal, 289–90
pluralism
  beyond tolerance of, 251–52, 254
  civic, 225, 245, 247–50, 253–54
  commitments and, 252–53
  defined, 134, 134n60, 235–36
  dialogue and, 253
  diversity *versus,* 248
  energetic engagement with diversity and, 250–51
  overview of, 244–47
  relativism and, 252
  shape of the table and, 248, 248–49n72, 254
  transformation and, 233
  "two pluralisms" proposal, 241–42, 249, 249n75
pluralization, 242
political science, 35
political secularism, 237
politics, Christianity within, 141–42
Popular Practice, 82n11
popular religion approach, 96, 97
Portugal, 110
potluck metaphor, 248
practical wisdom, 300–1, 304–5
practice of, *versus* study of, 184–85
prescriptive usage, of interreligious studies (IRS), 27–30
Protestants, 107, 108
Protestant Work Ethic, 323
psychic phenomena, 113

Q

questions of representation, 204n23

R

racism, 29, 274
reductionism, 15–16, 124
reflective turn, 185–89
reflexivity, 133–36
reincarnation, 113
relativism, 252
religion
  appreciative knowledge for, 153–54
  approaches to, 10–12
  belief principles within, 87

belonging and, 86
concept of, 200
conclusions regarding, 19–21
conversation regarding, 150
critiques regarding, 19–21
as culturally embedded, 32n103,
    65–66
defined, 10–12, 204
dimensions of, 16–17
diversity of, 64–65, 121, 135–36
dynamics of, 65
essentialist approach to, 12–13
everyday aspect of, 101
family resemblance within, 222
fluid nature of, 61
freedoms within, 13
functionalist approach to, 13–16
global landscape of, 40–48
internal coherence within, 87–88
'just the basics' approach to, 160
levels of, 71–72
as linguistically constructed, 66
lived-practice-based approach to,
    240
living, 275–77
nature of, 64–66
pacification through, 13–14
prominence of, 39–40
putting human face on, 137–38
shaping power of, 226
statistics regarding, 39, 40, 41,
    105–10
stereotyping and, 155
study of, 159, 257–58, 260, 302n59
    (See also Religious Studies
    (RS); theology)
syncretism of, 67–78
temporal nature of, 68–69
usefulness of category of, 19
the way and, 86–87
Religions in Schools Task Force
    (American Academy of Religion),
    60
religious, spiritual and secular (RSS)
    identity, 204

Religious and Life Stance Communities,
    211
religious appropriation, 224
religious authority, 129–30
religious blending, 88–94, 112
religious but not spiritual (RBNS), 110
religious difference, 128–36, 134,
    253–54, 274
religious diversity
    awareness of, 325
    blame to, 225
    dignity of difference and, 225–30
    engagement and, 250–51
    indifference and, 287
    overview of, 213
    of traditions, 224
religious diversity training, 145
religious hybridity, 89–92
religious identity
    articulation of, 52
    authentic, 53–54
    complexity of, 55–61, 63
    feminist thought and, 60
    forging solidarities within, 52–53
    formation of, 59
    oversimplification of, 124
    overview of, 48–50
    personal, 50–51
    river analogy regarding, 77–78,
        78n63
    social, 50–51
religious illiteracy, 142–43, 160
religious leaders, public opinion
    regarding, 107
religious literacy. See also interreligious
    literacy
    abilities of, 147
    benefits of, 159
    in business, 144n20, 148, 152
    characteristics of, 147
    conversation and, 156–57
    cultivation of, 151
    defined, 139, 143, 145–46
    degrees of, 143
    in education, 157–58, 159

encounter and, 161
energy from, 145
forms of, 149
goal of, 150
in healthcare, 144, 152
interreligious literacy *versus,* 155
as job skill, 156
lokahi (harmony through diversity)
    and, 146, 154–55
myth of, 160
as operative knowledge, 298
overview of, 140–48
social cohesion and, 150
social value of, 148
sufficiency of, 157–61
tolerance and, 158
value of, 148–53
in the workplace, 145, 149, 151–52,
    156
Religious Literacy Movement (RLM),
    152–53
religious orientations, 79–88
religious pluralism, 230–31, 245
religious practices, 112, 114
religious reflexivity, 133–36
Religious Studies (RS), 35, 256, 257, 260
religious violence, 125, 155, 219, 307
research, 30, 32n103
researcher, authorial identity of, 33
resilience, 167
rituals, 10
robustness, 166, 168
rock climbing, 168–69, 171n18, 181
Roman Catholicism, 107, 108

S

salad bowl metaphor, 248
Satan, 107–8
scholar-activism, 175
scholar-practitioner model, 190–93
scholars, as critical caretakers, 25
secular context, 237–38
secularism, 237–39
secularity, 236–44

secularization, 133–36, 136–37n80,
    239–42
secular worldview, 207
segregation, 228
self, 49–50
self-actualization, 333
self-awareness, 286, 301, 325, 335–36
self-critical faith, 125–27
self-discovery, 326–29
self-implicating usage, of interreligious
    studies (IRS), 30–34
self-implication, 127–28
self-improvement industry, 326
self-knowledge, 300–1
self-reflection, 187, 188
self-transcendence, 300–1
sense of meaning, 208
September 11, 2001 events, 122, 227–28
single religious belonging (SRB), 83
single religious identity (SRI), 83
skiing, 221
"skin in the game," 180–81, 192
slavery, 29
The Sneetches and Other Stories (Seuss),
    214–16, 218–19
social identity, 50–51
sociology, 35, 315n11
solidarities, 279–83
Spain, 47
sparring, 170–71, 192
spider silk, 167
spillover effect, 278–79, 283
spiritual beings, belief in, 12. *See also*
    God
spiritual but not religious (SBNR), 110
spiritual energy, in physical things, 113
spirituality, 33, 100–1
stereotypes, 120–24, 155
storytelling, interreligious
    communication and, 132–33
Strategic Religious Participation in a
    Shared Religious Landscape, 84
strong practitioner dimension, 190
student-learning outcomes (SLOs),
    23–24

study of, *versus* practice of, 184–85
substantivist approach, 12
sustainability studies, 183–85
Sweden, 47, 110
Sword of Damocles, 168
syncretism
    defense of, 74, 76–77
    defined, 68, 75
    fear of, 269n40
    hard, 69–70
    overview of, 67
    problem and promise within, 73–78
    resistance to, 75
    scholarly voices regarding, 70–73
    soft, 69–70
    subjective, 73
    term use of, 67–69
    traits of, 68

T

tacit knowledge, 315, 315n11
Talmud Torah, 177–78
tarot cards, 113
"Taxonomy of Interfaith," 172n21
teams, diversity within, 229–30
textualized worldview, 207
theological pluralism, 245, 261
Theological Studies (TS), 36, 256, 260.
    See also theology
theological worldview, 259
theology
    Anselm and, 259
    approaches to, 257–58
    defined, 257
    doing, 256–60
    as faith seeking understanding, 259
    as interreligious, 74–75
    methods of, 260
    name of God and, 258
    particular perspective and, 258
    as pluralistic discipline, 259–60
    rejection of, 209–10
    as religious difference engagement
        mode, 272

religious reality and, 258
    study of religion *versus*, 260
    as ultimate ground and goal of all
        reality, 259
theology of religions, 260, 261–64
tolerance, 158, 251–52, 254
traditions, 200, 224, 243, 287
transdisciplinary usage, of interreligious
    studies (IRS), 34–38
transformation, 231, 233, 242–44
transreligious, defined, 203–4
transreligious theology, 260, 269–71
tribalism, 225, 226–27, 228, 279
Trinity, doctrine of, 13, 103
"two pluralisms" proposal, 241–42, 249,
    249n75

U

unaffiliated religious identity, 40, 41, 43,
    46–48, 110–11
United States
    atheism within, 47
    Buddhism within, 43
    Christianity within, 41–42
    Hinduism within, 43
    immigration within, 231–33,
        232n56
    Islam within, 244
    Jews within, 44
    religion statistics regarding, 105–10
    secularization and, 241
    unaffiliated religious identity within,
        43
unity, 229
universalism, 225, 226–27, 228
upāya (skillful means), 326

V

valueless relativism, 252
value roots, 322
vernacular architecture, 100
vernacular religion, 99–100
violence/religious violence, 125, 155,
    219, 307

virtue, 289, 291–94
virtue ethics, 291
virtuoso, 291

W

the way metaphor, 86–87, 86n27
way of life, 206n33
Way of Life wheel, 210
Western Europe, 110–12
Where's Waldo? metaphor, 95
wherewithal, 289–90
wisdom, born, 315–16

workplace
  interfaith interaction within, 320–21
  religious literacy within, 145, 149,
    151–52, 156
  value roots within, 322
World Council of Churches, 130
World Religions paradigm, 11n5, 11n7,
  96
worldview, 204–11, 205n28, 259

Y

yoga, 113, 325, 329–33